Philosophers
and Scholars

WITHDRAWN

Philosophers and Scholars

Wolfson, Guttmann and Strauss on the History of Jewish Philosophy

Jonathan Cohen

translated from the Hebrew by Rachel Yarden

LEXINGTON BOOKS

A division of
ROWMAN & LITTLEFIELD PUBLISHERS, INC.
Lanham • Boulder • New York • Toronto • Plymouth, UK

LEXINGTON BOOKS

A division of Rowman & Littlefield Publishers, Inc.
A wholly owned subsidiary of The Rowman & Littlefield Publishing Group, Inc.
4501 Forbes Boulevard, Suite 200, Lanham, MD 20706

Estover Road, Plymouth PL6 7PY, United Kingdom

The Hebrew edition of this book was published with the generous assistance of the Melton Center for Jewish Education and the Federman Fund of the Institute for Jewish Studies of The Hebrew University of Jerusalem. Aid toward the publication of the English edition was provided by Hebrew University's School of Education.

British Library Cataloguing in Publication Information Available

Library of Congress Cataloging-in-Publication Data
Cohen, Jonathan, ha-Dr.
    [Tevunah u-temurah. English]
    Philosophers and scholars : Wolfson, Guttmann and Strauss on the history of Jewish philosophy / Jonathan Cohen.
        p. cm.
    Includes bibliographical references and index.
    ISBN-13: 978-0-7391-1998-3 (cloth : alk. paper)
    ISBN-10: 0-7391-1998-2 (cloth : alk. paper)
    ISBN-13: 978-0-7391-1999-0 (pbk. : alk. paper)
    ISBN-10: 0-7391-1999-0 (pbk. : alk. paper)
    1. Wolfson, Harry Austryn, 1887–1974. 2. Guttmann, Julius, 1880–1950. 3. Strauss, Leo. 4. Philosophy, Jewish—Historiography. I. Title.
    B154.C6413 2007
    181'.06--dc22
                                                                              2007017102

Printed in the United States of America

♾™ The paper used in this publication meets the minimum requirements of American National Standard for Information Sciences—Permanence of Paper for Printed Library Materials, ANSI/NISO Z39.48-1992.

In memory of my father,
Hartley Cohen,
who directed me on the paths which led to this book

Contents

Preface

Two fertile and thought-provoking courses I took at The Hebrew University in the early 1970s served as the source and the inspiration for this book. One of the classes, taught by Prof. Seymour Fox, analyzed the conceptual frameworks guiding scholars in various scientific fields. The fundamental concepts used in this course were developed by Fox's teacher, Prof. Joseph Schwab of the University of Chicago. The other course, taught by Prof. Eliezer Schweid and the late Prof. Rivka Schatz-Oppenheimer, comprised an exhaustive, in-depth historiographical survey of the development of scholarship in the fields of Jewish philosophy and kabbalah.

Prof. Fox's course, under the aegis of the School of Education, was the beginning of a rich and sustained relationship. He generously agreed to advise me in my doctoral work, much of which has been incorporated in this volume. I am grateful for the scholarly and methodological insights garnered from conversations with him, which have left their mark on the text. I regret that Prof. Fox, whose recent and sudden passing has stunned and saddened all who knew him, could not share in my gratification at the publication, in English, of the work he helped so much to cultivate.

During the period of my studies in the Department of Jewish Thought, I participated in the instructive classes of Prof. Shalom Rosenberg, who also agreed to guide me in my doctoral work. I thank him for his incisive remarks, which enhanced the precision and clarity of the work. The late Prof. Nathan Rotenstreich urged me to publish my research, and his keen observations have left their imprint, particularly on the book's introduction. It grieves me that he did not live to see the publication of either the Hebrew or English editions. I will always remember his unstinting dedication to encouraging and promoting the work of his students.

I have the pleasant obligation of expressing my thanks to my colleagues at the Melton Center for Jewish Education, and particularly to Prof. Michael Rosenak and Prof. Mordechai Nissan, who also encouraged me warmly to publish my research. Their loyal support, along with the Center's readiness to contribute to the publication of this book, are but one expression of the many kindnesses I have been shown by my teachers and colleagues at the Center from my student days until the present. In addition, I am grateful to the "Jerusalem Fellows" program, which enabled me to dedicate large amounts of time to research, and to the Memorial Fund for Jewish Culture. The book's new revision and publication were facilitated by a post-doctoral fellowship from the Schonbrun Fund and by a grant from the Federman Fund of the Institute for Jewish Studies. I am grateful to these bodies for their assistance, which was extended with a generous spirit.

Mr. Moshe Kleinman, Mr. Avraham Ben-Zvi and my wife Michal Padoa-Cohen all had a hand in editing the language of the text in its various Hebrew versions. I am indebted to their sharp eyes and their good taste. Michal's encouragement, as well as our discussions on the content of the book, enriched my thinking. And these are among the things that are beyond estimation.

I am also grateful to the editors at Lexington Books, for their professional and expeditious processing of the English edition.

Introduction

A Systematic Approach to the History of Philosophy

In the course of the following study, we will seek to locate and articulate the principles which guided the scholarship of Harry Austryn Wolfson (1887–1974), Yitzhak Julius Guttmann (1880–1950) and Leo Strauss (1899–1973) in the field of Jewish philosophy. There is no need to dwell at length on the contribution of these three figures to the study of Jewish philosophy. Regarding the works of Harry Wolfson, Isadore Twersky has written, "Wolfson's firm method of philological analysis (minute textual study modeled after the Talmudic mode of study), his original conception of the history of philosophy, and his clear definition of subject matter joined together to produce an impressive, magisterial sweep and extraordinary expertise possessed of great resilience and force."[1] As for Yitzhak Julius Guttmann's classic composition, *The Philosophies of Judaism*, Eliezer Schweid states that "In many ways, it should be seen both as a summary of the scholarship in Jewish philosophy of the nineteenth and early twentieth centuries, and also as the normative standard guiding academic research in Jewish philosophy to this day."[2] Shlomo Pines notes the place of Leo Strauss in the study of Jewish medieval philosophy as follows: "There are considerable doubts regarding many of Maimonides' main ideas, now that the old and less-old certainties of several of his nineteenth and twentieth century commentators have been exploded, by virtue of the progress in scholarship which has been achieved first and foremost through the methods employed by L. Strauss."[3]

Our purpose in this work is not to trace the contribution of these scholars to the study of Jewish philosophy, nor to plot their personal intellectual development. Neither will we merely present their findings and conclusions, as the writings of Wolfson, Guttmann and Strauss themselves are freely accessible to the reader without intermediaries. Instead, we propose to approach the works of these scholars as *models of a systematic construction of the history of Jewish philosophy.*

Presenting the objective of this work in such a fashion raises the question of why a scholar should be concerned with the history of Jewish philosophy. What is the difference between giving a systematic-philosophic account of past thought and engaging with that same body of thought for other reasons?

Nathan Rotenstreich lists a number of plausible motives for scholarship in the history of philosophy, none of which have anything to do with systematic reflection.[4] Among the motives he mentions are the cultural-educational motive: the acquisition of a culturally requisite knowledge of the history of philosophy. Being conversant in such a field can nourish the discourse of the cultured and the elite, in a manner similar to the acquisition of language. Within the framework of national culture, certain philosophical works can serve as models for imitation or paradigms of cognitive excellence, functioning as expressions of national self-awareness. A more extreme example is that of a scholastic-dogmatic subjection to a particular philosophical system, acceptance of whose authority presupposes an acquaintance with its tenets.

There are scholars whose interest lies in the philological aspect of Jewish philosophic texts. When philological research is conducted in isolation, divorced from all systematic principles, it reflects an impulse to a kind of antiquarianism, a valuing of history for its own sake. The very existence of phenomena—ideas that were broached, systems that were constructed and thinkers who created—is considered sufficient justification for their study and for their precise empirical description.

In Rotenstreich's opinion, the systematic approach to the history of philosophy is driven by other factors, first and foremost the viewing of past systems as exemplars of reflection, instances of confrontation with perennial philosophic problems shared also by the scholar himself. Although Rotenstreich believes that in-depth, comprehensive philosophical reflection is possible independent of past philosophical models, he nevertheless holds that philosophy, by its very nature, has an internal motivation to investigate its past. There are three grounds for this motivation.

First, philosophy, the "conscious knowledge of knowledge," is reflective in its essence. This is both its method and its content. As such, philosophy is interested in manifestations of reflection, since this is the way in which it comes to know itself. Such manifestations are inherent in articulated systems, which are effectively summaries of reflective activity directed towards permanent problems. Many of these systems came into being in the past, although the fact of their belonging to the past is not a decisive factor here. Secondly, reflection engenders in human beings a consciousness of their own historicity and of that of their works. Human beings and their works are situated on a continuum of time: Not everything began in the present, and not everything will be completed in the present. Philosophy, which (ontologically speaking) endows human beings with a historical consciousness, is concerned with this historical perspective "within its own house" as well, when it undertakes to contemplate the history of philosophy. And finally, philosophical reflection leads to an awareness of the conceptual and systematic heritage that informs contemporary philosophical activity. Conscious knowledge of this situation directs us to investigate the source of current philosophic concepts and systems.

The various orientations towards the history of philosophy—the cultural-educational, the philological, the theological and the systematic philosophical—have spawned diverse methods of ordering the thought of the past. In what follows, we will survey several possible ways of organizing the history of Western philosophy. As will become clear below, the ongoing debate among students of the history of Western philosophy affords us a perspective from within which to descry similar trends in the ordering of the history of Jewish philosophy.

WRITING THE HISTORY OF PHILOSOPHY: APPROACHES AND ISSUES

John Passmore distinguishes between six approaches to the study of the history of philosophy.[5] A "polemical" orientation reflects the writer's attempt to mobilize support for his own basic viewpoints by harnessing past controversies to justify present positions. Past thinkers become the writer's allies in his efforts to corroborate his own arguments. Scholars who adopt this approach are mainly concerned with issues occupying their own philosophical community, and they display little interest in the rules of historical-philological research. It is clear from Passmore's writings that he believes that this approach detracts from historical precision.

In contrast with the polemical approach, the system of merely chronicling the history of philosophy is devoid of all polemical intent. The historian relinquishes any quest for meaning or causality in the development of thought, limiting himself to the description of viewpoints articulated by past thinkers. He either adheres to some kind of chronological order in his description, or presents a number of different schools of thought with no ideological continuity between them. Passmore terms this kind of chronicling "doxography." The scholar here has no systematic interest in the subjects of his research; he makes do with what he considers to be the accurate reporting of historical data.

Since Hegel, any attempt to distinguish sharply between a conceptual viewpoint belonging solely to the present and one originating solely in the past has become problematic. Hegel's assumption that stages in the history of culture and society reflect stages in reason's development towards objective self-awareness renders the history of philosophy itself a part of the philosophical system. Every philosophical system, of whatever time period, concludes its function upon being subsumed under a more comprehensive philosophic system. From this perspective, mere doxographic writing turns out to be of purely antiquarian interest, lacking any significance for the systematic philosopher. Further, a philosophical system cannot be accessed as a "support" for contemporary philosophers' opinions, although it may conceivably have played a role in advancing philosophy to its current state. From this standpoint, the disclosure of a lawful pattern that can provide an account of how the various systems came into being, as well as of their history and influence, becomes imperative. In this case, the doxographic chronicle can conceivably serve as raw material for a more dramatic narrative of teleological development.

In contrast with Hegel's "retrospective" approach, Passmore identifies another type of writing, which he calls a "classifying history." The latter reflects the belief that the history of philosophy is not a dialectical process in which clashing theories are reconciled within the framework of more comprehensive theories, on a higher level of synthesis. The history of philosophy cannot be described as a story of ineluctable progress towards harmony. Accordingly, it is the task of the historian of philosophy to identify perennial, substantive and eternal disputes which recur in different periods in varying conceptual garbs.

Scholars concerned with the "history of culture," on the other hand, are not seeking out conflicting eternal essences. Rather, they attribute the origins of intellectual systems to the fluctuating socio-historical environment. They also do not believe that social and cultural movements reflect developments in human thought. Their act of reductionism is in the opposite direction: Manifestations of reason are not considered to have any independent ontological status, as they are merely the derivatives of local or cultural contexts. Consequently, according to this position as well, whoever tries to apply ideas derived from ancient theories to contemporary issues would be falsifying the truth. Since Greek philosophers lived in cultural surroundings far removed from our own, a scholar may not employ a Platonic idea to help resolve a given philosophical problem that engages him in the present. He should content himself instead with a "horizontal" examination of the influences stemming from the context in terms of time and place; he should not concern himself with a "vertical" process of cumulative development. This kind of historical consciousness may engender a severe form of relativization, which can prevent scholars from identifying with any past system.

Finally, Passmore presents the approach he considers most worthy, the type he calls the "history of problems." In his view, this orientation avoids falling prey to the errors or the extremes of the other approaches. Its reach extends beyond that of doxographic writing: It searches out the reasons which led philosophers to focus on particular problems at particular times. However, it makes no dogmatic assertions that the centrality of certain issues can be explained on the basis of relative cultural factors alone. Neither does it go to the opposite extreme of affirming that the search for truth is an entirely autonomous enterprise, transcending history. Hegelian extremism, which subordinates the "history of problems" to a rigid scheme reflecting the movement of "universal" reason, is also rejected.

Nonetheless, argues Passmore, one can approach writing the history of philosophy with the assumption that there has been some kind of progress in the history of thought. Over the course of time philosophers come to see their problems more clearly, and they become aware that it is no longer possible to content themselves with solutions which seemed plausible in the past. Moreover, outstanding thinkers are mindful of the manner in which their problems have been influenced by developments in science, culture, religion and the social order. Passmore does not ignore the fact that there have been dark periods in the history of philosophy, yet he openly acknowledges that the "historian of problems" is more interested in periods of progress. Notwithstanding his respect for philological-historical research, whose function it is to prevent scholars from drawing arbitrary conclusions, he would prefer that the history of philosophy be written by active philosophers who are implicated in philosophical problems and their resolution, despite the risk of distortion this could entail. Historians who are not engaged by philosophy will tend to write "doxographies."

Passmore's distinctions highlight a whole series of questions which will interest those concerned with the systematic writing of the history of philosophy:

1. Is it possible to consciously forswear writing about the history of philosophy from some philosophic standpoint? If so, is it desirable?
2. To what degree is philosophy an autonomous activity, liberated from social, political or cultural influences? What is the connection between philosophy and its religious, scientific or national frame of reference?
3. Has there been comprehensive or only partial progress in the history of philosophy? Has that progress been in the direction of attaining the truth, or only towards achieving a clearer grasp of fundamental problems and dismissing inadequate solutions?
4. Is there a trend towards unifying harmony underlying the various philosophical theories from the past, or are there perhaps clashing eternal archetypes, whose conflicts are both irreducible and irreconcilable?

If we undertake a short comparison between the programmatic introductions of two historians of Western philosophy who wrote comprehensive studies in the field, Wilhelm Windelband and Frederick Copleston, we will see that these questions already arose for them.

PROGRESSIVE AND TRADITIONAL TRENDS IN WRITING THE HISTORY OF PHILOSOPHY: WINDELBAND AND COPLESTON

Windelband answers the above four questions on the basis of a certain definition of philosophical activity.[6] He is aware of the wealth of definitions of philosophy and holds that the late definition of Kant, that philosophy is "critical consideration by reason of itself" is "apparently final."[7] Nevertheless, he amplifies this definition in light of Hegel's conception that the process of the elevation of reason to self-awareness regarding its own processes is realized within the expanse of historical time. Accordingly, philosophy is "laboring to bring to conscious expression the necessary forms and principles in which human reason manifests its activity, and to transfer these from their original form of perceptions, feelings, and impulses, into that of conceptions."[8] For Windelband, philosophy is essentially historical in character. When the efforts to reach "a formulation in conception of the material immediately given in the world and in life" are absorbed by history, "the constitution of the mental and spiritual life" is gradually disclosed to us.[9]

From here we learn that in Windelband's eyes, doxographic writing—however well grounded it may be in philological-historical scholarship—does not represent "a genuine science."[10] Windelband's historical-idealist orientation mandates that the historian of philosophy arrange the various theories revealed through research in a "rational, developmental and cumulative scheme."[11] His words clearly reflect his aim of identifying progress in the course of human thought. However, he does strive to moderate some of the more blatant tendencies of Hegel's schematic historiosophy.

Windelband does not believe there is any hard and fast correlation between the dialectical processes of rational thought and the religious, social and political structures which succeed one another upon the stage of history. He maintains that historical data should not be subsumed in advance under a scheme which posits that the manifestations of human culture reflect the trajectory of the "universal spirit." Windelband identifies three factors which exert an influence on the direction and quality of the history of philosophy.

First, there are eternal problems with which thought is faced when it comes to examine the degree of consistency of its own processes, as well as the degree of correspondence between its processes and the "raw material" tendered it by experience. Critical thinking discovers that there are internal contradictions between the categories of reason itself (termed "antinomies" by Kant). For instance, reason examines its objects by means of the categories of part and whole and of causality, which are related to the dimensions of space and time. However, it also seeks to abstract and universalize its concepts. This abstraction and universalization nullifies all spatial division and all causal motion. In addition, thought wonders at the degree of correlation between its categories and the nature of the phenomena themselves, and discovers (through Kant) that there is no necessary connection between them. These problems are eternal, and the continuous attempts to resolve them within the framework of systems that tilt the scales in a given direction (such as Cousin's four-fold scheme of sensualism, idealism, skepticism and mysticism)[12] accelerate the process of the disclosure of the basic principles of reason and impel it forward. Windelband calls this the "pragmatic" factor, as it is anchored in the impulse to resolve theoretical problems.

A second factor is a process which Passmore assigned to the category of "cultural history." Windelband explicitly declares his intention to highlight the role of motifs and models characterizing the self-understanding of cultures and civilizations as factors in the generation of philosophical systems. He does not believe in reducing cultural phenomena to developments in the sphere of "universal reason." Neither does he appear to favor the opposite reduction of treating systems of thought as the "superstructures" for civilizational or cultural forces. He seeks only to ascribe to the "history of culture" some kind of causal role in stimulating philosophic thought, without offering any systematic prescriptions for the relationship between this factor and "pure thought."

Finally, in the face of Hegel's rationalism, Windelband stresses the factors of the individual and the particular, which have genuine causal effect in moving the history of philosophy forward. The individual philosopher with his unique personality, who lives in a singular set of circumstances, never to be repeated, is a genuine source of his own philosophical system. Even if individual philosophers struggle with a fixed set of problems connected with timeless logical tensions, and even if they are influenced by a collective cultural self-image, their individual uniqueness ensures their personal contribution to philosophical development. Here as well, just as in the category of the "history of culture," Windelband does not purport to provide a systematic resolution to the question of the universal ideational factor versus the individual biographical factor as sources for the history of philosophy, or to posit any kind of relationship between these two aspects. He contents himself with indicating the importance of both, insisting that both be taken into account in the articulation of the history of philosophy.

According to Windelband, then, doxographic writing is not "historical" in the scientific sense of the word. The history of philosophy proper involves tracing the gradual disclosure of the movements of thought. Nevertheless, philosophy is not an entirely autonomous enterprise, for it also draws on trends in the history of culture and on biographical elements connected with the personality of the thinker. Although he pronounces Kant's definition of philosophic activity "final" and appropriates Hegel's model of stage-by-stage development, Windelband never explicitly claims that philosophy is marching towards some harmonious, unified system within which all other systems will be absorbed.

In Copleston we have an example of an attempt to give an account of the history of Western philosophy from a religious point of view.[13] Copleston declares outright that his book is primarily designed to transmit the Western philosophical tradition to students in Catholic seminaries, in order to foster a respect for man's quest for the truth. He senses, however, that the very attempt to review the history of Western philosophy from an avowedly Thomistic stance requires justification. He has no choice, then, but to address the questions posed above.

Copleston also has reservations about composing a history which merely "chronicles" the past. Details revealed through historical research cannot be "understood" in isolation, without paying attention to their causes and effects, and without relating to the motifs which create continuity between them. Furthermore, Copleston claims, it is unthinkable to write history from anything other than a principled position. Like Windelband, he warns historians against "inserting" the facts into a predetermined scheme and stresses the importance of the aspiration to objectivity. Yet he thinks it inconceivable that a historian could approach his task without principles in hand to help him select and organize the "facts" and themes included in his account.

To illustrate his claim, Copleston surmises that two historians, one a "transcendentalist" and the other an "atheist," working with an identical set of findings, will arrive at different conclusions regarding the contribution of Neoplatonic philosophy to the tradition of Western thought, despite the fact that both are trained professionals who sincerely aspire to objectivity. There is, then, no intrinsic reason why a trained historian with a religious point of view should not undertake to articulate his version of the history of Western philosophy.

Copleston's faith-based assumptions include a commitment to Thomistic philosophy as the *Philosophia Perennis* [eternal philosophy]. With this frame of reference, he addresses the issues mentioned above regarding the degree of autonomy enjoyed by philosophy, the progress revealed within it over time and its ability to encompass different and even conflicting systems within a single framework.

Copleston appears to devote more attention to demonstrating the autonomy of philosophy in relation to revelation than to distinguishing between philosophy and the history of culture. Revelation, to the extent that its source is transcendent, reaches man as perfection. Philosophy, in contrast, is the result of a human striving for ultimate truth. Accordingly, it is imperfect at the outset and completes itself through the dimension of time. Copleston does not reduce philosophy, even Thomistic philosophy, to theology. Philosophy is not "the theology of revelation," which systematically illuminates the revealed principles of faith. It represents an internal human aspiration, and in this sense is "autonomous" vis-a-vis revelation. This aspiration does have religious value, however, as it reflects—perhaps unconsciously—a human quest to know the structure of reality, to know the absolute.

This supposition enables Copleston to view most of the philosophical systems that have arisen in history with sympathy. Even if every theory lays claim to the absolute truth, and even if there exists a deep antagonism between their conclusions, they join forces in a joint project propelled by a unified impulse. Even if the Thomistic philosopher is constrained, in principle, to reject the systematic materialism of Marx, this does not prevent him from admiring the Marxist attempt to offer an absolute, comprehensive solution to human suffering, and to learn from it regarding the relative contribution of economic motives to the creation of thought-systems.

With regard to the issue of progress, Copleston's theory is fraught with tension. On the one hand, he believes that philosophy develops and generates real innovations that are not merely the applications of traditional ideas to new problems. Philosophy is the "labor of the human spirit," and accordingly is never complete at any given point in time; it is constantly growing and developing. Over the course of time, "new expanses" of study open up, and new "lines of approach" to problems ensue. New "facts" and "human situations" arise which require a new response.

On the other hand, when we scrutinize the "innovations" Copleston adduces in support of his argument, we discover that in his view, philosophical "development" merely signifies the application of principles derived from the *Philosophia Perennis* to new spheres, rather than a substantive change in orientation. For instance, the philosophy of government could not be perfected within the framework of the Thomistic system until the advent of the modern experience with liberal and totalitarian states, nor could it be implemented without addressing the various theories advanced by modern political philosophy. The observations of Thomas himself on the state are fairly circumscribed, and a Thomistic philosopher will not develop his own theory if by so doing he contravenes the tenets of Thomism. Consequently, a "developed" articulation of Thomistic political philosophy must necessarily be deferred until political and theoretical developments allow for its completion. This completion will not be accomplished within the framework of the "original," "closed" Thomistic system, but rather with reference to the diverse theories of government which merit discussion in contemporary political philosophy, and through their agency.

At first glance, this is a "liberal" approach, which would seem to champion innovation and mandate the principle of development. However, on closer inspection it appears that Copleston's aim is in effect to introduce the Thomistic approach into modern philosophical discourse, without considering the possibility of accepting the latter's fundamental assumptions. Admittedly, Thomism undergoes a certain improvement by virtue of the fact that it is compelled to evaluate certain modern phenomena and to "translate" its traditional concepts into modern terms. Yet such a "completion" or "development" does not constitute a significant turning point or a fundamental innovation. Copleston also states that if a non-Thomistic philosopher reaches "valuable" conclusions through the use of "true" principles, the fruit of his efforts should be regarded as part of the "eternal philosophy" itself. He believes that in this fashion he can embrace portions of the theories of Spinoza and Hegel without sharing their pantheistic assumptions. Yet it seems that the yardstick for judging conclusions to be "valuable" and principles to be "true" will always remain in the hands of the Thomistic tradition. It would seem, then, that the framework Copleston proposes does not really allow for genuine "progress" in the history of philosophy.

As for the question of the theoretical and cultural breadth of philosophy, Copleston holds that a philosophical system is not an autonomous creation which can be understood solely from within itself. It is necessary for us to examine its degree of continuity with previous systems or to compare it with other systems prominent in the same time period. Otherwise our understanding of the individual system itself will be defective. Moreover, he argues that philosophy should be not be viewed as "incorporeal spirit," and that the autonomy of the philosophic quest is limited by personal and socio-historical factors.

CONTEMPORARY PHILOSOPHERS' OBSERVATIONS ON WRITING THE HISTORY OF PHILOSOPHY: RICHARD RORTY AND ALASDAIR MACINTYRE

Somewhat more recently, a dialogue was held on the proper relation between contemporary philosophical inquiry and past philosophic works.[14] Two of the contributions to this discussion, by Richard Rorty and Alasdair MacIntyre,[15] demonstrate that the issues underlying Passmore's distinctions, which had already engaged Windelband and Copleston, continue to be a source of controversy.

Rorty's explanation of living philosophers' use of the writings and theories of the "great dead philosophers"[16] is based on an analysis of "needs" which have nothing to do with the quest for an ultimate, unified truth. There are those, says Rorty, who turn to past theories in order to undertake a kind of "rational reconstruction."[17] This type of scholarship seeks to reconstruct the hypothetical opinions of selected philosophers on contemporary philosophic issues. Naturally, these philosophers did not voice their opinions on questions currently under discussion. Also, given the development of rational discourse since their time, we can say today that they erred in many of their important conclusions. Yet we can assume that if these same philosophers were to further explore the consequences of their own theories, and if we were given the opportunity to show them the faulty reasoning underlying certain of their claims, they would acknowledge our theories to be the more rational. Rorty holds that this model of turning to the past stems from the "need" to believe in the possibility of progress in rational discourse, so that we regard ourselves as "differing from our ancestors on grounds which our ancestors could be led to accept." It is important to us to view the history of human thought as a continuous rational dialogue, in which the great philosophers of yore gain satisfaction from their dwelling-place on high at our present successes, as they draw gratification from the fact that their seminal ideas are being developed and their errors are being set aright.

Rorty presents another possible model of inquiry into the history of philosophy; a model whose justification also stems from the way it fulfills a certain "need." Here the aim is to reconstruct, to the extent possible, the conceptions of a past philosopher within the frame of reference of the terms and thought processes of his times, without creating any connection between the issues which concerned him and the problems on our agenda. Scholarship of this type takes upon itself a severe limitation, which Rorty presents by means of a quotation from Quentin Skinner: "No agent can eventually be said to have meant or done something which he could never be brought to accept as a correct description of what he had meant or done."[18] True, even within the framework of this limitation one can conceive of an imaginary dialogue between a philosopher from the past and a contemporary philosopher who "speaks the same language," with the first philosopher providing hypothetical responses to his colleague's hypothetical critique. Nevertheless, one cannot really ask: "What would John Locke have said about John Rawls' theory of justice?"[19] According to Rorty, this model, which he terms "historical reconstruction,"[20] does not necessarily conflict with the model of "rational reconstruction." Historians of this stripe need not necessarily accuse their colleagues of being "anachronistic," nor need those who engage in "rational reconstruction" necessarily charge advocates of the second approach with antiquarianism for its own sake.

Just as "rational reconstruction" serves the need "to partake of a comprehensive and progressive rational dialogue," so "historical reconstruction" assists the contemporary scholar to achieve "self-awareness" regarding the historical relativity of his conceptions. Although the contemporary scholar believes correctly, in Rorty's view, that we know a lot about many subjects regarding which our predecessors' ideas were flawed, it is appropriate that he also sense that our own conceptions are the product of a particular, limited "system of arrangements," just as our predecessors' theories were. From this point of departure, Rorty defines doxography[21] in the following manner: an attempt to ensure that certain figures regarded by the author as genuine philosophers express their opinions on a fixed array of subjects, or that an outdated canon of philosophers be recruited to deal with problems currently considered central. Yet aside from doxography, we find two other legitimate sorts of writing about the history of philosophy. One is "Geistgeschichte,"[22] or history of spirit, whose most prominent representative was Hegel. Here, as in the case of "rational reconstruction," the historian has a "need" to justify himself. Yet he is not interested merely in defending his way of addressing a specific philosophical problem while basing himself on a great past thinker's approach to the same problem. The writer seeks instead to corroborate his general outlook regarding what constitutes philosophy's legitimate field of activity. In order to establish his claim that these problems, and not others, and this subject of inquiry, and no other, be considered philosophy—not cultural or intellectual history—he presents the reader with a historical narrative. The continuity obtaining between the philosophical systems composing the narrative tells a dramatic tale of growth and development in the direction of the writer's conception of "true" philosophy.

Rorty also discusses the writing of what he calls "intellectual history."[23] This form of history is not interested in drawing strict distinctions between philosophers *par excellence* and writers, theologians or scientists. Its objective is to afford the reader a taste of the intellectual life in a given location, so that he can become acquainted with the options available to intellectually alert young people in a particular locale or during a particular epoch. The "need" driving this kind of writing is again "awareness," yet this time in relation to the model of the "history of spirit." By studying intellectual history, the author of the "canon," who subscribes to a particular view of philosophical activity, becomes aware that many of the thinkers he considers "great" were devoid of influence in their own time. It may be that the leading intellectuals of a given age do not feature among the towering figures of the canon. The thought that perhaps the canon exaggerates the worth of certain philosophers' contributions creeps into the historian's mind, creating a healthy check on the "Geistgeschichte."

In sum, Rorty introduces two new propositions into the discourse on the writing of the history of philosophy:

1. Modes of constructing the philosophical past service the author's present pragmatic needs; they do not articulate "truths," whether philosophical or historical.

2. The various modes of construction are not counterposed one against the other, as in Windelband—the pragmatic factor, the factor of the history of culture and the individual factor—and there is no reduction of one particular factor to another (e.g., the reduction of problems to culture, or of culture to rational thought processes). Instead, a functional relationship prevails among them, a relationship of mutual balance. "Historical reconstruction" prevents us from refracting the past solely through the prism of our current problems, fostering a healthy relativism which prevents the canonization of the contemporary agenda. "Rational reconstruction" expands the framework of present philosophic discourse by way of insights gleaned from past thinkers. "Geistgeschichte" directs our attention to philosophy as a whole, demanding a systematic correlation between the chosen works of the canon and the problems the historian pronounces to be authentic. "Intellectual history" serves as a control on the "excesses" of "Geistgeschichte," providing it with raw material for new canons.

Unlike Rorty, who sees the reason for the different approaches to writing the history of philosophy as residing in the need of the European philosophic community for an expanded rational society with its own identity, dialogue and self-justification, Alasdair MacIntyre offers a starting point for evaluating philosophic works which dates back to philosophy's earliest inception, rather than referring to its end point. He begins by listing the factors that create distance between the contemporary historian and works of the past: changes in the definition of the agreed-upon applications of philosophy, changes in the internal divisions between the various branches of philosophy and changes in the literary form in which philosophy is written.[24] The variation of historiographical canons from one period to another, as well as the difficulty in translating terms and concepts from a system with a known systematic and historical context into the thought processes and assumptions which characterize the philosophical discourse of our times, are additional examples of this distance.[25] In the final analysis, argues MacIntyre, we are faced with a severe problem: it would seem that every thinker who strives to formulate or evaluate a theory that reaches us from a conceptual world of the past must consider the theory either from within itself or from within a perspective external to it. However, philosophically speaking, we have no criterion external to the two theories, from whose point of reference it would be possible to assess the degree of rational validity of the old or the new theory. Overcoming this problem is conditioned, in MacIntyre's view, on the possibility of overcoming the phenomenon of the incommensurability—as defined by Kuhn—of diverse conceptual frameworks.[26]

In response to these difficulties, MacIntyre suggests that perhaps our very ability to discuss two conceptual frameworks and pronounce them incommensurable, even on the most abstract level of worldviews, is contingent upon certain elements of continuity which serve as their backdrop. In MacIntyre's words, "Even the most radical of philosophical conflicts occur within the context of not dissimilar continuities."[27] If classical and modern concepts for "emotions," for instance, are irreconcilable because they are imbedded in incommensurate systems, we nevertheless feel that all of the terms in some way correspond to our understanding of "anger" or "fear." When a translation from one conceptual world to another fails, we must be able to provide an account not only for the failure, but also for the shared elements between the concepts which enable us to judge the failure a failure.

Even if we should assume that the variance obtaining between conceptual frameworks and the terms embedded in them can only be measured against the backdrop of continuums of focus, if not of definition, the following questions still remain: What tools do we have at our disposal to determine one conceptual framework's rational superiority over another? How could any account of the history of philosophy presume to determine whether a particular "early" system or another "later" system is the more rational? Here MacIntyre draws a comparison between theories in the natural sciences, which apply to a prescribed subject matter and do not attain the scope of an entire worldview, and philosophical systems, which are characterized by a higher level of abstraction.

Regarding theories in the natural sciences,[28] MacIntyre would agree with Kuhn that one cannot, for example, rule medieval theories of motion to be inadequate explanations of physical reality on the basis of the assumptions of Newtonian theory of motion, since these theories conflict with one another on fundamental principles. When, then, can a theory be deemed adequate or inadequate with regard to the range of phenomena it purports to explain? Here, however, the history of science provides a way for the scientific enterprise itself to consider certain theories rationally superior to others. The new perspective afforded by Newtonian theory enables us to give an account of the failure of medieval theories from within these very theories themselves. The historian of science, who is acquainted with the premises of both theories, can go back and scrutinize the previous theory from its own vantage point, and point out its internal inconsistency and inapplicability to the full range of phenomena it purports to explain. MacIntyre assumes that the historian can set aside his commitment to a later framework, assume the spectacles of the earlier system and evaluate it on the basis of its own assumptions. This affords him an advantage over those past thinkers who were committed to the system during the period of its ascendancy. He does not elaborate regarding the essence and nature of this advantage, or regarding the possibility that the later viewer's empathy might be flawed by prejudices rooted in his own commitments. Yet the upshot of his discussion is that the historical dimension of the sciences is "sovereign" over the sciences themselves. Only by "looking backwards," namely, by way of an internal examination of the theories which were dismissed because of their inconsistency and their incompatibility with their subject matter, will scientists be able to validate the superiority of the theories which have been adopted by the scientific community. Unlike Kuhn, MacIntyre does not believe that political, economic or social factors are of crucial importance in paradigm shifts,[29] and this explains his tendency to search for more rational and universal criteria.

In MacIntyre's view, this historical dimension is important not only for the rational corroboration it provides for scientific theories, but also for purposes of evaluating more comprehensive philosophic systems. Although in science later theories are generally preferred over earlier ones, it may be that such was not always the case, and there is no rational requirement that this be so. And certainly, argues MacIntyre, there is no necessity that the later should supersede the earlier in the case of philosophical worldviews. If in the sciences we are accustomed to judge theories according to their proximity to theories currently considered valid, in the history of philosophy it is permissible to direct our glance "backward" to the very beginning of the enterprise, and to judge systems according to the degree of their compatibility with the founding Platonic system or their deviation from it. In his words,

It would be fatal to our whole project to allow the philosophical present to determine what was to be counted as the philosophical past. Yet this does not mean that we are resourceless. For whereas the natural sciences derive their minimal unifying definition from the point that they have now reached, philosophy is able to derive a similar minimal unifying definition from its starting-point. Nobody is to count as a philosopher who does not have to be judged in the end against standards set by Plato. I do not say this only because Plato does already in fact to a surprisingly large degree provide philosophy both with its starting-point and with the definition of its scope and subject matter. But Plato transcends, in just the way I have described, the limitations of Pre-Socratic philosophy and in so doing sets a standard for all later attempts to transcend his limitations in turn. This is how he made Aristotle possible; this is indeed how he made philosophy possible. Hence all philosophers after Plato must confront a situation in which if you cannot transcend the limitations or what you take to be the limitations of Plato's fundamental positions, then you have no sufficient reason for failing to recognized yourself as a Platonist—unless, that is, you abandon philosophy altogether.[30]

To sum up, there is a striking clash between MacIntyre's quest for a "minimal unifying definition," rational and universal in character, of that which is to be included in the history of philosophy, a definition grounded in the enterprise's founding moment, and Rorty's opinion that philosophy's legitimate domain is determined by the philosophical community's present "needs." If we return to the questions posed at the outset of this discussion, Rorty champions "progress" in the annals of philosophy, on the claim that advances in rational discourse have rendered us better equipped than our predecessors to identify their mistakes. In contrast, MacIntyre draws his standard of rationality from the originator of the obligation to rationality (Plato) and regards them as the touchstone for evaluating deviations from rationality. Rorty is willing to accept plural models for the articulation of the philosophic past, since he believes that they serve the "function" of mutual correction. MacIntyre, on the other hand, claims that that history of philosophy which would judge the success of a system on the basis of its ability to supersede Plato's assumptions, is the only meaningful history there could be, and it has yet to be written. While Rorty ascribes no value to the autonomous status of philosophy, except to the extent that the philosophical "society" feels the need to endow philosophy with special significance,[31] MacIntyre is unwilling to relinquish a singular definition of philosophy which renders the field unique from within itself. Ultimately, Rorty regards philosophizing as an infinitely progressive process, which can expect no unified harmonious results, only plural genres. MacIntyre, by comparison, would seek to explain all plurality of expression in terms of what he considers to be a primordial unity.

Both Windelband in his day and Rorty in ours are "end-oriented," meaning that they assess developments in the history of philosophy on the basis of a definition of the field garnered from its most recent achievements. This, despite the contrast between Windelband's adherence to Hegelian thought patterns and Rorty's predilection for pragmatic modes of thinking. Similarly, both Copleston and MacIntyre display a "beginning-orientation,"[32] which judges philosophical developments by their linkage to an early theoretical archetype, whether Platonic or Thomistic. The chapters below purport to show how disputes such as these regarding the articulation of a history of Western philosophy are also reflected in scholarship concerned with the history of Jewish philosophy. The full force of this debate will become apparent later on, when we undertake a close analysis of the works of Harry Wolfson, Julius Guttmann and Leo Strauss, with a view to extrapolating the systematic worldviews that guided them in their research.

SYSTEMATIC PREMISES IN "THE SCIENCE OF JUDAISM"

We have reviewed above certain schools of thought concerning the study of the history of Western philosophy, in order to create a context for our examination of the theoretical trends that can be extrapolated from scholarship dealing with the history of Jewish philosophy. However, before attempting a theoretical analysis of contemporary scholarly works in the field, the analysis must be anchored, however briefly, in another context. The reference is to orientations which have guided scholarship in the field of Jewish studies. This introduction is not the proper framework for a comprehensive, in-depth review of the various scholarly approaches that have informed academic Jewish studies in the nineteenth and twentieth centuries, even if we were to restrict ourselves to the area of Jewish philosophy. Yet, in order to gain some perspective on the scholarship of Wolfson, Guttmann and Strauss, it is important that we take note of a few points raised by contemporary scholars and thinkers on the question of ideology in Jewish studies and on the systematic trends of thought that have influenced research in the field.

According to Nathan Rotenstreich, the founders of academic Jewish scholarship during the first half of the nineteenth century aspired to uncompromising objectivity.[33] They denied Jewish tradition all normative status; they did not consider its content capable or worthy of shaping the worldview and lifestyle of the modern Jew. They sought no continuing connection with the tradition; they were not out to amend or reform the Jewish religion and were no longer even caught up in the struggle to liberate themselves from the past in order to achieve objectivity. In Rotenstreich's words, "the severance of all connections with the world of tradition" was an "accomplished, incontrovertible fact."[34] In his view, the first scholars of Jewish studies, whose most prominent representative was Leopold Zunz, were also not decisively influenced by the romantic trend underlying historical research in Germany at the time, the same trend which used the past as a kind of platform for nationalist values in the present. Pursuant to the late eighteenth-century ideal of the Jewish enlightenment, the founders of Jewish studies nurtured among themselves an objective neutrality, refraining to the greatest possible extent from making any value judgments, positive or negative.

Nevertheless, argues Rotenstreich, the quest for objectivity did not release these scholars from certain systematic assumptions which guided their work. He lists them as follows:

1. From the enlightenment, Zunz and the members of his generation borrowed the ideal of rationality, namely, the obligation to evaluate the phenomena of life in accordance with reason. The assumption was that mere existence, without the achievement of knowledge and self-awareness, is not humanly adequate.
2. Knowledge or awareness of the past is not attained by assembling historical details and arranging them in order next to one another.

Historical details are not comprehensible unless they are associated with a guiding idea. The creation of this connection between events and the idea behind them constitutes the historian's "artistic" function.

3. Every event that is investigated may be classified within the framework of a historical evolutionary process. The event's comprehensibility is contingent upon the scholar's connecting it to the dimension of time preceding it.

4. These premises, which apply to history in general, hold true with regard to the history of Judaism as well, as the details of Judaism are guided by an overarching idea, by an "essence."

5. The course of Jewish history can be viewed as a teleological development in the direction of the growth of Jewish self-awareness: the awareness of a people (or at least its intellectuals) concerning the essential idea constituting Judaism.

6. This awareness of the guiding idea of Judaism develops from a concrete and particularistic viewpoint to a more abstract and universal perspective.

7. There is value in the study of religion, for religion harbors true rational ideas in the form of images.

8. Judaism should not be regarded as a separate phenomenon, but as part of universal human culture.

Gershom Scholem dwelled extensively on the tensions characterizing the field of Jewish studies from the outset, and which continued to beset it for many years.[35] In his evaluation, the aspiration to objectivity bespoke a destructive bent, although some of the fundamental tenets enumerated above joined together to form a positive, constructive gesture, at times against the will of the scholars themselves. From Scholem's point of view, Zunz and Steinschneider represented a "demonic-destructive" impulse. Historical criticism, which functionally relativizes events and ideas to the context of time and place alone, promotes the disintegration of Judaism as a living organism. This approach lent the study of traditional Jewish texts the aspect of a funeral rite; consequently, the texts were seen to exercise influence only inwardly, among themselves, rather than radiating outwards and becoming the basis for a renewed confrontation with the past by subsequent generations. Nevertheless, the field of Jewish studies also manifested a constructive tendency, namely, the re-collection of sources and values that had been marginalized and their transformation into a renewed source of cultural nourishment. Such an inclination could gather momentum once a national framework was created which would induce the Jewish people to seek out the sources of their vitality as they were in themselves, without resort to metaphysical or moral apologetics. Yet in the days of Zunz and Steinschneider there was no national ground on the basis of which it might be possible to develop this constructive inclination, such that any such reclamation of textual material occurred only unintentionally and a posteriori.

Scholem believed that during the second half of the nineteenth century there was a turning point in Jewish studies, which can be explained in part by social and institutional factors. Zunz and Steinschneider were unencumbered by any theological orientation and were not affiliated with the institutions for higher learning of any of the streams of German Judaism, whether liberal or moderate. Over the course of time, however, it became apparent that the German universities were not opening their gates to scholars of Jewish studies. Such scholars could receive appointments only in Jewish institutions, and each of these had a particular theological commitment. As a result, maintains Scholem, even the best scholars of this generation, such as David Kaufman and David Neumark, reflected the apologetic tendencies of their institutions. There was a general trend towards "sentimentalizing" the affiliation with Judaism and "spiritualizing" Judaism itself. Every historical stream which could not portray itself as a rational combination of progress and moderation was considered a "marginal" or "pagan" phenomenon, which reflected "external influences." In Scholem's view, only an approach which neither sought too actively to revive Judaism, nor too actively to destroy it, was capable of achieving the public support of the German Jewish bourgeoisie.

An analysis of the first chapter of David Neumark's *Toldot Ha-Filosofiah be-Israel* (*A History of Jewish Thought*), entitled "The Functions of Jewish Philosophy in Contemporary Times,"[36] would seem to confirm Scholem's view. Neumark is an example of a scholar who declares his motives for scholarship to be of an explicitly theological and apologetic nature. According to Neumark, the study of contemporary Jewish history should not be animated by the pursuit of historical knowledge for its own sake, nor even by the wish to encourage a connection with past thought or identification with its contents. True, said Neumark, there might be some continuity between essential principles of faith, common to the "ethical monotheism" of ancient and medieval times and to modern Jewish theology. As far as "historical teachings" are concerned, namely, developmental and empirical ways of thinking applied to issues like miracles and the Divine origin of the Law—a large gap divides the modern educated Jew from his medieval counterpart. Whatever continuity exists between past and contemporary Jewish philosophy finds its expression in aims rather than content. The aim is explicitly apologetic: to purge Judaism of idol worship and mythology.

In Neumark's opinion, Judaism's contribution to human culture was and is "the expansion of the boundaries of theoretical and logical thought" at the expense of "mythological thinking."[37] For him, the Jewish religion is "systematic, logical and theoretical" in character, and the narrative of the history of Judaism is the narrative of the development of abstract thought. Lucid reasoning is Judaism's weapon against mythology.

Neumark does indeed vehemently denounce "a priori constructs" in the study of history. He does not posit a scheme which regards the latest way of thinking as the "redemption of the historical process," a la Hegel. Yet neither does he accept the perspective, which he coins the "end of prophecy" approach, whereby spiritual perfection is held to reside in a given period of the past, or within the thought of a certain great man.[38] However, despite his sensitivity to a priori constructs, Neumark nevertheless held that a certain progress can be perceived in the development of Jewish philosophy. The prophets of Israel advance the cause of self-conscious rationality through their war against irrational myths. Medieval thinkers' struggle against erroneous opinions led to the development and expansion of ethical monotheism from a "life-perspective" to a full cosmological "worldview." This progressive process conducts itself by way of some kind of dialectical law: At a certain stage the repudiation of mythology brings a new mythological reaction in its wake. This reaction again prompts Jews to distance themselves from the concrete, in the direction of the abstract. This additional step forward generates another reaction, and so forth.

For Neumark, then, Jewish philosophizing had the same function in the past as it does in the present: to protect the principles of Jewish faith and to conduct an ideological crusade against the ever-present idolatrous impulse. It is the task of contemporary Jewish philosophy to engage in a comprehensive, incisive debate with the proponents of "coarse materialism" who deny "spiritual realism."[39] Such philosophizing must serve the theological objective of "responding to the Epicurean"—today as before. It may be possible to employ ancient philosophical arguments to this end, yet in many matters, Neumark contends, it will be necessary to "adapt" the heritage of the past to present categories, and to conduct a "systematic articulation of the principles of Judaism" based on a "modern philosophical worldview."[40] It would seem, however, that Neumark's objective is to employ modern concepts to embellish the fixed ideological core of Judaism, rather than to reformulate Jewish viewpoints on the basis of new systematic premises.

If the endeavor succeeds, says Neumark, it will afford the educated modern Jew a certain intellectual equilibrium. The longing for "a definite, comprehensive worldview"[41] underlying the philosophic quest will be satisfied once the individual finds answers to eternal philosophical questions within his own religion. For surely it is not desirable that one's consciousness should be plagued by a persistent compartmentalization or struggle between one's philosophy or general outlook and the main articles of one's faith.

One can easily understand why Gershom Scholem so fiercely opposed approaches like Neumark's. Scholem was searching for the roots of Jewish vitality precisely in the "mythological" aspects of Jewish thought and regarded the "spiritualization" of Judaism that Neumark exemplified as a sign of an exilic detachment from the national life force. In his view, living organisms are in a perpetual state of tension and internal struggle, and one should not expect them to achieve equilibrium. Unlike the founders of the field of Jewish studies, however, Scholem sought to deliberately pursue the conflict between the "destructive" and "constructive" impulses within Jewish scholarship. The cruel relativization wrought by philological-historical research subverts all sentimental or apologetic attachments to Judaism, forcing the modern Jew to face the "mythological" chapters of the past which he preferred to repress. This state of affairs, created through wholly "secular" tools, also facilitates the forging of a new, more authentic religious connection between the Jew and his literary sources.[42]

In light of Rotenstreich and Scholem's remarks, one can regard Wolfson, Guttmann and Strauss as a distinct group of scholars, succeeding Kaufman and Neumark. To begin with, none of them was affiliated with a Jewish institution of a definite theological cast for the bulk of his productive years. Wolfson's base was Harvard University, and his ambition was to redeem Jewish studies from the "Oriental Studies" departments and constitute it as a field of study in its own right. Guttmann, although he received rabbinic ordination in Breslau and headed the College for Jewish Studies in Berlin, held a university appointment, first in Breslau and later at the Hebrew University of Jerusalem. Strauss, who was Guttmann's pupil in Berlin, found his place at the "New School of Social Research" in New York, and subsequently at the University of Chicago. It may be that the affiliation of these scholars with research universities liberated them from the need to identify with a particular theological stream.

Second, all three scholars were exposed to the movement for national Jewish revival. However, this exposure does not seem to have had any decisive or formative influence on their work. Wolfson regarded himself, at least at the beginning of his career, as a nationalist Hebrew intellectual committed to the revival of Jewish uniqueness in the modern period. According to Ze'ev Harvey,[43] this "Hebrew" orientation accompanied Wolfson throughout his life, and this is the explanation for Wolfson's theory regarding the "Hebrew" character of all of Western philosophy. Nevertheless, the national element seems almost completely absent from the substance of his research. The clear focus of his interest was on the Jewish religion as a system of theological doctrine. Neither the national Jewish experience, the people's reflections on itself nor the people's deliberations on its fate engaged him. Although Guttmann, in contrast, came to the land of Israel, was active at the Hebrew University and participated in forums on the question of the Jewish character of the settlement in Palestine,[44] the national component of the Jewish experience does not carry significant weight in his scholarship. His principal concern, as the next few chapters will clarify, was with the character of Jewish religiosity, and its attempt to understand itself through recourse to philosophical reflection. Strauss was a Zionist in his youth[45] and wrote of the State of Israel's importance for the restoration of Jewish dignity. Yet his systematic views led him far beyond any form of nationalism, and he came to regard Judaism as a purely religious gesture, diametrically opposed to philosophical reflection.

Scholem's critique of the assumptions of Neumark, Kaufman and their generation did not detract from his estimation of them as scholars of high stature. He also expressed the opinion that Wolfson, Guttmann, Strauss and others of their generation paralleled Neumark and Kaufman in theirs.[46] However, it is not our intention here to address the influences that a certain generation of scholars might have had on its successors. Our subject is the systematic basis of the writings of Wolfson, Guttmann and Strauss, the same basis on which N. Rotenstreich included these three scholars in his book *Iyunnim ba-Machshavah ha-Yehudit ba-Zman ha-Zeh* (*Studies in Contemporary Jewish Thought*), alongside R. Kook, Soloveitchik, Leibowitz, Buber and Hugo Bergman.[47]

Where do Wolfson, Guttmann and Strauss stand in relation to the questions we posed at the outset regarding the systematic articulation of the history of philosophy, and with regard to systematic trends in Jewish studies? What was their approach to questions such as the construction of the history of thought on the basis of a pre-existing worldview, the autonomy of philosophy vis-a-vis theology and culture, the question of progress in the history of philosophy and possible ways of reconciling the conflicting streams within it? In order to answer these questions, we will undertake a careful analysis of the works of these scholars in the chapters that follow.

An examination of the writings of Wolfson, Guttmann and Strauss reveals that all of them approached the study of the Jewish philosophic past from a systematic standpoint. They structured this past on the basis of strong theoretical assumptions regarding the essence of religion, the essence of philosophy and their patterns of interaction. They also conducted their research on the basis of definite assumptions concerning the manner in which past religious philosophy manifested and disclosed itself. Their scholarship represents living testimony to Copleston's declaration that significant historical writing is possible only from a principled starting point. Each of them had his own viewpoint regarding the extent of philosophy's dependence on or independence from religion or culture, as well as the degree to which religion is enriched by its contacts with philosophy. Similarly, each of them staked out a position concerning the possibility of synthesis between religion and philosophy, or between different trends in the history of Jewish thought. On the question of the degree of progress manifested in the history of Jewish philosophy, Guttmann's perspective also differs from that of Wolfson, and Strauss takes issue with both views. Although their approaches to these fundamental questions were fundamentally different, they all adhered to a systematic theoretical position and it was this standpoint that guided their scholarship.

A FRAMEWORK FOR ANALYZING SYSTEMATIC PREMISES

In disclosing the systematic substructures informing the works of Wolfson, Guttmann and Strauss, we have found it useful to employ a framework suggested by Joseph Schwab for analyzing theoretical doctrines in the sciences. This framework is based on the assumption that the transition between human modes of conceptualization and the phenomena of the external world is not unmediated. Every piece of research which aims to provide a satisfactory explanation for a range of specific phenomena on the basis of some kind of comprehensive principle is controlled by a particular conceptual structure. This conceptual structure, or in Schwab's terminology, "substantive structure,"[48] determines what questions will be asked within the framework of a given piece of research. These questions in turn prescribe for the scholar what type of facts he should seek. And finally, once the facts have been assembled, the scholar interprets them and accords them significance in keeping with the substantive structure that guided his research.

Substantive structures, then, mediate between consciousness and phenomena. An elaboration of this principle is the fact that different substantive structures necessitate different canons of proof. Not only do the criteria for proving a historical fact differ from the criteria for proving a fact in the empirical sciences, but even within the framework of the same discipline, sometimes different means of verification are required to prove different types of facts. In order to illustrate this point, Schwab brings an example from the field of history. The way of proving the truth of a historian's claim (to the extent that it is possible to attain the "truth" at all) concerning the location of President Roosevelt on the last day of his life differs from the methods of verification which would be employed in order to prove Roosevelt's order of priorities for his decisions at Yalta. The process of verification in the first case would be guided by the concept of history as a mere list of chronological events. By way of contrast, in the second case the search would be guided by the assumption that in order to understand history it is necessary to reveal the inner aims and intentions of significant historical figures.[49]

The complex of problems concerning the pathways to verification and canons of proof whereby a certain disciplinary orientation gathers what it considers to be valid knowledge is termed "syntactic structure" by Schwab.[50]

In order to disclose the substantive structure underlying a scientific theory, according to Schwab, one begins by "identifying the terms and distinctions which constitute the skeleton (the structure) of a theory."[51] The theory is considered to apply to some definite "whole," such as the "soul" or the "short story," which has been isolated from other phenomena and targeted for special research.[52] Within the overall framework, the theory identifies parts or elements, such as the parts of the soul according to Aristotle or Freud, or elements such as "plot," "character," "style" and "message," which are addressed by certain approaches to narrative. The theory also attributes special qualities to the whole and to its parts and asserts the existence of a particular relationship among the various parts that make up the whole.[53]

There are cases in which the relationship is characterized as mutual dependence, or as the dependence of several parts on a single part (such as the dependence of the "ego" and "super-ego" on the "id" as a source of energy, according to Freud's theory of personality). At times, one part is dominant, and other parts subordinated to it, not by virtue of the dominant part's serving as a source for others, but by its being the end to which the others aspire, an end which bestows some of its special qualities on others. (See, for example, the preferential status accorded the cognitive part in Aristotle's theory of the soul.)[54]

In addition, there are certain parts which partake of a pattern of movement in time, such as the dialectical movement forward which leads to the realization of the goal of freedom at the end of the historical process in Hegelian and Marxist theory. (In Hegel's system, the parts are states or peoples, whereas in Marx they are classes).[55]

The disclosure of the elements comprising the skeleton or architectonic structure of a given theory, as well as the articulation of the elements' characteristics and of the relations among them, is accomplished through a critical rhetorical analysis of the texts in which the theory is embedded. Such analysis is concerned to uncover the principles and basic assumptions underlying the theory, and to trace the manner in which these principles govern the research process. The reader's task is to penetrate beyond the data and interpretations offered by the researcher and to discover his position regarding the essence of the discipline itself.[56]

We will begin by identifying the component elements of Jewish philosophy according to the systems of each of the thinkers—Wolfson, Guttmann and Strauss—and continue with a description of the properties of those elements and a characterization of the relationships obtaining among them. These steps will lead us to pose the following question: Does the dimension of time exert an influence on the elements' properties or relationships? Lastly, we will examine the canons of interpretation employed by each scholar, namely, his criteria for drawing interpretive conclusions as mandated by his conception of the discipline's structure. Three chapters will be devoted to the analysis of the system of each scholar (epistemological perspectives, historiosophical components and guidelines for interpretation).

The analysis of Guttmann and Strauss in parts 2 and 3 also includes comparative remarks.

In the chapters dealing with aspects of epistemology, the discussion will revolve around the scholar's outlook on the character of religious and philosophical knowledge and the possible interactions between them. In this manner we will analyze the relevant "totality," that of Jewish philosophy with regard to both of its "elements": the Jewish religion and philosophy. During the course of the analysis, each scholar's unique conception regarding the character of the Jewish religion and of philosophy will become apparent. It will become clear that the different ways in which they understand the properties of the elements comprising Jewish philosophy lead the three scholars to characterize the relationship between Judaism and philosophy in three distinct ways. We will attempt to show that Wolfson subordinates one of the elements (philosophy) to the other (Judaism), Guttmann conceives of a mutual influence and a limited interpenetration of the two, while his pupil Strauss asserts that the two elements necessarily repel each other (although he believes that the instrumental use of one element by the other is both possible and necessary).

The focus on historiosophy in the second chapter of each analysis brings the dimension of time into the discussion of the elements of Jewish philosophy. Within this framework, principles of movement in time are disclosed, and their influence (or lack of influence) on the elements of Jewish philosophy is described. Along with the differences in the epistemological sphere noted above, in Wolfson's view Jewish philosophy acquired its fundamental contours at the time of its inception, in the works of Philo. (All subsequent thought, Christian and Muslim as well as Jewish, is merely the unfolding and application of a pre-existing foundation). Unlike Wolfson, Guttmann attributes an evolutionary movement to Jewish philosophy. Transitions from one period to another bring improvement and refinement in their train. Strauss, in contrast to both, argues that in thought of the highest order there is only an external appearance of movement in time, and that every outstanding thinker (whether thoughtful Jew or philosopher) is a totally meta-historical phenomenon.

The third and concluding chapter in the analysis of each theory will focus on canons of interpretation and will trace the processes by way of which each scholar organizes the data of his choice, and how he weaves his data into patterns that create what he considers to be valid meaning. We will seek to understand, among other things, how each scholar accounts for logical contradictions in the texts he studies, how he integrates a scholarly detail into a "totality" which endows it with meaning, how he characterizes the relations between form and substance in a philosophic work, and what type of causality serves him as a source of explanation.

A short introduction will be appended to the study of each scholar's works, containing necessary background information.

We will consider ourselves amply rewarded if this project, which highlights the systematic plurality prevailing in the discipline of the history of Jewish philosophy, contributes to an increased recognition of the weight of the systematic element as a guiding factor in research and instruction in the field.

NOTES

1. Isadore Twersky, foreword to Harry Austryn Wolfson, *Repercussions of the Kalam in Jewish Philosophy* (Cambridge, MA: Harvard University Press, 1979), ix.

2. Eliezer Schweid, "Ha-Philosophia ha-Yehudit ke-Echad ha-Zeramim ba-Philosophia shel ha-Meah ha-Essrim," *Da'at* 23 (Summer 1989): 101.

3. Shlomo Pines, "Ha-Ma'amar ha-Teologi-Medini le-Shpinoza, ha-Rambam ve-Kant," in *Bein Machshevet Israel le-Machshevet ha-Amim* (Jerusalem: Bialik Institute, 1977), 307.

4. The following discussion of systematic reasons for studying the history of philosophy is based on Nathan Rotenstreich, *Al Tchumah shel-ha-Philosophia* (Jerusalem: Hebrew University Press, 1969), 160–79; and on his remarks at a conference on "Hora'at ha-Philosophiah be-Veit-ha-Sefer ha-Tichon u-va-Universitah," *Iyyun* 23 (January 1972): 33–43.

5. John Passmore's distinctions, although in a different order, first appeared in his article "The Idea of a History of Philosophy," *History and Theory—Studies in the History of Philosophy, Beiheft* 5 (1965): 1–32. Later they appeared in more concise and refined form in his article, "Historiography of Philosophy," in *The Encyclopedia of Philosophy*, vol. VI, ed. Paul Edwards (New York: Quentin Macmillan Co., 1967), 226–29. An additional article which appeared in the same collection of *History and Theory*, which relates to the history of philosophy as a type of "unique history" with partial autonomy and internal continuity which cannot be reduced to the "history of culture," is: Maurice Mandelbaum, "The History of Ideas, Intellectual History, and the History of Philosophy," 33–66.

6. The discussion of Windelband's theories is based on pp. 1–22 of Wilhelm Windelband, *A History of Philosophy* (New York: Harper, 1958).

7. Windelband, *A History of Philosophy*, 7.

8. Windelband, *A History of Philosophy*, 9.

9. Windelband, *A History of Philosophy*, 9.

10. Windelband, *A History of Philosophy*, 8, 10.

11. Windelband, *A History of Philosophy*, 8, 10–11.

12. Windelband draws here from the book by Victor Cousin, *Cours de l'histoire de la philosophie* (Paris: Pichon et Didier, 1829), particularly from the fourth lesson in the first volume, pp. 133–72.

13. The discussion of Copleston's views is based on Frederick Copleston, *A History of Philosophy* (London: Burns & Oates, 1946) i, 1–22.

14. Later published as Richard Rorty, Jerome B. Schneewind and Quentin Skinner, eds., *Philosophy in History—Essays on the Historiography of Philosophy* (Cambridge: Cambridge University Press, 1984).

15. Richard Rorty, "The Historiography of Philosophy: Four Genres," in Rorty, Schneewind and Skinner, *Philosophy in History*, 49–76; Alasdair MacIntyre, "The Relationship of Philosophy to its Past," in Rorty, Schneewind and Skinner, *Philosophy in History*, 31–48.

16. Rorty, "Historiography," 49.

17. Rorty, "Historiography," 49–53.

18. Rorty, "Historiography," 50, quoting from Quentin Skinner, "Meaning and Understanding in the History of Ideas," *History and Theory* 8 (1969): 28.

19. Rorty, "Historiography," 51.

20. Rorty, "Historiography," 53–56.

21. Rorty, "Historiography," 61–67.

22. Rorty, "Historiography," 56–61.

23. Rorty, "Historiography," 67–73.

24. MacIntyre, "The Relationship of Philosophy," 31–32.

25. MacIntyre, "The Relationship of Philosophy," 32–39.

26. MacIntyre, "The Relationship of Philosophy," 40–41.

27. MacIntyre, "The Relationship of Philosophy," 46.

28. MacIntyre's discussion of the natural sciences can be found in "The Relationship of Philosophy," 41–45.

29. For Thomas Kuhn's approach, see his famous book *The Structure of Scientific Revolutions* (Chicago: University of Chicago Press, 1970), particularly pp. 79–81 concerning political and social factors in the exchange of "paradigms" in the history of science. Kuhn elaborates a bit on the communal factor in "paradigm shifts" in the book's epilogue, pp. 139–65.

30. MacIntyre , "The Relationship of Philosophy," 45.

31. Rorty, "Historiography," 59, 73.

32. The terms "end-orientation" and "beginning-orientation" are taken from Seymour Fox's book, *Freud and Education* (Springfield, IL: C. C. Thomas, 1975), pp. 31–45, where he characterizes Freud's thought as beginning-oriented.

33. Nathan Rotenstreich, *Tradition and Reality* (New York: Random House, 1972), 21–35.

34. Rotenstreich, *Tradition and Reality*, 22.

35. Gershon Scholem, "Mi-Toch Hirhurim al-Hochmat Israel," in his *Devarim be-Go* (Tel Aviv: Am Oved, 1976), 385–403. See also Scholem, "The Science of Judaism—Then and Now," *The Messianic Idea in Judaism* (New York: Schocken Books, 1971), 304–13.

36. David Neumark, *Toldot ha-Filosofiah be-Israel* (New York: Shtiebel & Others, 1921), 3–14.

37. Neumark, *Toldot*, 3.

38. Neumark, *Toldot*, 10–12.

39. Neumark, *Toldot*, 3.

40. Neumark, *Toldot*, 7.

41. Neumark, *Toldot*, 9.

42. Scholem, *Dvarim be-Go*, 400–402; Scholem, *Messianic Idea*, 312–13.

43. Regarding "Hebraism" as the basis for Wolfson's orientation, see Warren Zev Harvey, "Hebraism and Western Philosophy in H.A. Wolfson's Theory of History," *Immanuel* 14 (Fall 1982): 77–85.

44. See Guttmann's article, "Binyan Eretz Israel ve-ha-Yahadut," *Ptachim* 12 (Spring 1970), 19–26.

45. See Strauss's autobiographical comments in his introduction to the English edition of his book *Spinoza's Critique of Religion* (New York: Schocken Books, 1965), 1–7.

46. Scholem's comments about Wolfson and Guttmann appear in his book *Messianic Idea*, p. 313. His remark about Strauss appears in his book *Mi-Berlin li-Yerushalayim—Zichronot Neurim* (Tel Aviv: Am Oved, 1982), 171. In addition, his admiration for Strauss's talents and originality is documented in a letter to Benjamin published in Steven B. Smith's article, "Gershom Scholem and Leo Strauss: Notes Toward a German-Jewish Dialogue," *Modern Judaism* 13, no. 3 (October 1993): 226–27, note 6.

47. Nathan Rotenstreich, *Iyyunim ba-Machshavah ha-Yehudit ba-Zman ha-Zeh* (Tel Aviv: Am Oved, 1978). His chapter on Wolfson is called "Mechkar Histori ke-Omanut Cohanim" (pp. 104–9); on Guttmann, "Toldot ha-Toda'ah ha-Datit u-Mahutah" (pp. 132–38); on Strauss, "Bein Atuna li-Yerushalayim," (pp. 139–43).

48. Schwab's epistemological remarks on the question of the quality of human knowledge, along with his definitions of the term "substantive structure," can be found primarily in the following works: Joseph Schwab, "Dialectical Means vs. Dogmatic Extremes in Relation to Liberal Education," *Harvard Educational Review* 21, no. 1 (Winter 1951): 37–64, especially 39–41; Joseph Schwab, *Science, Curriculum and Liberal Education* (Chicago: University of Chicago Press, 1978), 184–228, 229–72; Joseph Schwab, "The Concept of the Structure of a Discipline," in *Conflicting Conceptions of Curriculum*, ed. Elliot W. Eisner and Elizabeth Vallance (Berkeley, CA: McCutchan, 1974), 162–75; Joseph Schwab, "Problems, Topics, Issues," in *Education and the Structure of Knowledge*, ed. Stanley Munson Elam (Chicago: Rand McNally, 1964), 4–43 (especially 8–10, 35–38).

49. On diverse "substantive structures" in the discipline of history according to Schwab, see Joseph Schwab, "The Practical: Arts of the Eclectic," *School Review* 81 (August 1973): 537–38; Edward Carr, *What is History?* (New York: Vintage, 1961); Fritz Stern, ed., *The Varieties of History* (New York: Meridian, 1956).

50. Among other places, Schwab discusses the term "syntactic structure" in his article "Education and the Structure of the Disciplines," 246 (see n. 48 above).

51. See Joseph J. Schwab, *The Practical: A Language for Curriculum* (Washington, D.C.: National Education Association, 1970), 12.

52. See Schwab, "What Do Scientists Do?" in *Science Curriculum and Liberal Education*, 186. There he terms this aspect of a given theory, which is exposed through critical analysis, "bounding."

53. In the same article, Schwab calls the identification of the parts and their characterization "analyzing." Concerning Freud's theory of the soul, see Sigmund Freud, "The Ego and the Id," in *The Standard Edition of the Complete Psychological Works of Sigmund Freud*, ixx, trans. and ed. James Strachey (London: Hogarth Press, 1961), 13–66. For one approach to the elements of a short story, see Hollis Summers, ed., introduction to *Discussions of the Short Story* (Boston, MA: Heath, 1966).

54. For an extensive analysis of the relationship between the elements of the soul, according to Freud's theory of personality, see Fox, *Freud and Education*. On pp. 2–24 of the introduction to the book, Fox, following Schwab, explores the possible

relationships between the parts which make up a theory. In his words, parts can be ranked in terms of the degree of influence one part exerts on the others, and they can also be classified according to the criteria of activity (the part "controls its own destiny") and passivity (it requires an external stimulus in order to function). Regarding the pride of place accorded the cognitive component in Aristotle's theory of the soul, see Aristotle, *On the Soul*, trans. W.S. Hett (London: William Heinemann, 1964), book 3, chapters 4–7, 163–79; Aristotle, *The Nichomachean Ethics*, trans. H. Rackham (London: William Heinemann, 1926), book 2, chapter 4, 83–87; book 10, chapter 7, 613–19. See also Schwab's comments in his article "The Practical: Arts of the Eclectic," 521–22 (note 49 above).

55. Joseph Schwab, "The Practical: Arts of the Eclectic," p. 537 (note 49 above); see also W.H. Walsh, *Philosophy of History* (New York-Evanston, IL: Harper Torchbooks, 1967), 156.

56. For a theoretical characterization and practical illustration of the process of "rhetorical analysis," see Joseph Schwab, "Enquiry and the Reading Process," *Journal of General Education* 11 (1958): 72–82.

I

ORIENTATION BY ORIGINS: BIBLICAL THEOLOGY AND ITS UNFOLDING IN THE SCHOLARSHIP OF HARRY AUSTRYN WOLFSON

INTELLECTUAL BACKGROUND

Harry Austryn Wolfson was born in 1887 in the village of Ussertine, Lithuania.[1] As a young man he studied in religious seminaries in Grodno and Byalistok, proceeding from there to the Slobodka yeshiva in the city of Kovno. Of a Zionist/nationalist orientation, he belonged to a Hebrew Zionist circle of senior seminary students.

In 1903, the Wolfson family emigrated to the United States, and Harry Wolfson studied in Rabbi Yitzhak Elhanan's yeshiva in New York. He subsequently found a position teaching in the Hebrew school in Scranton, Pennsylvania, while himself studying in the public high school. During this period Wolfson composed Hebrew poetry, and several of his poems were published in Hebrew periodicals.

In 1908, by virtue of his outstanding academic achievements, Wolfson was awarded a scholarship to Harvard University. He completed his bachelor's degree in 1911, and his master's in 1912. That year he won a Sheldon scholarship, which enabled him to devote almost two years to the study of ancient Hebrew manuscripts in the great European libraries. In 1915, Wolfson received his doctorate for his thesis on the Jewish medieval thinker Rabbi Hasdai Crescas, and from 1915–1925 he served as a lecturer in temporary appointments.

In 1925, Wolfson became the first professor in the United States to occupy an academic chair devoted entirely to Jewish studies. Throughout the period of his tenure at Harvard until his death in 1974, Harry Wolfson strove to transform the field of Jewish studies from its status as an adjunct to classical and Christian studies into an independent theoretical discipline in its own right.[2]

Ze'ev Harvey, in his article on Wolfson's theory of history,[3] holds that Wolfson's early Hebraic orientation informed the entire corpus of his works. During his initial studies at Harvard, he was significantly influenced by his teacher, the philosopher George Santyana, himself the pupil of the famous pragmatist William James. Harvey asserts that it was this influence which prompted Wolfson to argue the superiority of Rabbi Yehuda Ha-Levi's worldview over that of Maimonides, in his first published article in the field of Jewish studies.[4] He portrays Ha-Levi there as the emissary of the Hebraic spirit, which is fundamentally ethical in character. It views the world as a dynamic current and demands the subject's involvement in his relationship with God. According to Wolfson, then, Ha-Levi's Judaism is pragmatic and functional in nature, having the power to shape the daily deeds of human beings. Maimonides, in contrast, represents a cosmological, Hellenistic orientation, which sees the world through the prism of static structures and points humans towards objectivity and detachment. In Wolfson's opinion, the pragmatic value of this speculative Hellenistic approach is very limited.[5]

His major work on R. Hasdai Crescas, published in 1929, still bears the imprint of this early point of view. Crescas is also presented as a Hebraist who openly challenges philosophy.[6] However, by the 1930s, in his book on Spinoza, and even more so by the 1940s, Wolfson had changed his approach. From then on, Hebraism and the Greek philosophical tradition are depicted as being on friendly terms, with Greek philosophy being taken under the wing of Biblical theology, deferring to the latter's fundamental principles of belief. Here as well, writes Harvey, Hebraism maintains its primacy in Wolfson's thought. Henceforth, Wolfson would no longer seek to prove the superiority of an independent, fully crystallized Hebraic worldview to Hellenism, but rather the ascendance of the Hebraic orientation within the Greek philosophical tradition itself.[7] In the sections below we will analyze this thesis, which Wolfson promoted and disseminated for most of his life.

Nathan Rotenstreich, in a chapter of his book *Studies in Contemporary Jewish Philosophy*, seeks to clarify Wolfson's choice to specialize in medieval religious philosophy given his prior immersion in Talmudic studies.[8] He relies on an article Wolfson published in 1920 in the Harvard Jewish students' periodical, the *Menorah Journal*, which is also quoted in Leo Schwarz's bibliographical article. Wolfson states there that while the Talmud and its accompanying literature are the most fertile ground for original research in Jewish studies, "I believe that aside from the Bible, medieval Jewish philosophy is the only important branch of Jewish literature which ties us to general world literature. This is the mutual foundation of our culture, European culture and the cultures of Asia and Africa."[9]

For Rotenstreich, this statement demonstrates that in Wolfson's view, philosophy written in Hebrew "occupies an important place in the expanse of partnership and intimacy."[10] Alongside his desire to emphasize the uniqueness and dominance of the Jewish worldview, he seems also to have aspired to commune with the best in Western culture and civilization.

Nevertheless, his student Isadore Twersky reminds us that throughout his life Wolfson viewed himself primarily as a scholar of Jewish philosophy, which he regarded as the foundation of Western philosophy.[11] This thesis of his will be discussed at length in subsequent chapters.

Within the framework of this background survey, we will not attempt to ascertain which biographical influences were most formative in shaping Wolfson's beliefs. We will proceed at this point to consider his scholarly writings as reflecting a unified, systematic and coherent approach to religious and philosophic knowledge, historiosophy and exegesis. We will be more interested in the internal connections between the elements of his system, and in illustrating its application to specific scholarly issues, than in tracing a connection between his life circumstances and his worldview. In analyzing his works, we will base ourselves on his principal scholarship in the field of religious philosophy—his books on Crescas, Philo, Spinoza, the Church Fathers, the Kalam, the repercussions of the Kalam in Jewish philosophy and collections of his articles.[12] We will not presume to pass scholarly judgment on Wolfson's observations concerning the views of the thinkers he studied. We will restrict ourselves to sketching Wolfson's own theoretical system as it emerges from his writings, without seeking to evaluate it according to scholarly canons external to his approach.

NOTES

1. For a detailed biography of Wolfson, see Leo Schwarz, *Wolfson of Harvard* (Philadelphia: Jewish Publication Society of America, 1978). For a survey of Wolfson's writings, with an evaluation of his literary style, see Leo Schwarz, "A Bibliographical Essay," in *Harry Austryn Wolfson Jubilee Volume*, vol. I, ed. Saul Lieberman (Jerusalem: American Academy for Jewish Research, 1965), 1–46.

2. The significance of this fact is noted in the appreciative words penned by his student Isadore Twersky in the prologue to Schwarz's book, *Wolfson of Harvard*, p. xxii.

3. Warren Zev Harvey, "Hebraism and Western Philosophy in H.A. Wolfson's Theory of History," *Immanuel* 14 (Fall 1982): 77–85.

4. Harry Wolfson, "Maimonides and Hallevi—A Study in Typical Jewish Attitudes Towards Greek Philosophy in the Middle Ages," *Jewish Quarterly Review* II (1911–1912): 297–337.

5. Harvey, "Hebraism," 103–6.

6. Harry Austryn Wolfson, *Crescas' Critique of Aristotle* (Cambridge, MA: Harvard University Press, 1929), 13.

7. Harvey, "Hebraism," 106–8.

8. Nathan Rotenstreich, *Iyyunim ba-Machshavah ha-Yehudit ba-Zman ha-Zeh* (Tel Aviv: Am Oved, 1978), 104–9.

9. Harry Wolfson, "The Needs of Jewish Scholarship in America," *Menorah Journal* 7, no. 1 (February 1921): 5.

10. Rotenstreich, *Iyyunim*, 105.

11. In his preface to the collection of Wolfson's articles he edited, Twersky testifies that "Wolfson regularly insists that he is primarily a student of medieval Jewish philosophy." *Studies in the History of Philosophy and Religion*, vol. I (Cambridge, MA: Harvard University Press, 1973), viii.

12. The reference is to the following works: *Religious Philosophy—A Group of Essays* (Cambridge, MA: Harvard University Press, 1961); *Studies in the History of Philosophy and Religion*, vol. I (Cambridge, MA: Harvard University Press, 1973); *Studies in the History of Philosophy and Religion*, vol. II (Cambridge, MA: Harvard University Press, 1977). For a bibliography of Wolfson's main writings, see: Schwarz, *Wolfson of Harvard*, 259–69.

1

Epistemological Perspectives— Religious and Philosophical Knowledge

Their Character and Modes of Interaction

RELIGIOUS KNOWLEDGE—ITS CHARACTER, ORIGINS AND INTERPRETATION OF REALITY

For research purposes, Harry Wolfson chose to occupy himself with a particular type of religious knowledge, a lucid characterization of which appears in the beginning of the preface to his book *Philo*:

> To medieval philosophers of the various creeds, religion was not an outworn survival of primitive times, which, with the magic wand of philosophy, they tried to transform into something serviceable. Nor was it to them a peculiar kind of human experience, which, by philosophic probing into the mysterious workings of the subnormal or supernormal human mind, they hoped to track down to its hidden sources. Nor, again, was religion to them a floating wreckage of an ancient term, gutted out of its original contents, which, in accordance with the salvage-laws of language, they appropriated and used as a designation for their own particular brands of philosophy. It was to them a certain set of inflexible principles, of a divinely revealed origin, by which philosophy, the product of erring human reason, had to be tested and purged and purified.[1]

Wolfson is polemicizing here against several schools of scholarship in the philosophical pragmatism of his time. He rules out those definitions of religion which serve modern extra-religious interests, seeking instead an authentic characterization of historical religion as it understands itself. According to Wolfson's definition, the content of religion is a set of principles which together constitute a coherent *system* of beliefs and opinions. These principles do not change and are not subject to the influence of place and time; their origin lies in Divine revelation. Only religious knowledge is

absolute knowledge, by virtue of its Divine source, while human philosophic knowledge is not absolute. Accordingly, it is only fit that religion be
the arbiter of reason. Wolfson rejects, with not a little scorn, instrumental theories of religion.
Religion is not, Wolfson asserts, a means of legitimizing the intellectual or
social proclivities of human beings. Its source is not to be found in human
experience, particularly not in some mysterious or esoteric psychic realm.[2]

In setting forth this characterization of religion, Wolfson focuses on that
aspect of the religious phenomenon which he considers worthy of research.
While in one of his early articles he also states that the Talmud (which embodies the legal aspect of the Jewish religion) provides a more fertile
ground for research from an internal Jewish perspective than the philosophic works, the overall body of his work testifies to his affinity for the
doctrinal aspect of religion.[3] Just as he did not focus on the law or the commandments as the media of religious life, he did not concern himself with
the living personal connection between the believer and his God. If we
adopt the distinction drawn by Mendelssohn and Buber between "belief" in
the sense of the believer's trust in a personal God and "belief" in the sense
of an internal conviction that a particular assertion regarding the nature of
Divinity is correct, Wolfson's works are dedicated entirely to "belief *that*"
rather than to "belief *in*."[4]

The question then arises as to the factors that are likely to influence a person's principles of belief. On what basis do people reach decisions about issues such as God's infinity, general and individual providence, Divine omnipotence and the truth of God's revelation to man?

Wolfson suggests that even though the empirical sciences show progress
in uncovering recurring natural processes, and even if the historical sciences
have focused our attention on the similarities between the myths of ancient
peoples and certain Biblical motifs, from the standpoint of pure logic, the
lawlike causality of nature can be viewed as the product of the will of an
omnipotent God (who can abrogate the laws of nature if He so wills), and
the Bible can be viewed as a unique book which bears witness to its Divine
source. Consequently, basic religious knowledge is not necessarily dependent on fluctuating empirical and historical knowledge.[5]

If empirical and historical science is not relevant to the fundamentals of
belief, what does influence the basic content of doctrinal religious knowledge? For Wolfson, the starting point of every religious doctrine is a prior
human commitment on metaphysical questions such as the existence of
God and how we can attain knowledge of God. This commitment usually
derives from an involvement with pagan or Biblical literature, accepted as
sacred scripture, or rejected in a gesture of rebellion.[6] One's position on this
issue conditions one's interpretations of natural processes as well as one's
orientation to canonical texts.[7]

Philo, whom Wolfson regarded as the founder and supreme representative of Western religious thought,[8] lists three possible fundamental positions on the issue of the foundation of religious knowledge. The first two approaches are derived from a pagan outlook, which holds that the source of religious knowledge about God, as well as the means by which human beings seek for knowledge of God, are immanent in human beings themselves. Within the framework of this pagan outlook, there are two further alternatives: the "atheistic" approach and the "theistic" approach.[9]

According to the "atheistic" approach, belief in God is a subjective fabrication rooted in the human imagination. Religious belief was concocted by a "sly ruler" in order to instill reverence for the law and obedience to its dictates in the masses. The "theistic" approach, in contrast, holds that the source of knowledge about God is not the subjective imagination but reason. It is within the power of reason to discover, by way of logical inferences, the existence of a God immanent in nature who exists independent of our awareness of Him.

According to this fundamental premise, human beings contemplate the natural world around them and seek to draw rational inferences regarding its origins. Plato, who envisioned a unified and eternal primordial matter underlying the diversity of our world, concluded that a Deity exists who fashioned this matter. Aristotle, who regarded the world as an eternal object in constant motion, reasoned that there must be an Unmoved Mover. The Stoics as well, who experienced the world as an ordered system possessed of beauty and purpose, inferred the existence of a God who represents the intellect or soul of the world. All of the foregoing are interpretations of the facts of nature, interpretations based on the assumption that from the conditions of the world's existence we can rationally infer the existence of an absolute being which is its source.[10]

Wolfson's attitude towards the pagan-theistic approach is ambivalent. From the short sermon with which he chose to conclude his collection of articles, *Religious Philosophy*, one could infer that the distance between the atheistic and theistic brands of paganism is not particularly great. The Greek philosophers who relied on reason, such as Plato, Aristotle and the Stoics, as well as certain modern philosophers, are all portrayed as "atheists." By this Wolfson means that they deny the existence of a God who created the world and presides over it. Instead of acknowledging the transcendental God, or openly professing their heresy, they propose substitutes such as the "Unmoved Mover" or the "soul of the world imprisoned within the entrails of the world," etc.[11]

After the example of "Scripture-bred religious thinkers," Wolfson holds that such formulations are generally "polite but empty phrases for the honest atheism of the fool in Scripture."[12] It would seem, then, that the sole determinant of a person's fundamental principles of faith is his acceptance or rejection of the transcendent and manifest God of the Bible. If we pursue this line of thought and ask on what basis human beings accept or reject the God of the Bible, Wolfson appears to consider the matter as dependent on their degree of their intellectual pride or modesty. Heretics refuse to admit that human beings are not capable of understanding things beyond their ken or of penetrating the intent of the Omnipotent God.[13] It is this moral quality which determines whether God will be seen as fundamentally resembling nature or as distinct from it. In effect, then, tenets of faith are contingent upon a person's moral character.

This moral-psychological stance is also manifest in the opening essay of the collection *Religious Philosophy*, "The Philonic God of Revelation and His Latter-Day Deniers."[14] The essay depicts two classes of human beings: those who accept the truths that Wolfson finds so obvious—that the Bible is distinct from myth, and that God is beyond human comprehension and above nature—and those who adamantly reject these truths. There are those who acknowledge Philo's "God of Revelation" and those who deny him, as their intellectual energy issues from a negative, "heretical" impulse.

Elsewhere, however, Wolfson is far more sympathetic to the pagan theistic orientation. Even in the above sermon he points out that Philo differentiated between believers and heretics among the Greeks themselves, classifying Plato, Aristotle and the Stoics in the camp of the believers. Philo also acknowledged the possibility of attaining a certain awareness of God through reason, despite the fact that perfect awareness can be achieved only by way of revelation.[15] In the second chapter of his book on Philo, Wolfson stresses statements by the latter to the effect that reason and philosophy were Divine gifts bestowed on the Greeks, gifts which enabled them to attain on their own certain truths which the Bible revealed to the people of Israel. Wolfson asserts that "Philosophy is thus just as much a gift of God to non-Jews as revelation is to the Jews. This is in accordance with his general view, based upon Scripture, that all knowledge comes from God."[16]

From here it seems that even knowledge about God acquired through the human intellect originates in some form of revelation, whence its truth value. Wolfson's ambivalence regarding religious knowledge achieved through reason derives from a fundamental ambivalence towards classical and modern philosophy, which claim to represent the fruits of reason. This subject will be explored at greater length when we address the status of reason from the standpoint of religion.

As for the third fundamental position, that of the Bible, Wolfson ascribes a number of basic principles to it which were first formulated by Philo. Philo arrived at these principles while grappling directly with the doctrines of the Greek philosophers. He contends that these Philonic principles were accepted by all of the monotheistic religions. First, as already mentioned, from the Biblical standpoint, the most profound form of religious knowledge is attained through revelation. There are two facets to this revelation: the one-time event at Sinai and the protracted revelation transmitted through Divine inspiration across the generations.

The experience of Sinai was in itself a one-time event, yet the Divine revelation continues. The original revelation had to be conveyed by way of human language, which is flawed by its very nature. The ambiguity inherent in language necessitates interpretation in order to ascertain the true meaning of the written word. This problem led to the genesis of the Oral Law, which began as an attempt by the human intellect to uncover the hidden meanings of the text of the Written Law. From this point on, Divine revelation consists of a response to these efforts, aiding and encouraging human interpretation.[17]

Through both the one-time and continuing revelations, human beings attain a more perfect knowledge of God than the philosophers did by way of reason. Only through revelation can humans grasp the true infinity of God, while all conceptions of Divinity derived from reason portray the Deity as possessed of various finite and limited qualities. Only the revelatory conception, such as that articulated in the work of Philo and the medieval "scriptural" philosophers, presents the Deity as unknowable and beyond description.[18] While Greek philosophy portrays the Deity as bound by obligatory laws external to him in everything concerning his relation to the world, the revelatory approach depicts him as a deliberate and purposive agent possessed of absolute freedom.

From the Aristotelian perspective, which assumes the eternity of the world, the world would seem to represent an alternate source of power alongside the Deity, thereby limiting his omnipotence. "Scriptural philosophy," in contrast, affirms that the world was created ex nihilo for a reason, and that God is free in principle to alter the primal order of things. Even God's goodness is grasped as truly infinite only through revelation. From the scriptural perspective, God not only presides over nature as a whole by way of organized laws; in his loving-kindness he extends his Providence over individual human beings as well.[19]

In sum, Wolfson concerns himself largely with the doctrinal aspects of religion and considers fundamental principles of faith to be the systematic embodiment of religious knowledge. In his view, the factors which mold a person's basic beliefs do not derive from developments in other realms of knowledge, such as the empirical or philological sciences. They originate in one's commitment to or alienation from basic religious tenets, whether pagan or Biblical. The source of religious knowledge is certainly not the imagination, which by its very nature is incapable of giving rise to an objective concept of God. Reason is also limited in its capacity to generate principles of faith, although it does have the capacity to reach partial conclusions about God on the basis of his revelation in nature, through its power of inference. Only revelation, which issues from an unlimited source, affords us a concept of Divinity which is truly unlimited.

PHILOSOPHIC KNOWLEDGE AND ITS STATUS
IN THE RELIGION OF REVELATION

We have already explored Wolfson's view of the limited capacity of reason to stake out substantive metaphysical positions. The Bible, consequently, must serve as the high court of the intellect, the final arbiter of the judgments of reason. In fact, we find that according to Wolfson's account, the most prominent spokesmen of the historical religions of revelation saw philosophy as a pursuit possessed of both positive and negative aspects.

The architect of scriptural philosophy, Philo of Alexandria, held that philosophy as well was a revelatory gift to the Greeks from God. The fact that the metaphysical conclusions of the major Greek philosophers closely approximate the Biblical concept of the Deity lends credence to this position, in his eyes. In his works Philo points out many commonalities that can be found between the concepts of Divinity held by Plato, Aristotle and the Stoics and the Biblical conception of God, particularly with regard to the issue of God's unity and the absolute dissimilitude between him and any other being. From this perspective the rational metaphysics of the philosophers should not be seen as a continuation of the popular pagan mythological religion, but as a disavowal of the latter. In this sense, Plato, Aristotle, the Stoics and all those who arrived at the concept of a unitary God are termed "spiritual proselytes."[20]

Another instance of the esteem in which the "scriptural thinkers" held philosophy can be found in Wolfson's description of the Church Fathers, who inherited the Philonic orientation. The Church Fathers were faced with a difficulty which did not concern Philo—the problem of heretical sects, which were considered to be the noxious fruit of philosophical thought. We might therefore have expected the Church Fathers to reject philosophy outright; yet we find that philosophy maintained its respectable status even among the Church Fathers. Origen (who for Wolfson represented the theory of "one [rationalistic] faith") held that faith combined with philosophical knowledge is superior in quality to simple belief.[21] Another group, headed by Clement of Alexandria, affirmed that a faith accompanied by logical proofs and a faith devoid of all rational basis are equal in value. (Wolfson terms this the "double faith theory.")[22] Even Tertullian, who advocated an approach favoring simple faith alone, did not completely rule out the use of philosophy. Wolfson notes that Tertullian did not hesitate to make use of the philosophical knowledge he acquired before his conversion to Christianity to defend and explicate Christian tenets. Despite his preference for a simple faith, he ascribed a certain limited value to philosophy as a pedagogic and apologetic tool in the hands of proselytizing Christians with philosophic training.[23] In a different article on heretical Christian sects, Wolfson shows that the same Church Fathers who appear to dismiss the Arian heresy on account of its resort to Aristotelian syllogistic reasoning did not dismiss logical thinking per se. They only warned against the misapplication of Aristotelian rules of logic, which might generate specious conclusions when applied to Christian doctrine.[24]

On the other hand, Wolfson does not mince words when speaking of those thinkers who regard reason as the ultimate judge in matters of belief. On more than one occasion, in contemptuous tones, he assails those classical and modern philosophers who sought to deprive religious leaders of authority in matters of belief. In the opening remarks to his article, "The Philonic God of Revelation and His Latter-Day Deniers," Wolfson writes ironically about the prevalent attitude towards Philo in the world of philosophic scholarship:

> And because he was not professionally a teacher of philosophy, some modern students of his works say that he was not a philosopher. Still, while we may deny Philo the honorific title of philosopher, with the privilege of wearing ostentatiously a special garb like that affected by ancient Greek philosophers, we cannot deny him the humbler and more modest title of religious philosopher.[25]

According to Wolfson, philosophers who rely on their own reason yet deny the transcendent God of the Bible are in no way superior to simple pagans. He presents the approach of Cyril, the theologian, to those philosophers who reject the Biblical concept of God in the following manner: "To Cyril, evidently, philosophers did not constitute a special class of men, with a special discipline of their own. They were to him simply heathen."[26] On the subject of the English philosopher Hume, he notes that, "Hume, like many ordinary people who are not known as profound philosophers, did not believe that the world was created by God."[27]

In other words, from the vantage point of the advocates of revealed religion, philosophy is considered to be a form of partial revelation which attains partial truths. It may be capable of assisting in the formulation and justification of religious truths, so long as it doesn't lay claim to independent authority. In the passages below we will address the various models Wolfson presents as possible interactions between the principles of revealed religion and the conclusions of philosophy.

THE INFLUENCE EXERTED BY THE PRINCIPLES OF REVEALED RELIGION ON THE CONTENT OF PHILOSOPHY

In the second chapter of his book *Philo*,[28] the fourth chapter of his book *The Church Fathers*,[29] and elsewhere as well,[30] Wolfson uses the phrase "the handmaid of Scripture" to characterize the appropriate status of philosophy vis-a-vis Biblical religion. This status is based on the epistemological premises of Philo and his disciples, according to which the concepts of consciousness are necessarily contingent upon sense data, which are prone to error and distortion. In addition, there are numerous questions which the senses cannot resolve, such as the origin and essence of the soul, the creation of the world and so forth. This state of affairs accounts for the endless controversy among philosophers on these matters. Hence, according to Wolfson, we cannot rely on reason as an absolute source of metaphysical knowledge, and its conclusions should always be corrected by recourse to a truly perfect source of knowledge, namely, revelation.[31]

This subordination of philosophy to revelation was expressed in the history of European thought by the fact that the various "scriptural philosophers" did not consider themselves first and foremost members of recognized schools of philosophy. On the contrary: They judged the various schools according to the degree to which their respective conclusions approximated Biblical doctrines.[32] These "scriptural philosophers" assumed from the outset that there must be a basic correspondence between the teachings of revelation and the conclusions of "the second revelation," i.e., reason, as embodied in the works of the great philosophers. They assumed that every contradiction between these two sources of knowledge could be ascribed either to the limitations of reason, or to the inherent indeterminacy of human language, which serves as the mode of expression for revelation. Wolfson, however, is less interested in the Biblical philosophers' analyses of the language of the Bible, and more in their critique of the Greek philosophical tradition in light of basic Biblical premises.[33]

This critique is amply demonstrated in the last chapter of his book on the founder of "scriptural philosophy," entitled "What is New in Philo?" In that chapter Wolfson constructs an ideal type he calls "the synthetic medieval philosopher," a type who embodies those elements of Jewish, Christian and Muslim philosophy which betoken a critical stance towards the Greek philosophic tradition. This "synthetic medieval philosopher" views certain elements of Greek philosophy, particularly the philosophic proofs for the existence, unity and incorporeality of God, with great satisfaction. However, at times his satisfaction with the philosophers' positions is somewhat attenuated, as in the case of Plato's view of the relation between God and the world. While Plato does refer to God as the Creator, he leaves the ideas, which have independent creative powers, intact alongside Him. Aristotle's position, which conceives of God more as a prime mover than as creator, is even more problematic. If we drop down a rung in the degree of scriptural philosophy's satisfaction with Greek philosophy, we find the "synthetic medieval philosopher" evincing even stronger criticism of the theses of the eternity of the world and the immutability of laws of nature, as they would seem to limit the freedom of God as creator and leader of the world, and deprive human beings of free will.[34] We are faced, therefore, with an independent and homogeneous orientation known as Biblical philosophy, possessed of an internal certainty which appropriates or rejects philosophical positions in accordance with its own perspective. We will now proceed to examine this phenomenon in greater depth.

The degree of "scriptural" philosophy's satisfaction with central motifs in Greek philosophy determines the extent to which it introduces changes into these opinions and incorporates them. This principle is a central axis of Wolfson's article "Philo Judaeus" in the *Encyclopedia of Philosophy*,[35] in which he describes the revision wrought in the substance of the Western philosophical tradition due to the ascendance of the Philonic orientation.

Certain doctrines were altered hardly at all. For instance, with regard to the creation of the world, Philo finds fairly strong parallels between the Biblical narrative and Plato's description of the creation in the *Timaeus* dialogue. Plato portrays God there as an eternal being who existed before the world came into being, a spiritual and transcendent being who continues to exist beyond the dimensions of the world. In light of this, Philo saw no reason not to interpret the Biblical account in accordance with Plato's views. However, the Platonic postulate of eternal ideas which exist outside of the Deity was not compatible with the Biblical creed. Philo, who sought to appropriate the concept of the ideas (which to his mind was not foreign to the Jewish tradition) without stripping the Deity of His uniqueness as an eternal and creative being, synthesized the two theories into a single harmonious doctrine. He posits two levels of existence for the ideas: an eternal existence, as spiritual entities embedded in the Divine intellect, and a created existence as entities existing in a reality external to the Divine intellect.[36]

In other cases, the change or revision which the revelatory perspective wrought in the substance of Greek metaphysics was more explicit. Instead of attempting to harmonize without detracting from either view (the ideas remain eternal, so long as they are subsumed within the Divine intellect), particular philosophic conceptions were reinterpreted or considerably expanded. For instance, in the *Timaeus* Plato depicts the creation and preservation of the world as deriving from the will of God. According to Wolfson, we can assume that by the term "will" Plato meant the necessary expression of the Divine nature. Philo, however, interprets "will" as absolute freedom. There was no necessity, then, for the world to be created, nor need it continue to exist if God were to wish otherwise.

Philo also expands the concept of "natural law" employed by the Greek philosophers. Most of the Greek philosophers held that positive laws which were legislated by men of intelligence in accordance with their rational inclinations, talents and aspirations may be called "natural laws," but only in a restricted sense. No system of human laws, even if it were the product of the greatest philosopher's intellectual exertions, could completely match the comprehensive and eternal laws according to which the cosmos is conducted. Philo accepts this premise while expanding the concept of "natural law" and applying it to Divine revelation. Positive laws originating in revelation can therefore be considered wholly "natural laws," since they stem from God.

Scriptural philosophy carried out a more drastic revision of conventional philosophic concepts on the issue of the possibility of the knowledge of God by human beings. In Wolfson's opinion, Philo introduces an entirely new concept in the history of philosophy, namely, that the Deity is not given to knowledge or description. Wolfson contends that it can be proved that in the Platonic and Aristotelian systems, God is essentially knowable.[37] It was Philo who first formulated the distinction between proving the existence of God through reason and knowing the essence of God, which is beyond the scope of reason due to the latter's immanent limitations. For Wolfson this distinction is a genuine innovation in the Western philosophic tradition. Its source, however, lies not in Philo's creative powers, but in the Bible's view of God as essentially "different" from any other being. According to conventional philosophic thought, the essence of a phenomenon can be known only by comparing it with other phenomena within the framework of the categories of "genera" and "species." God, by virtue of his incomparability to any other phenomenon, cannot be defined according to these categories, and consequently his essence cannot be known. Thus the radical revision which Philo wrought in Greek philosophy takes the form either of introducing new ideas into the tradition or of making fundamental alterations in existing ones.

This revision was conducted by way of a negative process as well. Philo and his successors effectively purged the Greek tradition of views which are incompatible with Biblical faith. This negative revisionism is illustrated by the following passage from the book *Philo,* in which Wolfson describes the latter's approach to recognized Greek concepts of God:

> Philo, as we have seen, rejects the Aristotelian conception of God on the ground of its incompatibility with the Scriptural conception of God as a creative, and not merely as a motive, cause of the world. He rejects also the Stoic conception of God on the ground of its incompatibility with the Scriptural conception of God as an incorporeal being. His conception of God is like that of Plato, a being who is both incorporeal and creative. But, as we shall see, he does not follow Plato in ascribing a soul to the world as a whole.[38]

So far we have witnessed one type of interaction between revelation and philosophy according to Wolfson's conception, namely, a reshaping of philosophic propositions in conformity with Biblical principles, following the encounter between philosophy and the Bible. However, revelation is also not left unaffected by its encounter with reason. We turn, then, to those changes that transpired, according to Wolfson, in the form and substance of the revelatory message as a result of its interaction with philosophy.

THE INFLUENCE OF PHILOSOPHY
ON THE FORM AND CONTENT OF REVELATION

Philo and his successors in the school of "scriptural philosophy" changed the shape of Biblical faith. In his preface to *The Church Fathers*, Wolfson writes that "Philo has recast the principles of Jewish religion in the form of a philosophy."[39] In an article on the modern repudiation of Philo's God of revelation, Wolfson stresses that "Philo was the first who tried to reduce the narratives and laws and exhortations of Scripture to a coherent and closely knit system of thought and thereby produced what may be called scriptural philosophy in contradistinction to pagan Greek philosophy."[40]

Although in terms of content, scriptural philosophy retains a unique identity which is well-differentiated from pagan Greek philosophy, in terms of form, the Bible's literary and juridical modes of expression are transformed into a coherent philosophic system with logical derivatory links. Moreover, the Bible's fundamental doctrines are articulated by way of the terms and distinctions typical of the philosophic tradition.[41]

In Wolfson's evaluation, this change in form does not seriously alter the substantive principles of the Biblical worldview. While the Biblical outlook effects an essential revision in the content of Greek philosophy, philosophy, when engaged in the disclosure and formulation of Biblical ideas, actually enhances the expressive power of revelation itself. Metaphysical ideas originating in the pagan world do not usually penetrate "Biblical philosophy" unless the latter is internally predisposed to adopt them.[42] The substantive changes that can be ascertained in the revelatory message as a result of its encounter with philosophy have the effect of expanding, deepening and actualizing the philosophical potential of fundamental Biblical principles.

One of the clearest examples cited by Wolfson in illustration of this process is the transition made from the Biblical doctrine of the "dissimilarity" between God and every created being to the philosophic concept of God as "incorporeal." Admittedly there is no explicit mention of the latter concept in the Bible in either its Platonic or Aristotelian form. However, Wolfson argues that the concept is already incorporated in the Biblical declaration that no other being can be likened to God. He considers the doctrine to be implicit in the verses "For you saw no shape when the Lord your God spoke to you at Horeb out of the fire" (Deut. 4:15); "You shall not make for yourself a sculptured image, or any likeness of what is in the heavens above, or on the earth below, or in the waters under the earth" (Exod.

20:4); "To whom can you compare Me, or declare Me similar? To whom can you liken Me, so that we seem comparable?" (Isa. 46:5). Wolfson holds these verses to be possessed of "great philosophic potential," a potential which is "easily discernible." As soon as a thinker like Philo, who was weaned on the Bible, encountered the conventional philosophic distinction between form and matter, a transformation occurred, and the concept "dissimilar" turned into the philosophic concept "incorporeal." The transformation proceeded as follows: Philo learned from the philosophers that all worldly phenomena are composed of certain elements, and that these elements are made up of a combination of form and matter. Given this assumption, the proposition that God is unlike anything else in the world becomes equivalent to the proposition denying any element of matter in God, that is, affirming his incorporeality.[43] Consequently, the encounter between the Bible and philosophy does not result in any deviation from Biblical tenets. Quite the contrary: The philosophic potential of the Biblical doctrines themselves emerges, as the philosophic principles inherent in Biblical formulations are disclosed by recourse to known philosophic distinctions.

Wolfson suggests a similar process as background for the development of the concept of the unity of God in Philo's philosophic commentary on the Bible. In the Bible itself, the famous verse, "Hear, O Israel, the Lord is our God, the Lord is one" refers to numerical unity alone. God is one in the sense that his unity precludes the possible existence of multiple deities, and in this sense the verse can be interpreted primarily as a polemic against polytheism. There is no logical or metaphysical discussion in the Bible on the question of the internal unity of God, whether he is composed of different substances such as matter and form, or whether he is defined by the categories of "genera" and "species." For Aristotle, however, the concept of unity signifies both internal unity and a non-composite simplicity. This understanding of the Aristotelian conception is particularly valid with regard to the unity of God. Given that the Aristotelian God is incorporeal, and that internal complexity is a property of bodies alone, God would appear to be one not only relative to other beings, but in an absolute internal sense as well. When Philo encountered the Aristotelian concept of the simplicity and non-composite nature of God, he argued that this absolute unity is the same unity implied in the Bible. For Wolfson, Philo's stance is not a deviation from the Biblical conception, but a broadening and deepening of the original Biblical view of the unity of God.[44]

Wolfson, then, is willing to accept that the revelatory message changes in both form and content pursuant to its encounter with philosophy. However, unlike the revision undergone by philosophy following its encounter with revelation, the changes sustained by revelation following the encounter with philosophy do not, in the main, strike at the foundations of the Biblical perspective. Quite the opposite: philosophy becomes the hand-maid of revelation, by helping revelation to transmit its message in a more communicative fashion.

So far we have reviewed the changes which transpire in both Biblical religion and philosophy following the interaction between the two. However, if we continue to trace the ways in which philosophy serves the Biblical faith, we will see that it not only effects formal and substantive alterations in the latter by way of conceptual articulation;[45] it also furnishes justifications and external corroborations which lend rational support to the foundations of Biblical faith.

One type of support, for instance, is the scriptural philosophers' adoption of classic philosophic proofs for the existence of God. Their aim here would seem to be to show that the fundamentals of the Biblical perspective can be logically demonstrated.[46] On the other hand, the Philonic school holds that the Bible's key articles of faith are not the *product* of logical discourse but a kind of authoritative *prologue* to all rational discussion. In keeping with this assumption, it need not be absolutely necessary or altogether possible to ground faith in logical proofs. At times the scriptural philosophers set themselves a more modest objective: to show that their beliefs do not contradict reason and are not absurd. For instance, regarding the belief in immortality and the resurrection of the dead, the Church Fathers held that these phenomena belong to the category of miracles which God might perform in His world. In their view, miracles are not absurd, given the principle that God is omnipotent and "everything is possible for him."[47]

The only categories which, rationally speaking, seemed to them to lie outside the province of the omnipotent God were the non-existent, the unimaginable and the contemptible. Since immortality and the resurrection of the dead are not phenomena which belong to these categories, they were not considered absurd matters that necessarily contravene reason.

Philosophy was mobilized to justify the Biblical faith not only for the purpose of grounding the latter's beliefs, but also in order to refute hostile opinions. By way of example, the Church Fathers, who were, according to Wolfson, the first heirs to the Philonic Biblical perspective, are portrayed as a united front that took it upon itself "to refute the Epicurean" on the subject of the immortality of the soul. On the one hand, Wolfson is willing to acknowledge the substantial differences of opinion existing among the Church Fathers, as well as the fact that there is no direct polemic in their writings against the heresy of the corporeality and temporality of the soul. Nevertheless, Wolfson's major scholarly efforts are devoted to highlighting their points of agreement and to presenting their positions as a coordinated preemptive campaign against Epicurean views. For instance, most of the Church Fathers view the soul as incorporeal, while Tertullian insists that it is material in nature. Nevertheless, argues Wolfson, the difference between

Tertullian and the majority is only a matter of semantics. The incorporeality at issue there is not absolute, like the incorporeality of God; it is, rather, an incorporeality relative to ordinary material objects. On the other hand, Tertullian's corporeality is of a special sort, totally unlike corporeality as commonly understood. Accordingly, for Wolfson, both sides were "refuting the Epicureans" (even though their writings betray no such specific intent) by demonstrating the soul to be of a different quality than the body. Logically, then, the soul exists independently of the body and is therefore capable of separating itself from the latter and gaining immortality. To take another example, although the Church Fathers differ among themselves on the question of the origin of the soul (whether souls are specially created for individual persons and are ready and waiting to be distributed to human beings, or whether they partake of a single archetypal soul), they would nevertheless all concur in portraying the manner in which the soul dwells in the body as an existence within a "garment," "home," "palace," or "temple," according to the Biblical and Philonic concepts. All of these expressions testify to the soul's existence as distinct from the body, and, potentially, independently of it.[48]

INTERIM SUMMARY:
RELIGIOUS PHILOSOPHY AS THEOLOGY

To sum up Wolfson's theory of the nature of religious and philosophic knowledge and the legitimate interaction between them: philosophy in the West has been largely a *theological* enterprise. In order to clarify Wolfson's argument, we shall examine two modern definitions of theology, most prominently that of Emil Fackenheim, who, in Michael Rosenak's words, "quests for a clear delineation of theology and its modes of thought, and systematically distinguishes between theology on the one hand, and philosophy and science on the other."[49] The Catholic theologians Rahner and Vorgrimler have also commented on the theological enterprise in a manner which may shed light on Wolfson's thesis.[50]

Fackenheim addresses the distinction between religious belief, philosophy and theology in a number of places in his writings. He terms religion "the life of faith itself." The substance of the Jewish faith, in his view, is "the direct relation, not only of man in general, but also of Israel in particular, to God." The pure form of religious belief is described by him as "immediate," and in periods when the immediacy of faith was strongly felt, there was hardly any need to clarify it with intellectual tools or to reflect on its essence. In those periods, revelation was considered the legitimate source of religious truth, and it served as the basis for a direct, immediate and particular encounter between human beings and God.[51]

The categories of philosophy, in contrast, are universal and intellectual. Philosophers regard the "objective" posture of the thinker as more valid and more comprehensive than the personal stance of the believer. As a result, philosophy can never regard revelation as an "irreducible source of truth," and the tangible connection between human beings and God necessarily escapes its purview.[52]

Theology, though identical neither with religious belief nor with philosophy, carries a commitment and responsibility to both of them.[53] Theological thought, to the extent that it is specifically theological, cannot be objective, as the faith commitment is one of its immanent presuppositions.[54] On the other hand, in Fackenheim's words, "Theological thought is indeed thought, and it cannot therefore be merely a type of sermonizing or personal confession." The element of thought in theology is its systematic approach, through which belief is rendered organized and coherent, the antithesis of vagueness and arbitrariness.[55] Accordingly, the manner of expression that theology chooses in order to construct and defend its claims is generally an explicitly discursive one. It is interesting that this same "double commitment of theology" is also voiced in an article by the Catholic theologians Rahner and Vorgrimler: "The Christian, because he is already a believer and has already organized and unified his life in the light of his faith, cannot hold that the Church and her doctrine are irrelevant to his philosophy and have not authority over him as a philosopher." While, on the other hand: "The theologian who believes that he does not need to 'philosophize' either falls back unthinkingly on one of the existing, dominant philosophies of his time or else simply talks in an edifying way and consequently does not carry out the real task of theology."[56]

What, then, are the positive functions of theology? First, Fackenheim affirms, it is up to theology to frame, explain and illuminate the principles of religious belief. It is theology's job to construct an organized and systematic formulation of faith which is comprehensible in terms of current concepts and thought patterns. In addition, it must articulate the implications of its commitment to such fundamental beliefs as revelation. The second function of theology is to justify the commitment upon which faith is based and to show that its cardinal properties are not absurd, but are compatible with philosophic scrutiny. This justification often involves defending the foundations of faith against competing contemporary thought-systems.[57]

Fackenheim's distinctions and the remarks made by Rahner and Vorgrimler would seem to support our contention that Wolfson views the orientation of European philosophy as theological in nature. For Wolfson, the Philonic-scriptural philosophy which dominated Europe for 1700 years fulfilled functions similar to those described by Fackenheim. As regards the functions of "formulation and illumination," we have found that in Wolfson's evaluation, Philo and his heirs transformed the "narratives, laws and exhortations" in the Bible into "a coherent and closely knit system of thought."[58] They also interpreted Biblical doctrines in accordance with philosophical distinctions and derived implications and consequences from fundamental articles of faith. Moreover, we have seen how scriptural philosophy attempts to justify articles of faith, whether by recourse to logical proofs or by attempting to explain why given doctrines are not absurd. Another facet of the effort at justification, and the confrontation with other viewpoints, is expressed through Wolfson's example of the way the Church Fathers collectively refuted the Epicurean position on immortality.[59]

Fackenheim's distinctions between religious belief, philosophy and theology can also be of assistance in understanding the theological orientation that Wolfson imputes to European philosophy. To recall, Fackenheim defines religion as "the life of faith itself," the direct relation between human beings and God. It would not be fair to say that Wolfson entirely ignores simple faith (that kind of faith that is devoid of systematic formulation and intellectual scrutiny). In his description of the various sects of Alexandrian Judaism, he praises those who clung to a simple traditional faith, and seeks to demonstrate that the gap between them and the orientation of philosophically-minded believers was not very large. In Wolfson's opinion, Philo held that both the simple believer and the philosophic believer were equally capable of serving God out of love. And certainly he would have preferred the simple believers over the extremist philosophers, those alienated intelligentsia whose identification with their Greek surroundings led them to adopt a critical stance towards the Bible.[60]

It may be that in place of Fackenheim's direct encounter, Wolfson considered the legal dimension of Judaism, with its precise formulations, to constitute part of the elemental experience of the Jewish religion. Perhaps this is how we should interpret the remark in one of his early programmatic articles, that from an internal Jewish point of view the Talmud offers more fertile ground for research than Jewish philosophy.[61] Notwithstanding this point, however, Wolfson did not choose to make either the phenomenology of belief or the study of the Talmud the focus of his academic interest. It is evident from his scholarship that he limited his field of vision to religion as expressed in its doctrinal formulations.[62] In his article on "Cyril of Jerusalem," Wolfson briefly depicts the process of the "theologization" of Christianity. His statement here would appear to be valid for all the monotheistic religions, which in Wolfson's view constituted a single homogeneous unit, a continuation of Philo's project:

> Christian doctrine ever since the middle of the second century, beginning with the Apologists, was presented as a philosophy. The Apologists, and others after them, following the example of Philo in his treatment of Scripture, introduced new philosophical concepts and new philosophical terms into Christianity. . .

All these gradually became part of Christian belief. Christian terminology and formulas became laden with deep philosophical meaning. All those who used them were thus unconsciously philosophers.[63]

Wolfson seems to be implying here that his decision to focus on the doctrinal aspects of religion does not mean that he is distorting the religious phenomenon, as it presented itself in Western history. In his view, after a certain historical period, the essence of religious belief itself came to involve a consideration of the truth value of various types of religious knowledge. For example, in the tradition of the Church Fathers (based on definitions drawn from Aristotle and the Stoics) faith is grasped as a gesture of consent. For, say, Clement of Alexandria, there were two kinds of consent. The first was depicted as the assimilation of the teachings and commandments of the Bible "through faith," while the second was termed consent "through scientific faith." Given that the teachings of the Bible are assumed to issue from the "voice of God," they can be grasped "through faith" as truths whose validity and authority stems from their very source and essence. Or, alternatively, they can potentially be proven through philosophic proofs, by way of "scientific faith." In either case, we are faced with different kinds of evidence, which are meant to serve as the underpinnings for the believer's consent to given principles or commandments.[64] It goes without saying that the personal dimension—that direct link between God and human beings which Fackenheim terms the "life of faith itself"—is missing from Wolfson's analysis. This is not to imply that Wolfson ignores the phenomenon of faith. He rather grasps that phenomenon as a gesture of rational consent. By transforming faith into an issue of principled commitment, Wolfson effectively submerges it within the realm of theology, thereby depriving it of any existence independent of conceptual formulations and syllogistic inferences.

Philosophy as well is deprived of any independent status in Wolfson's thought and is also submerged within theology. First, from Wolfson's remarks on the subject it would appear that philosophy lacks the capacity to supply its own premises and fundamental principles. The subject matter and substance of philosophic systems does not issue from the independent activity of reason as it develops across the generations. The significant changes which have transpired in the fundamental problems which occupy philosophy have stemmed primarily from changes in the religious literature on which philosophy draws. Until the period immediately preceding the rise of Christianity, argues Wolfson, the religious literature that left its imprint on Greek and Latin philosophy was pagan Greek literature. From then on, the religious literature whose influence became conspicuous in citations, references and allusions in philosophical texts is monotheistic literature: the Bible, the New Testament and the Koran. The Bible's influence is so strong, Wolfson contends, that it succeeds in changing the literary form of philosophic expression itself. Note, for example, the shift from the mode of discourse or dialogue to philosophic explications of the Biblical text. Such a change in the source from which philosophy is nurtured is no mere external development, according to Wolfson, but heralds a substantive shift in the philosophic doctrines themselves.[65] One of the main indications of this Wolfsonian perspective is that he hardly mentions Greek philosophy without adding the adjective "pagan" and consistently characterizes medieval philosophy as "scriptural philosophy."[66] In Wolfson's view, modern philosophers who have deliberately detached themselves from the Bible as a source have been compelled to return to positions which are substantively pagan. It is no accident that Wolfson perceives Spinoza to have returned to the Aristotelian view of an impersonal Deity devoid of will (a sophisticated version of the popular Greek religious conception). Hume, for his part, is portrayed as having resurrected the Epicurean proposition that the world came into being by accident.[67] Wieseltier is justified in saying that Wolfson even divided up historical periods in accordance with philosophy's willingness to place itself at the disposal of the monotheistic scriptures.[68] Thus philosophy cannot supply its own subject matter or fundamental premises, but must necessarily draw them from the literary traditions of the historical faiths.

Evidently, then, Wolfson denies the possibility of the existence of an independent rational starting point which is not informed by the commitment and consent of faith. The following passage from the article "Spinoza and the Religion of the Past" illustrates his approach nicely:

> Behind the imposing facade of Spinoza's philosophic system, with all its intricacies of design and vocabulary, there is thus a simple philosophic faith. . . In opposition both to the religious faith, which professed a belief in the creation of the world by the will of an eternal God, and to the Epicurean faith, which professed a belief in the emergence of the world out of the accidental collision of aimlessly drifting eternal atoms, Spinoza's philosophic faith protested that the world in its present form existed from eternity.[69]

To return to Fackenheim's classification, Wolfson cannot countenance an objective universal stance which is not responsible to faith. The universal, neutral aspect of philosophy is expressed in its logical-discursive method, which can be employed for good or evil.[70] But as for substantive fundamental premises, Wolfson assimilates philosophy to theology, which is responsible to faith, just as he assimilates faith to the systematic formulations of theology.

Perhaps the most obvious sign of the blurring of boundaries between revealed religion, philosophy and theology in Wolfson is the manner in which he uses these terms interchangeably in his writings. For instance, the original title of chapter 2 of his book *Philo* is "Handmaid of Scripture," while in his article "Greek Philosophy in Philo and the Church Fathers," philosophy is presented as "the handmaid of *theology*."[71] Furthermore, in the first two sections of his article "The Knowability and Describability of God in Plato and Aristotle," the speculative tradition which deliberates on the essence of God is variously called "religious philosophy," "philosophy," and "theology."[72] In addition, while one collection of his articles appeared under the title *Studies in the History of Philosophy and Religion*, another collection was named *Religious Philosophy—A Group of Essays*. Elsewhere, in contrast, Wolfson terms all religious thinkers before Spinoza, whose beliefs and opinions are discussed in the above collections, "rationalist theologians."[73]

In terms of content, the bulk of Wolfson's scholarship was assuredly devoted to theological matters. If to employ the double definition coined by Dagobert Runes, we can say that on the one hand, most of Wolfson's research was concerned with the "study of the question of God and the relation of God to the world of reality," while on the other hand Wolfson considered the works of Philo and his heirs to be "the theoretical expression of a particular religion."[74] This theological orientation also prevails in those articles, chapters and headings which fall under the rubric of studies in "religion" or "philosophy." Such a phenomenon, in the case of a scholar who scrupulously distinguished between philosophic concepts in the body of his works, could only stem from an unwillingness to grant independent status to either religion or philosophy.

Before we proceed to analyze Wolfson's view of the development of religious thought over the generations, it is worth emphasizing the link between his theological orientation and his epistemological assumptions. The Philonic perspective, which guided religious thought in Europe until the advent of Spinoza, is "empirical," in assuming that rational knowledge is based on sense data. With regard to "spiritual" issues such as Creation, or the nature of the soul, the senses are unable to provide us with any kind of data. Even with regard to other, "non-spiritual" issues they may provide distorted or necessarily incomplete data. On the other hand, the religious knowledge transmitted through revelation (which is considered an unchallenged fact in the Philonic tradition), is entirely perfect. Accordingly, reason is not capable of providing humans with the foundation for an all-encompassing objectivity, and consequently philosophy—the product of reason—should not be treated as an independent field capable of severing itself from the metaphysical assumptions it absorbs from the religious traditions. Admittedly, the major Greek philosophers covered considerable ground in distancing themselves from popular religion and in their striving for a monotheistic and transcendent worldview. Yet elements of polytheism, immanentism and pagan fatalism remained among them nevertheless.[75] However, it seems that for Wolfson religious belief cannot stand entirely alone either. If it wishes to be an effective force in the history of thought, it requires the assistance of the second form of revelation, reason, to provide a systematic articulation of its principles and a rational foundation for its claims. Reason is meant to subordinate itself to religion, which serves it as both a "material source" and as a "negative norm" demarcating the boundaries of philosophy.[76] However, religion also undergoes a certain transformation in the course of its encounter with reason, wherein it is reshaped into a "coherent and closely knit" theological-doctrinal system.[77]

NOTES

1. Harry Wolfson, *Philo: Foundations of Religious Philosophy in Judaism, Christianity and Islam*, vol. I (Cambridge, Mass.: Harvard University Press, 1947) v.

2. For a clearcut example of how religion can be viewed as a "human experience," an approach Wolfson encountered as a student at Harvard when William James' influence there was very pronounced, see William James, "The Varieties of Religious Experience—A Study in Human Nature," (London and Glasgow: Collins, 1960). It is possible that certain passages in the book, such as this one (p. 45), prompted Wolfson to polemicize against studying religion as the study of "the subnormal or supranormal human mind":

> In the psychopathic temperament we have the emotionality which is the *sine qua non* of moral perception; we have the intensity and tendency to emphasis which are the essence of practical moral vigor; and we have the love of metaphysics and mysticism which carry one's interests beyond the surface of the sensible world . . .
> If there were such a thing as inspiration from a higher realm, it might well be that the neurotic temperament would furnish the chief condition of the requisite receptivity.

As for Wolfson's opposition to the use of religious terminology to denote modern philosophical viewpoints, it may be that he is reacting to attempts such as that of Mordechai Kaplan to provide a functional interpretation of the traditional concept of God. On this subject, Kaplan's opinion is diametrically opposed to that of Wolfson:

> Words, like institutions, like life itself, are subject to the law of identity in change. It is entirely appropriate, therefore, to retain the greater part of the ancient religious vocabulary, particularly the term "God." As long as we are struggling to express the same fundamental fact about the cosmos that our ancestors designated by the term "God," the fact of its momentousness or holiness, and are endeavoring to achieve the ideals of human life which derive from that momentousness or holiness, we have a right to retain their mode of expression.

See Mordechai Kaplan, *Judaism as a Civilization*, (New York: MacMillan, 1934), 398.

3. Harry Austryn Wolfson, "The Needs of Jewish Scholarship in America," *The Menorah Journal* 7, no. 1 (February 1921): 28–35.

4. See Moses Mendelssohn, *Ktavim Ktanim be-Inyanei Yehudim ve-Yahadut* (Ramat Gan: Masada and Bialik Institute, 1947), 102–3; Martin Buber, *Two Types of Faith*, trans. N.P. Goldhawk (New York: Harper Torchbooks, 1961), 43–50.

5. Harry Wolfson, "The Philonic God of Revelation and His Latter-Day Deniers," in *Religious Philosophy: A Group of Essays* (Cambridge, MA: Harvard University Press, 1961), 25–26.

6. Wolfson, *Philo*, vol. II, 441–46.

7. Wolfson, "The Philonic God of Revelation," *Religious Philosophy*, 25–26.

8. See the condensed version of his thesis regarding the centrality of Philo's influence on European philosophy in his introduction to the collection entitled *Religious Philosophy* (p. v). This point will be elaborated later on. As we can infer from the title of the article "The Philonic God of Revelation and His Latter-Day Deniers," as well as from its content, Wolfson's identification with the position of Philo and Philonism is most pronounced. This point as well will become self-evident further on.

9. Wolfson, "The Philonic God of Revelation," *Religious Philosophy*, 2–3.

10. Wolfson, *Religious Philosophy*, 2–3.

11. Wolfson, "Sermonette," *Religious Philosophy*, 270–71.

12. Wolfson, *Religious Philosophy*, 270–71. Wolfson's comments here refer to the "scoundrel" in Psalms 14:1.

13. Wolfson, "The Philonic God of Revelation," *Religious Philosophy*, 25–26.

14. Wolfson, *Religious Philosophy*, 25–26.

15. Wolfson, *Religious Philosophy*, 3–4.

16. Wolfson, *Philo*, vol. I, 143. See also Wolfson's article "Greek Philosophy in Philo and the Church Fathers," in *Studies in the History and Philosophy of Religion* (Cambridge, MA: Harvard University Press, 1973–1977), 71–72. The article shows that the Church fathers also adopted this evaluation of philosophy from Philo.

17. Wolfson, "The Philonic God of Revelation," *Religious Philosophy*, 6–10.

18. See on this issue Wolfson's article, "The Knowability and Describability of God in Plato and Aristotle," *Studies*, 98–114.

19. Wolfson "The Philonic God of Revelation," *Religious Philosophy*, 6–10.

20. Wolfson, *Philo*, vol. I, 177–80; vol. II, 447–48.

21. Wolfson, *The Philosophy of the Church Fathers* (Cambridge, MA: Harvard University Press, 1970), 106.

22. Wolfson, *Church Fathers*, 112.

23. Wolfson, *Church Fathers*, 104–6.

24. Wolfson, "Philosophical Implications of Arianism and Apollinarianism," *Religious Philosophy*, 126–30.

25. Wolfson, "The Philonic God of Revelation," *Religious Philosophy*, 1.

26. Wolfson, "Philosophical Implications of the Theology of Cyril of Jerusalem," *Religious Philosophy*, 105.

27. Wolfson "Causality and Freedom in Descartes, Leibniz and Hume," *Religious Philosophy*, 207.

28. See vol. I, 143–54, for a clarification of the source and sense of the expression "handmaid of Scripture."

29. See in particular pp. 97–99 (see note 21 above).

30. See, for instance, Wolfson, "Greek Philosophy in Philo and the Church Fathers," *Studies*, 75–77.

31. Wolfson, *Philo*, vol. I, 151–54.

32. Wolfson, "Arianism and Apollinarianism," *Religious Philosophy*, 136–37.

33. Wolfson, *Philo*, vol. II, 447–49.

34. Wolfson, *Philo*, vol. II, 447–54.
35. The discussion in the next few pages is based on Paul Edwards, ed., *The Encyclopedia of Philosophy*, vol. VI (New York: Quentin Macmillan, 1967), 151–55.
36. See also Wolfson, "Extradeical and Intradeical Interpretations of Platonic Ideas," *Religious Philosophy*, 37–38.
37. Wolfson brings detailed proofs for this claim in his article "The Knowability and Describability of God in Plato and Aristotle," *Studies*, 98–114.
38. Wolfson, *Philo*, vol. I, 326.
39. Wolfson, preface to *Church Fathers*, v.
40. Wolfson, "The Philonic God of Revelation," *Religious Philosophy*, 1.
41. Wolfson, *Philo*, vol. II, 95.
42. Harry Wolfson, *The Philosophy of the Kalam* (Cambridge, MA: Harvard University Press, 1976), 70.
43. Wolfson, *Philo*, vol. II, 95–96.
44. Wolfson, *Philo*, vol. II, 98–99; see also "Arianism and Apollinarianism," in Wolfson, *Religious Philosophy*, 144–45.
45. The concept of "articulation" as one of the central functions of discursive thought was proposed orally by Prof. Nathan Rotenstreich in one of his talks with the "Jerusalem Fellows" in the 1985–1986 academic year.
46. Wolfson, *Philo*, vol. II, 92–93, 448.
47. Wolfson, "Immortality and Resurrection in the Philosophy of the Church Fathers," *Religious Philosophy*, 98–99.
48. Wolfson, *Religious Philosophy*, 83–84, 90–92.
49. Michael Rosenak, "Tifkudam shel Teologiah Yehudit Bat-Zmaneinu be-Hibur Philosophiah Hinuchit Datit ba-Tfutzot," (Ph.D. diss., Hebrew University of Jerusalem, 1976), 17, 21–24.
50. Karl Rahner and Herbert Vorgrimler, eds., *Dictionary of Theology* (New York: Crossroad, 1981).
51. Emil Fackenheim, "An Outline of Modern Jewish Theology," *Quest for Past and Future* (Scarborough, Ontario: Indiana University Press, 1968), 99–100.
52. Emil Fackenheim, "Review of *Franz Rosenzweig, His Life and Thought*" (ed. N. Glatzer), *Judaism*, II, no. 4 (October 1953): 369.
53. This formulation is based on Rosenak, "Tifkudam," 21.
54. Fackenheim, "Outline," 99.
55. Fackenheim, "Outline," 98.
56. Rahner and Vorgrimler, *Dictionary of Theology*, 385.
57. Fackenheim, "Outline," 97, 99, 101, 104.
58. Wolfson, "The Philonic God of Revelation," *Religious Philosophy*, 1.
59. Wolfson, "The Philonic God of Revelation," *Religious Philosophy*, 46–48.
60. Wolfson, *Church Fathers*, 100; Wolfson, *Philo*, vol. I, 66–67.
61. Harry Austryn Wolfson, "The Needs of Jewish Scholarship in America," *The Menorah Journal* 7, no. 1 (February 1921): 28–35.
62. On this issue we tend to agree with Leon Wieseltier in his article "Philosophy, Religion, and Harry Wolfson," *Commentary* 61 (April 1976): 64.
63. Wolfson, "Theology of Cyril of Jerusalem," *Religious Philosophy*, 105–6.
64. Wolfson, *Religious Philosophy*, 108–9.
65. Wolfson, *Philo*, vol. II, 442–45.

66. Wolfson, "The God of Revelation," *Religious Philosophy*, 1–2.

67. Wolfson, *The Philosophy of Spinoza*, vol. II (Cambridge, MA: Harvard University Press, 1934), 346; Wolfson, "Causality and Freedom," *Religious Philosophy*, 207–10.

68. Wieseltier, "Philosophy, Religion," 60–62.

69. Wolfson, *Religious Philosophy*, 254–55.

70. See Wolfson, "Arianism and Apollianarianism," *Religious Philosophy*, 129.

71. Wolfson, *Philo*, vol. I, 87; Wolfson, *Studies*, 75.

72. Wolfson, *Studies*, 98–99.

73. Wolfson, *Philosophy of Spinoza*, vol. II, 334.

74. Dagobert David Runes, *The Dictionary of Philosophy* (New York: Philosophical Library, 1942), 317.

75. By polytheistic elements, Wolfson is referring to the fact that according to Aristotle, for example, natural law remains a kind of second source of power which binds the Deity itself (see pp. 43–44 above). Alternatively, substantial "immanent" elements can be discerned in the Stoic tendency to ascribe a general "soul" to the world, which constitutes its divine element (see above pp. 44–45 and below pp. 95–96). "Fatalistic" elements, on the other hand, find expression in the lawful necessity informing the creation of the world and its stewardship in Aristotle, a necessity which allows no place for the Divine will (see pp. 43–44 above).

76. The terms are those of Rahner and Vorgrimler, *Dictionary of Theology*, 385.

77. See Wolfson, "The Philonic God of Revelation," *Religious Philosophy*, 1.

2

Historiosophical Elements

Chronicling the Articulation of Jewish Philosophy over Time

INTRODUCTION

We will now turn from the epistemological issue of the mutual relations prevailing between religious and philosophic knowledge to the question of the philosophy of history. We will seek to clarify how Wolfson saw time as a factor in the development of religious thought, what he considered to be "the beginning of time" and "the end of time" for these purposes and why. In attempting to ascertain the historical parameters of religious philosophy, according to Wolfson, we will further inquire: During what period did religious philosophy reach its peak? What was its most creative period, when the works of greatest value were composed? From what perspective, according to Wolfson, can we see religious philosophy as thought in motion, and from what perspective could it be seen as thought at rest? During which key periods in its history was there movement in religious philosophy, and in which periods was there rest? And finally, what type of motion characterizes human thought once it participates in the dimension of historical time? Is it possible to speak of decisive turning points or of gradual growth in the direction of valued ends as typifying the historical course of religious philosophy?[1] Or must we content ourselves with characterizing the history of religious philosophy as chiefly a reworking and further elaboration of original foundations?[2]

At the outset of our discussion we will explore the character of religious philosophy as a general human phenomenon, as the product of an interaction between reason and revelation. Towards the end of the chapter we will examine Wolfson's view of the specific contribution made by Jewish philosophy to religious thought, as well as his theory of the role of philosophy in the Jewish religious tradition.

THE EARLY PERIOD:
THE FOUNDING OF RELIGIOUS PHILOSOPHY

For Wolfson, philosophy's point of origin is the human quest for knowledge about God, his relation to the world and to human beings.[3] Without delving into pre-historic details, Wolfson asserts that the "primitive" period of religious thought was that in which the Deity was grasped as the arbitrary ruler of the world, a ruler subject to no natural laws whatsoever.[4] The "philosophic" period in human thought about God begins when the attempt to understand the nature of God joins forces with the general philosophical impulse to plot out a unified and systematic picture of all of reality. The search for a unified explanation for the structure of existence commenced with the early Greek philosophers' attempts to single out one all-encompassing element (water or fire, for instance) as the material basis of all beings.[5] It proceeded with Aristotle's reduction of all the changes which transpire in the world to four types of movement, themselves aspects of the power of locomotion. This power of locomotion was perceived to be contingent upon an Unmoved Mover, thereby laying the foundation not only for the physical unity of the universe, but also for the unity of the laws of nature operating within it. This Unmoved Mover, or God, was now grasped not as an arbitrary ruler but as the necessary causal force underlying movement and change in the universe.[6]

The major Greek philosophers, then, succeeded by dint of their human intelligence in arriving at a concept of God of the highest order. Plato and Aristotle perceived God as possessed of absolute internal unity; He is an incorporeal being, totally independent of all factors external to him.[7] A logical tension arises, therefore, between the quest for the unity of being typical of philosophers[8] and the need to maintain the existence of an original shaper of primordial matter who is himself independent of this matter, a "First Cause" not contingent upon the movement it generates. This tension has fueled numerous philosophical debates over the generations and is one of the main driving forces animating religious philosophy. However, in Wolfson's evaluation, this period is still only the "preliminary" period of religious philosophy. Wolfson even intended to publish a volume on Greek philosophy as a sort of preamble to his works on scriptural philosophy. According to his student Twersky, Wolfson's main arguments regarding the "preliminary" character of Greek philosophy vis-à-vis religious philosophy are contained in two articles, which formed the nucleus of the planned book.[9] The one that I will address here is the "Describability and Knowability of God in Plato and Aristotle."[10]

In this article Wolfson seeks to prove that "it is not yet possible" to identify the idea that God is unknowable and indescribable in the writings of Plato and Aristotle. For instance, in one place Plato observes that it is difficult to attain knowledge of God and unwise to disseminate such knowledge indiscriminately, yet the implicit assumption, according to Wolfson, is that such knowledge is theoretically attainable.[11] While Aristotle goes to great lengths to distinguish between those predicates which can be used to describe God and those which can only be applied to material beings, he does not hold it impossible to describe God at all. Wolfson contends that inherent in the definition of God as the "Unmoved Mover" is the assumption that God can be defined through the categories of "genera" and "species."[12] The distinction between the possibility of proving the existence of God and the possibility of knowing his essence is therefore constrained to "wait" until the appearance of Philo. Following the Bible's lead, Philo articulates the principle of the impossibility of expressing the nature of God, a principle which was subsequently adopted by the Church Fathers, the Kalam and medieval Jewish philosophy.[13] This phenomenon, among others, led Wieseltier to declare somewhat critically that just as Hegel viewed every philosophic work preceding Christianity as a preparation for the latter, Wolfson viewed every philosophic work preceding Philo's "scriptural" philosophy as preparation for the latter.[14]

Accordingly, from Wolfson's perspective, ancient Greek philosophy, whose areas of inquiry included religious subjects, nevertheless cannot be considered religious philosophy in the full sense of the word.[15] True religious philosophy—that which subjects itself to heteronomous doctrinal assumptions—begins only with Philo. As already noted, Wolfson maintains that the "autonomous-pagan" orientation in the quest for God is capable of generating only two possibilities: either an atheistic paganism (which denies the objective existence of God outside of man's imagination), or a theistic paganism (reason's attempt to construct a concept of God on the basis of inferences from the natural world).[16] Consequently, the historical period when philosophy was not yet in need of the knowledge of revelation can only be regarded as a preamble to the age of the birth of religious philosophy itself. The metaphysical achievements of the main Greek philosophers are evaluated in Wolfson's writings entirely according to their success in approximating the Biblical worldview. Given that the Bible articulates an abstract, transcendent concept of God, as a single, non-contingent and non-composite being, yet also as characterized by infinite compassion (through revelation and individual Providence), the Platonic and Aristotelian concepts of the Deity only approximate the Biblical conception, without ever fully attaining it. In Plato, for instance, the ideas maintain their creative power outside of God, and in Aristotle, God is connected to the world by the bonds of a necessary causality and does not possess an absolute will.[17]

Human thought, then, equipped with the two elemental building blocks it inherited from the ancient period, is on the verge of establishing a genuine religious philosophy. The first building block is naturally the Bible with its message of revelation, which on the metaphysical level signifies an anti-primitive and anti-mythological concept of divinity. The "progress" the Biblical concept of God represents over the "primitive" conception is expressed by the fact that in the Bible God is not an arbitrary ruler, but a ruler who implants laws within the structure of his world, laws of whose continuity he is the guarantor.[18] Progress can also be discerned with regard to the "mythological" concept of God, which portrays God as one who gives birth to the world from within himself, in a fashion analogous to the birthing of creatures on earth. In contradistinction to this "mythological" orientation, the Biblical worldview preserves the transcendence and otherness of God, by conceiving of him as a creative artisan.[19]

The second building block is Greek philosophy, which succeeded—through the use of the second divine gift, reason—in arriving at descriptions of God that closely approximate the Biblical concept. However, both philosophy and the Bible must undergo another stage of development, correction or improvement, in order for the religious truth about God to be revealed to the world in its full clarity.[20] The Bible must see its "narratives and laws and exhortations" reduced to a "coherent and closely knit system."[21] This requires the two special virtues of philosophy: the quest for systematic unity and the logical-discursive method of exposition. Philosophy itself, however, is required to correct its imperfect doctrines about God in accordance with the Bible, in order that a concept of divinity which is not at all contingent upon powers external to itself (whether they be ideas or causality) be disclosed to the world. Philo is the main figure in the annals of human thought who effected this encounter between the Bible and philosophy, an encounter that amended the fundamental doctrines of philosophy in light of the Bible and enhanced the Bible's powers of articulation by means of philosophy. With Philo, the "preliminary" period comes to an end. Philo heralds the foundation of the true religious philosophy, namely, systematic thought about the nature of God and his relation to man and the world that subordinates itself to transcendent revelation.[22] It is true that Wolfson sometimes calls the "scriptural philosophy" founded by Philo a "new school" or "new version" of Greek philosophy, and such expressions might suggest that he gauges philosophy's development in accordance with how far it distances itself from its classic origins.[23] Yet as we have seen, his touchstone for evaluating the achievements of ancient philosophy and for criticizing the new philosophy is the Philonic system. In Wolfson's view, "scriptural philosophy," which spans five languages and 1700 years, has more common elements distinguishing it as a whole from Greek "pagan philosophy" in its entirety than there are elements distinguishing the various Greek schools of thought from one another.[24]

Similarly, Wolfson returns time and again to his assertion that following the foundation of "scriptural philosophy," no real innovations in European philosophy are discernible until Spinoza: "For well-nigh seventeen centuries this Philonic philosophy dominated European thought. Nothing really new happened in the history of European philosophy during that extended period."[25] And elsewhere: "Philo revolutionized philosophy and remade it into what became the common philosophy of the three religions with cognate scriptures, Judaism, Christianity and Islam. This triple scriptural religious philosophy, which was built up by Philo, reigned supreme as a homogeneous, if not a thoroughly unified, system of thought until the seventeenth century, when it was pulled down by Spinoza."[26]

THE PERIOD OF ELABORATION:
THE ARTICULATION AND DEFENSE OF PHILONIC PRINCIPLES

With the establishment of Philonic philosophy, the founding period of religious philosophy draws to a close. Philo's work constitutes both the sole turning point and the sole climax in the history of religious thought. Here the stage-by-stage evolutionary movement, which progressed from the "primitive" and arbitrary concept of divinity by way of the "rationalist-determinist," though perhaps not entirely transcendent, concept of divinity to the systematic formulation of the transcendent Biblical God-concept, comes to a halt. From here on, a fundamental stasis sets in in the history of religious doctrines. The tenets of scriptural philosophy acquire a meta-temporal and meta-locational validity in different periods and different cultural regions.

The basic unity of the tenets of Philonic philosophy, independent of the dimension of time, is a recurrent motif in all of Wolfson's scholarly works. In the third chapter of his book *Philo*, these tenets are explored in detail, and the claim is advanced that most of them were adopted as building blocks of Christian and Islamic theology. Philo is said to have proposed eight Biblical articles of faith as a sort of "preamble to faith" for all religious philosophy. The first article is that of the existence of God. This is counterposed against all of the theories that either maintain, following Critias, that belief in God was conjured up by human rulers in order to foster fear of sin, or those who argue, in the wake of Protagoras, that human beings with their senses and intellect are "the measure of all things." The second article is the unity of God, which implies the negation of primordial creative beings outside of God, the negation of corporeal complexity within the divine essence and the negation of the ability of the human intellect to comprehend this essence. The third article is the belief in providence, in the sense of deliberate individual providence, and not in the sense of the necessary telos that informs the laws of nature. The fourth is the creation in time of a world that need not have been created. These four tenets, affirms Wolfson, are anchored directly in the Bible and the Jewish tradition, and thus the fifth tenet is that of revelation itself. Two other doctrines, that of the unity of the world and that of the ideas, are held to reflect a clear Greek influence. Wolfson contends that support for the doctrine of ideas can be found in the rabbinic tradition, while in his opinion the principle of the unity of the world is not deeply entrenched in the Jewish tradition, despite Philo's assertion that the creation narrative teaches it. The eighth and final doctrine is that of the eternal character of the Torah, which underlies the entire Pharisaic enterprise.[27]

According to Wolfson, five of the eight doctrines mentioned above have been adopted, with some modifications, by the religious philosophies of Judaism, Christianity and Islam. The teaching concerning the existence of God has been accepted together with the negation of atheistic, skeptic, Stoic and Epicurean positions. However, there have been attempts to reconcile the Bible's concept of the Creator with Aristotle's concept of the Unmoved Mover. The doctrine of the unity of God, with all of its accompaniments—the negation of polytheism, the negation of the corporeality and complexity of God and the negation of his dependence on external agents—was also accepted, although disputes arose concerning the issue of complexity.

With the institution of belief in the trinity in Christianity and the Islamic teaching regarding the positive attributes of God, assorted interpretations have been advanced for the third doctrine, the idea of providence. For the most part, however, the Philonic viewpoint on individual providence was adopted. As for the doctrine of the creation (the fourth doctrine), not all thinkers embraced Philo's somewhat Platonic version, which espouses a creation within time, yet from primordial matter. Certain philosophers were quite vehement in their defense of the principle of creation ex nihilo, while others held that the creation did not necessarily transpire within time. Yet the great majority regarded the creation as the willful act of an absolute sovereign, rather than as a necessary sequence of events. Similarly, all of the theologians of the monotheistic religions championed the revelatory character of the Bible.[28]

Although Wolfson refrains from saying so explicitly, two of the three doctrines that were not completely accepted by monotheistic theology, in his view, are the same doctrines to which he imputes a Greek background: the existence of the ideas and the unity of the world. As for the eternal character of the Bible (the fourth doctrine), this is the basic stumbling block which divided the Jewish rabbinical tradition from the Christian and Muslim faiths.[29] In his book *The Philosophy of the Church Fathers*, Wolfson also includes the doctrine of the ideas among the "scriptural presuppositions" which serve as a precondition for all philosophizing on the part of Christian theologians.[30] In *The Philosophy of the Kalam*, he explains that the doctrine of the ideas reemerges in Christian theology in the guise of the doctrine of the trinity. The idea of the unity of the world, although not specifically enumerated among the articles of faith of the Church Fathers, is an implicit underlying principle for them. A similar structure informs the Kalam: the eternal validity of the Pentateuch is emphatically denied, the unity of the world is assumed to be true and the doctrine of the ideas becomes the theory of divine attributes, while Philo's five other doctrines were adopted more or less intact.[31] Wolfson's last book, *The Repercussions of the Kalam in Jewish Philosophy*, primarily addresses the ways in which Jewish philosophers, both rabbis and Karaites, defended the purity of the Philonic articles of faith against slight deviations which arose in the Islamic environment.[32]

One of the most daring premises in Wolfson's historiosophy holds the Philonic articles of faith to be almost completely impervious to the forces of time and place. Transformations in human political and cultural history do not affect the inner life of theological deliberations at all. As already noted,[33] even historical developments in the natural sciences fall outside of the theologian's purview, since the former have no logical connection to basic metaphysical commitments. The most colorful expression of this creed of Wolfson's can be found in an article addressing the history of the theory of ideas from Plato to Spinoza. When making the transition from the theory of ideas as formulated in Christian theology to the Muslim theory of divine attributes as a later reflection of the Platonic ideas, he writes: "Six hundred and twenty-two years roll by since the rise of Christianity, and a new religion appears—Islam."[34] And again, when making the transition between Christian scholasticism to the reflection of the ideas in the theories of Descartes and Spinoza, "Centuries roll by and the scene is shifted from the schoolmen, who were professional teachers of philosophy, to Descartes and Spinoza, who were free-lance philosophers."[35]

There is no trace here of the Muslim conquest, of the rise of nation-states, of the scientific revolution or of the cultural differences prevailing between medieval Islamic countries and seventeenth-century France. The time simply flows, and places change, until a religious-intellectual phenomenon manifests itself which continues a previous phenomenon. However, in the very same article Wolfson speaks of four "events," a term which is commonly understood to mean some happening of political or social significance. For Wolfson, however, an "event" is, for example, the publication of a theological book which effects "the introduction of the problem of divine attributes into medieval Christian philosophy."[36] It's difficult not to get the impression here that this is a deliberate reinterpretation of an accepted historical term, for purposes of constructing a "parallel history" of theological concepts possessed of its own inner vitality.

Wolfson's conscious disregard of the cultural-historical context of religious thought is also what lies behind the meta-historical figure he terms "the synthetic medieval philosopher," or "the hypothetical scriptural philosopher." In the last chapter of his book *Philo*, this general representative of homogeneous medieval philosophy is charged with adopting Greek philosophic ideas amenable to the Biblical perspective, such as the proofs for the existence of God, his unity and incorporeality, and refuting antagonistic ideas, such as necessary natural providence.[37] By way of contrast, in Wolfson's article "The Philonic God of Revelation and His Latter-Day Deniers," the figure's function is not to engage religious doctrines formulated prior to the development of "Philonism," but to confront in advance the subsequent heresy of Spinoza, Hume and Mill regarding the substantive and ethical perfection of God.[38] This same inclination to create typological figures also appears in Wolfson's article "Immortality and the Resurrection of the Dead," where the Church Fathers are mobilized as a united front in order to address both ancient heresies—Epicurean doctrines denying the eternity of the soul—and modern ones—in the figure of the "rationalist" student of religious studies who is incapable of believing in the resurrection of the dead due to its purported lack of a "scientific" basis.[39]

Accordingly, the stage-by-stage evolutionary motion that had held sway in the preliminary period of religious philosophy was transformed, with the founding of scriptural philosophy, into a condition of almost total repose. Despite the fact that he describes Biblical philosophy as homogeneous, however, Wolfson himself simultaneously asserts that it was "not thoroughly unified."[40] And in fact, even within "Philonism" itself, a certain movement can be discerned, which manifests itself in the form of endless theological disputes. Yet this movement does not proceed in linear fashion towards a valued objective, as it had previously until reaching its pinnacle with Philo. In the main, it is nothing more than the unfolding of the implications of the Philonic system itself as applied to the topics on the agenda of religious philosophy. In Wolfson's words:

> The endless discussions to be found in the voluminous literature of the various languages in which mediaeval philosophy is embodied are only elaborations upon these principles—explanations of these principles in their manifold implications, discussions of various difficulties arising from these principles, homilies on various scriptural proof-texts advanced in support of them, and discourses on various philosophical passages which appear to be either in agreement or disagreement with them.[41]

The role of medieval theology, then, is not to create new religious doctrines, as Philo did vis-à-vis Greek philosophy, but to explain and justify existing creeds.

However, if we examine Wolfson's other writings, we find that he also notes additional factors as responsible for motion in the history of religious philosophy. As already noted, the enterprise of scriptural philosophy is imbued with immanent inner tension: On the one hand, in the wake of Greek philosophy (but also in the wake of the Bible) most of the "rationalist theologians" tended to regard nature as a unified lawful system. On the other hand, following the Bible's lead, they proclaimed the sovereignty of God over nature (through the doctrine of creation and miracles), and human independence from the lawfulness of nature (through the doctrine of free choice).[42] Religious philosophy, then, was fueled by two impulses that are logically in tension with one another: the philosophical impulse to include all factors in the universe within one unified system and the Biblical understanding that radically separates between God, the cosmos and human beings. This tension persisted as long as a prior loyalty to the Biblical worldview predominated among philosophers. It was abrogated by Spinoza, who in repudiating the revelatory message "succeeded in bringing both God and man under the universal rule of nature."[43]

Various religious thinkers sought to resolve this tension in different ways for different issues. This could explain the motion apparent in religious philosophy, i.e., the theological give-and-take which transpired in the chronicles of scriptural philosophy. The different solutions proposed by the theologians were not chosen according to exclusively logical criteria. They always reflected an a priori loyalty to fundamental premises drawn from the religious traditions, whether Jewish, Christian or Muslim. For instance, Philo accepted the traditional Jewish concept of God as Creator according to the analogy of a craftsman. Thus in Wolfson's view the Philonic "logos," which serves as the location of the ideas that bear the patterns of existence, shifted from its first stage, when it was part of the divine thought, to its second stage, when it acquired an independent existence outside of the Deity, through an act of creation. The Philonic logos is never identical with its creator, just as an object created by an artisan is not identical with the artisan himself. Here the "scriptural" impulse to separate between the Creator and his creation overcame the "pagan-philosophic" tendency to derive all of being from a single foundation. In contrast, the apologists, first-century pagan philosophers who converted to Christianity, subscribed to a "mythological" concept of God as processed by Christian theology. They portrayed God as one who begets things from within himself, according to the analogy of natural reproduction. Consequently, the logos as well was held to make the transition from its first to its second stage through an act of procreation, with the entity being born bearing a certain resemblance to the being that begets it. Here, under the influence of pagan mythology, an inclination to identify between various agents in the universe that all partake of a single system was preferred over an inclination to distinguish absolutely between the Creator and the created.[44] Some three hundred years later a heretical Iranian sect adopted the "Philonic-Jewish" concept of the logos, while returning to the original Biblical worldview.[45]

With regard to the question of human free will, a difference arises between Philo's system and that developed by Christian theology. Philo, following the Jewish tradition of the Land of Israel, deems human beings to be torn between the "good inclination" and the "bad inclination," forces which Wolfson identifies as the poles of intellect and emotion.[46] God, however, who is separate from nature, as the Lord who created its lawfulness out of complete freedom, apportioned something of his essential nature to human beings, rendering them also independent of nature through the gift of free choice.[47] Here the Biblical division between God, nature and man is clearly upheld. Greek philosophy, by comparison, even in its more exalted forms, viewed human beings as part of nature. The definition of free will in Aristotle, for instance, is only a relative definition: Human deeds are free when performed without external coercion. However, the individual's internal decision-making process is always an expression of his predetermined essential nature.[48] Despite the fact that they had been nurtured on pagan philosophy, the Church Fathers generally endorsed the Philonic view on this subject. Human free will is absolute, not relative, and the concept of divine grace is considered, in Philo's wake, as a form of assistance provided human beings in mastering their inclinations. This assistance is accorded them in reward for previous successes in this realm achieved through their own efforts.[49] Augustine was the one to turn Christian thought once again in the direction of paganism, by depicting Adam's punishment as the loss of free will. He considered humans to be altogether subject to deterministic natural forces, particularly the sexual urge, and thus to have lost some of their status as separate from nature. All divine assistance in overcoming this inclination is conferred not as a reward for previous good deeds, but out of pure grace. Like the Arian sect in the matter of the logos, here as well a certain "heresy" developed, which resurrected the prior Biblical orientation. Pelagius argued that humankind had not lost its freedom of choice by virtue of Adam's sin, thereby restoring the human species to its unique status.[50]

From Wolfson's scheme we can infer that there was a certain motion in the direction of a divergence from the Philonic system within the framework of Christian theology. Under the influence of traditions Wolfson calls "mythological," Christian theology sometimes deviates in the direction of excessive homogeneity in the relations between God, the world and humankind. Nevertheless, it bears mentioning that for Wolfson such minor deviations do not suffice to remove Christian theology from the domain of "scriptural philosophy." All of the theological debates among the Church Fathers were conducted within the framework of what Rotenstreich calls "the ground rules," the six doctrines enumerated above shared by both Philo and the Church Fathers.[51] This is also the case in Islam, within whose orthodox school slight "deviations" from the Philonic framework work also manifested themselves, deviations which also spawned "purer" Philonic reactions on the part of rival groups. In the theology of the Kalam, however, the deviations were not only in the direction of mythology, but also in the direction Wolfson dubs "primitive," namely, the portrayal of an arbitrary Deity, whose links with the world and with human beings are not mediated by rational lawfulness. One example of this is the negation of the "intermediate causes" by most of the Kalam theologians. Here as well, the deviation from the concept of the Biblical God is rooted in a commitment to sacred texts. In Wolfson's view, the Muslim Koran stresses power as the first and primary attribute of God, in the course of a polemic with believers in false gods, who are characterized by impotence. This power was understood by them to mean absolute dominion, making God the direct and exclusive cause of everything that transpires in the world. When the theologians of the Kalam encountered Greek philosophy, they confirmed the opinion of most philosophers concerning the existence of God, thus ruling out the Epicurean theory that denies the rule of God and ascribes all worldly events to chance. However, they opposed the idea supported by most philosophers that imputes causal force to natural agents outside of God, thus diminishing God's exclusive reign in the world.[52]

The Kalam consequently developed the concept of an absolutely willful Deity, capable of arbitrarily changing the primal order of things at any moment and directly responsible for all occurrences. This is in contrast to the original Philonic conception, whereby God, through an act of will, embedded "intermediate causes" in the world, possessed of independent causal power. A minority opinion then also emerged within the Islamic tradition that once again mandated the principle of causality (as in the approach of Ibn Rushd), along with various intermediate positions.[53]

However, once scriptural philosophy had deviated from the basic Philonic approach, under the influence of certain "mythological" and "primitive" Christian and Islamic traditions, the opposing, non-orthodox groups—the Arians, Pelagius, the Muatazillah or Ibn Rushd—had an only partially corrective effect. The most important guardian of the tenets of scriptural philosophy was medieval Jewish philosophy. Wolfson's last book, *The Repercussions of the Kalam in Jewish Philosophy*,[54] demonstrates that the opinions of the Kalam philosophers—to the degree that they deviated from the original Philonic prescription—did not penetrate Jewish philosophy, despite their common cultural platform. As Twersky emphasizes in his introduction to the book, Wolfson scrupulously distinguished between "influence" and "repercussions." The Kalam did not influence the essence or content of Jewish philosophy, yet it supplied the conceptual-philosophical arena and the impetus to defend the central Philonic doctrines for R. Sa'adiah Gaon, R. Bahiah Ibn Pakudah, Maimonides and their contemporaries.[55]

In conclusion, then, according to Wolfson there was no stage-by-stage developmental motion in scriptural philosophy after Philo. To the extent that there was movement, it was expressed on the one hand by the unfolding of the doctrines of Philonism itself in all of their implications and the defense of them against other philosophical viewpoints. On the other hand, we find a diverging movement in the direction of "primitive" or "mythological" paganism, and a counter-attempt to return scriptural philosophy to its Philonic foundations.

THE PERIOD OF DISMANTLING: SPINOZA AND THE NEUTRALIZATION OF SCRIPTURAL PHILOSOPHY

Now we arrive at the period which Wolfson considered the "end of time" for scriptural philosophy, a period connected primarily with the figure of Spinoza. Wolfson admittedly states that scriptural philosophy did not come to an end all at once—there was a certain regression in its beliefs and opinions even before Spinoza, and it continued to exist in some fashion even after Spinoza.[56] However it was Spinoza who systematically undermined it, with regard to all of its characteristic concerns, on the basis of his profound knowledge of its language and literature.[57] In terms of the history of religious philosophy, two of Wolfson's theses on Spinoza are of particular import. The first is his vehement assertion that Spinoza had no new message for Western philosophy. The second is his observation that Spinoza effectively returned philosophy to its "preliminary" period.

In contrast with Philo, who revolutionized philosophy, Spinoza demolished scriptural philosophy on the basis of arguments which had arisen and been applied within the framework of the Philonic tradition itself. Spinoza's distinction lay in the fact that he carried these arguments to their full logical conclusions, even when they led him beyond the Biblical premises that had hitherto served as the source and boundary for all philosophizing.[58]

Spinoza's daring, in Wolfson's eyes, found expression in four major themes. First, throughout the entire history of philosophy numerous thinkers maintained the existence of a unified material substructure underlying the whole universe. The theories on this subject developed from the Greek philosophers' concept of "formless basic matter" to the proposition that a single material constitutes both earthly and supernal bodies (in the view of Crescas, Bruno and Descartes). Nevertheless, according to Greek philosophy, medieval philosophy and Renaissance philosophy prior to Spinoza there is a discontinuity in the unity of the universe, a gap between God and the world. In consequence, medieval philosophic systems arose that espoused the existence of pure spiritual intellects beyond material existence, in an attempt to bridge the divide between God and the world.

Along with the above, almost all philosophers believed in a spiritual God who cannot be comprehended within matter external to himself. Wolfson makes it clear that these rationalist theologians were aware of the logical tensions created by this dualism, but, as Fackenheim put it, they "stubbornly" refused "to cross the boundaries set up by tradition" regarding the otherness of God.[59] Spinoza, who was quick to make use of the weaponry that had accumulated in the storehouses of philosophy itself, affirmed that the Deity has an attribute of bodily extension and an attribute of consciousness. Instead of two coexistent kingdoms, the divine spiritual and the worldly material, he envisages the universe as one kingdom, with every instance of speculative thought or of physical movement reflecting a unified logical-mathematical web.[60]

Wolfson repeatedly reminds us that the "scriptural philosophers" also championed the unity of the laws of nature and sought to uphold this principle at every possible opportunity. Some of them went even further by asserting that the Deity chose to limit his own will, in order to adapt it to the rational rules that he himself had laid down for the world from the outset. They were nevertheless faithful to the Biblical portrait of God as Creator, who presides over all aspects of the cosmos, performs miracles and grants human beings free will. They therefore insisted on claiming, at times even against their own powers of reasoning, that portions of the constitution according to which God rules the world are not intelligible to human beings. This breach in the unity of natural law was abolished by Spinoza, who argued that no physical or metaphysical event in the universe can deviate from the laws of nature.[61]

Additional issues treated by Spinoza, such as the essence of the soul and the issue of freedom of choice, serve to reinforce the principle of the unity of nature which had been ruptured in the writings of the scriptural philosophers. The rationalist theologians, who viewed God as a pure spiritual entity entirely detached from the material world, also regarded the human soul, in its status as "part of God above," as a spiritual element distinct from the body which separates from it at death. This spiritual soul distinguishes human beings from nature, preventing them from being completely included within it. Spinoza, who had no difficulty in conceiving of God as including within a single logical-causal system the two attributes of existence, thought and extension, also had no difficulty, in the wake of this doctrine of cosmic unity, in conceiving of the speculative and physical aspects of humans as entwined in an inseparable unity.[62]

Human beings are part of nature in another way as well, according to Spinoza. The inner logic coursing through every being in the universe—whether inanimate, plant, animal or human—is the principle of self-preservation. Existence, instead of being contingent upon the will of a transcendent ruler for its creation and perpetuation, includes within itself the principle of its existence and perpetuation, and this inner impulse is what activates human thoughts and motions. Just as God has no will, in the sense of a principle of goal-oriented action not contingent upon a necessary intellectual causality, human beings also have no "will." Irrational humans are controlled by certain natural forces outside of themselves or by emotional excitations which sometimes work against their own interest, i.e., against their continued existence. A rational person is one who permits the general divine principle of self-preservation to guide him as well, and to determine the behaviors required to keep him in existence.[63]

For Wolfson, then, Spinoza did not create a new metaphysics. He simply latched on to one of the traditional impulses of scriptural philosophy itself, the impulse towards the systematic unification of being. Medieval philosophy, however, had countered this impulse with an opposing Biblical impulse, one which conferred a special ontological status upon God and humankind vis-à-vis nature. The rationalist theologians were aware of the logical tensions created when God is grasped as a perfect eternal being who nonetheless effects changes within time, yet they were loath to relinquish either of the doctrinal poles which jointly produced this tension. Spinoza's unwillingness to tolerate logical tension, together with his detachment from basic Biblical premises, induced him to cling to only one of the poles of the dialectic of scriptural philosophy, thus effectively annihilating its motion and its vitality.

Wolfson's second thesis regarding Spinoza is an extension of the first. Not only did Spinoza not introduce any real innovation into the history of philosophy; he returned Western philosophy to Aristotelian presuppositions. For in Wolfson's system, the primary criterion for assessing the historical value of a given philosophic system is its theory of divinity. As he states at the end of his book on Spinoza: "In its most essential feature, the theology of Spinoza may be regarded as a return to the theory of Aristotle, with its conception of an impersonal deity devoid of will and acting by necessity, against which the medievals constantly argued."[64]

However, at the end of his later article, "Spinoza and the Religion of the Past," Wolfson goes to even greater lengths. He applies the above thesis to almost all of the typical subjects of religious philosophy, arguing that Spinoza returns not only to Aristotle, but also to the doctrines of Greek philosophy in general:

> Spinoza is daring, but he introduces no novelty. His daring consists in overthrowing the old Philonic principles which by his time had dominated the thought of European religious philosophy for some sixteen centuries. But in overthrowing these principles, all he did was to reinstate, with some modification, the old principles of classical Greek philosophy. That is what he did in dealing with the concepts of God, the soul, freedom, ethics, and immortality, though, in the case of immortality, he follows a medieval variation of the Platonic conception of immortality.[65]

It may be that according to the yardstick of pure philosophy—logical consistency free of tensions and comprehensive systematic unity—Wolfson regarded Spinoza as the philosopher par excellence. However, precisely because he strove for consistency and uniformity, he ultimately sent philosophy back to its mythological roots. The mathematical-logical web, from which no physical or intellectual act can escape, is a sort of new version of "the rationalized conception of fate which prevailed in the philosophies of Plato, Aristotle and the Stoics."[66]

Wolfson's thesis regarding Spinoza, that he returns human thought to its "introductory" period instead of enhancing and perfecting it, is also expressed in his discussion of Hume's project: "The Philonic conception of divine causality . . . is directly discussed and rejected by Hume, and he similarly rejects the classical Greek conception of fated causality. . . . In their place, he revives the Epicurean denial of causality."[67]

Wolfson's contention, then, is that in his bid to depose the medieval Philonic system, the modern philosopher does not offer a loftier or more refined worldview to replace it. Instead, he resurrects a pre-Philonic Greek teaching, whether deterministic ("mythological") or one which highlights the role of chance ("primitive").

At this point we shift to Wolfson's perspective on the modern period in Western philosophy. Wolfson doesn't dismiss all of the attainments of human thought in the modern period. So long as the human intellect confines itself to the physical, biological or political realms without presuming to metaphysical authority, it progresses in evolutionary-cumulative fashion, registering valuable achievements. Nothing would preclude a Philonic theologian from adopting contemporary ideas in the field of physics, for example. Regarding the structure and composition of the physical cosmos, Philo himself embraced the prevailing Aristotelian conception. In the waning days of the middle ages, after the advent of the Copernican revolution, scriptural philosophers engaged in an attempt to prove that there is no contradiction between their traditional metaphysics and the new notions regarding the structure of the cosmos.[68] For Wolfson, Crescas preceded Bruno and Newton in propounding a new physical theory of infinite space.[69] At the end of his article on Maimonides and R. Yehudah Ha-Levy's conceptions of creation, Wolfson speculates how well disposed these two thinkers, both quintessential representatives of the Philonic tradition, might have been to adopt some kind of evolutionary theory. He concludes that they would have been willing to accept evolution as a biological theory, so long as it did not involve metaphysical assumptions regarding the eternity of the world or some kind of mechanistic causality. If evolution can be regarded as a process originating with a willful first cause, and whose lawfulness is teleological, then there is no substantive reason that would compel a scriptural philosopher to reject it.[70] In the political arena, Wolfson considers modern ideas such as democracy and international federalism to be so positive that he anoints Philo as their author.[71]

However, even if Newtonian space, evolution and democratic federalism are grasped as positive developments, Wolfson stipulates that every attempt to tender a unified explanation for physical phenomena is ultimately based on an ancient Jewish outlook. In his opinion, the scientific method that seeks lawfulness in a nature perceived to be uniform is the application of the traditional Jewish method of reading texts that are also grasped as the product of unified and deliberate thought.[72]

As noted above, the main shortcoming of the modern period in Wolfson's eyes is the tendency to detach itself from Biblical authority when it comes to metaphysical beliefs, and to set up human reason as the ultimate judge in such matters. At the dawn of the modern period, certain thinkers had already begun to gnaw away at the Philonic worldview. For instance, Descartes, in most of his metaphysical positions, comes across as a traditional "Philonic" philosopher. Despite his view of the body as a machine, he believed that God implanted a separate soul in human beings. Through miraculous means, the Deity also bestowed upon humans the power of free will to assist them in their struggle with their bodily desires, which conform to the patterns affecting all bodies. Descartes held that God rules over his world, if not through secondary causes with independent creative powers, at least according to patterns of continual re-creation that he had in mind at the time of the original creation. With regard to one central issue, however, Descartes explicitly dissents from the Philonic tradition: the issue of miracles. While willing to acknowledge the miraculous character of free choice, Descartes obstinately refuses to admit that God is capable of performing miracles within nature itself.[73] One might speculate that in Wolfson's view, the logical inconsistency in Descartes' system stems from the fact that he ascribes metaphysical value to the scientific picture of the world, one devoid of all surprises.

However, if deviation on isolated issues creates logical tension, an overall rejection of the Philonic framework of Biblical authority engenders wholesale historical regression. As we have seen, Spinoza goes back to Aristotle and Hume returns to Epicurus. Yet this does not exhaust Wolfson's critique of contemporary metaphysical "arrogance." First, all modern attempts to replace the Biblical God with "gods" that are ultimately the projections of human consciousness (however they are termed: "man's idealized consciousness," "man's aspiration for ideal values," "the unity of ideal ends") are characterized by Wolfson as "atheism."[74] It is considered a waste of time to append labels of absolute meaning to limited human aspirations. Even if these thinkers ultimately aim to rehabilitate religion in the modern context, the logical status of such concepts of divinity, rooted as they are in human impulses, is no different from that of outright atheism. Thus there is no distinction between "modern religious humanism" and Marxism, which views religion as the "opiate of the masses."[75]

Wolfson is less disparaging with regard to "all modern forms of religious rationalism."[76] In their case, at least, God is deemed to exist independently of human understanding, and he serves as the object of human intellectual aspirations. As examples of this type of theory of divinity, Wolfson cites Spinoza's "substance," Leibnitz's "central monad," the "spirit" of German idealism, Bergson's "elan vital" and Whitehead's "principle of concretion."[77] What all of these concepts have in common is the fact of their being powers "devoid of personality," which are immanent in the cosmos." These labels as well, then, are no substitute for the transcendent, personal and heteronomous God of the Bible. Here again we encounter Wolfson's ambivalence regarding everything to do with religious rationalism, whether classic or modern. On the one hand, as we have seen, the mind is capable of autonomously attaining a lofty and abstract, though less than perfect, concept of divinity. On the other hand, Wolfson assumes that an ordinary person, one who is not overly reflective and not over sophisticated, should know his Creator naturally, without resort to philosophizing. This is the only plausible explanation for his fierce critique of the efforts of both classic and modern philosophers to "devise deities," as if these efforts issue from a malicious heretical impulse. The parallel between the post- and pre-Philonic periods in this matter is obvious here:

> those who called themselves lovers of wisdom, philosophers, made quibbling about the meaning of God one of their chief occupations. Ever since Xenophanes rejected the gods of popular religion and put something else in their place to which he gave the name God, it became the practice of the Greek lovers of wisdom not to deny God but to change the meaning of God. . . . Nowadays, lovers of wisdom are still busily engaged in the gentle art of devising deities.[78]

The blunt and critical tone of articles such as "The Philonic God of Revelation" or "Sermonette" leaves little room for doubt that Wolfson viewed the modern return to "pagan Greek philosophy" in a negative light. The question therefore arises whether he envisioned the possibility of reviving scriptural philosophy following its subversion at the hands of Spinoza. The answer to this question would appear to be fairly complex. Wieseltier contends that Wolfson sought to demonstrate in his scholarship that Judaism, whose principles were formulated in Philonic philosophy, is qualified to grapple with contemporary philosophic trends, and that all of his writings reflect a "traditional religious intention."[79] Harvey, in contrast, writes that Wolfson's position was more pessimistic.[80] In the early days of his philosophic scholarship, when he was under the influence of pragmatists like James and Santayana, he did indeed strive for a renaissance of Jewish philosophy. In his first article on Maimonides and R. Yehudah Ha-Levi, there is a tendency to treat the medieval Jewish philosophic tradition as an expression of Hellenism, and the critiques of R. Yehudah Ha-Levi and Crescas as confrontations with Hellenism on the part of "Hebraism."[81] At the time he considered the "Hebraic" worldview of R. Yehudah Ha-Levi and Crescas, with its concept of a personal commanding God, to be of higher pragmatic value than the Greek "cosmological-objective" conception. The works of most of the medieval philosophers are held to be irrelevant to the new age, as they lack pragmatic effectiveness, i.e., the ability to influence people's daily lives. Only "personal, ethical and subjective" conceptions of God, such as those of R. Yehudah Ha-Levi and Crescas, are capable of serving as a springboard for the renaissance of religious philosophy and religious life. Eventually, after he had formulated his mature theses regarding the "Jewish-Philonic" character of scriptural philosophy in its entirety, from Philo to Spinoza, Wolfson's approach changed. In Harvey's opinion, by then Wolfson had despaired of the possibility of a renaissance in religious belief, which is a precondition for a renaissance in religious philosophy, which requires a "preamble of faith." Consequently, and because he had become totally absorbed in the philological-historical research required for the formulation of his theses, Wolfson gave up on the attempt to "revive" religious philosophy, contenting himself with a mere description of the grand philosophy of the past.

To us it appears that Wolfson's writings could support either reading. Just as Wolfson felt ambivalent about the virtues and vices of philosophy, so he was ambivalent about the possibility of reviving scriptural philosophy in our time. On the one hand, his protestations that he speaks only as a historian notwithstanding, he himself takes on the role of theological defender of several elements of the Philonic system against modern "heresies." Entire essays by Wolfson were devoted to the attempt to show that all the arguments advanced against Philonic doctrines in the modern period were already known "in advance" to medieval theologians, such that there is no modern heretical opinion that cannot be responded to.[82] Theological-scholarly efforts like these would seem aimed at grounding and justifying Philonism as a serious intellectual option that can compete with modern systems.[83] In this context, the artificial resuscitation received by the Church Fathers in the conclusion of Wolfson's article "The Immortality of the Soul and the Resurrection of the Dead" is worth recalling. Their role is to "answer" the student of religious studies regarding the immunity of traditional Jewish-Christian beliefs from the revelations of modern science.[84]

In addition, in the preface to his book *Philo*, Wolfson makes explicit statements regarding the potential vitality of Philonism in the modern period:

> The preamble of faith with which the philosophy of Philo begins, though no longer universally accepted unchallenged, has not completely disappeared. It is still the preamble of the living philosophy of the greater part of mankind. At the present time, under the name of one of the most distinguished of mediaeval Christian exponents of Philonic philosophy, a modernized version of that philosophy, in its metaphysical as well as in its ethical and social teachings, based upon the same principles of the same old preamble of faith, is ably defended by an organized school of thought. While it is to be admitted that for

one who believes, or is willing to believe, in the principles of the old preamble of faith, it is no more difficult to build up and defend a Philonic type of philosophy at the present time than it was for many a century in the past.[85]

Nevertheless, Wolfson concludes his book on a more pessimistic note. If at the outset he claimed that Philonism is still a living philosophy for many non-reflective believers, and that a professional philosophic school, Thomism, is engaged in defending it, at the end of the book his view of modern versions of Philonism is less enthusiastic, and he sees no great chance of reviving the latter, at least not in official philosophic circles:

> It is only recently that Philonic philosophy, through the increasing influence of one of its most distinguished Latin exponents, began to gain vogue and currency in quarters where it is not an inherited tradition, but that is due only to the breakdown of philosophy as a learned discipline, from which some inquiring minds try to seek escape in scholasticism as a substitute for scholarship.[86]

We find a number of value judgments in this passage that are the key to Wolfson's view of the modern period in philosophy. First, philosophy as a "learned discipline" is in a state of collapse. In light of our survey up to this point, we can infer that this collapse stems from the loss of the tension and vitality generated by the confrontation between the fragmented worldview of the Bible and the unified worldview of Greece. The loss of this tension, and the lack of interest in religious questions attendant upon the disintegration of religious faith, led to a preoccupation with what Wieseltier calls "small truths definitively apprehended."[87] For Wolfson, such a preoccupation is not philosophy in the classic sense, whose domain is precisely those metaphysical issues that the analytic philosophers regard as meaningless, since they are not given to empirical verification. Second, even if Thomism were to become fashionable in certain circles, that in itself would not presage the revival of Philonism as a living tradition. Given that Philonism, once based on the "preamble of faith," is no longer a living tradition (and, according to Wolfson, significant thought is conditioned upon the adherence to and processing of living intellectual traditions), any attempt by members of the academy to return to Philonism as a modern way of thought would be an inauthentic form of escapism.[88]

WOLFSON'S HISTORIOSOPHIC SCHEME— "ORIENTATION BY ORIGINS"

To sum up the course of religious thought from Wolfson's perspective, it can be said that prior to the rise of Philonism, the principle of stage-by-stage evolution towards a valued end was its law of motion. Yet once Philonism

established itself, it remained at rest, with every motion within it interpreted as an articulation of its own principles (together with minor pagan
deviations that were easily correctable). In contrast, with the advent of Spinoza the Philonic structure was destroyed and official philosophy reverted to
an autonomous paganism, liberating itself from heteronomous revelation
in the process. All this transpired despite the hypothetical possibility of constructing a theoretical defense of Philonism, and despite the fact that mul-
titudes unreflectively assume the Philonic "preamble of faith" to this day.
Wieseltier and Harvey are right to argue that this historiosophical structure
serves as a Jewish response to the periodization of Hegel and his disciples.
Instead of every pre-Christian or extra-Christian phenomenon being
grasped as a backdrop to Christianity, which is the main event for Hegel
and his followers, for Wolfson every phenomenon preceding scriptural philosophy is itself a backdrop, and scriptural philosophy engulfs all manifestations of religious philosophy in the monotheistic world.[89] Nevertheless,
Wieseltier's claim that Wolfson's conception affords a "perspective of the
middle," whereby the attainments of classical and modern philosophy are
judged according to criteria established by medieval philosophy, seems true
only in part.[90] The characterization is accurate only when presented as a way
of comparing Wolfson's theory to other conceptions.

In contradistinction to Hegel, for instance, who views both Greek philosophy and Christian scholasticism as leading inevitably to the worthy
goal embodied by Teutonic philosophy,[91] Wolfson considers religious philosophy's locus of value to reside in a system that held sway—in terms of
conventional divisions of time—between classical and modern philosophy.
Yet this is a translation of Wolfson's historiosophy into conventional scholarly terms. Wolfson employed the categories of "ancient times," "the middle ages" and "the modern period" only for external polemical purposes.
This can be clarified by a close reading of the preface to the compendium
Religious Philosophy, where he writes as follows:

> If we are to follow the *conventional method* of dividing philosophy into ancient,
> medieval, and modern, then medieval philosophy is to be defined as that sys-
> tem of thought which flourished between Greek pagan philosophy, which
> knew not of Scripture, and that body of philosophic writings which ever since
> the seventeenth century has tried to free itself from the influence of Scripture.
> Medieval philosophy *so defined* was founded by Philo.[92]

Wolfson seems to endorse the conventional time division instituted by political historians, which Christian scholars applied with certain modifications
to the philosophy of religion.[93] This division in itself reflects a lack of enthusiasm for the middle ages, which are presented as falling between two important
periods, the classical and the modern. Yet Wolfson, in a clever polemic, turns
the division on its head. While it's true that formally speaking the middle ages

falls between the two other periods, he says, it is nevertheless the most consequential of the three precisely by virtue of its being subjected to the Bible, while both the ancient and the modern periods are primarily pagan.

The above passage, then, was formulated in protest against the conventional time divisions. In our view, Wolfson's true conception regarding the internal development of religious philosophy should be sought in his ongoing scholarship, as instanced above. In these works the main topic of study is the formation of the Philonic philosophy, its articulation and disintegration. Thus the ancient period is characterized by Wolfson not as having generated an integral thought-system worthy of study in its own right, but as a kind of introduction, a preparatory stage for scriptural philosophy. According to this perspective, the advent of scriptural philosophy signals the onset of the most momentous period in the chronicles of philosophy. In Wolfson's opinion, the pinnacle of philosophic creativity is to be found not in the midst of the most significant period (in the thought of Maimonides, for example), but at its outset, namely, upon the founding of the religious philosophy that bound itself to the yoke of heteronomous truths.

Since the inception of Philonism, it has persisted and continued to articulate its ramifications despite all vicissitudes of time and place, so long as it has been sustained by a belief in the authority of revelation. However, once one of the original pillars of true religious philosophy becomes dislodged, when Spinoza, Hume and Mill discard the Biblical "preamble of faith" in their rejection of revelation, scriptural philosophy effectively exits the stage of the history of philosophy. Wolfson's is not a "perspective of the middle," then, but a "perspective of beginnings," i.e., an orientation according to origins.[94] The original elements which joined together to found the Philonic philosophy—the Greek quest to comprehend all of the cosmos within a single logical system and the Biblical outlook that stressed the sovereignty of God over the world and human freedom in relation to the world—are what continued to supply it with the tension that nurtured its discourse. The disengagement from these elements, first from belief in the Bible and more recently from metaphysical speculation in general, were the cause of its death, or at least of the death throes of Philonic philosophy. Wieseltier, then, seems to be on firmer ground when he describes Wolfson as having been "occasionally unfair to the complexity of his subject by defining it solely in terms of origins" and on less firm ground when he imputes to him a "perspective of the middle."[95]

JEWISH SOURCES IN WOLFSON'S HISTORIOSOPHY: PARTICULARISTIC TRENDS

The tendency to concern himself with origins, ascribed by Wieseltier to Wolfson, is substantively connected to the latter's presentation of the Bible and the rabbinic tradition as early sources of Western philosophy. Although in many places Wolfson tends to present theological issues and opinions as universal human options, one cannot ignore the particularistic bent that emanates from his research. Much of his scholarship represents an attempt to prove the direct connection between the unique Jewish tradition embodied in the written and oral Laws, and Philo's convictions and interpretive methods—later bequeathed to the entire Western world. According to this point of view, Judaism, as the most ancient and originary monotheistic faith, is the primary source of Christian and Islamic theology with regard to both content and method. As we have seen, the minor deviations from the Philonic framework found in the Church Fathers and the Kalam are considered to be of secondary importance, and Western philosophy at its best is characterized by Wolfson as unmistakably Jewish.

We will now expand our discussion of Wolfson's particularism by way of two foci. First we will concentrate on the historical role of Jewish religious literature, the written and oral Law, as early sources of the beliefs and interpretive methods appropriated by the entire Western world. Second, we will dwell on Wolfson's assessment of the contribution of distinguished Jews to the foundation, preservation and dismantling of scriptural philosophy.

THE HERITAGE OF THE BIBLE

We saw that Wolfson holds Philonic philosophy to be a reduction of the narratives, laws and homilies of the Bible to a "tight and coherent" system. The five doctrines of Philonic philosophy adopted by the Church Fathers and the Kalam—the existence of God, his unity, a willed creation, individual providence and the principle of revelation—all have their sources in the Bible. The Bible, then, is the chief source of content for the religious philosophy that dominated the West for 1700 years. To bolster this concept, Wolfson argues that Philo, the figure who bequeathed the Biblical perspective to Western philosophy, was acquainted with the Bible in its original Hebrew, although he brings only circumstantial proofs to this effect, acknowledging the lack of any direct evidence on the subject.[96] Similarly, he goes out of his way to refute the claims of scholars such as Goodenough that Philo was essentially a Greek mystic, who articulated his faith in the Bible by way of a sophisticated interpretive structure.[97] Wolfson, in contrast, asserts that Philo is the faithful transmitter of the Biblical perspective, of which he had read in the Hebrew original, and that he simply employed terminology he drew from the Greek mystics and philosophers of his generation.[98]

To make use of the theological terminology of Rahner and Vorgrimler, once again, the Bible was not only a "material source" for Western religious philosophy, but also a "negative norm."[99] Every religious philosophy that arose after Philo subordinated itself to the fundamental tenets of the Bible, by committing itself not to deviate from them. This self-restraint was predicated on the idea that human reason is limited, while the content of revelation is perfect.[100]

The Bible, then, bequeathed Western thought not only a doctrinal framework, but also a practical objective. This viewpoint of Wolfson's can be discerned from statements he made in one of his articles about heretical Christian sects and from his discussion of the concept of God in scriptural philosophy. In his article on the heretical sects he makes the following observation: "the entire history of the religion of Israel as depicted in Scripture itself is an attempt to eradicate all mythological conceptions of God. God is a creator of things; He is not a begetter of things."[101]

In other places already mentioned, Wolfson presents scriptural philosophy, including its Christian and Islamic permutations, as a continuation of the Bible's polemic against mythological concepts of divinity. In the main, the Church Fathers inherited their anti-mythological view of God from Philo. They defend the principle of the unity of God against the depredations of popular polytheism and gnosticism. Following Philo's example they argue for the non-dependence of God on factors outside of himself, both before and after the creation. They consider the world to have been created by God and not begotten from within him, although there was no necessity that it be created. The Church Fathers doubtless strayed from the Bible's anti-mythological message when they described the logos as having been born from within the Deity. Yet on most theological issues, a basic fidelity to Biblical monotheism is preserved. Regarding the creation of the world, they were even more zealous than Philo himself in their defense of the principle of creation ex nihilo.[102] In the Kalam, the situation was hardly different. The deviation in the direction of a mythological approach is even less marked in the Kalam. Admittedly, the Kalam orthodoxy did understand the attributes of God—the qualities of "life," "wisdom" and "ability," for instance—to be real eternal entities existing within the Deity and in distinction from its essence. Yet they opposed the Christian tendency to ascribe an independent divine status to every part of the Deity.[103] With regard to the creation, most of the sages of the Kalam accepted the principle of creation "ex nihilo," yet the Mu'tazilites were willing, after the lead of Philo himself, to accept the Platonic idea that the world was created from primordial matter. They did attach a certain reservation, also of Philonic origin, that this primordial matter was itself created as well.[104] The overall picture, then, is one of a Christian and Islamic struggle against polytheism and mythology by means of philosophical tools. This struggle is the direct extension of the original Biblical struggle, which Wolfson regards as the guiding theological thrust of the Jewish faith. It transpired, then, that the Jewish faith bequeathed not only fundamental concepts and norms of thought to Western religious philosophy, but also an objective and a program.

THE RABBINIC HERITAGE

Wolfson amplifies his thesis concerning the Jewish underpinnings of Western religious philosophy by stressing the proximity between Philo (who bequeathed scriptural philosophy to the Church Fathers and the Kalam) and the beliefs and interpretive methods of the Jewish rabbinic sages. For instance, Wolfson contends that the appearance of the theory of ideas in Philo's teachings should not be accredited exclusively to the influence of Plato. There was a position in the rabbinic tradition that espoused the prior existence of patterns of being, argues Wolfson, that Philo was surely aware of. To support his claim, Wolfson cites midrashic sources concerning the ideal form of the Temple that had been transmitted to Moses at Sinai, along with sources on the prior existence of the Torah, the Throne of Glory, the patriarchs, the Messiah, etc. Accordingly, Alexandrian Jews, and Philo in particular, must have had an inner predisposition to adopt Plato's theory of ideas.[105] The Philonic theory of ideas, which Wolfson regarded as the source of central Christian and Islamic beliefs such as the trinity and the theory of divine attributes, is tightly connected to rabbinic traditions.[106] Further, the Philonic division of the ideas into two categories, those patterns or forces that express goodness and mercy as opposed to those signifying judgment and retribution, corresponds to the accepted distinction in rabbinic tradition between the divine attributes of compassion and judgment.[107] Elsewhere in his book *Philo*, Wolfson remarks on the connection between Philo's concept of free will, "divine assistance" "the merit of the patriarchs" and other rabbinic statements on these subjects.[108]

In Wolfson's opinion, Philo inherited not only beliefs and opinions from the sages of the Land of Israel, but an entire interpretive orientation. Wolfson asserts that the source of the philosophical-allegorical commentaries of Philo and the medieval sages, as well as their holistic-harmonistic approach to the text, can be located in rabbinic literature.[109] There is no point in belaboring the distinctions between different types of allegories, he argues; they can be simply defined as follows: "the interpretation of a text in terms of something else, irrespective of what that something else is."[110]

The rabbis of the Land of Israel were presumably less well-acquainted with Greek philosophy than Philo was. Yet they were accustomed to interpret the Bible in terms of the things they had experienced and come to know, such as the cumulative wisdom of the generations, certain speculative meditations, the changing necessities of life and the ethical claims of conscience. The principle of the non-literal interpretation of texts was already well established in the rabbinic tradition by the time of Philo. Philo therefore inherited this original Jewish approach and endowed it with a philosophic orientation in keeping with his life experience in Alexandria. To quote from *The Philosophy of the Church Fathers*: "The allegorical method as applied by Philo to the Old Testament is thus a special type of midrashic method."[111] Thus the tradition of the non-literal midrash cleared the way for the philosophic-allegoric commentators on the Bible from among the Church Fathers and the medieval philosophers.[112]

Not only non-literal midrash, but also the holistic-harmonizing tendency typifying the medieval sages' approach to text (one that Wolfson recommends as a scholarly technique for the study of Judaism even today), are rooted in the literature and commentaries of the rabbinic tradition. Just as a scientist looks for unity and continuity in nature, so the rabbis and their successors over the generations assumed that every serious text reflects thought characterized by unity and continuity.[113] Consequently, instead of imputing the poles of inner contradiction in an ordinary text to intellectual negligence or "historical layers," traditional commentators sought to harmonize. This harmonizing orientation informed Philo's attempts to reconcile two interpretations of Plato's theory of ideas that had crystallized by his time, as well as Augustine's attempts to reconcile conflicting statements in the Gospels.[114]

The rabbis' terse and elusive writing style also had its effect on the preeminent works of scriptural philosophy. For example, in order for the reader to understand Crescas' book *The Light of God*, Wolfson reasons, he must not assume that Crescas recorded all of his conclusions. The book should be treated as a sort of protocol of discussions Crescas held with his students, in the same way that the deliberations of study halls in the Talmudic period were recorded.[115] With reference to Spinoza's *Ethics*, Wolfson observes that "In its concentrated form of exposition and in the baffling allusiveness and ellipticalness of its style, the *Ethics* may be compared to the Talmudic and rabbinic writings upon which Spinoza was brought up, and it is in that spirit in which the old rabbinic scholars approach the study of their standard texts that we must approach the study of the *Ethics*."[116]

Perhaps the main asset the Oral Law bequeathed to Western scriptural philosophy, in Wolfson's view, was the theoretical framework pertaining to creativity within a tradition.[117] Gershom Scholem expresses himself in a similar vein when describing the premises of the Talmudic and midrashic sages regarding continuity and creativity within time:

> we have arrived at an assumption concerning the nature of truth which is characteristic of rabbinic Judaism. . . . Truth is given once and for all, and it is laid down with precision. Fundamentally, truth merely needs to be transmitted. The originality of the exploring scholar has two aspects. In his spontaneity, he

develops and explains that which was transmitted at Sinai, no matter whether it was always known or whether it was forgotten and had to be rediscovered. The effort of the seeker after truth consists not in having new ideas but rather in subordinating himself to the continuity of the tradition of the divine word and in laying open what he receives from it in the context of his own time. In other words: Not system but *commentary* is the legitimate form through which truth is approached. . . . Truth must be laid bare in a text in which it already pre-exists.[118]

To return to Wolfson's historiosophical analysis, it seems that the status of Philo's system in his scheme parallels the status of the Written Law in the rabbinic corpus. "Nothing really new happened" in Western philosophy since the founding of the Philonic system.[119] All of the theological debates that fill the philosophic literature of the medieval period are merely the articulation of the implications of the Philonic "ground rules."[120] The works of the Church Fathers, Kalam theologians and Jewish medieval philosophers are merely commentaries on Philonic positions on such themes as the theory of divinity, creation, providence and the immortality of the soul, commentaries formulated in light of the problems engaging religious philosophy across the generations. In view of the above, Wieseltier would appear justified in his thesis that there is a connecting thread running through the interpretive system of the Talmudic sages (that sought to reconstruct the thought process of the Tannaitic scholars from the chapter headings provided by the Mishnah), the medieval philosophic commentaries ("circumscribed on all sides by sacred texts, whether they were those of Aristotle or those of the Old and/or New Testaments") and the scholarly techniques of Wolfson himself, informed as they are by an attitude toward the text "bordering on reverence" in the effort to uncover meaning considered to inhere in the text a priori.[121]

JEWISH THINKERS: THE JEWISH PARAMETERS OF THE HISTORY OF RELIGIOUS PHILOSOPHY

It appears, then, that Wolfson deliberately underscored traditional Jewish influences on the founder of scriptural philosophy, Philo, in order to lend a Jewish cast to all of Western philosophy. Yet not only are the roots of medieval philosophy Jewish, in Wolfson's eyes, but the historical parameters of this critical period in the annals of philosophy are marked by the personalities of two distinguished Jews. Scholars who have examined Wolfson's approach did not ignore the fact that he framed the boundaries of scriptural philosophy with the figures of Philo and Spinoza, and they consider this hardly accidental. In the opinion of Twersky, Wolfson's student and editor, this framing testified to Wolfson's stance regarding the pride of place of Jewish philosophy in the history of philosophy, and to the fact that he always regarded himself first and foremost as a scholar of Jewish philosophy.[122] Harvey also maintains that the Jewish character of scriptural philosophy is stressed by Wolfson through the positioning of two Jews at its historical extremes.[123] Rotenstreich, however, does not content himself with these observations. He considers the framework of Philo and Spinoza to be laden with irony: Greek and modern philosophy, itself devoid of any link to the Bible, constructs "substitutes" for the Biblical God. Philo's special virtue lies in knowing how to use philosophy to deepen and strengthen Biblical monotheism; he adopted philosophy in order to fashion a concept of God that was unitary, absolute and indivisible. Rotenstreich believes that for Wolfson, Philo was the exemplar of a type of Jewish philosopher, one who chose the route of synthesis "in order to deepen the meaning of the Bible and the meaning of the ties to it." Spinoza, in contrast, is the exemplar of a philosopher who went the way of the Greeks. The ironic aspect to this structure is that only a Jew like Spinoza, who was acquainted from the inside with the attempt by Philo and his successors to produce a "synthesis whose orientation was the primacy and originality of the Bible," was capable of "breaking the unity and having it disintegrate" in a thorough and comprehensive fashion. In Rotenstreich's conclusion: "a single Jew refuted the effort of the single Jew."[124]

WOLFSON'S CONCEPT OF JUDAISM AND PHILOSOPHY

An analysis of Wolfson's epistemological and historiosophical view of the course of the encounter between reason and revelation in the chronicles of Western philosophy, and of the special role of Jewish tradition in its establishment, maintenance and dissolution, leads us to some overall conclusions. First, from Wolfson's standpoint, Judaism in its Philonic theological version is no less than the crucible of Western philosophy, and provided it with its primary energy and motivation for well-nigh 1700 years. Judaism is not dependent for its development on the rising and falling fortunes of Platonic or Aristotelian schools, whose source lies in Greek pagan philosophy.[125] It is itself a driving, active, critical and dominant force in the navigation of Western religious thought. Jewish philosophy has no need to respond to developments in the realm of general philosophy in order to defend itself; it is Judaism that generates and actively preserves the fundamental tenets that have served as the underpinnings of European thought for 1700 years. Perhaps the best example of this orientation of Wolfson's is his presentation of Neoplatonism. It was not the Neoplatonism of Plotinus that shaped the consciousness of Jewish philosophers like Ibn Gvirol and Bahiyah Ibn Pakudah.[126] Rather, Neoplatonism is a sort of pagan stepson by way of Christianity, whose inception lies in the original Jewish Philonic conception of the theory of ideas.[127]

For Wolfson, then, all of the conventional distinctions between "Jewish philosophy" and "general philosophy" break down. The most significant form of general philosophy is that which addresses theological problems, while the contents and interpretive methods of Western theology were drawn first and foremost from its Jewish founder, Philo. Jewish philosophy is *in itself* "general" philosophy, with the exception of insignificant pagan deviations. Consequently, Wolfson does not regard philosophizing as an activity foreign to the spirit of Judaism. Through philosophy the message of the Bible is formulated clearly and systematically. In positive terms, philosophy has the power to strengthen and deepen the Biblical concept of God and disseminate it abroad. In negative terms, the philosophic effort is also a direct extension of the Biblical aim to refute mythological concepts of God. As the legal heir of the Bible, Jewish philosophy performs a parallel function in the realm of beliefs and opinions to that of the Oral Law in the realm of the law. It's hard to determine whether Wolfson completely identifies with the concept of an "oral philosophic tradition" which he claims to find in Maimonides.[128] Yet in view of the above, one could speculate that he did consider Jewish philosophy to function in this manner. We recall how he termed philosophic allegory a "type of philosophically-oriented midrash." In his opinion, philosophic commentary grew naturally out of the inner Jewish tendency "to interpret something in terms of something else," and from the rabbis' orientation towards non-literal and non-anthropomorphic commentary. For example, when Wolfson discusses Spinoza's thought processes, he portrays medieval philosophy in terms that harken back to the assumptions of traditional Talmudic inquiry: "He lived in an age when the traditions of philosophy were still alive, and what we nowadays have to discover by the painstaking methods of research came to him naturally as the heritage of a living tradition."[129]

Accordingly, in Wolfson's view philosophy is not an exotic growth artificially implanted in the soil of Judaism in order to help it cope with external challenges. It also need not be considered, although at times it makes itself out to be, an autonomous tendency of the intellect that substantively opposes the believer's commitment to heteronomous revelation.[130] On the contrary, Jewish philosophy is a legitimate, internal Jewish phenomenon. This is evidently the origin of Wolfson's call to expand the canon of sacred Jewish books such that they might include the philosophical literature authored by Philo.[131]

NOTES

1. Joseph Schwab mentions this possibility in his article "The Practical: Arts of the Eclectic," *School Review* 81 (August 1973): 537.

2. This is Gershom Scholem's view of the way the rabbinic tradition approached the Written Law. See Scholem, "Tradition and Commentary as Categories in Judaism," in *The Messianic Idea in Judaism* (New York: Schocken Books, 1971), 282–303.

3. Harry Wolfson, "The Philonic God of Revelation," in *Religious Philosophy: A Group of Essays* (Cambridge, MA: Harvard University Press, 1961), 2–3.

4. Harry Wolfson, *The Philosophy of Spinoza*, vol. II (Cambridge, MA: Harvard University Press, 1934), 334.

5. Wolfson, *Philosophy of Spinoza*, vol. II, 332.

6. Wolfson, *Philosophy of Spinoza*, vol. II, 333–34.

7. Harry Wolfson, *Philo: Foundations of Religious Philosophy in Judaism, Christianity and Islam*, vol. II (Cambridge, MA: Harvard University Press, 1970), 446–49.

8. Wolfson, *Philosophy of Spinoza*, vol. II, 331–33.

9. Harry Wolfson, *Studies in the History and Philosophy of Religion* (Cambridge, MA: Harvard University Press, 1973–1977), viii.

10. Wolfson, *Studies*, 98–114.

11. Wolfson, *Studies*, 103.

12. Wolfson, *Studies*, 108–9.

13. Wolfson, *Studies*, 114. See also Wolfson, "Albinus & Plotinus on Divine Attributes," in *The Harvard Theological Review*, vol. 45, no. 2, 115.

14. See Leon Wieseltier, "Philosophy, Religion, and Harry Wolfson," *Commentary* 61, no. 4 (April 1976): 62.

15. This may be the source of Wolfson's reservations about the assertion that Plato, for example, was the first theologian. As he puts it in his article "The Knowability and Describability," *Studies*, 98: "It may be true that Plato is the first systematic theologian. But if so, his theology has the peculiar characteristic that it dwells more on what may be considered the subordinates of God than on God himself. Compared with the part played by the ideas in the Platonic system of philosophy, that of God seems rather insignificant."

16. See pp. 36–38 above, according to Wolfson, "The Philonic God of Revelation," *Religious Philosophy*, 2–5.

17. Wolfson, *Philo*, vol. II, 448–49.

18. Wolfson, *Philosophy of Spinoza*, vol. II, 334; Wolfson, *Philo*, vol. I, 346–48.

19. Wolfson, "Arianism and Apollinarianism," *Religious Philosophy*, 145–46.

20. See above, pp. 52–54.

21. Wolfson, "The Philonic God of Revelation," *Religious Philosophy*, 1.

22. This is according to the definition of religion that Wolfson proposed in his introduction to *Philo*, cited on p. 35 above. Wolfson's theory might conceivably enable Greek philosophy as well to be termed "religious philosophy," as it engages in the study of divinity and draws on religious literature. However, it is not properly a religious enterprise according to Wolfson's definition of the latter as activity that involves a connection to a heteronomous revelation. Wolfson might consequently be more inclined to regard Greek philosophy as "pre-Philonic" thought, rather than as religious philosophy in the full sense of the word.

23. Wolfson, *Philo*, vol. II, 456–58.

24. Wolfson, *Philo*, vol. II, 456–58.

25. Wolfson, *Philo*, vol. II, 459.

26. Wolfson, preface to *Religious Philosophy*.

27. Wolfson, *Philo*, vol. I, 164–89.

28. Wolfson, *Philo*, vol. I, 194–97.

29. Wolfson, *Philo*, vol. I, 194–95.

30. Harry Wolfson, *The Philosophy of the Church Fathers* (Cambridge, MA: Harvard University Press, 1970), 81.

31. Harry Wolfson, *The Philosophy of the Kalam* (Cambridge, MA: Harvard University Press, 1976), 74–75.

32. Harry Wolfson, *Repercussions of the Kalam in Jewish Philosophy* (Cambridge, MA: Harvard University Press, 1979), 232–33.

33. See pp. 36–37 above.

34. Wolfson, "Extradeical and Intradeical Interpretations of Platonic Ideas," *Religious Philosophy*, 49.

35. Wolfson, *Religious Philosophy*, 64.

36. Wolfson, *Religious Philosophy*, 53–58.

37. Wolfson, *Philo*, vol. II, 444–56.

38. Wolfson, "The Philonic God of Revelation," *Religious Philosophy*, 11–25.

39. Wolfson, *Religious Philosophy*, 84–103.

40. Wolfson, preface to *Religious Philosophy*.

41. Wolfson, *Philo*, vol. II, 455–56.

42. Wolfson, *Philosophy of Spinoza*, vol. II, 331–32.

43. Wolfson, *Philosophy of Spinoza*, vol. II, 332.

44. Wolfson, "Extradeical and Intradeical," *Religious Philosophy*, 41–42.

45. Wolfson, "Arianism and Apollinarianism," *Religious Philosophy*, 145–46.

46. Wolfson, *Philo*, vol. I, 425–28, 449–51.

47. Wolfson, *Philo*, vol. I, 427–33, 454–56.

48. Wolfson, *Philo*, vol. I, 435–37. See also Wolfson, "Philo Judaeus," *Studies*, 63–64.

49. Wolfson, *Philo*, vol. I, 457–61.

50. Wolfson, "The Pelagian Controversy," *Religious Philosophy*, 163–69.

51. Nathan Rotenstreich, *Iyyunim ba-Machshavah ha-Yehudit ba-Zman ha-Zeh* (Tel Aviv: Am Oved, 1978), 106.

52. Wolfson, *Philosophy of the Kalam*, 518–21.

53. Wolfson, *Philosophy of the Kalam*, 551.

54. Wolfson, *Repercussions of the Kalam*.

55. Wolfson, *Repercussions of the Kalam*, viii–ix.

56. Wolfson, *Philo*, vol. II, 456–58.

57. Wolfson, *Philosophy of Spinoza*, vol. I, 8–13. Wolfson's outlook on this subject is clearly voiced in the following citation, pp. 12–13: "But it is quite certain that Hebrew literature was the primary source of his knowledge of philosophy and the main stock upon which all the other philosophic knowledge which he later acquired was grafted. . . . His nascent philosophic doubt arose as a reaction against the philosophy which he read in Hebrew."

58. Wolfson, *Philosophy of Spinoza*, vol. II, 331.

59. Wolfson, *Philosophy of Spinoza*, vol. II, 331. Regarding "midrashic stubbornness" as stemming from fidelity to "root experiences," see Emil Fackenheim, *God's Presence in History* (New York: New York University Press, 1970), 21–35.

60. Wolfson, *Philosophy of Spinoza*, vol. II, 331–33.

61. Wolfson, *Philosophy of Spinoza*, vol. II, 334–35.

62. Wolfson, *Philosophy of Spinoza*, vol. II, 335–36.

63. Wolfson, *Philosophy of Spinoza*, vol. II, 228-32.
64. Wolfson, *Philosophy of Spinoza*, vol. II, 346.
65. Wolfson, "Spinoza and the Religion of the Past," *Religious Philosophy*, 269.
66. Wolfson, "Causality and Freedom in Descartes, Leibniz and Hume," *Religious Philosophy*, 196.
67. Wolfson, *Religious Philosophy*, 207.
68. Wolfson, *Philo*, vol. II, 454-58.
69. In Wolfson's book *Crescas' Critique of Aristotle* (Cambridge, MA: Harvard University Press, 1929), the title of the sixth chapter is pregnant with meaning: "Foreshadowing a New Conception of the Universe." See particularly pp. 36-37, 118.
70. Wolfson, "The Platonic, Aristotelian and Stoic Theories of Creation in Hallevi and Maimonides," *Studies*, 249.
71. Wolfson, "Philo Judaeus," *Studies*, 70.
72. Wolfson, *Crescas' Critique*, 20-25.
73. Wolfson, "Causality and Freedom," *Religious Philosophy*, 200-202.
74. Wolfson, "Sermonette," *Religious Philosophy*, 270-71.
75. Wolfson, "The Philonic God of Revelation," *Religious Philosophy*, 2-3, 25-26.
76. Wolfson, *Religious Philosophy*, 2-3.
77. Wolfson, *Religious Philosophy*, 2-3.
78. Wolfson, "Sermonette," *Religious Philosophy*, 270-71.
79. See Wieseltier, "Philosophy, Religion, and Harry Wolfson," 57.
80. Warren Zev Harvey, "Hebraism and Western Philosophy in H. A. Wolfson's Theory of History," *Immanuel* 14 (Fall 1982): 75-85.
81. Harry Wolfson, "Maimonides and Hallevi: A Study in Typical Jewish Attitudes towards Greek Philosophy in the Middle Ages," *Jewish Quarterly Review*, II (1911-1912): 297-337.
82. See particularly Wolfson, "The Philonic God of Revelation," *Religious Philosophy*, 24-26.
83. See note 79.
84. Wolfson, "Immortality and Resurrection," *Religious Philosophy*, 101-3.
85. Wolfson, *Philo*, vol. I, vi-vii.
86. Wolfson, *Philo*, vol. II, 458.
87. Wieseltier, "Philosophy, Religion, and Harry Wolfson," 58.
88. In this context see particularly Wolfson, *Philosophy of Spinoza*, vol. I, 20, 24.
89. Wieseltier, "Philosophy, Religion, and Harry Wolfson," 61-62.
90. Wieseltier, "Philosophy, Religion, and Harry Wolfson," 61-62.
91. Wolfson refers to this point in his book *Philo*, vol. II, 439-41. In Hegel, see: Georg Friedrich Hegel, *Lectures on the History of Philosophy*, vol. I, trans. E. S. Haldane and F. H. Simson (London: Kegan Paul, 1892), 101, 109-10.
92. Wolfson, preface to *Religious Philosophy*.
93. Wolfson, *Philo*, vol. II, 439.
94. See note 32 to the introduction.
95. Wieseltier, "Philosophy, Religion, and Harry Wolfson," 60, 62.
96. Wolfson, *Philo*, vol. I, 87-93.
97. Wolfson, *Philo*, vol. I, 10-11. See on this subject Erwin Ramsdell Goodenough, *By Light, Light: The Mystic Gospel of Hellenistic Judaism* (New Haven, CT, and London: Yale University Press, 1935), 4-5.

98. Wolfson, *Philo,* vol. I, 85–86.

99. Karl Rahner and Herbert Vorgrimler, eds., *Dictionary of Theology* (New York: Crossroad, 1981), 385.

100. Wolfson, *Philo,* vol. I, 143–45, 150–54, 155–60.

101. Wolfson, "Arianism and Apollinarianism," *Religious Philosophy,* 145.

102. Wolfson, *Church Fathers,* 89–90.

103. Wolfson, *Philosophy of the Kalam,* 722.

104. Wolfson, *Philosophy of the Kalam,* 726.

105. Wolfson, *Philo,* vol. I, 181–85.

106. On this subject see Wolfson's article "Extradeical and Intradeical Interpretations of Platonic Ideas" in *Religious Philosophy,* especially pp. 38–64.

107. Wolfson, *Philo,* vol. I, 223–27.

108. Wolfson, *Philo,* vol. I, 447–51, 452–56.

109. Wolfson, *Philo,* vol. I, 133–37.

110. Wolfson, *Philo,* vol. I, 134.

111. Wolfson, *Church Fathers,* 36.

112. Wolfson, *Church Fathers,* 24; Wolfson, *Philo,* vol. I, 137–39.

113. Wolfson, *Crescas' Critique,* 26.

114. Wolfson, "Extradeical and Intradeical," *Religious Philosophy,* 30–31.

115. Wolfson, *Crescas' Critique,* 28.

116. Wolfson, *Philosophy of Spinoza,* vol. I, 24.

117. Wolfson, *Philo,* vol. II, 443–46.

118. Scholem, "Revelation and Tradition as Categories in Judaism," *The Messianic Idea in Judaism,* 289–90.

119. Wolfson, *Philo,* vol. II, 459–60.

120. Rotenstreich, *Iyyunim,* 106.

121. Wieseltier, "Philosophy, Religion, and Harry Wolfson," 58.

122. Isadore Twersky, foreword to Wolfson, *Studies,* viii.

123. Harvey, "Hebraism," 81.

124. Rotenstreich, *Iyyunim,* 108–9.

125. See again Wolfson's remarks on the subject in his article "Arianism and Apollinarianism," *Religious Philosophy,* 136–37.

126. Compare, by way of example, Julius Guttmann's opinion in his book *The Philosophies of Judaism* (Philadelphia: Jewish Publication Society of America, 1964), 9.

127. Wolfson, "Extradeical and Intradeical," *Religious Philosophy,* 46–47.

128. Wolfson, *Philosophy of the Kalam,* 47.

129. Wolfson, *Philosophy of Spinoza,* vol. I, 20.

130. This manner of viewing philosophy underlies the scholarship of Leo Strauss. See, for example, his remarks in the article "The Law of Reason in the *Kuzari*," *Persecution and the Art of Writing* (Glencoe, IL: Free Press, 1952),104–9.

131. See Wolfson's article "How the Jews Will Reclaim Jesus," *The Menorah Journal* 49, no. 1–2 (Fall–Winter 1962): 25–31.

3

Guidelines for the Interpretation of Jewish Philosophical Texts

Wolfson's epistemological and historiosophical premises manifest themselves in practice through particular modes of interpretation, several of which have already been alluded to in the exposition of his substantive positions. At this point, we wish to expand upon some of his typical interpretive moves. It has already been noted that Wolfson regarded all of the texts he studied—classical Greek, medieval, even modern—to be propounding theological positions. He portrays religion, in its theological version, as a coherent system of beliefs. He also deems the major religious philosophers to have composed and read theological texts with the same precision with which the rabbinic sages wrote and read legal texts. Accordingly, he himself was careful to read his sources as coherent tracts. In his article on the various interpretations of Plato's theory of ideas, Wolfson explicitly opposes two methods of reading that in his view, fail to rigorously address the problem of contradictions in philosophic texts.[1] The first approach reflects the inclination of modern scholars to divide every phenomenon into historical stages, even with regard to individual thinkers. Wolfson opposes the attempt by assorted scholars to ascribe conflicting strands in Plato's teachings to different periods in the development of his thought. The approach he terms "periodization," that attributes different dialogues to different stages in Plato's life, all too readily absolves the scholar from proposing a philosophic solution to the contradictions in Plato's work. But it is not only readers at some historical distance from the text who fall victim to overly convenient exegetical methods. Philosophers from the ancient period as well, who identified with Plato's system and regarded themselves as his disciples, found other ways to avoid addressing the contradictions on a theoretical level. Rather than imputing the polarities in their master's thought to stages in his philosophic development, they would choose that pole most compatible with their own perspective and pronounce it the true embodiment of Plato's philosophy, while ignoring the weight of conflicting utterances. Wolfson coins this method of interpretation "selection and rejection." He ascribes both of these manners of reading texts—not only the ancient, but the modern as well—to "pagan philosophers." Wolfson contends that the first person who began reading philosophic texts correctly was Philo the Jew. According to Philo's approach, characterized sympathetically by Wolfson as "less convenient but more precise," the scholar must grapple with both poles of a contradiction and accord weight to both of them, in an effort to construct a complex, harmonious theory that contributes to their mutual reconciliation.

Wolfson implemented this approach in his own research; his treatment of the issue of free will in Philo's work is an excellent example of this.[2] To begin with, Wolfson brings a passage from Philo's writings that is held by a recognized scholar to indicate Philo's retreat from a belief in free will. The passage asserts that ultimately, human moral commissions and omissions are determined by a single, Divine cause. While the Law adjures us to "choose life," this seemingly voluntaristic view should be seen merely as a didactic technique designed to instill discipline. How, then, is the true ontological reality to be reconciled with the pedagogic dictum of scripture? The answer to this, remarks Philo, lies in the realm of mystery. In Drummond's evaluation, Philo ultimately consigns belief in free will to the status of a "useful illusion of the uneducated." Wolfson himself acknowledges that the spirit of the passage seems to contravene other statements in Philo's writings that mandate the principle of free will. Precisely for this reason, Wolfson undertakes a close reading of the passage while comparing it to various excerpts from Philo's works, with the aim of showing that it does not pose a contradiction. He affirms at the outset that a close scrutiny of the passage shows it to address only the choice of the good, not the choice of evil. Accordingly, only the choice of the good is imputed to God, while the choice of evil remains within the province of human beings. And even with regard to the choice of the good, the principle of free will is not compromised. The passage declares that "no person chooses the good by way of himself, but in accordance with the Lord's consideration, for He confers the most pleasant things upon the deserving." A careful reading of the last few words of the sentence, contends Wolfson, reveals that only "the deserving" merit that "consideration of the Lord" which enables them to choose the good. Moreover, implicit in the concept of "the deserving" is the assumption that those people who merit "the Lord's consideration" first performed, through their own free will, deeds that rendered them "deserving" of Divine assistance. In other words, individuals who exerted themselves in the exercise of their free will in an effort to overcome sin merit, through an act of grace, an augmentation of that very power of choice from God. Wolfson maintains that an examination of Philo's other works confirms that this is indeed his position. It is not our purpose here to determine whether Wolfson's interpretation is correct, but to direct attention to the manner in which, through a careful and comparative reading, he arrives at a formulation of a thinker's opinion on a given issue, on the assumption that the latter's words were chosen with care and that his position is indeed consistent.

Accordingly, Wolfson opposed the fragmentation of philosophic texts into historical layers, favoring instead a holistic and harmonistic mode of reading. Yet in keeping with his assumption regarding the endurance and continuing historical influence of metaphysical frameworks formulated in an early period of Western thought, he was in the habit of attending, in the course of reading his sources, to the traces of those metaphysical foundations he believed to be embedded in the work of every thinker he studied.

Wolfson was aware of the influence of horizontal-environmental factors upon the writings and outlooks of the philosophers he studied. Philo, for instance, surely absorbed his expertise in the mythology and philosophy of Greece and his acquaintance with the mystery religions prevailing in the Hellenistic world from his Alexandrian surroundings. Yet these factors only provided him with a linguistic and conceptual framework for expressing his fundamental worldview that was drawn from his ancestral tradition.[3]

The emphasis placed by Wolfson on past traditions over present influences with regard to his sources is particularly striking in his treatment of two figures far removed from one another in time, place and orientation: the theologian Cyril of Jerusalem and the German philosopher Leibniz. Cyril, Wolfson acknowledges, had no interest in philosophic speculation, unlike certain Church Fathers who preceded him such as Clement of Alexandria, Origen and Augustine. The only work he left to posterity was a compendium of popular sermons, delivered in order to disseminate orthodox Christian doctrines to ordinary believers in fourth century Jerusalem.[4] Wolfson, however, is interested neither in Cyril's didactic strategy nor in the forms of the early Christian catechism. What concerns him is the possibility of identifying, in a tightly circumscribed number of sentences from Cyril's texts, echoes of classic theological arguments on fundamental issues such as the definition of the nature of faith. By way of example, in Wolfson's reading the passage in which Cyril defines faith as "the soul's assent with regard to certain matters" reflects a conceptual tradition extending back to Aristotle and the Stoics. In Aristotle, faith is defined as a judgment about the correctness of a given piece of information, according to the criteria of internal consistency and correspondence to reality. Faith in this sense can apply both to primary intellections and to inferences on the basis of logical proof. For the Stoics, the term "assent" has the same meaning that the term "faith" does for Aristotle. The Christian philosopher Clement of Alexandria later unified the two terms, defining "faith" as the "assent of the soul." He further applied the definition not only to logical or empirical knowledge attained through the senses or reason, but also to the knowledge gleaned from revelation as reflected in the precepts of scripture. This knowledge can also be treated as "primary intellections" that are self-substantiating by virtue of being "the word of God," or as a body of knowledge that can be verified through intellectual proofs. In light of the above, Cyril's definition recalls the definition of religion in philosophic terms, despite the fact that Cyril himself was not consciously a philosopher.[5] Thus Wolfson places Cyril on a venerable philosophical continuum,[6] without suggesting, for instance, that Cyril made an original contribution to the crystallization of orthodox Christian theology.

The German philosopher Leibniz is also judged in keeping with this approach. Wolfson does not investigate the influence of Leibniz's philosophic contemporaries (such as Descartes, Hobbes and Gassendi) on his ideas, for he is more interested in examining Leibniz's positions on the perennial problems of causality, miracles and free will in light of the Philonic tradition. With regard to the problem of causality and miracles, Wolfson holds that Leibniz adhered to an intermediate position somewhere between "Philonism" and "Neo-Philonism." The Philonic tradition holds that the laws of nature were implanted in reality during the creation as "intermediate causes," possessed of independent efficacy. The miracles are a sort of "one-time laws," also implanted in the world at the time of creation. According to the "Neo-Philonic" view, which first appeared within the framework of the Kalam, the Deity is the unmediated cause of every new event in the world, and any "intermediate causes" are stripped of all independent efficacy. Here as well there is no differentiation between miracles and other events, not because they are all comprised within a single lawful framework, but because they are all expressions of the unmediated will of God. Leibniz's approach approximates the original Philonic approach. Leibniz does not believe that the laws of nature (at least since they were first instituted by God) operate out of some inner necessity, but that every event comes into being spontaneously. Yet the harmonious patterns produced by the spontaneous evocation of individual events were designed in advance by God.[7] His explanation of miracles resembles that provided by the Philonists: They reflect a kind of primordial disharmony. Or in Leibniz's words, as cited by Wolfson: "One may say that miracles are as much in the [general] order as the natural operations."[8]

In this formulation Wolfson hears resonances of Jewish traditions articulated in Maimonides' *Guide of the Perplexed* and R. Yehuda Ha-Levi's *Kuzari*. Miracles there are either presented as natural, as emanating in some way from nature, or as coming into being through the eternal will of God. The origins of these traditions, in Wolfson's view, lie in certain rabbinic midrashim (homiletic texts). Wolfson asserts that Leibniz must have adopted these positions in the course of studying the Latin translations of *Guide of the Perplexed* and the *Kuzari* available in his day. He fails, however, to bring any proof that the philosopher was actually acquainted with these books.[9] To recall, Wolfson is interested in Leibniz not for any contribution he might have made to the European philosophy of his day, but for his ostensible role as heir to the Philonic tradition, which he adhered to on the issues of causality and miracles and diverged from on the issue of free choice.

The two interpretive principles we have described, that of holistic reading and of an attentiveness to conceptual and systematic resonances from the past, are also reflected in Wolfson's approach to the language of a philosophic text and to its literary form. While Wolfson treats every word in a classic philosophic text as uniquely significant, he is not interested in merely uncovering its meaning within the cultural-linguistic frame of reference in which the author wrote. For Wolfson, there is no necessary philosophic correlation between the author's idiomatic usages and the substantive traditional content inhering in them. Language and literary form, in his belief, are only an outer shell that reflects the unavoidable influences of time and place, indicating the author's wish to clothe his message in a medium that will be understood. Philo, whom Wolfson regards as the founding father of most of the formal and substantive modes of scriptural philosophy, serves as a paradigm here as well: "In the case of Philo, as in the case of any other author, while the outer speech of style may be the man, it is the inner speech of thought, and the latent processes of reasoning behind it, that is the philosopher."[10]

The scholar's task, then, is to penetrate beyond transitory linguistic usages and modes of expression in order to expose the pure logical thought modes that transcend time and place. It is true that Philo's philosophic system takes the form of public sermons on narratives from the five books of Moses, because his profession at the time was that of a preacher.[11] Once abstracted from their homiletical context, however, his theological doctrines formed the basis of Western philosophy for 1700 years,[12] without undergoing significant substantive changes.

The distinction that Wolfson draws between linguistic usage and fundamental beliefs is particularly germane to the way thinkers versed in the Bible employ typical modes of expression from their pagan surroundings. Philo, for instance, adopts a nomenclature about God linguistically identical to that used by the Greeks for their deities. God for him is the God of "liberty and hospitality, of suppliants and of guests," though these titles were commonly applied to Zeus. Philo portrays God as "victory-giver," "benefactor" and "savior," all epithets used in reference to the Greek deities. And while in form these terms are borrowed from Greek popular religion, in substance they express certain characteristics of God already found in the Bible.[13] Philo also employs current mythological language to describe the religion of the Bible. The covenant into which the people of Israel were introduced at Sinai is described as their initiation into "the mysteries," with the Greek distinction between "lesser mysteries" and "greater mysteries" also adopted here.[14] Yet for Wolfson such distinctions are idiomatic rather than substantive: "He uses terms borrowed from the mysteries in the same way as he uses terms borrowed from popular religion and from mythology, all of them because they were part of common speech."[15]

The use Philo the Jew makes of the terminology of the Greek and Hellenistic philosophical tradition resembles his use of the mythological and mystery traditions. One example of this is the connection, in Wolfson's view, between Philo's concept of the logos and a parallel concept used by the Stoics. In Philo the logos, thought, appears in three stages: as a quality of Divinity itself, as the totality of all created spiritual powers and as the totality of the Divine powers existing in the world itself. The third stage—the totality of the Divine powers existing in the world—bears a striking similarity to the Stoic logos, and Philo therefore portrays it in terms borrowed from the vocabulary of this philosophic school. Yet similarity does not mean identity. The Stoic logos is material in essence and identified with Divinity itself. The Philonic logos, in contrast, is immaterial (it combines with matter according to the analogy of Aristotelian form), and God Himself exists beyond it. Specifically in order that the reader not identify this stage of the logos with the Stoic logos, Philo takes pains to explain that it is only a stage and an expansion of the spiritual logos that is separate from the world, beyond which there exists a transcendent God.[16]

This distinction between linguistic idioms and substantive worldviews, that obligates the scholar to ferret out the philosophic positions underlying diverse forms of expression, originates, so Wolfson claims, in the nature of the connection between the Biblical Jew and his polytheistic milieu. Already in the Bible itself we find the use of modes of expression and worship borrowed from its pagan surroundings. The Biblical God is not always designated by a special name, but is often referred to by a general title commonly applied in the Biblical environment: "Elohim." His worship was to be focused in the "House" and the "Temple," as was the practice among other peoples. His worship involved sacrifices brought by priests, along with prayer and obeisance. Yet in the matter of fundamental beliefs, the Biblical Jew knew that only the God of Israel was the true God, while the deities of the gentile nations were of no substance. The adoption of the terminology and religious ritual of the particular historical context, then, argues Wolfson, is not evidence of a substantive pagan stance.[17]

Even Spinoza, who rejected the revelatory foundations of the Bible, continued the Jewish tradition of adopting modes of expression from the surrounding milieu without allowing them to influence his substantive beliefs. It may be that the sharpest formulation of this interpretive doctrine distinguishing between literary form and theoretical content appears in Wolfson's introduction to his book on Spinoza:

> Many students of Spinoza regard his use of the geometrical method as a logical consequence of his mathematical way of looking at things. . . . The geometrical method of demonstration, whether synthetic or analytic, need not necessarily be written in the geometrical literary form, and, conversely, the use of the geometrical literary form is not determined by the subject matter of which it treats. . . . There is no logical connection between the substance of Spinoza's philosophy and the form in which it is written; his choice of the Euclidian geometrical form is to be explained on other grounds. Primarily, we may say, the reason for its choice was pedagogical, the clearness and distinctness with which the geometrical form was believed to delineate the main features of an argument and to bring them into high relief. It was used for the same reason that one uses outlines and diagrams.[18]

Wolfson's conviction regarding the indifference of philosophic systems to linguistic and literary forms derives from his epistemological and historiosophic premise regarding the immunity of fundamental metaphysical positions—whether Biblical or pagan—to the vagaries of time and place. The same principles described above serve as guidelines for the interpretive process by way of which Wolfson arrives at scholarly conclusions. His special thesis concerning the character of scholarly knowledge and the function of interpretation in the history of philosophy contrasts starkly with the theory that animated scholarship in the field of Jewish studies at its inception. In his article on the origins of the "science of Judaism," Glatzer differentiates between "lower historicism," which he also terms "functional" or "practical," and "higher historicism," called "ideological" or "theoretical." "Low historicism" did not aspire to descry immutable, absolute or universal truths of eternal validity through the study of history. For scholars of this persuasion there was only the historical process itself, the flow of time and events. The specifics of history received their meaning from within the transitory context in which they transpired, and were held to be wholly the product of influences prevailing at a given point in time.[19] Truths once considered eternal became relative for the historian, of "practical" or "functional" value, in keeping with the conditions of time and place. "Time-honored institutions, usages, and beliefs were presented in the relative positions they occupied in the context of history."[20]

Yet alongside the disintegrative thrust of "lower historicism," the "science of Judaism" was also characterized by the tendency of "higher historicism" toward unification. This tendency sought to ascertain the place of every detail uncovered by the scholar within the universal expanse of the creations of the human spirit. Historical knowledge signifies "the awareness of the relationships between the particular and the universal and the conception of the place the singular occupies in the total."[21] Scholarship is meant to inform us of "how the detail emerges from its isolation to become an integral part of the spiritual creation of humanity."[22] The starting premise is that all of human literature, and not only works hitherto consecrated as sacred writings, constitutes a single universal fabric. It is the scholar's task to assign assorted types of literary items to their rightful place in this overall fabric.

Within the context of Jewish studies, this "theoretical" orientation took on a more specifically ideological thrust: the attempt to identify a point of contact between the Jewish people and the world and to establish Judaism as an integral part of world history. It was particularly important to expose the connections between Judaism and ancient culture and to trace the former's role in the origins and growth of Christianity and in the scientific activity of the middle ages.[23]

A perusal of Wolfson's historiosophical doctrines indicates that he did not abandon "high historicism's" ideological propensity to emphasize the links between Judaism and European culture. He can be said to have continued Jewish studies' original impulse to bolster the status of Judaism in the history of religion in general, and he showed an interest in Judaism's contacts with the ancient world, Christianity and medieval philosophy. Yet by virtue of his "Hebraic national pride," stemming from the national and literary revival of the early twentieth century,[24] Wolfson appears to have turned the tables; instead of seeking the origin of Jewish philosophers' beliefs and positions in the religious streams and philosophical schools of their Greek, Muslim or Christian surroundings, he deemed the Jewish Philonic tradition to be the source of fundamental doctrines that came to figure among the mainstays of Western religious thought. The apologetic impulse to remove Judaism from the category of "oriental studies" and cast it as an established element of Western culture, worthy of scientific inquiry, still exists in Wolfson.[25] Yet his is not an attempt to explore the place of Judaism in the chronicles of Western religious thought, but a declaration of Judaism's founding and sustaining role in the establishment and articulation of Western religious philosophy in general.

Moreover, Wolfson can be said to have a "theoretical" interpretive orientation, in Glatzer's terms. He did not regard himself to be merely recording the details of the historical events of religious philosophy; yet neither did he take it upon himself to penetrate the structure of the unique religious-philosophic consciousness of any particular thinker. Every item of scholarship (namely, every theological issue as conceived of by a given thinker) receives its meaning in Wolfson when he identifies its place in the totality that transcends it. This totality that unites the items of his scholarship is not "horizontal," for it is not based on facts or events connected with the time or cultural milieu of the scholar in question. On the contrary, as noted above, immediate political, social and cultural developments were excluded in advance from the total context that serves Wolfson as a framework for theoretical meaning. Wolfson's field of meaning is "vertical"; it takes the form of a sort of continuum linking specific beliefs and opinions to a restricted number of pre-existing metaphysical options from the distant past. In order to provide examples of this theoretical-scholarly bent of Wolfson's, we will review several articles that at first blush appear to have a different external structure. The article "Creation *Ex Nihilo* in the Writings of the Church Fathers, Arabic and Jewish Philosophy and Thomas Aquinas"[26] is an instance of diachronic scholarship, that does not focus on a single thinker. The main issue of the article is the theological question of creation ex nihilo. Ostensibly, Wolfson's aim here is to suggest to the reader diverse meanings of the concept at issue, as they emerge from the works of major scriptural philosophers. In fact, he does something else: He identifies each of the opinions he is surveying with one of four archetypal approaches formulated in the ancient world. The *Book of the Maccabees* presents the original Biblical position, whereby the world was created "from non-existent things." Two other archetypal stances are that of Plato (that the world was created from primordial matter that always existed alongside God) and that of Aristotle (the world in its entirety is primordial and always existed alongside God). The fourth ancient metaphysical standpoint is that of Plotinus, who conceives of the world as the eternal emanation of the Divine essence.[27]

Every individual reference to the topic of creation since Plotinus is characterized by Wolfson as the reflection of one of the four archetypal positions. The Church Fathers reject Plotinus' approach in favor of that of the *Book of the Maccabees*. Yet certain Christian thinkers, such as Duns Scotus, and certain Arab philosophers, such as Alfarabi, adopt Plotinus' view, striving to prove that the traditional formula of ex nihilo actually signifies *Ex Essentia Dei* ([an emanation] from the Divine essence). By comparison, the Jewish philosophers R. Saadia Gaon, Maimonides and R. Hasdai Crescas insist that the concept not be understood in this fashion, but in the sense of "a new creation from the void." This latter is also the view of Thomas Aquinas.[28] Thus the chronicle of opinions on the subject of creation features a recurring debate between the scriptural orientation towards the creation of the world and the mythological/emanationist orientation. Wolfson, then, feels that he has succeeded in conferring interpretive meaning upon a given scholarly item when he manages to categorize it as a reflection of one of the early archetypal approaches to the issue.

The same interpretive criteria are applied in the next article, concerning only a single thinker: "Ibn Khaldun on the Attributes and on Predestination."[29] As background material to Ibn Khaldun's theory of attributes, Wolfson adduces the latter's proof of the existence and unity of God. As mentioned above, in his work on Philo Wolfson stated that the scriptural philosophers rejoiced in the Greeks' proofs for the existence of God and put them to great use.[30] Until Ibn Khaldun's time, Wolfson avers, philosophers employed two types of cosmological proofs drawn from classical philosophy. One, the "Platonic type," posits that the world came into being after not existing. Its second premise is that everything that comes into being necessarily comes into being through a creator, and therefore the world came into being by means of a creator. The second, "Aristotelian type," starts from the premise that the world is eternal. Upon contemplation of the world, the conclusion emerges that all generation and corruption stems from some cause. This state of affairs, in an eternal world, necessarily leads to an infinite causal regression. Since such a regression is impossible, there must be a first cause that preceded all other causes. Although it isn't possible, in Wolfson's evaluation, to classify Ibn Khaldun's proof of the existence of God as either "purely Platonic" or "purely Aristotelian," it is nevertheless a composite of these two archetypes. Like Aristotle, Ibn Khaldun begins by contemplating the world, and concludes that everything derives from a cause that precedes it. Yet he does not go on to say, as does Aristotle, that this would lead to an untenable infinite regression. Consequently he adopts the Platonic assumption that the world is created, and that the chain of causes ultimately goes back to a first cause, also characterized as the creator of the world.[31]

In his article on the positions of three modern philosophers—Descartes, Leibnitz and Hume—on the theological issues of miracles and free will, the same pattern repeats itself.[32] The article begins by reviewing the various metaphysical options we have inherited from the ancient world: (a) The approach of Plato, Aristotle and the Stoics that posits an absolute, predetermined causality, precluding any possibility of miracles and free will. (b) The Epicurean approach that attributes all worldly phenomena to chance. (c) The Philonic approach, that posits causality, but a causality that was implanted in reality by a willing Deity (and that in principle may be abrogated by this Deity, whether through miracles or through the gift of free will to human beings).[33] The positions of Descartes, Leibnitz and Hume are therefore interpreted according to how closely they approximate the Philonic or Epicurean viewpoints.

These examples attest to the fact that Wolfson's rules of interpretation are clearly antithetical to "low historicism." In his conception, the opinions of the great Western theologians are not confined in significance and worth to their relative contexts of time and place. Their value is also not contingent upon their being innovations that reflect the unceasing creativity of human thought, or in Wolfson's language: "In thought, as in nature, there is no creation out of absolute nothingness, and there also are no leaps whatsoever."[34] Their true significance, for Wolfson, lies in their status as permutations and reflections of archetypal human orientations to God, the world and human beings.

The last point to be made when analyzing Wolfson's rules of interpretation is that his "anti-historicist" perspective is what animates his special approach to causality in the history of thought. A scholarly interpretation that ascribes intellectual phenomena to conditions of time and place would most likely endorse a causality model drawn from the natural sciences, which study bodies that move within time and space. The influence of a given intellectual phenomenon on another intellectual phenomenon can be proven, according to this historicist orientation, by pointing to an almost physical contact within time and space between thinkers and texts. Shlomo Pines, for instance, contends that important shifts that transpired in Jewish medieval thought should be attributed primarily to the relocation of the Jewish population from one historical-cultural environment (the Muslim one) to another (the Christian one).[35] At times, he observes, the impression may be received "that the doctrines and philosophical theories that have appeared in Judaism can be largely explained by the influence of Jewish thinkers that preceded them. . . . This impression is surely mistaken."[36] A clear instantiation of the position that one should look for the philosophic sources of Jewish medieval thinkers in their external historical-cultural surroundings appears in Pines' introduction to the English translation of *Guide of the Perplexed*. In Pines' words there, Maimonides did not view himself as part of a "specific Jewish philosophic tradition,"[37] drawing his philosophic positions as he did mainly from Aristotle and the latter's non-Jewish commentators. Maimonides ascribed supreme value to these thinkers, pursuant to his education within the framework of "the philosophic tradition of Spain and the Maghrib."[38] When Pines comes to prove his claims, he looks primarily for unmediated textual evidence. He learns of Maimonides' philosophic sources from an explicit letter to Ibn Tibbon indicating the former's admiration for Aristotle and his commentators, and from explicit citations and referrals to these same sources within the text of the *Guide* itself.[39] In order to affirm that Maimonides embraced the influence of certain philosophers, it is necessary to prove, so Pines argues, that he saw these philosophers' texts firsthand and studied them in depth. If, for instance, there are no explicit references to scholastic theories in Crescas, due to a literary custom of his or a reluctance to cite Christian sources, it is necessary to at least point to an explicit passage that demonstrates his acquaintance with the curriculum of Christian universities.[40]

Pines admittedly does not rule out the possibility that a philosopher of the distant past, such as Plato, might have had an overall influence on a medieval philosopher like Maimonides. Along with Strauss, he acknowledges that Maimonides' use of verbal codes for political reasons does indeed stem from Plato, yet refrains from activating his interpretive tools in order to prove this, as he does to prove the influence of other thinkers. In his words, "No attempt can be made . . . to delimit and define the influence exercised by Plato on the *Guide* in this field, as it is too generalized, too diffuse, and often too indirect."[41]

Pines is willing to trace the Platonic influence only by referring to the writings of one of Maimonides' contemporaries, Alfarabi. Here, then, we have an example of a scholar of a "low historicist" orientation, that expresses itself in a propensity to associate beliefs and opinions with highly particularized cultural surroundings. This propensity is naturally accompanied by an interpretive disposition to seek out a physical-empirical causality, namely, an unmediated physical contact between the influencing agent and the idea or thinker being influenced.

Wolfson, on the other hand, constructs his major doctrines precisely according to the interpretive principle of a "general and indirect causality." In his evaluation, it is possible to trace a significant link between the treatment of a theological problem during the ancient period in Alexandria, for instance, and the treatment of the same problem in the Islamic states in the middle ages, without having to prove that the medieval philosopher in question was directly acquainted with Philo. If the structure of the problem as formulated by Philo parallels the structure of the problem in the writings of a much later "scriptural philosopher," this is sufficient grounds for the conclusion that the later philosopher has adopted a "Philonic" approach to the problem.[42] According to Philo, for instance, the moment we subscribe to a belief in the voluntaristic creation of the world, from a logical standpoint there is no reason why the Deity could not effect miracles in a world whose lawfulness he himself has voluntaristically founded. The same argument, that miracles must be possible by virtue of creation, is sounded by Tertullian, Augustine, Maimonides and Aquinas,[43] but not because every one of them read and internalized the specific formulation of the problem and solution as it appears in Philo's works. There is a substantive logical tension here, intrinsic to the structure of every scriptural philosophy that accepts the doctrines of creation and miracles from the Bible on the one hand, and the doctrine of the stability of the laws of nature from philosophy (and also from the Bible) on the other. The causal connection between the problem as articulated in Philo and the manner in which it was formulated by the Church Fathers and medieval thinkers is not, then, of a physical-empirical character, but of a logical and transhistorical character.

In many places in his works, Wolfson certainly sought to demonstrate direct textual connections between terms and ideas. Origen, for instance, speaks "in almost the language of Philo" when insisting that passages from scripture that are incompatible with reason should not be interpreted literally.[44] Yet the positions of the Church Fathers on the question of reason as a criterion for interpreting the Bible are Philonic, not because they are based on Philo's explicit statements, but because no Biblical philosopher who engages in allegorical-philosophical commentary can avoid eternal problems such as the limits of allegorical interpretation or the authority of reason to interpret scripture in non-literal fashion. Since beliefs and opinions are not necessarily tied, in Wolfson's view, to particular historical and geographical "culture zones," their derivatives cannot be traced exclusively through textual evidence of direct empirical influence. Given that the principal problems of Western theology stem from the special logical structure of a worldview that measures the authority of scripture against the conclusions of reason, one could make an argument for causal connections between ideas even according to the criterion of logical-structural parallels.

We have seen, then, that Wolfson's theoretical premises regarding the character of religious philosophy and its articulation over time found expression in scholarly and interpretive methods that correspond to these premises. The assumption that human thought, like the lawful character of nature, is coherent and continuous, and that religion in its theological form is a systematic structure of doctrines, did not permit Wolfson to suffer unresolved inner contradictions in the texts of a thinker of recognized stature. His concept of the theological text as a theoretically coherent tractate led to his conscious negation of the interpretive options of "periodization" or "selection and rejection." His central conviction that the foundations of human thought on metaphysical questions had already been laid in the ancient world, and that the same limited number of theoretical orientations on core theological issues merely elaborate themselves over time—and do not undergo a process of evolutionary development—spawned four interpretive principles: First, the predilection to seek out terms, expressions and concepts whose origin could be ascribed to the philosophic heritage of Greece or of Philo. Second, the view of language and literary form as transitory cultural clothing for central and perennial intellectual standpoints. These two interpretive principles guided Wolfson in the very course of the reading, as we have seen above. He was also guided by two further principles when it came to assigning overall theoretical meaning to the items being studied. First, the integration of scholarly items within a vertical field of meaning composed of traditions of pure ideas (rather than a horizontal field of meaning composed of streams or schools that prevailed in a given time or place). Second, inferring connections between thinkers and topics according to the model of trans-historical logical causality, rather than that of physical-empirical causality.

NOTES

1. Harry Wolfson, "Extradeical and Intradeical," in *Religious Philosophy: A Group of Essays* (Cambridge, MA: Harvard University Press, 1961), 28.

2. The discussion below is based on Harry Wolfson, *Philo: Foundations of Religious Philosophy in Judaism, Christianity, and Islam*, vol. I (Cambridge, MA: Harvard University Press, 1947), 442–56.

3. Wolfson, *Philo*, vol. I, 85–86.

4. Wolfson, "Philosophical Implications of the Theology of Cyril of Jerusalem," *Religious Philosophy*, 104.

5. Wolfson, *Religious Philosophy*, 106–9.

6. As expressed in Wolfson, *Religious Philosophy*, 104–6.

7. Wolfson, "Causality and Freedom," *Religious Philosophy*, 203–7.

8. Wolfson, *Religious Philosophy*, 206; Wolfson, *Philo*, vol. I, 351–53, note 24.

9. Wolfson, "Causality and Freedom," *Religious Philosophy*, 204–5.

10. Wolfson, *Philo*, vol. I, 102.

11. Wolfson, "The Philonic God of Revelation," *Religious Philosophy*, 1.

12. Wolfson, *Philo*, vol. II, 459.

13. Wolfson, *Philo*, vol. I, 38–39.

14. Wolfson, *Philo*, vol. I, 43.

15. Wolfson, *Philo*, vol. I, 46.

16. Wolfson, *Philo*, vol. I, 326–29.

17. Wolfson, *Philo*, vol. I, 9–12.

18. Harry Wolfson, *The Philosophy of Spinoza* (Cambridge, MA: Harvard University Press, 1934), vol. I, 44, 45, 55.

19. Nahum A. Glatzer, "The Beginnings of Modern Jewish Studies," in *Studies in Nineteenth Century Jewish Intellectual History*, ed. Alexander Altmann (Cambridge, MA: Harvard University Press, 1964), 34.

20. Glatzer, "The Beginnings," 108.

21. Glatzer, "The Beginnings," 37.

22. Glatzer, "The Beginnings," 37.

23. Glatzer, "The Beginnings," 38.

24. Warren Zev Harvey, "Hebraism and Western Philosophy in H. A. Wolfson's Theory of History," *Immanuel* 14 (Fall 1982): 81–83.

25. Glatzer, "The Beginnings," 34. Wieseltier terms Wolfson's position here an aspiration for "scholarly correction." See Leon Wieseltier, "Philosophy, Religion, and Harry Wolfson," *Commentary* 61, no. 4 (April 1976): 61–62.

26. Harry Wolfson, *Studies in the History and Philosophy of Religion*, vol. I (Cambridge, MA: Harvard University Press, 1973–1977), 207, 221.

27. Wolfson, *Studies*, 207.

28. Wolfson, *Studies*, 208–17.

29. Wolfson, *Religious Philosophy*, 177–95.

30. Wolfson, *Philo*, vol. II, 446–49.

31. Wolfson, "Ibn Khaldun," *Religious Philosophy*, 177–79.

32. Wolfson, *Religious Philosophy*, 196–216.

33. Wolfson, *Religious Philosophy*, 196–98.

34. Wolfson, *Philosophy of Spinoza*, vol. II, 331.

35. Shlomo Pines, *Bein Machshevet Israel le-Machshevet ha-Amim* (Jerusalem: Bialik Institute, 1977), 7.

36. Pines, "Ha-Scholastikah she-Aharei Tomas Aquinas ve-Mishnatam shel Hasdai Crescas ve-shel Kodmav," *Machshevet Israel*, 178.

37. Moses Maimonides, *The Guide of the Perplexed*, ed. and trans. S. Pines (Chicago: University of Chicago Press, 1963), cxxxiii.

38. Maimonides, *Guide*, lxi.

39. Maimonides, *Guide*, lix–lxi (and also the other parts of the introduction).

40. Pines, *Machshevet Israel*, 299, note 99.

41. Maimonides, *Guide*, lxxvi.

42. Wolfson's remarks in his preface to *Philo* (p. vi) are particularly significant in this context: "The structure of the problems as herein presented will provide a general framework for the same problems as they appear in the works of later philosophers."

43. Wolfson, *Philo*, vol. I, 353–55, and note 33.

44. Harry Wolfson, *The Philosophy of the Church Fathers* (Cambridge, MA: Harvard University Press, 1970), 78.

II

A TELEOLOGY OF ENDS: RELIGIOSITY, CONTEMPLATION AND DEVELOPMENT IN THE SCHOLARSHIP OF JULIUS GUTTMANN

INTELLECTUAL BACKGROUND

Isaac Julius Guttmann was born in 1880 in Hildesheim, Germany, then moved to Breslau with his family in 1892. His father, Ya'akov Guttmann, served as the rabbi of Hildesheim, and subsequently as the rabbi of Breslau until his death in 1919. Ya'akov Guttmann's academic specialty was medieval Jewish philosophy; he wrote monographs on R. Saadiah Gaon, Ibn Gvirol, Ibn Daud and Maimonides and took an interest in the influence of Jewish philosophers on Christian scholastic thinkers. The young Julius Guttmann attended the University of Breslau and the same rabbinic seminary his father had attended. In 1903 he received his doctorate from the University of Breslau for a thesis on Kant's concept of God. In 1906 he was awarded rabbinic ordination by the seminary, yet after a short stint as a practicing rabbi he turned to an academic career. From 1911 to 1919 Guttmann was a member of the philosophy department of the University of Breslau. In 1918, on the recommendation of Hermann Cohen, he was offered the philosophy chair at the Academy for the Science of Judaism in Berlin, where he began teaching in 1919. In 1922 Guttmann assumed the academic direction of the Institute for Research in the Science of Judaism, championing a strict adherence to pure scientific standards in face of the trend to promote the existential character of Jewish studies as a force that could shape people's lives. In 1934 Guttmann left Germany following Hitler's rise to power, accepting a professorship at the Hebrew University of Jerusalem, where he taught until his death in 1950.[1]

According to Fritz Bamberger, author of a detailed personal and intellectual biography of Guttmann, Guttmann's original theory of religion was shaped by Kant and Hermann Cohen. Prior to the publication of his article on the relation between religion and philosophy in the teachings of R. Yehudah ha-Levi in 1911, Guttmann viewed religion as a gesture of faith in a sublime idea that ensures the realization of the truth of ethics within nature. Religion was not yet portrayed—as he was later to portray it—as a singular truth-dimension in its own right.

In his article on R. Yehudah ha-Levi, and even more so in a 1922 article on the relation between religion and science in medieval and modern Jewish thought, Guttmann begins, in the wake of Schleiermacher, to perceive religion as a realm characterized by a unique type of certainty—a kind of inner personal certainty that draws on a distinct religious consciousness. Yet his original adherence to Kant and Cohen, who enunciated the principle of a priori categories that shape the structure and content of human consciousness, prevented him from embracing existentialist thought, which is predicated on a direct, unmediated connection between human beings, the world and God. In his polemic against existentialism that appears in the chapter on Franz Rosenzweig in *Philosophies of Judaism,* and also in his article "Existence and Idea" in the *Religion and Knowledge* collection, Guttmann maintains that we have no choice but to ascribe unconditional rational and ethical validity to religious experience. This validity is necessarily grounded in ideas of truth and goodness that anticipate and condition any perception of an existential relation between Divine reality and human reality.[2] These topics will be addressed more extensively in the coming chapters.

According to Bamberger, Werblowsky and Rotenstreich, Guttmann preferred the phenomenological orientation of Husserl and Otto to the existentialist perspective of Heidegger and Rosenzweig for purposes of characterizing the unique structure of the religious consciousness.[3] In Rotenstreich's words:

> Guttmann asks: How are we to determine the character of the phenomenon— religion—that we seek to address, if we do not resort to data or given states of consciousness that derive from the religious life itself? How are we to identify this data, and categorize it as belonging to the field of religion, without knowing what we had in mind when we undertook to investigate the diffuse data of the religious life? What emerges in Guttmann's conception is a combination of a particular orientation of consciousness and its factual givenness. In this regard, his treatment resembles Husserl's phenomenological mode of discourse. Guttmann was aided and impelled by the assorted works of Rudolph Otto, whom he frequently cites in support of his arguments.[4]

In Bamberger's view, this approach enabled Guttmann to maintain a philosophic distance from the religious subject that so occupied him, so that, unlike the existentialists, he would not be tempted to express himself from within his own personal religious experience. Guttmann, however, saw no contradiction between the phenomenological method and the a priori categories of Kant. On the contrary: He regarded this method as an expansion of the Kantian framework from its formal foundations to include concepts constructed on the basis of actual religious life, as experienced by religious people.[5]

According to Eliezer Schweid, Guttmann's scholarship represents an exemplary summary of the orientation to the study of Jewish philosophy espoused by the "science of Judaism" in the face of nineteenth-century European culture.[6] Non-Jewish philosophy is portrayed as a single comprehensive entity, termed "general philosophy." This reflects the particular manner in which Jewish scholars of that period regarded European culture: as a general humanistic-universal movement. "Judaism," on the other hand, was considered to possess its own unique character, stemming from its discrete literary sources.

Scholars of this bent highlighted the influence of general philosophy on Jewish thinkers in their work, in order to illustrate how open Jewish culture was to the best products of the surrounding humanistic culture. They even sought to identify a reciprocal influence of Jewish thinkers on "general philosophy," to show how much Jews had contributed to enriching this culture. Yet at the end of the nineteenth and beginning of the twentieth century, a number of scholars, including Guttmann, were more anxious to stress the unique Jewish response to the intellectual challenges posed by general philosophy, and the "elements that distinguished Jewish thought by virtue of its reliance on religious sources." Nevertheless, writes Schweid, "The theory that positioned the philosophic movement at the heart of the confrontation between the sources of Jewish religion and general culture remained intact." Further on in his article Schweid criticizes this theory, preferring to regard Jewish thinkers as neither "imitating," "responding to a challenge" nor "aspiring to contribute," but as drawing simultaneously both on their Judaism and on their links to various non-Jewish streams of thought. Moreover, thought produced in a non-Jewish environment should not be treated as a monolithic entity, but as arising under the influence of different philosophical schools such as neo-Kantianism or existentialism, predicated on distinct national-cultural foundations (German, French, etc.) that relate to distinct religious traditions (Jewish, Catholic, Protestant, etc.). Notwithstanding this critique, Schweid reminds us that the old model, which focuses on issues of demarcation, absorption of influence and mutual adaptation between Judaism as a religious essence and general philosophy (of which Guttmann is one of the most prominent advocates), still exercises a crucial influence in the world of contemporary Jewish thought.

From this point on, when analyzing Guttmann's works as representative of a distinct scholarly orientation to contemporary Jewish philosophy, we will refrain from commenting on the intellectual background of his scholarship.

We will undertake instead an internal analysis of the components of his systematic construction of the history of Jewish philosophy, focusing on the main body of his work as assembled in the book *Philosophies of Judaism*, the collection *Religion and Knowledge* and in lectures published under the title *On the Philosophy of Religion*.[7]

NOTES

1. Sources for this early intellectual biography of Guttmann: Fritz Bamberger, "Julius Guttmann: Philosopher of Judaism," *Leo Baeck Institute Yearbook* 5 (1960): 3–34; Raphael Jehuda Zwi Werblowsky's introduction to Julius Guttmann, *The Philosophies of Judaism* (New York: Jewish Publication Society of America, 1964), vii–x.

2. Bamberger, "Philosopher of Judaism," 15–18.

3. Bamberger, "Philosopher of Judaism," 18; Werblowsky, introduction to *The Philosophies of Judaism*, viii.

4. Nathan Rotenstreich, "Toldot ha-Toda'ah ha-Datit u-Mahutah," in *Iyyunim ba-Machshavah ha-Yehudit ba-Zman ha-Zeh* (Tel Aviv: Am Oved, 1978), 134.

5. Bamberger, "Philosopher of Judaism," 18, 21.

6. The following analysis of the place of Guttmann's theory in Jewish studies is taken from Eliezer Schweid, "Ha-Filosofiah ha-Yehudit ke-Echad ha-Zeramim ba-Filosofiah shel ha-Meah ha-Essrim," *Da'at* 23 (Summer 1989): 101–10.

7. For a complete bibliography of Guttmann's works, see Baruch Shohatman, "Kitvei Professor Yitzhak (Yulius) Guttmann Zal (1903–1950)—Reshimah Bibliografit," *Iyyun* 2, no. 1 (January 1951): 11–19.

4

Epistemological Perspectives— Religious and Philosophical Knowledge

Their Character and Modes of Interaction

RELIGIOUS KNOWLEDGE—ITS CHARACTER AND ATTRIBUTES

In the process of investigating the world of religious thought, Wolfson distanced himself from the question of the living relation between the believer and his God. He chose to focus instead on the doctrinal formulations of the historical monotheistic religions, and on the logical tensions emanating from the confrontation of the philosophic quest for systematic comprehensiveness with the fragmented Biblical world-picture. Yet this very dimension of the living relation, informed by powerful emotions on the part of both humans and God, is what interested Guttmann. The religious consciousness for him could not be summed up in conceptual-objective terms that serve to ascertain whether a particular state of affairs is true or false. The way a person relates to the object of his faith is what was primarily important to him. From Guttmann's perspective, fundamental types of religious orientation lie at the root of metaphysical philosophic formulations, and these types can be distinguished and articulated. Let us proceed to examine the manner in which Guttmann characterized the religious consciousness.

In the second chapter of his lectures *On the Philosophy of Religion*, Guttmann opens his discussion of the character of the religious phenomenon by distinguishing between the "objective" and "subjective" aspects of religion. Religions present various beliefs regarding the nature of the Deity, the link between Him and human beings, the purpose of life and so forth. All these are associated with the objective content of religious faith. Apart from these formulations, however, religion has to do with human attitudes toward this content. A belief in the existence of God can only be termed religion if the believer feels connected to his God. While for the philosopher God is an object of knowledge, for the religious person God is one pole in a "personal" relationship characterized by love, trust and awe. Guttmann terms this aspect of religion, that rests on a Divine-human relationship with an emotional cast, the "subjective side" of religion. Hence his definition of religion as "a certain behavior of the soul—possessing an objective content."[1]

Just as it is impossible to ignore the question of the objective status of the referent of the religious consciousness, as did Shleiermacher in summing up all of religion as a feeling of dependence, or Natorp in characterizing the essence of religion as "an infinity of feeling,"[2] so it is impossible to merely identify religion with propositional formulations concerning the nature of God and his connection to the world and humankind, formulations that lay claim to rational validity. Wolfson's reaction to James' psychological reductionism[3] was to stoutly defend traditional religion's understanding of itself as objective truth rooted in revelation. Guttmann, in comparison, ascribed great value to the psychological and phenomenological attempt to view the religious propensity of individuals and communities as a fact of human consciousness worthy of investigation. Nevertheless he refused to content himself with a descriptive, empirical approach to these phenomena and sought to evaluate them according to criteria of objective truth as well.[4]

In *On the Philosophy of Religion* Guttmann labors to establish the status of religion as a unique phenomenon in human spiritual life.[5] He is interested first and foremost in ascertaining what does not characterize religion, as a prelude to identifying the positive attributes of the religious consciousness. As noted above, Wolfson held that the greatest flaw in the definition of religion was the attempt to locate its source in the human consciousness, whether as the manifestation of a given psychological constitution or as the carrier of a recognized philosophic truth. For him, historical religion perceived itself as heteronomous in origin and doctrinal in nature.[6] Yet in Guttmann's evaluation, distortions in the characterization of religion stem from the tendency to offer reductionist definitions that convert this unique human domain of consciousness into another such domain. The reductionist approach can be divided into two categories: philosophic theories, that seek to characterize religion on a wholly objective basis, and empirical scientific theories, that seek to characterize it on an entirely subjective basis.

The main philosophic theories are also of two types: those that identify religion with metaphysics and those that identify it with ethics. Many medieval religious philosophers started from the premise that religion is identical to the theoretical content of metaphysics. Guttmann agrees that there is some truth to this assumption, as, formally speaking, both religion and metaphysics treat of beliefs and opinions concerning the supreme object, God, and His relation to the world and humankind. From a substantive viewpoint as well, religion contains elements of the metaphysical view that sees God as the cause of all being. On the other hand, there are echoes in metaphysics of a peculiarly religious insight, that God is the "ground" of reality. The singular aspect of religion, however, lies in its understanding that the Supreme Reality is not only being and power, but ideal value as well. This indicates not merely the dependence of a limited reality upon an unlimited reality, but the moral and spiritual contingency of the human subject upon a qualitatively more sublime reality. This substantive uniqueness is accompanied by a "methodological" uniqueness, which also removes religion from the purely objective realm: While metaphysics progresses towards its conclusions by means of rational proofs, religious certainty issues from an unmediated personal experience of the presence of a personal God, the source of all value. This experience, despite its essentially personal character and its independence of proof, brings in its wake the greatest possible certainty, the kind that begets a readiness for self-sacrifice.[7]

Notwithstanding the above, the moral component of the religious experience should not lead us to equate religion with ethics. Here as well, Guttmann contends, the two realms have much in common. In its Kantian configuration, ethics also regards God as the source of moral value and of a way of life predicated upon such value. Yet subjectively speaking there is an essential difference between the ethical relation to God and that of the religious believer. From the standpoint of ethics, God is a necessary postulate of moral reason. In order to realize itself, the moral ideal requires a moral order and a guarantee of future moral order. However, Guttmann asserts, the fact that human beings have a moral ideal, accompanied by the aspiration that it be realized in the world of nature, does not necessarily entail that an entity exists that can guarantee such realization. It is not inconceivable that such a human ideal could remain suspended without there necessarily being any God to ensure its realization. The believer, in contrast, does not consider the moral order to be self-evident, nor does he create God in order to satisfy the requirements of the moral consciousness. He believes—sometimes in the absence of any rational or empirical indications—that there is indeed a "Redeemer," yet his conviction as to His existence stems from a personal experience of presence, rather than from systematic necessity.[8]

Moreover, the religious framework generates distinct moral concepts that cannot be found in ethical systems. Apart from moral wrongdoing, religion presents us with the concept of sin. Sin "defiles the whole essence of man" and alienates him from his Creator.[9] The love of one's fellow espoused by religion is not exhausted by the moral obligation to enhance his or her living conditions; it aspires also to "concern for the inner personality," the "image of God."[10] Finally, there are subjective dimensions to the religious experience that entirely transcend the moral arena. In addition to the moral relation expressed in drawing close to God by performing his will, there is also the unique religious relation of the soul's communion with its Maker.[11]

Guttmann not only challenges those schools of thought that identify religion with the objective content of metaphysics or morality; he also attacks the reductionist attempts of positivist, sensualist and psychoanalytic theories to depict religion as the projection of subjective human desires. From the standpoint of Comte, for instance, religion is a pre-positivist attempt to interpret the world and endow it with order. In this primitive "theological" stage, human beings ostensibly project onto nature personalized attributes of birth, love and violence, for they are as yet unable to explain these phenomena according to a rational lawful pattern. In the second, "metaphysical" stage of the development of human thought, human beings construe the cosmos as an expression of a rational order, yet this order is held to originate in rational-spiritual agents not accessible to sensory perception. Only in the positivist-scientific stage do human beings learn to construct a lawful pattern from empirical experience alone. For Comte, then, religion is a primitive attempt to provide a cognitive-objective explanation for reality, an attempt that fails by virtue of excessive subjectivity and "anthropomorphism." In Guttmann's view, however, to represent religion as "primitive science" is to ignore its primary characteristics, namely, the understanding of God as the embodiment of ultimate value, as characterized by mystery and as the correlative pole of a personal relationship—all perceptive modes that transcend the subject matter of science.[12]

According to Feuerbach, defined by Guttmann as a "sensualist," religion is a specious solution to human fears of the chaotic forces controlling our lives. People want to believe these forces are working on their behalf; they therefore project onto them personal qualities of accessibility, concern and involvement. In so doing, they activate their own subjective feeling and imagination. Prayer, sacrifices and the belief in reward and punishment and in the world to come are all ways of transforming the reigning powers in the world from hostile or indifferent forces to forces sympathetic to human beings and concerned with their happiness and redemption. For Feuerbach, the ideal human behavior is love, which we also project onto the Deity as an ideal attribute. Guttmann focuses his critique of Feuerbach on the philosopher's sensualist reductionism. In Guttmann's opinion, a systematic sensualism cannot explain the development of abstract concepts or of ideal ethical values that require self-sacrifice without contributing to sensual pleasure. Such a creed is also unable to either refute or confirm the existence of a genuine transcendent reality beyond subjective human senses and feelings, or to explain how such beliefs could have arisen in the history of human thought.[13]

Guttmann sees Freud's psychoanalytic reductionism as suffering from the same deficiencies. According to Freud, remorse over the murder of the "primordial father" leads to the creation of a substitute entity in the figure of the "totem." The tribe members' ambivalent feelings towards the father are projected onto the totem prior to their murder of the father from sexual jealousy. The tribe's adulation of the father, which gathers force in light of their regret over his death, is translated into a prohibition against approaching the totem and into rituals expressing concern for his life and well-being. Vestiges of the hatred and jealousy toward the father find expression in the ritual of eating the flesh of the animal identified with the totem one day a year. The guilt feelings over the murder are transmitted from one generation to the next and form the basis of an ethical consciousness. Yet in Guttmann's opinion, concepts such as "remorse" and "guilt" are not in themselves adequate to account for the transition to pure ethical distinctions between good and evil. Simple regret (over wasting money, for instance) is not a sufficient explanation for moral contrition over injustice or religious remorse over sin. Moreover, the principle of projection does not in itself suffice to explain the attribution of Divine qualities to the father, unless a concept of the Deity had existed before the projection onto the totem occurred.[14]

Guttmann, then, vehemently opposes the approach Fackenheim dubs "subjective reductionism,"[15] one that derives from positivist, sensualist or psychoanalytical motives. He was more amenable to the sociological perspective of Max Weber.[16] He applauds Weber's scholarly moderation and his willingness to refrain from reductionism. Weber generally "refrained from directly deriving the religious realm from the social realm."[17] While cautious about explaining religion in social terms, Guttmann nonetheless acknowledges that "changes in the social and political realms did exert a profound influence on religious development."[18] He calls Weber's theory, which ascribes attributes of the Jewish concept of God, such as universalism, personalism and ethical will, to His status as a party to the military covenant that united the tribes, a "model theory in every sense. . . . There are many correct understandings here, even in his sociological derivation of the Jewish portrayal of God."[19] Guttmann also accepts the assumption that the encounter between Israelite religiosity and Egyptian and Babylonian-Syrian religiosity compelled the Israelite "intelligentsia" to develop their own religious images to the point that they could hold their own in the face of alien religious beliefs.[20] This assumption proved useful to Guttmann himself when he embarked on a study of the "rationalization" of Judaism against the backdrop of medieval Islamic philosophic culture.[21] Yet he feels Weber went too far in supposing "all of the substantive essence of the God of Israel to derive from the role of the covenantal God." In Guttmann's view, "The description of a covenant between the people and God already assumes a familiar image of God, in order to enable the very description itself [of the covenant]."[22] While the political role of the covenantal God does highlight several of God's essential attributes, the sociological approach oversteps its bounds when it treats this political role as the source of the entire content of the God-image. "The genesis of the content of the God-image is none other than recognized religious experiences, in which an awareness of God and an awareness of God's relation to believers is imbedded."[23] Accordingly, any attempt to trace the connection between the socio-political environment and the quality of Jewish religiosity must maintain the perspective of "the reciprocal relations between social life and Jewish religiosity.[24] As further elaborated below, this principle, together with the principle of the encounter between different types of religiosity, found expression in Guttmann's studies of the history of medieval and modern Jewish philosophy. This dynamic-dialectic perspective is a far cry from that of Wolfson, who shut off the internal doctrinal discourse of Western theology from political and social influences. For Guttmann, in contrast, "The sociological structure of religious life has crucial significance for the connection between socio-economic circumstances and the development of religious ideas." Nevertheless, "[The sociological structure] has more to do with the triumph of religious ideas than with their genesis, as the influence of social circumstances on this genesis is more oblique than direct. The determining factor . . . is the inner connections within the religious consciousness."[25] In Guttmann's view, then, the socio-political context is not the source of religious orientation, yet the degree of sway exercised by different orientations among different strata of the Jewish people was greatly affected by differences in social and political conditions.

In the process of grappling with "objective" and "subjective" reductionism, Guttmann advances his thesis regarding the autonomy of the religious consciousness as a given phenomenon in human spiritual life. Neither cognition per se, nor the interests inhering in the biological or economic nature of human beings should be treated as the primary source of the religious consciousness. What, then, is the true source of "religious ideas"? For Wolfson the answer is clear: The cognitive content of religious doctrines is imbedded in a revelatory document of transcendent origin. Guttmann's approach, however, is more complex. In his view, religion is not a system of doctrinal beliefs but a "certain behavior of the soul," or the state of being in a live connection with God. Religion is not just a message, but a state of being. There are existential-experiential elements to this state of "being connected," that originate with a living God who initiates contact with human beings. Nevertheless, the relationship with God cannot be sustained without an autonomous-reflective contribution from human beings. On the one hand, Guttmann insists that "religious values all belong to the realm of existential values," in the sense that "faith is not in an abstract ideal" but in an "actual God."[26] Humans are granted an awareness of the living God only by God Himself. Belief in God is not the creation of the human spirit, nor is it an idea that we identify in our consciousness. "It is granted one only through the revelation of God and by hearing His word."[27] On the other hand, however, being connected to God is contingent upon a person's awareness and recognition of the fact that he is involved in such a relation, rather than in some sort of subjective vision that fulfills subjective psychological needs. According to Guttmann, there are a minimum number of autonomous and ostensibly objective criteria without which "there is also no possibility of a heteronomous concept of religion and morality." These criteria are drawn from both the cognitive and ethical spheres, that posit independent criteria for truth and goodness, as well as from the special domain of consciousness called "inner religious clarity," that is capable of identifying holiness, purity and sublimity. In his formulation, "Revelation remains mute for man, if he is unable to distinguish between truth and falsehood, good and evil, purity and defilement." In addition, "Every religious relation to God is based on the fact that man recognizes Him as possessed of these attributes [holiness, sublimity, mercy and goodness], and recognizes himself both in his distance from God and in his proximity to Him. Without this recognition and the clarity it brings, God is not the God of man, His word is no word for man and He has no commanding power over him."[28]

In his lectures on the philosophy of religion, Guttmann explains what he means by this special domain of religious consciousness. In his opinion, the religious consciousness enjoys a special epistemological status alongside theoretical and moral cognition. While theoretical and moral cognition at times also find expression within the framework of religion, once integrated with the religious consciousness they undergo a substantive change.[29]

Religious certainty is portrayed in Guttmann's works as personal inner evidence regarding the existence of a good and holy God, who charges human beings with a moral task and conditions intimacy with Himself upon the fulfillment of this task.[30] This certainty is provided humans through a spontaneous, unmediated experience.[31] It cannot be acquired by logical-discursive means, and it cannot be summoned at will. It erupts within a person unbidden, although it can be embraced and confirmed by a separate act of will. This personal certainty is self-corroborating. It has no need for external confirmation, whether in the form of rational proofs drawn from metaphysical theories or proofs drawing on a given external authority, such as miracles. Paradoxically, it is precisely this subjective clarity, essentially nontransferable in nature, which is experienced by the religious person as the highest and most comprehensive form of certainty, upon which his life and the meaning of his existence depend.[32]

Guttmann's own understanding of religion prevents him from fully articulating the positive essence of this certainty. Yet he takes it upon himself to defend the plausibility of its existence against its detractors. This, even with the knowledge that in the post-Kantian period the possibility of proposing a valid metaphysics has been undermined.[33] According to Guttmann science is limited to the realm of empirical experience, which is bound to the law of causality.[34] It can testify neither in favor nor against questions of values, or the possibility of the existence of a reality beyond experience.[35] As for ethics, the Kantian attempt to derive the moral imperative from cognitive foundations, and to assert that whoever fails to follow the categorical imperative is not living rationally, is insufficient to ensure the individual's responsiveness to his own ethical understanding.[36] The non-absolute nature of metaphysical and scientific truths and the inability of an ethics based upon cognition to create the necessary bridge from awareness to action reinforce the legitimacy of an absolute religious certainty, one relying on personal clarity concerning a transcendent presence that is the source of all values. Additional support for this type of certainty can be adduced from the argument that religious clarity is an equally prevalent human phenomenon in both "primitive" and "progressive" religions. Despite the diverse contents of the various religions, the special manner in which religious truth is grasped appears to Guttmann to be the heritage of humankind as a whole.[37]

The content of the religious experience itself, and not only the manner in which it is grasped, reveals itself in Guttmann's writings to have identifiable characteristics. In both "primitive" and "higher" religions, the Deity is portrayed as shrouded in mystery and concealed by a veil of secrecy on the one hand and as possessed of a manifest aspect intelligible to humans on the other. This paradoxical experience finds expression in both the cognitive and the moral realms. In Maimonides, for instance, intellectual contemplation leads one to the conclusion that it is impossible to ascribe positive attributes to God, given that his essence is hidden from human beings. On this point, Guttmann contends, there is no argument between Maimonides and R. Yehudah ha-Levi, for ha-Levi also notes that "Were we to know his reality—that would be a deficiency in Him" (*Kuzari* V, 21). The mystery and secrecy that envelop God become evidence for both of these thinkers that He possesses the positive attributes of grandeur and power.[38] In Neoplatonism, the absolute unity of God is derived through rational reflection, yet by its very nature this unity is beyond human comprehension.[39]

The revealed and hidden aspects of the Deity find expression in the moral arena as well. On the one hand, there is a human expectation that there be a certain correlation between the ways of God and the ways of human morality, an expectation that underlies Abraham's demand—"Shall not the Judge of all the earth deal justly?" (Gen. 18:25)—and Job's demand to understand the meaning of his suffering. The answer accorded Job expresses the two-sidedness of the religious experience. On the one hand, just as humans are incapable of fathoming the Creator's wisdom in establishing the world order, they are also incapable of grasping the wisdom concealed in human suffering. This does not mean, however, that God is arbitrary in principle, as espoused by Calvinism, for instance. The book of Job posits that all of God's works reflect wisdom and meaning, even if humans cannot understand them.[40]

These paradoxical dimensions of the Deity, as perceived by the singular faculties of the religious consciousness (since neither intellectual nor ethical cognition can tolerate contradictions), afford the human believer a connection with the Absolute that is also paradoxical in nature. Following the example of Rudolph Otto, Guttmann describes the link between the believer and his God as an inseparable combination of the Tremendum, the aspect of God that evokes awe, fear and aversion, with the Fascinosum, the side that arouses a longing for closeness and intimacy.[41] In one of his lectures on the philosophy of religion, Guttmann strives to prove that these orientations are found not only in the monotheistic religions, but in assorted forms in primitive animist and magical sects as well.[42]

Guttmann affirms that by their very nature religions have common characteristics, both with regard to their modes of certainty and with regard to the content of their experience of communion with the Absolute. Nevertheless, Guttmann distinguishes between different types of religious orientations. A comparison between Guttmann's distinctions and Wolfson's typology concerning basic metaphysical positions sheds light on the uniqueness of each. Both thinkers posited trans-historical typological distinctions with regard to religious knowledge. Both sought to accentuate not only the particularist element in the Jewish religion, but the universal element as well. Wolfson's typological distinctions, however, originate from a process of intellectual cognition. The question he poses is: How do human beings acquire cognitive doctrinal knowledge about the nature of God and his relations with the world and humankind? According to the "pagan-atheistic" approach, humans are incapable of attaining objective knowledge on these subjects. Whoever maintains the validity of religious knowledge is ultimately a victim of his own subjective imagination and may be driven by impure political motives as well. In contrast, the "pagan-theistic" approach suggests the possibility of attaining objective knowledge about God through a process of intellectual reflection, by drawing logical inferences about the Prime Mover from the lawfulness manifested in the world. The "theistic-Biblical" approach, on the other hand, contends that only revealed knowledge, that which reaches us from an Absolute source, can portray the Deity in truly absolute terms.[43]

Guttmann's typological distinctions, on the other hand, are phenomenologically based, and they refer to differences in the structure of experience and quality of the connection between the believer and his God. The primary distinction Guttmann draws is between pantheist or mystical religion (in its various forms) and personalist religion (also far from uniform in character). This distinction is summed up in chapter 1 of *The Philosophies of Judaism* in the following words:

> This difference is not a matter of choosing either a theoretical or an imaginative representation of the idea of God, but is a matter of fundamental religious attitudes, as is convincingly demonstrated by the completely different relationship between God and man which mysticism and pantheism affirm. Neither pantheism nor mysticism knows a personal, moral communion between God and man; in its place, there is union with the Godhead. It does not matter, for our present purpose, whether this union is experienced by man as an accomplished fact, or as the ultimate goal of his religious aspirations; whether it is envisaged as an essential identity of the self with the Divine life of the universe, or as a merging of the soul in the mysterious Divine ground of Being. The living relationship between persons is replaced by the extinction of personal individuality, which is felt to be the main barrier separating us from God.[44]

Up to this point we have examined the religious relation obtaining between human beings and God. Yet the relations between God and the cosmos are also of consequence for the believer's religious experience. The creating God, to whose will the world is subject, is experienced as "sublime," "exalted" and "majestic." In contrast, the pantheist God, perceived as a "life current" that fills and "floods" the world, sparks the reaction of a "mystic shudder before the hidden abyss of the Divine being."[45] Here as well Guttmann hastens to stress the difference between theoretical and religious distinctions: "In theoretical terms the difference is usually formulated by saying that for mysticism, the Divine 'ground,' or source, does not create the world, but rather emits it from its own substance. In religious terms, this means that God is not conceived as the will which determines the world, but rather as a transcendent self-subsistent Being, completely withdrawn into itself."[46]

Guttmann continues to develop these distinctions in *On the Philosophy of Religion*. While regarding religion as a separate domain of consciousness with its own unique inner lawfulness, when differentiating between diverse types of religiosity, he resorts to criteria drawn from other domains of consciousness. He contends that it is possible to classify different types of religious experience according to the degree of emphasis placed upon cognitive, aesthetic or ethical values.[47] Within the framework of pantheism, for instance, there are religious orientations that accentuate the value of cognition and contemplation. From a religious standpoint, reasons Guttmann, there is a religious similarity (despite the metaphysical difference) between the theories of Aristotle and Spinoza, given that both considered ultimate happiness to consist in intellectual union with the Deity. Hegel's theory also shares this orientation, for even if the Divine Intellect is dynamic in

Hegel, his worldview is also informed by a religious aspiration for the unification of the human and Divine spirits. In all three systems God is the Supreme Intellect, and knowledge of the truth is considered an ultimate value.[48] By way of contrast, there are types of religious pantheism that stress aesthetic values instead. In Guttmann's view, Giordano Bruno and Goethe all stressed the aesthetic side of pantheism, through an attachment to the beauty of nature and the order of the cosmos.[49] By way of contrast, in Judaism the focus is on moral values, which helps explain the "personal" character of the Jewish concept of God. While aesthetic and intellectual cognition apply to objective entities, the category of ethics reveals its distinctiveness only in its relation to personal entities. Morality applies only to personalities, never to objects. Accordingly, in Judaism God is perceived as a personal being, namely, "A God who possesses not only intellect and wisdom, but also *will* and perhaps *feeling*, too."[50]

But when Guttmann proceeds to a phenomenological analysis that highlights the unique nature of religious knowledge as a whole, and in the distinctions he draws between different types of religious ties, Guttmann transcends the boundaries of scholarly description. A close reading of his works suggests that he ascribes supreme value to the personalist type of religion, deeming this type, of which Judaism is the cardinal example, to represent the religious relation in its purest form. While in pantheism and mysticism, for instance, a person strives to identify with the Deity, this is an impossible movement within the framework of personalist religion, in which the distance between the human and Divine personalities is rigorously maintained.[51] Moreover, a religiosity that stresses the importance of cognition is necessarily elitist, as the spiritual level of the believer is determined by his individual intellectual attainments or mystic raptures. In comparison, a religiosity that stresses the worth of the moral act is in principle open to everyone.[52] One gets the impression that Guttmann is wary of the inherent moral pitfalls of attributing excessive religious value to individual experience. It may be, he surmises, that the driving force behind pantheist or mystical religion is the individual's need to overcome a sense of radical loneliness and lose himself in a larger and more comprehensive reality. By comparison, personalist religion is based on a sense of self-validation, with the human individual counterpoised against nature, and without any blurring of his singular qualities.[53] In addition to preserving the balance between the worth of the individual and his finite nature, personalism is regarded as superior to pantheism in its emphasis on the value of community, society, the nation and humanity, as opposed to withdrawing into a private spiritual world. In place of the individual worship of the mystic or the contemplative philosopher, Judaism offers religious involvement and moral-social activism within a community framework. Rather than emphasizing the aspiration for individual redemption, Judaism encourages hope for the redemption of the collective and of all of humanity. In place of the private enlightenment to which the mystic or the philosopher is privy, Judaism comes down on the side of public revelation, with the prophet functioning exclusively as the emissary of the Divine will.[54] Finally, in addition to the values of self-validation and humility on the personal level and public involvement on the societal level, Guttmann finds reasons for preferring Judaism on theoretical grounds as well. The mystical Deity (of the Neoplatonic tradition) is understood as subsisting entirely beyond the world, and is seen as producing the world from within Himself. This type of religiosity is capable of exhibiting greater tolerance towards the existence of "mediating entities" or emanations existing somewhere between the wholly transcendent Divine being and the world. Consequently, Neoplatonism was more amenable to syncretism and subject to polytheistic-pagan influences. By way of contrast, in Guttmann's words, "personalist monotheism can make no such concession,"[55] as it is based on a perception of God as voluntary Creator. This identification by Guttmann of the personalist Jewish religion with the pure religious phenomenon emerges clearly from the first chapter of *The Philosophies of Judaism*, in which the terms "religion" and "Biblical monotheism" are used interchangeably.[56] There is no remaining doubt, then, that if for Guttmann the special feature of the religious relation in general is the personal bond, then the personalist religiosity of Judaism, rather than the contemplative pantheistic religiosity that regards God as an object of cognition, represents the pure religious phenomenon.[57]

THE VALUE AND LIMITATIONS OF PHILOSOPHICAL KNOWLEDGE IN RELATION TO RELIGION

We have seen that Guttmann took pains to portray religion as a distinct and unique field of consciousness. Yet most of his scholarship was devoted to the representation and evaluation of theoretical systems that portray religion as a phenomenon of an intellectual-cognitive character. If Guttmann, in the wake of Husserl[58] and Otto, sought to make a phenomenological analysis of religious experience on the basis of data derived from the religious life, what point did he see in undertaking such a comprehensive review of the development of philosophical systems? What did Guttmann consider to be the essence of philosophy, what value did it have in his eyes, and how did he view its limitations?

Guttmann, like Wolfson, ascribes great significance to the recognized intellectual values that are part and parcel of the philosophic discipline. He commends the Talmudic sages, for instance, for the "capacity for conceptual thinking" manifested in their aphorisms.[59] He regards Ibn Gabirol as a thinker of stature by virtue of his "speculative power and originality of theoretical interests."[60] "The atmosphere of the late German enlightenment" is also commended because, in his words, it fostered an "aspiration for rational clarity in the concept of religion."[61] He criticizes Moritz Lazarus for focusing on the psychological aspects of the application of Jewish ethics to life and because he did not consistently adhere to a theoretical ethical system, qualities that "impair the methodological unity of [his] book."[62]

Still, for Guttmann philosophy was not merely a mode of logical argumentation whose aim is conceptualization, clarity, coherence and systematic thought. As distinct from Wolfson, he does not view philosophy as simply the handmaid of religion, which serves religion by disseminating its message in a clear and consistent conceptual language. However, reason does have a substantive role to play in justifying religious knowledge and establishing it on an objective plane.

In concluding his article on "The Relation Between Religion and Philosophy According to Yehudah Ha-Levi,"[63] Guttmann warns of the dangers inherent in grounding "the truths of faith on the clarity of religious sentiment alone." For "in this fashion the question of questions of our lives is turned over to the affirmation, which is not subject to criticism, of an entirely personal sentiment. . . . The power and truth of human reason will be thereby jeopardized, if it is indeed obliged to grant the voice of feeling the final say in questions of life perspective." Admittedly, it is impossible to derive the "directness of feeling" of the presence of God from the domain of reason. Yet reason does have the power to provide a justification of the "right to religious faith," or, in other words, the validity of religious faith before the judgment of reason.[64]

Reason rescues religion from the realm of subjectivity from another standpoint as well. We have seen that Guttmann recognizes Shleiermacher's contribution in characterizing religion as the personal connection between the believer and the object of his belief. Yet in Guttmann's opinion, Shleiermacher did not sufficiently address the distinctions between the various objects with which human beings maintain such a connection. He did not distinguish, for example, between the experience of dependency on God and other experiences of contingency. Consequently, argues Guttmann, an "objective" philosophical discourse is required, one whose task it is to distinguish between different objects of religious sentiment. Only objective reason can prevent the transformation of the study of religion into a branch of psychology. Aside from inquiring into "the forms of experience, in which [religious] objects feature"[65] in human consciousness, there is also a need for a categorical analysis of the nature of these objects themselves. Only the comparative categories of reason are capable of distinguishing, for instance, between a God who brings forth the world out of Himself and a creator God.

Reason not only establishes the rational rights of faith and serves to distinguish between the different types of objects that provide a focus for religious feeling; it is also a true partner in the constitution of religious experience itself. In his article "Existence and Idea," Guttmann argues against the self-contained validity of the absolute immediacy of experience. Even fundamental existential experiences, such as the unmediated presence of human beings in the world and their presence "with things," according to Heidegger, are mediated, Guttmann reasons, by the categorical significance and objective validity accorded them by consciousness.[66] The existential religious experience of the presence of God and the apprehension of His word, as described by the religious existentialists, is also not unmediated. It is not merely a matter of a call bursting forth from an "infinite existence" that is then received by a "finite existence."[67] As noted above,[68] the possibility of revelation is contingent, in Guttmann's view, upon the spiritual-cognitive autonomy of human beings. They must willingly accept the word of God as obligatory, an obligation stemming from attributes of value, such as sanctity, sublimity, goodness and mercy, ascribed to God and his teachings by humans themselves. It is true that God is not the creation of human reason, and that faith is a genuine gift of God that emanates from revelation and the hearing of the actual command of God. Yet even if religious clarity and an awareness of the value-attributes of God are an authentic Divine gift, the gift itself is given with the aim of its being an autonomous capacity, and in order to serve humans as a prism through which they themselves can distinguish between the actual word of God and "false prophecy."[69]

Philosophy, then, is not just a discipline that endows the heteronomous religious message with a clear, communicative, reasoned and systematic character, as Wolfson claimed. In contrast with Wolfson, who denied the validity of philosophic systems that portrayed the human intellect as autonomous and sovereign in metaphysical matters, Guttmann contends that it is precisely the autonomous status of human consciousness that reflects its exalted source. Hence the positive contribution of moral and religious philosophy in shaping the substance of revelation and transforming it from a "mute" entity to one possessing validity and value for humankind. Within the framework of Guttmann's theory, the famous maxim "The Torah speaks in the language of human beings" can be interpreted to mean that the heteronomous voice of God is itself apprehended by humans only through the agency of the autonomous, objective and ideal categories of truth and goodness. Only through them can human beings come to recognize and understand the Divine voice and submit themselves to its authority. It is only through the active collaboration of these categories, which afford the presence of God and his words both cognitive significance and ethical validity, that the process of revelation itself achieves completion.

Moreover, philosophy is not only a systematic method of distinguishing truth from falsehood and good from evil; it is first and foremost a central expression of the religious nature of human beings. Further on[70] we will encounter Strauss' view that the source of philosophy lies in a thoroughly secular ethos, one that aspires to theoretical independence and negates any reliance on heteronomous revelations that transcend human perception. Guttmann, on the other hand, believes that many of the manifestations of the philosophic quest are fueled by a religious impulse. *On the Philosophy of Religion* portrays the theories of Aristotle, the Neoplatonists, Spinoza and Hegel as expressing a type of intellectualistic religiosity. These systems conceive of God as truth, as the bearer of truth or as sublime intellect. The source of knowledge lies in God, and the person who acquires adequate knowledge is thereby demonstrating his connection with God. This affords him the most sublime form of happiness: the intellectual love of God. According to Hegel, both religion and philosophy aspire to fuse the human spirit with the Divine spirit, and the difference between them is one of form, not content.[71] In the Neoplatonic and Aristotelian philosophy of the middle ages, the theory of the immortality of the acquired intellect reflected a mystic longing for the negation of individuality and the participation of the intellectual soul in the bliss of the Active Intellect.[72] It is not surprising, therefore, that Guttmann (again, in complete contradiction to Strauss) depicts the kind of philosophic education that could be obtained in certain medieval Arab states as having exerted a broad cultural influence. Philosophy itself is presented not only as the queen of the sciences, but as "the highest form of religious knowledge."[73] It would seem, then, that from Guttmann's vantage point no absolute distinction should be drawn between "religious knowledge" and "philosophic knowledge." The philosophic quest for a coherent-theoretical understanding of the cosmos is an expression of the universal human drive for contact with the foundation and source of the world.

While for Wolfson, then, philosophy is a tool of religion, for Guttmann philosophy is a fundamental and constitutive force in the establishment of religious knowledge. Guttmann does not, however, ignore the dangers and limitations of philosophy. First, he argues that metaphysics lacks the ability to either corroborate or refute religious truth. According to the Kantian orientation, on which Guttmann relies, there can be no such thing as an objective metaphysics. Human beings can only know that of which they have experience, while religion calls for a connection to a realm beyond experience.[74] Second, philosophy developed from within the pagan mythological cosmogonies, thereby continuing the efforts of mythology to furnish a speculative explanation for the creation of the world. This mythological quest provided a basis for later, rational metaphysical speculations.[75] Yet religion, at least in its pure Jewish version, is not inclined to provide a speculative explanation for the world.[76] The task of the Biblical creation narrative, in Guttmann's view, is to testify to the existence of an abiding relationship of will between God and the world.[77] This personalist relation cannot be derived from the scholarly philosophical argument concerning the eternity or creation of the world. Philosophy is disposed only towards intellectual adoration and conceptual communion with the Deity. For philosophic religiosity

God is an object of apprehension, and the difference between Him and other objects is only theoretical. (Namely, He is the most abstract and comprehensive object.) In contrast, as emphasized above, the God of religion is a living personality, and the religious person is called upon not to comprehend Him but to live in communion with Him.[78] It follows, therefore, that not only does philosophy lack the power to either substantiate or refute religion; it is also powerless to derive the religious relation by way of logical reasoning.

It should also be noted that according to Guttmann the limitations of philosophy do not result only from the fact that human powers of cognition are limited. According to Wolfson, as we have seen, the unreliability of the senses prevents humans from attaining to ultimate truth. Consequently, they require revelation, which constitutes a higher level of apprehension. Guttmann, on the other hand, sees religion to be a different order of knowledge. Thus even the most sophisticated form of cognition, endowed with infinite powers of abstraction, would be by definition incapable of generating the religious relation from within itself.

Just as philosophic knowledge is inherently limited, so too "philosophic religiosity," based on an intellectualistic aspiration to God, though not devoid of religious pathos, cannot express the essentially personal religious relation. At times this philosophic religiosity can even detract from personalist religiosity, or actually undermine it. Even in those philosophic systems in which the Deity is "of a religious type"—that is, those in which the element of "human dependence on God" and the direct relation to Divinity" exists—this religious character is weakened by the "intellectualism of the philosophic approach."[79] Interestingly enough, precisely those two Jewish philosophers that Guttmann most admires, Maimonides and Hermann Cohen, exemplify in his view the weakening of personalism by intellectualism. This, despite the fact that both thinkers devoted considerable scholarly effort to articulating certain aspects of Biblical personalism. On the one hand it is true that Maimonides paved the way, in the philosophic conceptual world, for the image of a personal, voluntaristic God who creates the world through an act of will. Yet to the same degree he also assisted in transferring the focus of religious sentiment from moral activism to contemplation.[80] Hermann Cohen "no longer holds back from speaking of God as a person," yet "the methodological bases of his thought restrain him from the possibility of interpreting God as a Reality."[81]

THE INTERACTION BETWEEN RELIGIOUS
AND PHILOSOPHIC KNOWLEDGE

We have seen that Guttmann accords reason a major role in the establishment of religious knowledge, rather than regarding it as a mere tool for the articulation of such knowledge. The question therefore arises as to how Guttmann conceives of the likely patterns of interaction between religion and reason. From Wolfson's vantage point we saw that religion, by way of Philo's Biblical doctrines, has exerted a substantial influence on philosophy, and that Wolfson understands the cardinal principles of Western philosophy to be thoroughly Biblical in character. While admittedly Greek philosophy also exerted an influence on Biblical religion, this was only on the level of form, that is, in the transition from narrative, law and exhortation to systematic exposition. The fundamental content of Biblical religion was left unchanged by its encounter with philosophy, whose typical discursive forms of expression served to transmit its message, without influencing its content.[82] For Guttmann, by contrast, philosophy is not only an avenue of communication equally suited to a Biblical or pagan content. Philosophical metaphysics has always been permeated with a religious ethos, held by Guttmann in high regard. He considers the mystical-pantheist orientation, that runs like a thread through Aristotle, the medieval Neoplatonists, Spinoza and Hegel, to be a major spiritual force possessed of a discrete religious ethos. This ethos effects far-reaching changes in the content of religious belief and in the religious orientation of Biblical personalism.[83] Philosophy is not just an expression of metaphysical "hubris," or an imperfect human version of the revealed truth; it constitutes one of the expressions of the universal human striving to connect with the source of being. As such, it is not foreign to Biblical personalism. There is a genuine encounter here; it is not, however, an encounter between a rational language first formulated in a pagan context and a system of Biblical beliefs and opinions in need of an expressive tool, but between two lofty spiritual phenomena seeking diverse paths of contact with the Absolute. In what follows, we will attempt to examine the patterns of influence left by the philosophic ethos on Biblical personalism, bringing examples primarily from Jewish medieval philosophy as depicted in Guttmann's writings.

Of course, Guttmann also believed that in the middle ages, philosophy often served as a tool for the defense of Biblical beliefs, without causing any substantive change in the beliefs themselves. In Guttmann's view, medieval Jewish philosophy grew out of the need to fortify Judaism against external intellectual streams of thought and internal Karaite heresies. The father of Jewish medieval philosophy, R. Saadiah Gaon, evidently wrote his *Book of Beliefs and Opinions* as a polemic against religions with anti-monotheist tendencies, such as Persian dualism and Christian trinitarianism, as well as against philosophic theories espousing cosmological teachings at variance with the Biblical worldview (such as the eternity of the universe).[84] Saadiah Gaon makes selective and eclectic use of arguments from other theoretical systems to defend Biblical principles. His proofs for God's role as Creator are taken from Aristotle, for instance, while the way he uses them to establish

the principle of the creation of the world in time is drawn from John Philo-
ponus, by way of the Arab philosophers of the time.[85] Up to this point
Guttmann adheres closely to a "Wolfsonian" model, one that portrays the
Biblical philosopher as a theologian who bases himself from the outset on
Biblical principles, and adopts the positions of various theoretical schools
according to purely Biblical considerations.

In addition, however, Jewish thinkers sometimes had occasion to inter-
nalize a certain thought pattern from the dominant philosophic creed of
their day, since that thought pattern served as a conventional starting point
for the interpretation of a great range of phenomena at that time. The Jewish philosopher, however, would often employ this pattern to characterize
a uniquely Jewish phenomenon. R. Yehudah ha-Levi, for example, appropriated the conventional Neoplatonic perspective that every natural phenomenon requires "preparation" in the realm of matter in order for its special form to be emanated by the Active Intellect.[86] Ha-Levi, however,
transferred this thought pattern to the unique realm of the relations between the "Divine entity" and the Jewish people, arguing that keeping the
commandments and living in the Land of Israel are a form of preparation
for the emanation of the "Divine entity" upon the people. Here as well, it
is not proper to say that Yehudah ha-Levi was influenced fundamentally by
the religious ethos or root-assumptions of Neoplatonism (and indeed,
Guttmann depicts ha-Levi as a thinker unaffiliated with any school).[87] In
this matter as well, however, there is no deviation here from the Wolfsonian model of selective absorption for the purpose of giving voice to
uniquely Jewish positions.

Yet, for Guttmann, the influence of philosophy on Jewish spiritual life, as regards both religious values and the realm of belief, runs deeper than mere external manifestations. Both learned people and the laity absorbed both concepts and entire religious outlooks from Arab religious and philosophical
culture, and these in turn influenced the inner quality of Jewish religiosity.

On the level of popular thought, for example, we find that Neoplatonic
concepts of inner-contemplative religiosity were introduced by way of R.
Bahya ibn Pakuda's book *Duties of the Heart*. The affinity that many simple
Jews showed for the book testifies to the degree of openness in the Jewish
public at the time to such an approach.[88] On the more sophisticated philosophic level, philosophic thought had a decisive influence on the religious
viewpoint of a personality such as Maimonides. In Guttmann's words,
"[Aristotelian] metaphysics is not only the articulation of a theoretical
worldview; it is also imbued with a special religiosity. . . . Through knowledge man is able to cleave to God, and through knowledge he becomes part
of the upper world." This "[philosophic] path to God" is, in Guttmann's
conviction, what animates the "pathos of religious intellectualism" that informs *The Guide of the Perplexed*.[89] Maimonides transmitted this propensity

for "religious intellectualism" to a broad circle of educated people, and its impact is discernible up to the onset of the modern period.[90] From Wolfson's standpoint, to recall, philosophy is a type of formal language, which lacks the power to influence the content of the Biblical worldview in any substantive way. Strauss' position, which we will explore at length, is that philosophy is a thoroughly secular orientation, predicated on the independence of human cognition from external sources of knowledge. Such an approach precludes the possibility that philosophy as such could genuinely influence the religious ethos of the public, or of its teachers and leaders. In Guttmann's thought, by comparison, philosophic theories are an expression of natural human religious longings, and they therefore do not conflict with personalist religiosity. It is even conceivable that one type of religiosity could profoundly influence another, despite the substantial differences between them, which Guttmann does not seek to blur.[91]

When we examine the type of influence the intellectual ethos of metaphysics exerted on the personalist ethos of Biblical religiosity, we find that there were different levels of such influence. Certain Jewish philosophers were not aware of the significant differences between the two outlooks, and they portrayed Judaism and philosophy as identical worldviews that are in complete agreement. Most of the Jewish philosophers associated with the Neoplatonic school show this tendency, in Guttmann's opinion.[92] Among the Aristotelians, this mode of thought is represented by Abraham ibn Daud. His inclination was to "to simply approximate or equate philosophic theories and religious ideas, circumventing rather than solving the problem of their difference," rather than "resolving them in substantive fashion."[93] The same inclination is discernible in the modern period in the case of R. Nachman Krochmal, who found no contradiction between Judaism and the idealist philosophies of Schelling and Hegel.[94]

In the case of other, more mature, thinkers, Guttmann perceives a deep awareness of the difference between the religious values of the two worldviews, an awareness that spawns an unequivocal affirmation of the religious ethos and a negation of the philosophic ethos. The thrust of R. Yehudah ha-Levi's *Kuzari*, for instance, is not to equate Judaism with rational truth, but to elevate the religion above the realm of reason, on the claim that it reflects the ultimate truth.[95] The modern representative of this approach, in Guttmann's view, is Franz Rosenzweig, who rejects the monism of traditional philosophy. His approach disputes reason's capacity to derive all of reality from human cognition. It is based not on human intellectual striving, but on the spontaneous, voluntary overture of God, a loving address that redeems the concrete human being from loneliness and fear of death.[96]

The most common paradigm that can be found in Guttmann's writings for the relation between metaphysics and personalism is that in which Jewish philosophy is drawn primarily to the pantheist schools, both with regard to its thought structure and with regard to most theoretical questions, while preserving the cardinal elements of personalism against the systematic impetus of metaphysics. In *On the Philosophy of Religion*, Guttmann presents a moderate version of this paradigm as the orientation characterizing all of medieval philosophy.[97] To begin with, Jewish medieval philosophy is explicitly portrayed as an encounter between pantheism, which understands the world as having emanated from God, and personalism, which perceives God as the Creator of the world. The contradiction between these two theories was resolved by the argument of Jewish philosophers that the principle of emanation applies only to created beings, while the world as a whole was established by a voluntary act of God. In this manner the original Jewish approach was preserved despite the absorption of the idea of emanation.[98] Up to this point no true synthesis between metaphysics and personalism had been proposed, aside from an artificial-defensive kind of demarcation whereby the pantheist principle of emanation was circumscribed prior to the point at which it would jeopardize the cardinal principle of creation. In *The Philosophies of Judaism* Guttmann offers a similar interpretation concerning Maimonides' theory of prophecy. Generally speaking, Maimonides adopts the Aristotelian-naturalist theory of prophecy, in which the phenomenon of prophecy is based on a natural-causal link between human consciousness and the Active Intellect. Maimonides finds two ways of defending fundamental Jewish doctrines on this issue, however. First, he preserves the idea that prophecy is a kind of mission originating in the will of God, by emphasizing that God can deny prophecy at will even to one who has reached a level of consciousness that would ordinarily mandate it. Second, he maintains the uniqueness and one-time nature of the revelation at Sinai, by rendering the Mosaic prophecy entirely supernatural, in contradistinction to that of the other prophets.[99]

On certain issues, however, metaphysical intellection and Biblical personalism attain a genuine synthesis. Maimonides' theory of negative attributes, which scrupulously denies the Deity any quality that could be construed as a multiplicity in His Being, follows the path of Neoplatonic theology.[100] On the basis of rational-philosophic thought, Maimonides attains a positive religious relation to the Divine Being; that which we can know about God is the fact that we do not know Him. Paradoxically, this intellectual lack of knowledge is transformed into positive religious knowledge. The secrecy and mystery that envelop the Deity are comprehensible to a person in depth only to the extent that he has experienced, through proper intellectual effort, how the aspiration to encompass God through cognition is beyond realization.[101] In this fashion an epistemological certainty grounded in rational proofs becomes an integral part of an inner, personal religious clarity. In Guttmann's words, "The levels of philosophic knowledge are the levels of religious certainty. Religious internalization is possible only by way of philosophic profundity."[102]

In sum, Guttmann portrays the influence of intellectual religiosity on personalist religiosity, by way of their encounter in medieval and modern Jewish philosophy, as having penetrated beyond the surface level. This was not merely a tendentious-external application of philosophic thought, whether for purposes of formulating the religious position in the conceptual language of the time or in order to defend Judaism from hostile theories via polemics. While both of these tendencies existed, metaphysical religiosity nevertheless had considerable inner impact on the quality of personalist religiosity. So much so, in fact, that personalism was compelled, at times almost arbitrarily, to defend its cardinal doctrines against the imperialism of metaphysics. With regard to thinkers of Maimonides' stature, however, metaphysical certainty became a central component in the religious consciousness, although not in all respects.

This understanding of the influence of the metaphysical ethos on personalism in Guttmann differs from that of Peter Slomovics, who writes in his work on Guttmann and Kaufman that "Philosophy was and remained subordinate to religion. . . . Judaism preserved its core essence throughout the medieval period, despite the challenge presented by Greek philosophers. The changes introduced into it by philosophy . . . were all, at best, superficial, and never affected the substance of religion."[103] According to Slomovics, Guttmann believed that Jewish philosophy "made use of epistemology for its own religious purposes,"[104] and that philosophy was merely the "handmaid" of religion.[105] The role of Jewish philosophy, as depicted in Guttmann's scholarship, is primarily a didactic one; its aim is "to inscribe the truth of Judaism in the hearts and minds of people; by employing the scientific methods of the time to render religious truth comprehensible to all."[106] In my opinion, Guttmann is portrayed here as taking the path of Wolfson, namely, that philosophy serves as the handmaid of religion in order to express the doctrines of the Biblical faith in contemporary terms. A rigorous comparison between Wolfson and Guttmann, however, points up the extent to which Guttmann's scholarship fails to fit this model. Admittedly, Biblical personalism continued to feature in the annals of Jewish philosophy, despite isolated instances of Jewish thinkers who became wholly swept up in the metaphysical ethos. And at the outset of new periods in Jewish philosophy, the initial trend was often theological-eclectic, as borne out by the examples of R. Saadiah Gaon and R. Samson Raphael Hirsch. Still, most of the major thinkers portrayed by Guttmann in his book *The Philosophies of Judaism*, such as ibn Daud, Maimonides, R. Levi ben Gershon, R. Nachman Krochmal and Hermann Cohen, were influenced not only by the thought categories of their times, but by the intellectual and pantheistic ethos as well, that runs like a thread through Western philosophy and most of its schools. The picture is not one of a Judaism confident in its own powers, borrowing at will from the varying philosophic languages in order to spread its message to its believers and to the world as a whole. The picture is of a spiritual-religious orientation that expresses the human yearning for connection with the Absolute in a most authentic manner, encountering another orientation, the "pantheistic-mystical" approach, an orientation of equal spiritual power. This encounter leaves its mark on the "inner substance" of Judaism: It adds an intellectualistic dimension to it, one that simultaneously enriches and weakens the emotional quality of personalism.[107]

Nevertheless, the impact of philosophy on religion was not exclusively one-directional in character. The personalist ethos also exerted a noticeable effect on the metaphysical scholastic thought-structure of the Jewish philosophers. Here as well Guttmann accepts elements of the Wolfsonian approach, while supplementing them. For instance, Guttmann agrees that in certain cases the energy animating the philosophic zeal of medieval thinkers stemmed from the need to uphold the Biblical approach in the religious debates of the time. Islam's claim, for instance, that nature and history are in perpetual flux, and that therefore the Divine revelation changes as well, begat sharp formulations among Jewish thinkers concerning the immutability of the Divine will.[108] Guttmann regards this development as natural, given that the Jews sought to uphold the authority of the revelation at Sinai as a one-time historical event, rather than to defend a cognitive creed. As a rule, argues Guttmann, Judaism did not create "negative norms," doctrines that restrict philosophic freedom of thought, the way Christianity did (and as Wolfson believed Judaism did as well). Nevertheless, the incontrovertible belief that the Torah came from God—not as a doctrine, but as an event—was contingent, and not only in a formal doctrinal sense, upon additional assumptions such as the belief in providence and in reward and punishment. Jewish theology accordingly took it upon itself to safeguard these beliefs.[109] Yet with regard to Maimonides, in contradistinction to R. Saadiah Gaon and the Kalam, we find that Guttmann does not portray him as seeking to uphold Jewish beliefs for apologetic reasons.[110] In Guttmann's view, Maimonides "takes his stand upon strict science—that is, the metaphysics of Aristotle."[111] Nevertheless, with regard to issues that Maimonides regards as rationally irresolvable, he consciously appropriates the traditional standpoint. For instance, concerning the question of the eternity of the world or its creation in time, "The religious motive, which demands the existence of a supernatural God," says Guttmann of Maimonides, "may for once decide the issue."[112] What we have here, then, is not an indication of Judaism's overall influence on the essence of the philosophic worldview, or of personalist religion's overall influence on pantheist religiosity. Here we see a clear preference for the personalist orientation, which pictures God as a voluntary Creator, but only in matters that cannot be resolved by the intellect.

In Guttmann's view, the function of religion is not merely to delineate the boundaries of reason, either a priori or after exhaustive philosophic deliberations. On the one hand, philosophic formulations represent a conceptual expression of basic psycho-religious states of soul. We have seen above that the philosophic doctrine of negative attributes deepens and enriches the link to God as a secret and mysterious being. Yet from the standpoint of the religious influence on philosophy, it should be added that the doctrine of negative attributes gives voice to the religious notion of God as "different" and "other" (Otto's *Das Andere*).[113]

Guttmann believes that the conflicts which sometimes arise between philosophic theories, and within philosophic theories, are not the product of logical tensions between Biblical and pagan doctrines, but the conceptual expression of inner conflicts in the religious soul. For example, the tension in medieval philosophy between the claim that the individual's soul merges with the Active Intellect, and the claim that the soul retains some measure of individuality even after death, is a conceptual expression of the inherent religious tension between the mystical aspiration to merge with God, and the longing to experience as an individual, the ecstasy of intimacy with God.[114] Consider an example from the modern period of Jewish philosophy. In the thought of R. Krochmal, tension arises between his traditional religious sentiment regarding the direct connection between "the Absolute Spirit" and the Jewish people, and his view of the condition of the gentiles, for whom the transition between History and Spirit is always mediated by the agency of finite spiritual entities.[115]

However, it is not only the contradictions between religious feelings drawn from two different types of religion that generate conceptual tension in philosophic theories influenced by both personalism and pantheism. In *On the Philosophy of Religion*, Guttmann demonstrates how the personalist orientation creates immanent rational problems, independent of its encounter with pantheism. Personalism itself, independent of any influence it may have received from the emanationist type of pantheism, has no interest in retreating from the view of God as infinite and absolute. Yet we are acquainted with the notion of personality only in its limited human form. How, then, can one ascribe personality to the infinite God? Guttmann writes, "Human ethics are based on relations between people who resemble one another [by virtue of their status as finite beings], and consequently it must be asked what relationship exists between the infinite being and the finite, between the Creator and His creatures."[116] Moreover, human moral decisions are always made within a finite context, so how could God, who knows everything in advance and is under the influence of no external agent, make a voluntary decision? Without attempting to provide an exhaustive solution to these issues, Guttmann speaks of the relation between the human and divine personalities as one of analogy, not identity. It seems, then, that the very experience of a personal link to the Deity (and not the doctrinal dispute as to whether the world is created or emanated) produces a series of philosophic problems, even before it comes into contact with a conflicting religious ethos.

With regard to the character of the mutual influence exercised by the Biblical and philosophic worldviews, then, Guttmann's approach differs substantially from that of Wolfson. Concerning philosophy's influence on Biblical religion, Wolfson sees it as primarily formal-expressive in nature. Philosophy articulates the Biblical perspective in the discursive language of the time, enabling it to express itself in an accessible conceptual mode, to situate itself and to defend its uniqueness within the frame of reference of the theoretical issues that occupied philosophic thought in a given period. For Guttmann, in contrast, philosophy brings with it its own religious ethos, an ethos of intellectual striving for the Absolute. Most of the Jewish philosophers in the medieval and modern periods belonged first and foremost to the various non-Jewish metaphysical schools, and the intellectual ethos of these schools, together with their fundamental beliefs on cardinal metaphysical issues, profoundly influenced the quality of their religiosity and the content of their worldviews. Personalism found itself on the defensive, as it was forced to defend basic doctrines such as creation, or prophecy as a Divine mission, within the framework of thought patterns of an intellectualistic cast. Nevertheless, personalism emerged from its encounter with pantheism enriched and more firmly grounded. Take, for example, Maimonides' success in merging philosophic certainty in the matter of negative attributes with religious clarity regarding the otherness of God. However, and here the difference with Wolfson comes out more prominently, personalism did not emerge from this encounter without paying a price. Interestingly enough, this can be shown by examples drawn from Jewish thinkers held by Guttmann in the highest esteem. In Maimonides, for instance, the focal point of religious values was transferred from moral and democratic activism to the elitist value of theoretical intellectualism.[117] In Cohen, despite his adherence to Divine transcendence as a concept that cannot be identified with nature (given that it guarantees the future unity between nature and morality), the idea of God is stripped of its personal character: "The love of God is understood as love for a moral ideal, and the concept of the love of God for man is only an archetype upon which the pure moral deed can model itself."[118]

In all that concerns the influence of religion on philosophy, there is also a marked difference between Wolfson and Guttmann. Wolfson contends that the basic Biblical worldview was transmitted by way of Philo to the theology of the three monotheistic religions, and thereby to all of Western philosophy as a whole. Guttmann, by way of comparison, does not consider it his scholarly mission to trace the influence of Jewish religiosity or of the Jewish worldview on non-Jewish schools of thought and religions. Still, one of his important claims is that Jewish philosophy, while open to non-Jewish schools of philosophic study, was particularly dedicated to examining the philosophic problems posed by its own religious orientation.[119] In Wolfson's evaluation, the Jewish religion was ideationally broadened by its appropriation of philosophic language and consequently broke through the boundaries of the Jewish lifestyle and the Jewish community to shape the thought of all of Europe.

Guttmann also maintains that the Jewish approach to philosophy was more specifically focused than that of Islamic or German thought, which made contributions to most of the traditional branches of philosophy. The distinctive character of Jewish thought consisted in substantiating its religious worldview and in investigating the contradictions between scientific and religious truth.[120] For lack of a geographical and national cultural domain, the Jewish people applied themselves philosophically to the questions sparked by the encounter between their religious-spiritual existence and reason. Religion, accordingly, exerted a central influence on Jewish philosophy, by determining not the substance of its doctrines, as Wolfson held, but the types of problems that it would address. Problems of the sort mentioned above—the tension between the immortality of the acquired intellect and individual immortality or between the Divine will and God's omniscient wisdom—found their sharpest articulation in Jewish religious philosophy.

INTERIM SUMMARY: GUTTMANN'S VIEW OF THE ESSENCE OF JEWISH PHILOSOPHY

Wolfson's concept of the essence of "scriptural philosophy" stems from his view of religion as doctrine and of philosophy as logical argumentation. Religious faith in and of itself, as characterized by Fackenheim, is not a subject of scholarly inquiry. Philosophy in itself, understood by Fackenheim as the attempt to interpret reality objectively and without prior commitments, is also denied scholarly status; for both religion and philosophy "collapse" into theology. Wolfson considers Jewish philosophy to be an articulation and justification, through philosophic concepts and by way of philosophic argumentation, of given scriptural doctrines that are authoritative a priori.[121]

Guttmann's concept of Jewish philosophy is entirely different. Fundamentally speaking, religion for Guttmann is a discrete phenomenon of the human consciousness, a phenomenon that represents "a behavior of the soul" (and not merely the kind of contemplation undertaken by the cognitive aspect of the soul), taking the form of a personal relationship with the religious object. In Judaism, the ethical component (of being commanded by a being possessed of supreme value, giving it the authority to command) is the central element characterizing this relationship. The religious person requires reason in order to distinguish between various possible religious objects; reason also performs the task of conceptualizing religious beliefs clearly and of lending objective validity to the substance of the religious experience. Yet from Guttmann's standpoint Wolfson erred in devoting himself excessively to the "objective" side of religion, that aspect that concerns itself with the nature of the religious object, while entirely neglecting the "subjective" side, namely, the phenomenological analysis of the structure of religious experience. Peter Slomovics here argues correctly that according to Guttmann religion encompasses all of the human personality, including the emotional realm.[122] This comprehensive religious consciousness cannot be confined within the framework of theology, which formulates creedal doctrines, as Wolfson sought to do.

Guttmann, then, does not reduce the independence and power of philosophy as does Wolfson. Philosophy for him is not merely a neutral, logical, expressive language that can be grafted onto either Biblical or pagan premises. According to Wolfson, as we have seen, the language of logic, born and nurtured in pagan surroundings, was transmitted to the world of Biblical thought through Philo and has since served as a tool for the articulation of new premises. From Guttmann's viewpoint, however, the quest for a theoretical explanation of the world is organically connected to the mythological-cosmogonic origins of philosophy. The latter inherited from mythology the aspiration for a theoretical explanation of the origin of existence and for identification with the cosmos by means of contemplation.[123] The science of logic came into being in the context of these mystical-pantheistic motivations, with the result that it is no mere neutral language but a spiritual ladder through which humans can achieve the heights of abstraction that connect them with the upper worlds.[124]

The question arises whether by organically connecting philosophy to pantheist religious strivings Guttmann is not reducing philosophy to religion, and thereby nullifying its value as an independent enterprise. Guttmann's response to this question seems ambivalent. On the one hand, in articles such as "Existence and Idea,"[125] Guttmann insists on the autonomy of cognition and morality and on their non-contingent role in affording existential religious experiences the force of truth and ethical value. Yet on the other hand, he portrays the major philosophic theories as expressions of "intellectual religiosity," which is represented as a certain type of religious yearning.[126]

In the same way that Guttmann seeks to defend religion as a separate field that cannot be reduced to the fields of metaphysics or morality, he also characterizes metaphysics and morality as autonomous and irreducible fields.[127] One can safely say, however, that from Guttmann's standpoint the independence of the philosophic enterprise vis-à-vis Biblical personalism does not derive, as Strauss maintained, from a rejection of the religious motivation in principle,[128] but from a certain type of intellectualistic religious striving that fuels it.

In any event, Guttmann, unlike Wolfson, maintains a clear distinction between the terms "theology," "religious philosophy" and "philosophy of religion." In his lectures on the philosophy of religion, Guttmann defines the term "religious philosophy" as a philosophy in which "religious feeling is present."[129] He asserts that in Greek philosophy, medieval Neoplatonism and certain philosophical theories of the modern period, such a religious sentiment was indeed active.[130] Religious philosophy, then, is a philosophic system fueled by that "behavior of the soul" that is the foundation of the religious gesture. In contrast, "philosophy of religion" is "a new departure in philosophy," whose aim it is to understand the uniqueness of religion "as a *given phenomenon* of the spirit," with the assistance of analytical tools. This endeavor is distinct from that of "theology," whose aim it is to "vindicate one faith" among others.[131] In *On the Philosophy of Religion*, Guttmann refrains from employing the term "theology" to describe the latter orientation, but he mentions the thought of R. Saadiah Gaon as an example of it. And in *The Philosophies of Judaism*, when addressing the motives for the recourse to philosophy in Saadiah's time, he says: "The great work of Saadiah Gaon . . . teaches us something of the degree of subtlety reached in the discussions between Jewish and Islamic theologians concerning the possibility of a plurality of mutually exclusive revelations."[132] From this we learn that Guttmann saw theology as a project of justification generated by interreligious polemic.

This is not to say that there is no overlap between the various orientations in Guttmann's writings. In his preface to *The Philosophies of Judaism* he is willing to bestow the title "modern Jewish philosophy" only on those modern thinkers who take upon themselves "those systems of thought specifically concerned with the interpretation and justification of the Jewish religion."[133] This is a statement of a distinctly theological cast, even by his own definition. From a certain point of view, even Guttmann's lectures on the philosophy of religion are a theological defense of Judaism as the religion whose personalist religious orientation constitutes the most quintessentially religious connection, and which carries obvious moral and intellectual advantages.[134] In essence, however, Guttmann regards Jewish philosophy as an encounter between two types of religious philosophy. Thus already at the beginning of his opus *The Philosophies of Judaism* he focuses on the personalist aspects of Biblical religiosity, while stressing that mysticism and pantheism "did not cross the path of Jewish religion until after the close of the Biblical period,"[135] namely, in the middle ages. This is also the reason that he portrays medieval philosophy as the arena for the encounter between the emanationist pantheism and Judaism, which is based on the concept of a voluntary creation. In essence, says Guttmann, Jewish philosophy is a religious philosophy struggling to maintain its personalist ethos, while the intellectualistic pantheistic ethos made a major impression upon it, of which it is not always aware and from which it cannot always free itself. That which Judaism gained from the encounter with contemplative intellectualism—self-clarification, self-preservation and in its most sublime forms, a near-synthesis between the two orientations—it lost in the attenuation of its original religious sentiment: the moral relation to the living God.

NOTES

1. Julius Guttmann, *On the Philosophy of Religion* (From a lecture series given at the Hebrew University during the 1946/7 school year, transcribed by Shulamit Tov, preface by Nathan Rotenstreich.) (Jerusalem: Magnes Press, 1976), 23.

2. Guttmann, *Philosophy of Religion*, 39–40. In his critique of Shleiermacher and Natorp, Guttmann writes, "A person might well declare: My attitude to religion is not objective but is purely subjective. However, the conclusion that religion is wholly subjective does not arise from here."

3. See Guttmann, *Philosophy of Religion*, 33–36.

4. Guttmann undertakes this task in chapter 6 of *On the Philosophy of Religion,* called "The Truth of Religion" (p. 95 on). There he affirms the necessity of examining religion's claims regarding the certainty and truth-content of its postulates, rather than merely the structure of the believer's religious experience.

5. On p. 11 of chapter 1, Guttmann states: "This question is not concerned with establishing the truth of one particular faith vis-à-vis others, but with the *nature of religion* as a field in its own right . . . its tendency is to regard religion as a *given phenomenon* of the spirit."

6. See Guttmann, *Philosophy of Religion*, 35–36.

7. Guttmann, *Philosophy of Religion*, 24–26.

8. Guttmann, *Philosophy of Religion*, 32–33.

9. Guttmann, *Philosophy of Religion*, 36. Guttmann mentions here the debt he owes his teacher Hermann Cohen. His treatment of the concept of sin draws on chapter 11 of Cohen's book *Religion of Reason: Out of the Sources of Judaism* (New York: Frederick Ungar, 1972) entitled "Atonement" (see particularly pp. 183–88). Cohen refers to the concept of the "sin before God" as a fundamental premise that generates the category of the flawed individual. In this manner the individual, the "I," attains greater stature in the ethical discussion than he or she would command within an ethical system that confers worth upon human beings only to the degree that they conform to a general categorical imperative. Guttmann, under the influence of Otto, speaks of sin in a more "personalized-experiential" language, as that which "pollutes the whole of the human essence," alienating the human being from God.

See further Rudolph Otto, *The Idea of the Holy* (London: Oxford University Press, 1923), 50–58, particularly statements such as the following: "Mere awe, mere need of shelter from the 'tremendum,' has here been elevated to the feeling that man in his "profaneness" is not *worthy* to stand in the presence of the holy one, and that his own entire personal unworthiness might defile even holiness itself." Or: "The same perverse action that before weighed upon us now *pollutes* us; we do not accuse ourselves, we are defiled in our own eyes."

10. Also with regard to the concept of one's fellow, and the obligations engendered by it, Guttmann expresses himself in decidedly religious language, as compared to Cohen. It is true that Cohen obligates us to feel compassion for the suffering individual. Yet he does this only so that such compassion can provide the energy and motivation for the pure moral will. This pure moral will still grasps the inner human personality as a rational entity responsible for realizing the categorical imperative. Yet with respect to Guttmann "Religious ethics considers one's fellow as being created like one's own self in the image of God: there is homogeneity among men, all come from the same source, One God is their Creator. Clearly, therefore, the love emanating from this conception will be different in character, for it possesses a kind of intimacy, sensitivity and respect with regard to one's fellow. We are as one before God."(Guttmann, *Philosophy of Religion*, 37). It may be that Otto's influence can be detected here as well, from the description in chapter 3 of his book of the feeling or consciousness of "creature-feeling" (Otto, *The Idea of the Holy*, 10): "The 'creature-feeling' is itself a first subjective concomitant and effect of another feeling-element, which casts it like a shadow, but which in itself indubitably has immediate and primary reference to an object outside the self." Natan Rotenstreich (in his introduction to *On the Philosophy of Religion*, 9), observes that "The various works of Rudolph Otto offered both aid and stimulus, and indeed he refers to them quite frequently."

11. Guttmann, *Philosophy of Religion*, 33–34. See also Guttmann's article "Al-Yesodot ha-Yahadut" in *Religion and Knowledge* [Hebrew, translated from the German], ed. S. H. Bergman and Nathan Rotenstreich (Jerusalem: Magnes Press, 1955), 271.

12. Guttmann, *Philosophy of Religion*, 61–63.

13. Guttmann, *Philosophy of Religion*, 62–68, 72–75.

14. Guttmann, *Philosophy of Religion*, 75–80.

15. See Emil Fackenheim, *God's Presence in History* (New York: Harper Torchbooks, 1970), 41–43.

16. Guttmann's evaluation of Max Weber's work appears in his article "Mishnato shel Max Weber al ha-Soziologiah shel ha-Yahadut ha-Atikah," *Religion and Knowledge*, 230–58.

17. Guttmann, "Mishnato shel Max Weber," 250.

18. Guttmann, "Mishnato shel Max Weber," 247.

19. Guttmann, "Mishnato shel Max Weber," 246.

20. Guttmann, "Mishnato shel Max Weber," 247.

21. See Guttmann, *Philosophies of Judaism* (New York: Jewish Publication Society of America, 1964), 48–56.

22. Guttmann, "Mishnato shel Max Weber," 246.

23. Guttmann, "Mishnato shel Max Weber," 247.

24. Guttmann, "Mishnato shel Max Weber," 231.

25. Guttmann, "Mishnato shel Max Weber," 252.
26. From Guttmann's article "Eksistensiah ve-Ideah," *Religion and Knowledge*, 300.
27. Guttmann, "Eksistensiah ve-Ideah," 300.
28. Guttmann, "Eksistensiah ve-Ideah," 300.
29. Guttmann, *Philosophy of Religion*, 13–16.
30. Guttmann, *Philosophy of Religion*, 93–95.
31. Guttmann declares this to be an "eternal value" to be learned from the teachings of R. Yehudah ha-Levi. See "Ha-Yahas Bein ha-Dat le-Vein ha-Filosofiah lefi Yehudah ha-Levi," *Religion and Knowledge*, 85.
32. Guttmann, *Philosophy of Religion*, 120–23.
33. Guttmann, *Philosophy of Religion*, 123–25.
34. Guttmann, *Philosophy of Religion*, 121–22, 127–28.
35. See Guttmann's critique of Feuerbach on this subject in *On the Philosophy of Religion*, pp. 66–67, and also pp. 124–26.
36. Guttmann, *Philosophy of Religion*, 121–22.
37. On p. 54 of *On the Philosophy of Religion*, Guttmann states that "All the fundamental aspects in religion already exist at the more primitive levels. . . . The religious approach is not confined to an advanced stage of development but is present in the spiritual development of the human race, beginning with the earliest stages of which we are aware."
38. Guttmann, *Philosophy of Religion*, 41–42.
39. Guttmann, *Philosophy of Religion*, 44–45.
40. Guttmann, *Philosophy of Religion*, 44–46.
41. Guttmann, *Philosophy of Religion*, 45–46.
42. Guttmann, "Distance and Proximity," in *Philosophy of Religion*, 47–60.
43. Guttmann, *Philosophy of Religion*, 38–40.
44. Guttmann, *Philosophies of Judaism*, 7.
45. Guttmann, *Philosophies of Judaism*, 7–8.
46. Guttmann, *Philosophies of Judaism*, 7–8.
47. Guttmann, *Philosophy of Religion*, 82–83.
48. Guttmann, *Philosophy of Religion*, 97–100.
49. Guttmann, *Philosophy of Religion*, 105–6.
50. Guttmann, *Philosophy of Religion*, 91.
51. Guttmann, *Philosophies of Judaism*, 6–7.
52. Guttmann, *Philosophy of Religion*, 93–95.
53. Guttmann, *Philosophy of Religion*, 104–5.
54. Guttmann, *Philosophy of Religion*, 95–96.
55. Guttmann, *Philosophies of Judaism*, 8.
56. Guttmann, *Philosophies of Judaism*, 10–11.
57. This characterization is confirmed by N. Rotenstreich in his introduction to Guttmann's *On the Philosophy of Religion* (p. 9):

He wishes to show that, in the area of higher religiosity, monotheism represents the supreme stage of religious development. Here once again we encounter Guttmann in a dual capacity—as a historian of that philosophy which concerns itself with religion, and as a religious thinker wishing to comprehend his own religious attitude against a comparative background on the one hand, and an analytical-conceptual one on the other.

58. On the limited influence of Husserl's methodology on that of Guttmann, see Rotenstreich's introduction to Guttmann's *On the Philosophy of Religion*, pp. 8–9.

59. Guttmann, *Philosophies of Judaism*, 38.

60. Guttmann, *Philosophies of Judaism*, 104.

61. Guttmann, "Kant ve-ha-Yahadut," *Religion and Knowledge*, 221.

62. Guttmann, *Philosophies of Judaism*, 352.

63. Appears in Guttmann, *Religion and Knowledge*, 84.

64. Guttmann, *Religion and Knowledge*, 85.

65. Guttmann, "Ha-Dat ve-ha-Mada be-Machshevet Yemei ha-Beinayim ve-ha-Et ha-Chadashah," *Religion and Knowledge*, 301.

66. Guttmann, "Eksistensiah ve-Ideah," 301.

67. Guttmann, "Eksistensiah ve-Ideah," 299.

68. Guttmann, "Eksistensiah ve-Ideah," 116–17.

69. Guttmann, "Eksistensiah ve-Ideah," 300.

70. Guttmann, *Philosophy of Religion*, 237–38.

71. Guttmann, *Philosophy of Religion*, 97–100.

72. Guttmann, *Philosophy of Religion*, 116–17.

73. Guttmann, *Philosophies of Judaism*, 47.

74. Guttmann, *Philosophy of Religion*, 123–26.

75. Guttmann, *Philosophies of Judaism*, 14–16.

76. Guttmann, *Philosophies of Judaism*, 14–16.

77. Guttmann, *Philosophies of Judaism*, 6. These are his words: "The Biblical idea of creation does not pretend to provide a theoretical explanation of the origin of the universe; it is the form in which the religious consciousness of the nature of the relationship between God and the world has become articulate."

78. Guttmann expresses this opinion by agreeing with R. Yehudah ha-Levi's opinion in the chapter on ha-Levi in his book *The Philosophies of Judaism*, pp. 125–26.

79. Guttmann, *Philosophy of Religion*, 47.

80. Guttmann, *Philosophies of Judaism*, 166–71, 176–79.

81. Guttmann, *Philosophies of Judaism*, p. 415.

82. Guttmann, *Philosophies of Judaism*, 94–97.

83. Regarding the attitude of Jewish and Muslim Neoplatonists and Aristotelians towards Greek philosophy, Guttmann states (*Philosophies of Judaism*, p. 84): "Greek philosophy was no longer the source of particular doctrines only, but the systematic foundation of their thought."

84. Guttmann, *Philosophies of Judaism*, 61.

85. Guttmann, *Philosophies of Judaism*, 65–66.

86. Guttmann, *Philosophies of Judaism*, 130–32.

87. Guttmann, *Philosophies of Judaism*, 120.

88. Guttmann, *Philosophies of Judaism*, 104.

89. Guttmann, *Religion and Knowledge*, 87–90.

90. Guttmann, *Philosophies of Judaism*, 152–53.

91. Regarding Guttmann's consciousness of the disparity between the spiritual worlds of personalism and metaphysics, see *Philosophies of Judaism*, 124–25, 151–53.

92. Guttmann, *Philosophies of Judaism*, 143–44.

93. Guttmann, *Philosophies of Judaism*, 143.

94. Guttmann, *Philosophies of Judaism*, 322–23.

95. On this subject see Guttmann's discussion of R. Yehudah ha-Levi in *Philosophies of Judaism*, 120–33.

96. Guttmann, *Philosophies of Judaism*, 368–71.

97. Guttmann, *Philosophy of Religion*, 107–10.

98. I would like to acknowledge my debt to Prof. Eliezer Schweid, who directed my attention to this particular aspect of Guttmann's theory in a class he gave on the historiography of Jewish philosophy at the Hebrew University of Jerusalem.

99. Guttmann, *Philosophies of Judaism*, 171–72.

100. Guttmann, *Philosophies of Judaism*, 158–59.

101. Guttmann, *Philosophy of Religion*, 41–43.

102. Guttmann, "Ha-Motivim ha-Datiim ba-Filosophiah shel ha-Rambam," *Religion and Knowledge*, 88.

103. Peter Slomovics, "Yitzhak Yulius Guttmann ve-Yehezkel Kaufman: Machshavah ve-Mechkar ve-ha-Kesher Beineihem" (Ph.D. diss., Hebrew University of Jerusalem, 1981), 13.

104. Slomovics, "Yitzhak Yulius Guttmann," 22.

105. Slomovics, "Yitzhak Yulius Guttmann," 67.

106. Slomovics, "Yitzhak Yulius Guttmann," 35, 94–97.

107. On this matter see Guttmann, *Philosophies of Judaism*, 169–170.

108. Guttmann, *Philosophies of Judaism*, 56–57.

109. Guttmann, *Philosophies of Judaism*, 42–43. Regarding negative norms, see 53–54.

110. Guttmann, *Philosophies of Judaism*, 157–58.

111. Guttmann, *Philosophies of Judaism*, 154–58.

112. Guttmann, *Philosophies of Judaism*, 169.

113. Guttmann, *Philosophy of Religion*, 46.

114. Guttmann, *Philosophy of Religion*, 116–17.

115. Guttmann, *Philosophies of Judaism*, 338–39.

116. Guttmann, *Philosophy of Religion*, 91.

117. Guttmann, *Philosophies of Judaism*, 176–79.

118. Guttmann, *Philosophies of Judaism*, 366.

119. Guttmann, *Philosophies of Judaism*, 3–5, 54–55.

120. Guttmann, *Philosophies of Judaism*, 4.

121. Guttmann, *Philosophies of Judaism*, 47–50.

122. Slomovics, "Yitzhak Yulius Guttmann," 40.

123. See Guttmann, *Philosophies of Judaism*, 15. "Jewish thought is not oriented towards metaphysical questions. The sloughing off of mythological cosmogonies eliminated all potential starting points for the growth of metaphysics."

124. Guttmann, "Ha-Motivim ha-Datiim," 90: "The Neoplatonic ideal of the soul's ascension to the Deity . . . It is knowledge that enables a person to cleave to God, and knowledge that renders him part of the upper world."

125. Guttmann, *Religion and Knowledge*, 292.

126. Guttmann, *Philosophy of Religion*, 97–100.

127. See particularly Guttmann, *On the Philosophy of Religion*, pp. 121–22.

128. See Guttmann, *Philosophy of Religion*, 246–47, and Leo Strauss' article "The Law of Reason in the *Kuzari*," in his *Persecution and the Art of Writing* (Glencoe, IL: Free Press, 1952), 12.

129. Guttmann, *Philosophy of Religion*, 11.

130. Guttmann, *Philosophy of Religion*, 97–100.

131. Guttmann, *Philosophy of Religion*, 11.

132. Guttmann, *Philosophies of Judaism*, 56.

133. Guttmann, *Philosophies of Judaism*, 3.

134. Guttmann, *Philosophies of Judaism*, 262–65.

135. Guttmann, *Philosophies of Judaism*, 8.

5

Historiosophical Elements

Following the Development of Jewish Philosophy over Time

Now that we have characterized Guttmann's perspective on the nature of Jewish philosophy, it is worth examining his approach to the development of Jewish philosophy over the course of historical time. We will examine his views concerning the pre-historic and early periods of Jewish philosophy and clarify his position on the question of the continuity or conclusion of Jewish philosophic activity in the modern period. In addition, we will try to ascertain how Guttmann portrayed the type of developmental "motion" exhibited by Jewish philosophy with the passing of historical time. Our findings will be based primarily on a structural and substantive analysis of his major historical work, *The Philosophies of Judaism*. Selected articles from the collection *Religion and Knowledge* will also prove useful, particularly those that shed light on Guttmann's criteria for distinguishing between the medieval and modern periods in Jewish philosophy. Here as well we will draw comparisons between Guttmann's historiosophic theory and that of Wolfson.

PRE-HISTORY

Wolfson limited his field of research to the theological-doctrinal manifestations of religious belief, those same creedal doctrines Guttmann termed the objective side of religion. Wolfson did not seek to probe the nature of the believer's religious experience or to determine the quality of the religious connection between the believer and the object of his faith. The goal of his scholarship was to articulate how the history of medieval Western philosophy was shaped by Philonic theology. He therefore devoted no space to a discussion of Biblical thought in its own right, as gleaned from the text of the Bible itself. From Wolfson's perspective the Bible contains no systematic set of beliefs and opinions, thus there is no reason to treat it as a "pre-history" of Western philosophy. The Biblical worldview enters the domain of philosophy and exerts a cardinal influence in the realm of beliefs and opinions only thanks to its theological-doctrinal reworking at the hands of Philo. To the extent that there exists any "preamble" to Western philosophy in the sense of its being a set of systematic beliefs and opinions, this preamble would be Greek philosophy, which was the first to formulate metaphysical beliefs in a systematic conceptual fashion. It was succeeded by the "real" beginning-period of Western philosophy, namely the advent of the Philonic worldview, which ultimately conquered the doctrinal arena and was the first to apply systematic reasoning to Biblical presuppositions.

Guttmann, in contrast, is concerned with the "religious motifs" and "behaviors of the soul" underlying the abstract formulations of metaphysics. Jewish philosophy for him was a dramatic account of the encounter between the personalist religiosity of Biblical faith and the mystical-pantheist religiosity of the Greek metaphysical tradition. Consequently it is important for him to trace the roots of religiosity as a unique phenomenon of the human spirit, independently of its later systematic expressions. Given that the foundations of this orientation were already established, in Guttmann's view, in the pre-philosophic Biblical period, he elects to devote the first chapter of his historical work to "The Basic Ideas of Biblical Religion."[1]

At the beginning of the chapter Guttmann stresses that the genesis of personalist religiosity should not be sought in a process of philosophic speculation; its source lies rather in "the unmediated religious consciousness itself."[2] It has no affinity, consequently, for an abstract idea of God, conceiving instead of a supreme Divine will that rules history. The Biblical Deity is characterized by His moral will: He demands, adjures, promises and threatens human beings. He compels humans to submit to His will, and it is this awareness that underlies the God-consciousness of Biblical man. The essence of this consciousness consists of the "voluntaristic"[3] ethical connection between two distinct moral beings. This connection between two "moral wills" appears in various forms in the Biblical corpus. The book of Amos accentuates both the glory and majesty of God and his distance from human beings. Hosea and the Psalms, by comparison, convey a sense of closeness and intimacy.[4] Yet both the distance and the closeness are determined by moral criteria inhering in God's qualities as judge and as lover. The relation of God to the world is "personalistic." His free will is the sole reason the world came into being. It follows that His relation to the world is that of sovereign and creator, a unique transcendent being. The world itself lacks Divine qualities, and it becomes the work of God's hands.[5]

Further on in the opening chapter of *The Philosophies of Judaism*, Guttmann contrasts this personalist Biblical orientation with two other orientations to the relation between God, the world and human beings. The mythological-magical approach, for instance, was contemporaneous with the Bible itself. To defend personalism against its critics, Guttmann stresses the Bible's crusade against the magical and mythological view of the Deity. In order that we not view personalization as the indiscriminate projection of human characteristics onto the Deity, Guttmann takes pains to distinguish between the moral personalization of the Divine-human relation, which he deems legitimate, and the animistic personalization of inanimate nature. Similarly, he differentiates between the relation between two free wills and the attempt to subordinate the Deity to a natural causal system that ostensibly influences His will in accordance with human interests.[6] Yet before describing the Bible's early engagement with mythology and magic, Guttmann undertakes a comparison between Biblical religiosity and the mystical-pantheist religiosity that fueled the medieval Neoplatonist and Aristotelian philosophies. Although pantheism posed no challenge to personalism prior to the middle ages, Guttmann compares the two at the very beginning of his work, for two reasons. His first, declared, reason is to clarify the essential character of personalism itself.[7] Yet the reader senses that Guttmann is also preparing him for the more significant history of religious philosophy, as expressed in the dramatic dialectical encounter between ethical-personalist religiosity and contemplative-pantheist religiosity in medieval and modern times. This encounter could take place only once Judaism had encountered philosophic thought, for to Guttmann's way of thinking, religious consciousness can escape subjectivity only by way of reflective thinking.[8]

Guttmann's chapter on the Bible exposes us for the first time to his inclination for judging spiritual phenomena in light of their final, highest, development, in contradistinction to Wolfson's tendency to evaluate doctrinal systems in light of their origins. This evolutionary-developmental orientation manifests itself in three spheres. First, Guttmann emphasizes the fact that Biblical religiosity also has its own pre-history. While stating explicitly that within the framework of a book largely devoted to chronicling medieval and modern Jewish philosophy he has no intention of delving into the origins of the Biblical idea of God, Guttmann does note that a considerable amount of time elapsed before the Jewish concept of God developed from its early form as the God of nature to its later form as a personal God in the consciousness of the people. The transformation of the God of Israel into the God of the entire world was also an extended process. Once the Deity was grasped in personal terms, signs of evolutionary development are still discernible within Biblical thought itself. In earlier times the Deity had been conceived of as a sort of craftsman who created the world. This image subsequently underwent a process of spiritual refinement, and the world was later depicted as coming into being through the word of God alone. Moreover, the God who was attached first and foremost to His people became a God who presides over all peoples, intervening in the moral fate of every individual.[9] Despite his aim of tracing pure personalist religiosity back to a very early period, Guttmann nevertheless adheres to thought patterns that posit a development in history from "low," particularist and anthropomorphic phenomena, to "high," universal and more spiritual phenomena.

Guttmann's evolutionary point of view leads him to seek in early phenomena the nuclei of later, more developed phenomena. Thus not only does the Bible have a developmental pre-history and exhibit an inner development; it also contains the foundations of developments that find expression only in later periods. The problem of theodicy, for instance, paves the way for beliefs in the immortality of the soul and the resurrection of the dead, beliefs which find conscious and deliberate expression only in the rabbinic period. The problem of theodicy itself, as articulated in the book of Job, is treated by Guttmann as an example of pre-reflection. In his view, the deliberations over theodicy in the book of Job are not an instance of reflective thought for its own sake; they rather bespeak a religious consciousness that has recourse to rational tools in a time of crisis, while ultimately resolving its spiritual struggles by way of unmediated experience.[10]

The encounter between Judaism and Greek Hellenistic philosophy is also deemed a pre-historic element in Jewish philosophic development by Guttmann. Together with the short chapter on the Bible that precedes it and the short chapter on the religious ideas of Talmudic Judaism that follows it, the chapter on Hellenistic Jewish philosophy serves as a link in an introductory section termed "Fundamentals and First Influences" in the English translation of David Silverman.[11] Silverman is referring here to the fundamental concepts of Biblical personalism in its pristine state and to the early influences exerted by the Greek contemplative-pantheist ethos on the spiritual world of Judaism.

According to Guttmann's thesis, Hellenistic Jewish philosophy was only an episode in the annals of Jewish philosophy, both in terms of the length of time that it appeared on the historical stage and in terms of the influence it exercised on the continuing development of Jewish spiritual life.[12] As becomes apparent further on, in Guttmann's view both the episode of Hellenistic Judaism and the development of Biblical personalism through Talmudic Judaism are preparatory phenomena for the main chapter in the history of Jewish philosophy.

This incremental-evolutionary structure is evident within the chapter on Hellenistic Jewish philosophy as well. The chapter opens with a polemic against the claim that the book of Ecclesiastes reflects a marked Greek influence. Here Guttmann argues explicitly that aside from certain points of contact with popular Greek philosophy, the Palestinian Judaism that produced the book of Ecclesiastes was not influenced in any profound way by Greek philosophy.[13] While admitting that the book The Wisdom of Solomon from the Apocrypha employs explicitly philosophic terms, cites Greek sources on occasion and contains a number of ideas foreign to Judaism, Guttmann nonetheless contends that the book's basic stance is thoroughly Jewish.[14] Also in Fourth Maccabees the influence of philosophy is held to be detectable more through its discursive-rhetorical oratory, while the book's content displays a vital connection to the personal Biblical God.[15] Only Philo of Alexandria is depicted by Guttmann as having effected "a thoroughgoing philosophic reconstruction of Judaism," through a significant rationalist "sublimation" of the concept of God.[16] Yet in comparison with Wolfson, Guttmann's estimation of Philo's contribution to the history of Jewish philosophy is far more modest in scope.[17]

Guttmann's summation of Philo's worldview is undertaken from within the scholarly perspective that informs his more extensive work on medieval and modern Jewish philosophy. Unlike Wolfson, Guttmann does not hold that the Biblical worldview succeeded in conquering the conceptual-systematic world of philosophy. In his opinion, the engagement of personalism with intellectualist pantheism was a genuine encounter in which personalism underwent fundamental changes, not only in its style of discourse, but in its basic content as well. In accordance with this premise, Guttmann divides the opinions of a given thinker into "traditional-personalist" and "contemplative-metaphysical" elements.[18] This approach is already recognizable in his analysis of Philo's teachings. On the one hand, the Philonic concept of God is characterized by a high degree of abstraction that effectively voids it of all positive content. Logically speaking, this concept precludes any possibility of regarding the Deity in personal terms. Yet when discoursing on the subject of God, Philo frequently expresses himself in explicitly personalist terms. This phenomenon, says Guttmann, testifies not only to a systematic inconsistency, but to real tension between Philo's intellectualist worldview and his personalist religious sentiment. With respect to creation, Philo adopts the Platonic-Stoic synthesis of Posidonius that posits the formation of the world from primordial matter. Philo's God, however, is not the immanent *pneuma* (soul) of the Stoics, and He is far more exalted than the Platonic ideas. In the spirit of the Jewish tradition, Philo's God has no material aspect whatsoever and is portrayed as a thoroughly transcendent being. The idea of the logos in Philo's teachings constitutes an original contribution to religious philosophy and is understood by Guttmann as an attempt to mediate between Philo's abstract idea of God and the physical world.[19]

Philo views the ideal religious life through the prism of the mystical-contemplative approach. Ethics for him is a way of liberating oneself from the bonds of sensuality and ascending to a pure spiritual plane. Yet when describing the ideal relation of the religious person to his God, Philo stresses the values of submission through faith, humility and obedience, values that for Guttmann bespeak a traditional Jewish religiosity. Nevertheless, Guttmann contends that within the framework of Philo's theory, the soul attains to a mystical union with God.[20]

The Philonic concept of revelation also has two sides to it. On the one hand, Philo perceives the state of mystical communion with God as revelation. This type of revelation, however, is a far cry from the Jewish concept of a one-time historical revelation that encompasses all truth within itself. On the other hand, this original Jewish idea is also preserved in Philo, though it is given a "mystical interpretation."[21] Ultimately, then, Guttmann's Philo and Wolfson's Philo bear no resemblance to one another. Wolfson devotes considerable effort to demonstrating that Philo's teachings are characterized by an inner logical consistency. Guttmann, on the other hand, is willing to countenance the possibility that there may be palpable internal contradictions in Philo's thought, and he ascribes a portion of these contradictions to the tension obtaining between Philo's religious sentiments and his philosophic ideas.[22]

Guttmann's approach to Philo is distinguished from that of Wolfson not only by his more critical assessment of Philo's philosophic works. Neither does the main difference lie in the fact that Guttmann classifies Philo's views according to a dialectical rhythm which contrasts the "personal" and the "contemplative" sides of his teachings. The most striking difference between them manifests itself in their historiosophic perspectives. Did Philo effectively establish the discipline of Jewish religious philosophy, or did he merely introduce trends of thought that would reach full systematic development only in later periods? For Wolfson, "significant time" in religious philosophy begins with Philo's work; Philo, in his view, shaped the course of "scriptural philosophy" throughout the medieval period. It was he who systematically subordinated philosophy to revelation, and he who formulated the five cardinal principles that were accepted by the Church Fathers, the Kalam and Jewish medieval philosophers.[23] In Guttmann's evaluation, on the other hand, Philo never subordinated philosophy to religion in principle, though he frequently had recourse to Greek philosophic theories.[24] Moreover, Philo was not held to have exercised any great influence over the subsequent development of religious philosophy.[25] As we shall see further on, Guttmann prefers contextual, horizontal criteria for ascertaining intellectual influence to the "trans-historical" criteria applied by Wolfson.[26] Since medieval thinkers were not directly acquainted with the writings of Philo, there can be no justification for crowning him the father of medieval philosophy. His contribution should be assessed within the framework of Greek philosophy in the Hellenistic period—to which he belonged in terms of time and place. He should not be understood as having had a trans-historical influence.[27] Nevertheless, in accordance with his understanding that early phenomena often contain the seeds of later phenomena, Guttmann is willing to award Philo the title of "first theologian," from a historical perspective. While the substance of Philo's teachings did not attain to foundational status in the chronicles of Jewish philosophy, the model whereby he raised the problem of the connection between revelation and reason foreshadowed certain features of medieval thought. He was the first to present revelation and philosophy as dual sources of truth and the first to try to reconcile the two from a systematic point of view.[28] Even on the substantive level, Philo advanced toward concepts and values that became focal points in Jewish medieval philosophy, particularly with regard to the negation of positive divine attributes, mediation between the abstract Deity and the physical world by way of spiritual intermediaries and the emphasis on mystical contemplation as an element of the religious ethos.[29]

The third chapter of the opening section of Guttmann's book is called "The Religious Ideas of Talmudic Judaism." This is noteworthy in itself, for at no point does Wolfson dedicate a separate chapter to the study of the Talmud, in keeping with his decision to confine his scholarship to the formal-theological realm. However, this should not be interpreted to mean that Wolfson did not believe the Talmud had made a contribution to Jewish philosophy. As we have seen, Wolfson held that some of the fundamental methodological trends of medieval philosophy originated in the Talmud's midrashic and hermeneutical tendencies. The rabbis' non-literal interpretive techniques and their commitment to the systematic resolution of logical contradictions left their mark on the Biblical theologians of the three monotheist religions.[30] Yet just as Wolfson nowhere devotes a separate chapter in his scholarship to the Bible, despite his insistence that the most basic premises of medieval philosophy (on topics such as the nature of God, creation and revelation) stem from the Bible, so the Talmud also never served Wolfson as a subject for thematic research.

Guttmann's chapter on the Talmud is modest in scope relative to the book as a whole. Nonetheless, it is important to him to present the Talmud as an intermediary link that continues the personalist religiosity of the Bible, while also nudging Jewish thought to progress in the direction of the abstract and systematic thought of the medieval period.

The Talmud, then, perpetuates the religious ideas of Biblical personalism, including such doctrines as the transcendent nature of God, the connection between humans and God grounded in the ethical commandments of the Torah, the wisdom and righteousness of God embodied in his sovereignty over the world, the status of the Jews as the Chosen People, and the anticipation of a Kingdom of Heaven on earth in the historical future. Certain Biblical tenets, however, are developed in the Talmud well beyond their

Biblical formulation. The vital quality of the concept of God is articulated in even further depth by way of a consciously anthropomorphic approach, one that describes God, among other things, as learning Torah and partaking of the exile of His people. (Guttmann, despite his appreciation for abstract thought, finds no flaw in these kinds of anthropomorphisms. In his view they testify to a live and healthy religious encounter with God.)[31] The Biblical problem of theodicy prompts the explicit formulation of a belief in the immortality of the soul and in the resurrection of the dead.[32]

Yet the Talmud's focusing of religious expectations on the world to come effects a change in the religious ethos, a change that moves Jewish ethics in a more dualistic direction. This world, while maintaining its status as the arena of the moral, commandment-oriented activism of Judaism, nevertheless becomes a corridor to the next world. The soul is portrayed as a spiritual entity that comes to us from the world beyond and returns there after death. The body is depicted as a vessel for the desires that engage us in this world. This dualistic conception spawns a morality directed towards controlling one's desires in order to prepare the soul for life in the next world. Talmudic morality, then, begins to approximate the anti-sensual morality of medieval Neoplatonism. True, the Talmud refrains from advocating a morality of ascetic purification or from fostering expectations of unification with a world of incorporeal beings; these religious ideals emerged in Jewish culture only during the medieval period. Still, the morality of the Talmud creates an opening for the introduction of these ideas into the Jewish domain.[33]

Talmudic ethics anticipates not only the purification morality of the middle ages, in contradistinction to the historical-activist morality of the Bible. It anticipates the autonomous moral consciousness as well, which in Guttmann's opinion achieves full development only in the ethics of the modern period, specifically in the works of Kant and Hermann Cohen. In certain maxims, such as "Serve the master without thought of reward," the Talmudic sages stress the importance of a pure ethical motivation for observing the commandments and performing good deeds, as distinguished from a utilitarian motivation. Other teachings, such as that which speaks of "laws which had they not been given should have been given," point to the independence of morality from heteronomous decrees. Yet traces of what Guttmann terms a "primitive" approach, whereby a person is judged according to the quantitative "balance of his deeds," still remain in the Talmud, alongside the more "mature" trend stressing that the quality of the moral act stems from the intrinsic value of the other ("Beloved is man, who was created in the image of God," "Love thy neighbor as thyself—this is the supreme principle of the Torah").[34]

Guttmann distinguishes two additional important fields in which the Talmud creates a theoretical basis for systematic and abstract thought, one that reaches fruition only in medieval religious philosophy. First, the Talmud—more than the Biblical book of Job—employs conceptual-reflective thought in its treatment of religious problems. Talmudic thought is capable of compressing theoretical issues into pithy sayings characterized by a high degree of abstraction and comprehensiveness, such as "Everything is in the hands of Heaven except the fear of Heaven." Similarly, the Talmud tends to class the commandments under the rubric of comprehensive moral principles, such as, "That which is hateful unto thee, do not do unto thy neighbor; this is the entire Torah, and everything else only a commentary on it," or, "Thou shalt love thy neighbor as thyself—this is the supreme principle of the Torah."[35] Nevertheless, the Talmud lacks the systematic approach to beliefs and opinions that is the hallmark of medieval Jewish philosophy. The compressed Talmudic proverbs certainly shed light on particular issues, and they attest to the attempt of religious thought to penetrate the structure of religious experience. This is not merely an instance of recourse to reflective thought in time of crisis, but the adoption of a position outside of the circle of religious life itself in order to examine certain topics from a reflective perspective for its own sake. Nonetheless, such statements do not qualify as theology in the full sense of the word, as Talmudic thought does not yet consider the content of religion from a comprehensive, systematic philosophic perspective.[36]

Ultimately, the Talmud's non-systematic treatment of theological issues served as the foundation for a certain type of intellectual pluralism, which in Guttmann's evaluation differentiated medieval Jewish philosophy from its Islamic and Christian counterparts. True, the unchallenged belief in revelation was inextricably intertwined with other implicit beliefs such as the belief in Providence, miracles and reward and punishment. Yet these very assumptions determined the parameters of the wide-ranging intellectual freedom characteristic of the medieval Jewish philosophers. These beliefs prevented Jewish philosophy from becoming entirely swept up in the pantheist current, given the powerful influence of Neoplatonist and Aristotelian trends in the Islamic world. While Islamic philosophy sometimes succumbed to the Greek tradition, the Jewish philosophers, although they imbibed no small amount of influence from the outside, generally tried to maintain the fundamental convictions stemming from the commitment to the Divine origin of the Torah. Nevertheless, these parameters were not so restrictive as to substantially limit intellectual freedom, as did the dogmatic Christian tradition in the case of the scholastics.[37]

Guttmann's pre-historic chapters, then, address the religious ideas of the Bible, Philo and the Talmud. The Bible marks the first appearance of the personalist religious relation, namely, a consciousness that equates morality with commandment. It demands of the human individual as a moral personality in his own right a practical activism within history, instead of

fusion with a metaphysical-spiritual world subsisting outside of it. This consciousness continues to develop from the inside, both by way of the anthropomorphic formulations of the Talmud testifying to a highly charged
relationship with God and by way of the rabbinic doctrines of the world to
come and the resurrection of the dead. These doctrines emerge organically
from the Biblical debate over the question of reward and punishment. So
much for the foundational elements of Jewish personalism. These elements
would be put to the test in the momentous encounter with Greek metaphysics that took place in the middle ages. Already in the pre-historic period, however, before this encounter reached its full scope and intensity,
there were certain developments within the Jewish world that enabled the
assimilation of the intellectual-contemplative influences which to a large
extent shaped the cognitive approach of medieval thinkers. The book of
Job, which in Guttmann's view did not yet bespeak the independence of reflection from religious immediacy, represents a kind of first attempt to employ intellectual speculation in order to address religious-ethical conflicts.
In the Talmud, the ethos of overcoming one's desires in the "vestibule" of
this world as a way of preparing for the next world, and the great value ascribed to a spiritual life that originates in a form of intellectual deliberation,
provided an opening for the dualist and contemplative trends that entered
the Jewish world by way of the Neoplatonic and Aristotelian schools. Philo,
while preserving a personalist religious sentiment, articulated an abstract
speculative concept of God devoid of all positive attributes.

THE MEDIEVAL PERIOD

The historical drama of Jewish philosophy per se begins from Guttmann's
standpoint in the middle ages: in the Islamic world of the early ninth century.[38] Guttmann dates the inception of Jewish philosophy from then,
rather than from the time of Philo, for several reasons. First, Guttmann is
interested in types of human religiosity and in the transformations occur-
ring in the human religious orientation in various historical periods. He is
not concerned merely with philosophic systems built from individual elements joined together into logical constructs, but with the quality of the human relationship to the object of its faith. According to Guttmann, the religious orientation of an entire stratum of educated Jews was transformed
in the middle ages, with the assimilation of philosophic trends. As he put
it, "Throughout this period philosophy profoundly influenced the spiritual
life of Judaism. . . . Out of this philosophic interpretation of Judaism there
grew a philosophic form of religion which, although admitting the un-
questionable authority of Divine revelation, nevertheless represented a considerable transformation of Biblical and Talmudic Judaism, and in the

course of time reached a broad circle of educated Jews."[39] Jewish medieval philosophy follows in the footsteps of Islamic religious philosophy, likewise establishing a kind of "believing rationalism whose ultimate religious ideal was similar to that of its opponents [namely, those philosophers who rejected revelation outright], but which held . . . revelation to be the sole true realization of this ideal."[40] This new type of religiosity is not the exclusive province of a limited number of spiritual giants. Through commentaries, homilies and religious poetry it penetrated the very fabric of Jewish culture.[41]

From Wolfson's viewpoint, to recall, significant time in religious philosophy begins when Biblical doctrine dominates the conceptual-systematic world of philosophy. Guttmann, in contrast, argues that Jewish religious philosophy crystallizes when the rational religiosity of the philosophic thinkers, while not entirely overwhelming traditional Jewish personalism, exerts a decisive impact on it. Wolfson relies on a single thinker, Philo, who succeeded in reformulating the narratives, laws and exhortations of the Bible in conceptual-philosophic terms and in organizing the fundamental Biblical tenets into a coherent system to mark the beginning of Jewish philosophy. Since then no significant transformations have occurred, and Jewish philosophy has continued to unfold and articulate its problems in diverse philosophic languages (the problem of the Philonic logos becomes the problem of the Christian trinity, and the problem of the trinity becomes the Islamic problem of the attributes, and so forth).[42] Guttmann, on the other hand, argues that historical periods cannot be demarcated by the systematic efforts of an individual thinker. A new era in religious thought can be said to begin only when a change is felt in the overall religious ethos, a change of some historical-cultural moment, namely, a change that heralds a new beginning in the religious consciousness of significant numbers of Jews.

In Guttmann's view, then, the middle ages begin with a turning point in Jewish religiosity, a turning point with broad repercussions for the spirituality of educated Jews. Guttmann emphasizes nevertheless that this change was not an organic development from Biblical and Talmudic personalism. Religious rationalism did not emerge from the essence of personalism, as did, say, the rabbinic belief in the world to come, which was a natural outgrowth of the Biblical problem of theodicy.[43] Biblical personalism per se was not interested in theoretical-metaphysical speculations concerning the origin of the world. According to Guttmann, the Biblical account of creation is not intended to supply a scientific explanation of how the world came into being, but to articulate the abiding connection between the Creator and created beings. Metaphysical speculation, on the other hand, grew out of the Greek cosmogonies, which were fueled by a theoretical motivation.[44] Educated Jews began to take an interest in metaphysical questions only when the need arose to defend the Bible against the rationalist critique of religion that had developed within the framework of the Islamic cultural world. In other words, it was the encounter with the outside culture that compelled Jewish thinkers to offer pre-Socratic and/or Neoplatonist commentaries on the creation narrative and to wonder whether God created the world from eternal spiritual elements or from some kind of primordial matter.[45]

Wolfson regards the emergence of philosophy among Jews, when it first made its appearance in the first century, as a natural, internal extension of the rabbinic-midrashic effort to interpret the Bible in contemporary terms.[46] Guttmann, in contrast, affirms that Jewish philosophy proper was born only when the need arose to respond to a serious external challenge. In his words, "The Jewish people did not begin to philosophize because of an irresistible urge to do so. They received philosophy from outside sources, and the history of Jewish philosophy is a history of the successive absorptions of foreign ideas."[47] And while Guttmann praises numerous philosophers, such as R. Saadia Gaon, Maimonides and Crescas, for their philosophic independence in providing a systematic grounding for original Biblical personalist elements,[48] he explicitly states that every such Jewish reading is advanced within the framework of external philosophic systems. Jewish philosophy "remained closely bound to the non-Jewish sources from which it originated."[49] Accordingly, the transition from the pre-history to the history of Jewish philosophy takes place only with the rise of the major influential schools of Islamic philosophy—the Kalam, Neoplatonism and Aristotelianism. And indeed, that part of *The Philosophies of Judaism* that addresses the medieval period is not structured in strict chronological fashion (although a measure of historical chronology is maintained in a general way), but according to the place of the Jewish thinkers in the major philosophic schools. One axis in the movement of medieval Jewish philosophy is therefore the way Jewish thinkers responded to the succession of philosophic schools. Since Philo followed no definite school in a systematic fashion, and therefore left behind him no Jewish responses to any such school, he is not featured in the chronicle of Jewish philosophy. Guttmann did not believe that the causal forces behind the historical movement in religious philosophy stemmed from the logical tensions inherent in the Philonic system. It is the continuing developments in the external cultural world that drive Jewish thought as well. While Wolfson's "scriptural philosophers" only used the philosophic schools to render a conceptual-logical interpretation of the Biblical worldview,[50] Guttmann portrays these philosophers as far more dependent on these schools themselves. We will now explore Guttmann's understanding of the place of central Jewish philosophers in the succession of schools, in order to understand what he considered to be the principles of the historical movement of Jewish philosophy.

SAADIA GAON

R. Saadia Gaon, not Philo, is the "father of medieval Jewish philosophy" in Guttmann's eyes, for several reasons. First, both in his substantive positions and in the overall structure of his work, Saadia continued the intellectual tradition of the Mu'tazilite Kalam. He nevertheless refrains from adopting the Kalam framework in its entirety and shows philosophic independence and great freedom in rejecting elements of the Kalam hostile to Biblical principles, such as the theory of atomism.[51] Still, this is not equivalent to total independence, of the kind Wolfson attributed to the scriptural philosophers, namely the evaluation of schools of thought according to Biblical criteria alone.[52] In Guttmann's view, Saadia should be considered a full-fledged member of the school of the Kalam, despite the fact that on certain topics—such as the world to come and the resurrection of the dead—he remains true to original Jewish-Talmudic points of view.[53]

A further reason for Saadia's privileged status consists in the fact that he was the first to systematically articulate what Guttmann regarded as the proper method for characterizing the relation between cognitive and revealed truth. In Wolfson's view, to recall, philosophy is the handmaid of revelation.[54] The premises of revelation are authoritative, and philosophy must ever submit to revelation on cardinal issues.[55] According to Guttmann's analysis, however, the relation between intellectual and revealed truth in medieval thought was complex and highly fraught with tension, this tension first becoming apparent in Saadia. To begin with, according to Guttmann's interpretation of Saadia, metaphysical truth and moral truth can be apprehended entirely by way of independent reason. Contrary to Wolfson's belief, reason does not require any kind of revelatory corrective in order to attain a pure transcendent God-concept. Revelation does not harbor a higher or deeper theoretical content than that which reason has gained. It does serve a pedagogical function by endowing these truths with absolute authority, so that persons who are not philosophers will live in accordance with them. It is also a religious imperative to assimilate these truths, due not to the normative force of the Bible, but to the sheer force of reason itself. Admittedly, Saadia holds that the Jewish approach to philosophy is predicated on the assumption that the Biblical tenets are true a priori, and that the task of philosophy is to interpret and corroborate them.[56] Yet Saadia himself presents another perspective as well, one that is somewhat at odds with this orientation, and which becomes more prominent during the subsequent development of medieval religious philosophy. As Guttmann puts it, "The supremacy of reason becomes quite evident in the question of the interpretation of revelation. According to Saadia, one of the instances in which Scripture may be interpreted against its literal sense is precisely when the latter contradicts reason."[57] The implication is that reason is granted the status of an external, independent criterion in establishing the content of revelation itself. True, says Guttmann, Saadia himself did not venture much farther afield in his interpretations than the fundamental ideas of Biblical personalism. Yet he provided a methodological opening that enabled his successors to attribute doctrines to the Bible that, according to Guttmann, were a far cry from its original premises.[58]

Saadia, then, signals the dawn of medieval Jewish philosophy, as he follows a recognized external philosophic school, and lays the methodological foundations for the tension obtaining in medieval thought concerning the problem of reason and revelation. His status as founder, however, derives also from the systematic consistency with which he unfolds the "beliefs and opinions" he undertook to defend. For example, the correspondence between revelation and reason is expressed in Saadia by the mobilization of Kalam and Aristotelian proofs for the creation of the world in time. From the creation idea Saadia deduces the unity of God, for if there had been two creative powers possessed of absolute free will, they would hardly have collaborated in the creation of a single world.

Logically speaking, the creation idea also entails the three main attributes of life, power and wisdom, and Saadia wrestles with the issue of the attributes in the same manner as his contemporaries in the Kalam. On the one hand, he struggles to preserve the personalism of the Deity by not entirely depriving Him of positive attributes, as was the rule in the Neoplatonic world and in Maimonides' Aristotelian teachings. By the same token, however, Saadia is loath to play down the idea of the absolute unity of God. He therefore argues that the division into attributes is purely a function of the limitations of human language. Sometimes the inner logic of his theory drives him to the conclusion that even the primary attribute of Creator is only an expression of the human understanding that the world is the result of creation and has no inherent connection to the Deity. Nevertheless, Guttmann insists that Saadia remains faithful to the idea of a personal God. On this topic as well, Saadia is the first thinker to give voice to a tension characteristic of medieval Jewish philosophy, a tension that he sensed, yet was unable to resolve.[59]

In contradistinction to Wolfson's approach, Guttmann is willing to discuss past thinkers from an external critical standpoint as well. As a student of the neo-Kantian school of Hermann Cohen, he sees such thinkers through the prism of modernity. Saadia, for one, draws criticism for his "primitive" moral theories. Instead of ascribing moral value to human actions on a qualitative basis according to a person's awareness of his absolute obligation at the time of his action, Saadia judges a person's morality according to quantitative criteria, in conformity with the Talmudic tradition: "[A person is judged] according to the balance of his deeds." Here, Guttmann asserts, Saadia is continuing a "primitive" tradition of the rabbinic sages (who were evidently insufficiently "advanced" to recognize the

Kantian morality of pure obligation). Guttmann's critique is sometimes predicated on the assumption that the systematic ability of the first Jewish philosophers was inadequately developed, and that their thinking was sometimes fraught with unconscious inconsistencies. For example, Saadia strives to establish a eudaemonist morality based on the principle of happiness in conjunction with a morality of obligation that is not based on happiness, though the two cannot really be reconciled.[60] At times the ardor of his polemic against beliefs and opinions hostile to Judaism induces him to lodge contradictory charges against his disputants.[61]

Even on those occasions when Guttmann praises Saadia, the praise emanates from an external critical stance and is contingent upon the degree to which Saadia anticipates later theories. For instance, Saadia's basic postulates on the subject of theodicy—the existence of God, free will and the world to come—anticipate the three doctrines that were to underlie European religious thought from the eighteenth century Enlightenment onward.[62] Similarly, Guttmann stresses Saadia's ethical-activist orientation, according to which the theoretical-metaphysical truths of the Bible are merely a foundation for the ethical content of revelation. This theory supposedly prefigures the Kantian perspective, which places ethical issues at the focus of philosophical discourse, given that human thought is incapable of establishing absolute metaphysical truth.[63]

THE NEOPLATONIST SCHOOL
(ISRAELI, IBN GABIROL, IBN PAKUDA)

Guttmann's evolutionary approach to the development of Jewish philosophy, as well as the importance he ascribes to transformations in the general culture, again find expression in his treatment of the thinkers of the Neoplatonist school. First, the absorption of the Neoplatonist orientation into Jewish philosophy corresponds in time and place to the transition from the tenth to the eleventh century and the transfer of the center of Jewish philosophic activity from Babylon to Spain.[64] These changes in time and place exerted a certain influence, though not a decisive one, on the character of Jewish philosophic discourse. Moreover, the transition from the period of the Kalam to the Neoplatonist period heralds a new stage in the opening of Judaism to philosophy. The Kalam thinkers' approach to the philosophic tradition resembles that of Wolfson. Their approach was first and foremost theological, out of a predilection for validating and confirming a priori Biblical truths. They applied the various Kalam theories selectively and eclectically. For the Jewish Neoplatonists, on the other hand, Greek philosophy was not merely a source for the formulation of doctrines on certain topics, but the systematic foundation of their thought. The Neoplatonist system was now adopted in full, even if it underwent certain changes in order to adapt it to Biblical worldviews or to render it into popular theology.[65]

Furthermore, an inner stage-by-stage evolution can be discerned within the Jewish Neoplatonist school. Guttmann dubs the first Neoplatonist, Isaac Israeli, who was active in the tenth century, "an eclectic compiler."[66] Israeli interests Guttmann not for having produced a philosophic system of any profundity, but as a kind of historical signpost that marks the onset of a certain process. Israeli was the first thinker to attempt to transplant Neoplatonism onto Jewish cultural soil.[67] The religious thrust of his theory already bespeaks a quintessentially Neoplatonist orientation. For him, the religious ideal of philosophy is to draw near to a God who may be attained through the cognition of theoretical truth. Yet Israeli's bid to reconcile Neoplatonist doctrines such as the theory of emanation with Biblical tenets such as creation ex nihilo reveals an undeveloped thought system. His creation theory is an unwitting and unstable mixture of Neoplatonist and Biblical elements. While the Deity is held to have directly created the element of consciousness in the world, all of the other elements are said to emanate from consciousness itself. Israeli fails to explain why the Deity's creative powers stop or are arrested upon the creation of consciousness, and he himself is ignorant of the tension and arbitrariness inherent in his theory.[68]

The mature Neoplatonist theory was accepted by Jewish philosophic thinkers in the eleventh century, whose most prominent representatives were Solomon Ibn Gabirol and Bahya Ibn Pakuda. In Guttmann's view, Ibn Gabirol is a striking example of the extent to which Jewish thinkers internalized the Neoplatonist orientation as a platform for their views. There are almost no discernible Biblical-voluntaristic elements in his theory.[69] From this standpoint, Ibn Gabirol's theory serves more as a link in the development of general metaphysics than it does as a marker in the annals of Jewish philosophy. Ibn Gabirol's talent lay not in justifying Biblical beliefs or in the creation of a synthesis between Biblical voluntarism and the causal determinism of metaphysics. To Guttmann's way of thinking, his value as a philosopher lies in the systematic vigor and theoretical originality with which he developed the foundations of the Neoplatonist system itself.[70] Ibn Gabirol, consequently, marks the Jewish assimilation of the Neoplatonist system, an assimilation expressed by the works that were produced within its framework. Once the system was appropriated, it became an accepted tradition passed down from one generation to the next.

Here, Guttmann's evolutionary dialectic takes an interesting turn. While Ibn Gabirol is portrayed as having distanced himself from Jewish elements in his thought, becoming a Neoplatonist philosopher virtually through and through, Bahya Ibn Pakuda is depicted as a philosopher who enlisted the Neoplatonist tendencies of his time for the enrichment of traditional Jewish religiosity. For one thing, Bahya's Neoplatonism is no longer purely metaphysical in character, but a somewhat adulterated version that has absorbed voluntaristic elements (primarily the creation idea). Moreover, Bahya is interested not in the metaphysical aspects of the system per se, but in the religious motifs coursing through it, those motifs that might help guide the community to the true service of God.[71] The same dialectic in Guttmann that juxtaposes the metaphysical-determinist characteristics of Ibn Gabirol against the Biblical-voluntaristic elements of Bahya is operating in his sketch of the basic outlines of Bahya's theory itself. On the one hand, Guttmann argues that Neoplatonist philosophy and Islamic religious asceticism merely provided Bahya with modes of expression and conceptual categories that validated his traditional Jewish religiosity. Bahya's religiosity stems first and foremost from the prophetic and Talmudic demand for religious inwardness and the direction of the soul to God. This, for him, surpasses all external practical systems in importance. The distinction between the Duties of the Limbs and the Duties of the Heart may have been taken from the Mu'tazilites, but it ultimately reflects an ancient, internal Jewish inclination.

On the other hand, writes Guttmann, Bahya goes beyond the Talmudic ethos in the direction of Neoplatonist ethics. While the Talmud treats this world as a vestibule within which one acquires merits in preparation for the world to come, positive value is ascribed to observing the practical commandments in the interpersonal sphere. In this fashion, Guttmann contends, the Talmud maintains the "activist" character of Jewish morality. In Bahya, by way of contrast, the purgative value of morality eclipses its practical value in the interpersonal realm. The primary task of moral behavior is to liberate the soul from the bonds of the sensual world in anticipation of its spiritual communion with God. Here as well, Guttmann underscores the Jewish elements in Bahya's teachings. Bahya's asceticist morality is still a far cry from the self-mortification of Neoplatonism and the Islamic religious sects. It is forbidden for a person to seclude himself completely and forswear human companionship solely for his own personal purification. He must participate in the life of society, without relinquishing the development of an inner attitude of indifference to temporal pleasures.

In his theology as well, the dual nature of Bahya's thought becomes apparent. While the conceptual definition of God as the one Absolute empties the Deity of all personal qualities, Bahya's religious sentiments ascribe to Him attributes of vitality and will more characteristic of the Jewish concept.[72]

YEHUDA HA-LEVI

The drama of medieval Jewish philosophy enters a new developmental stage with the appearance of R. Yehuda ha-Levi. Ha-Levi epitomizes the transition from Neoplatonism to Aristotelianism, a transition that also exercises substantial influence on the philosophy of religion in its modern version. Formally speaking, Guttmann classifies ha-Levi with the Neoplatonic school, yet he opens his essay on the latter with the following caveat: "The singular figure of Yehuda ha-Levi belongs to no philosophic school."[73] Ha-Levi is included in the chapter on Neoplatonism for two reasons. First, because he internalized formal Neoplatonist thought patterns in order to explain singular religious phenomena. He believed that the way to connect with God is by observing the practical commandments bestowed upon us through revelation, in a direct Divine initiative. Ha-Levi did not consider the commandments to be merely a kind of training that equips us to rise to the cognitive knowledge of God. The commandments, in conjunction with the climactic conditions of the Land of Israel and the special capacity for religious experience innate to the Jewish people, serve to foster a type of knowledge fundamentally different from theoretical knowledge. While theoretical-scientific knowledge views the Deity as an object of thought possessed of supreme logical status, religious knowledge—or "the Divine matter," in ha-Levi's words—calls for "life with God," the experience of an unmediated presence in a manner analogous to sensual perception. Still, in order to describe how the commandments, together with national and geographic particularity, do indeed foster this unique religious consciousness, ha-Levi resorts to explanation-categories drawn from the conceptual world of Neoplatonism. Just as the Active Intellect implants forms only in matter that is prepared to receive them, and that has attained the desired disposition, so the "Divine matter," the ability to experience the Divine presence in an unmediated fashion, is actualized only in those persons who have succeeded, aided by the three sources of assistance provided by God, in achieving the disposition required to receive this influence. Yet the use of conventional Neoplatonist forms of exegesis in order to create a unique religious category is insufficient reason to classify Yehuda ha-Levi as a Neoplatonist.[74]

The second reason for the connection Guttmann draws between ha-Levi and the Neoplatonist school, and on account of which he follows his discussion of ha-Levi with the chapter on Aristotelianism, stems largely from Guttmann's historiosophical premise whereby the Neoplatonist school in Jewish philosophy developed in three stages. The preliminary stage opened when Isaac Israeli made a first attempt, devoid of any real systematic awareness, to implant Neoplatonist ideas in Jewish soil. Ibn Gabirol represents the period in which the Neoplatonist theory was genuinely assimilated, as expressed through the production of original works within its framework, while Bahya signifies the period in which the theory was passed down, with certain Biblical modifications, for purposes of enriching traditional Jewish spirituality. However, from Guttmann's standpoint Jewish philosophy is not capable of giving a profound, self-conscious account of the contradictions between religious and scientific-theoretical truth within the Neoplatonist framework, nor of resolving them systematically. This is by virtue of the fact that the ethos informing the Neoplatonist system is fundamentally religious in character. While the Neoplatonist Deity is indeed an object of cognition, this cognition is supposed to lead humans to a religious connection and communion with God. The mystery of the recondite unity of God serves as a focal point for religious longings. In consequence, the tension between philosophic and revealed religion is not highly developed in Neoplatonism. The Aristotelian school, however, comes across in Guttmann as more intellectualist than Neoplatonism. The soul's ascent to metaphysical knowledge is largely contingent upon the study of logic and physics, and communion with God is tightly bound up with the Aristotelian premise of the happiness inhering in cognition per se. Thus when al-Ghazali and Yehuda ha-Levi polemicize with philosophy, and portray it as the enemy of revealed religion, they are referring to Aristotelian philosophy. From a historical standpoint it is not surprising, observes Guttmann, that these attacks are leveled in proximity to the systematic formulation of Aristotelianism by Ibn Sina.[75]

To Guttmann's way of thinking, then, ha-Levi serves as a vital link in the chronicles of medieval Jewish philosophy. His role in this drama is to articulate the basic conflict between the theoretical connection to the Deity as an object of cognition and the religious relation of "living with God" with full intensity.[76] Jewish philosophy, as an entity with a developing self-awareness, is insufficiently aware of the conflicts between the elements that exist within it, until ha-Levi arrives and articulates them in depth. This provides fertile ground for the subsequent attempt within the framework of the Aristotelian school, primarily by Maimonides, "to seek a solution that would overcome [the conflicts] from within."[77]

Yehuda ha-Levi's second main function, in Guttmann's opinion, is to anticipate trends in the modern philosophy of religion. In his attempt to penetrate to the structure and quality of religious phenomena and events, ha-Levi presages the phenomenological approach of Guttmann himself. Particularly noteworthy is the distinction he draws between theoretical knowledge, which recognizes only conceptual distinctions between objects, and the direct, intuitive and concrete God-experience of the pious Jew. In Guttmann's words, "The power and majesty of God are conveyed solely through the unmediated experience of God, for only through it can there arise the joy and bliss of communion with God."[78] Here ha-Levi, in the wake of al-Ghazali, moves the philosophy of religion forward by introducing an epistemological category that represents a discrete realm of human consciousness, a realm distinct from scientific and ethical consciousness. As Guttmann reminds us, ha-Levi is not able to transcend the boundaries of medieval discourse on the question of the relation between religion and science. In the middle ages religion presented itself as a revealed source of truth, rather than as a unique form of perception possessed by humans as such. The latter orientation would have to wait for the advent of the modern, "universalist" period. The special status of religious truth that ha-Levi refers to derives first and foremost from a heteronomous process of revelation, one directed exclusively to the Jewish people and embodied exclusively in the Torah.[79]

THE ARISTOTELIAN SCHOOL

We have seen that even if ha-Levi had recourse to Neoplatonism in the presentation of his teachings, his principal engagement was with Aristotelian philosophy. In the period succeeding his death, from the mid-twelfth century onward, the Aristotelian school gained pre-eminence in the philosophic circles of the Islamic world. Guttmann begins his essay on Aristotelianism and its opponents in characteristic dialectical fashion. He first surveys the subjects concerning which Aristotelianism was influenced by Neoplatonism, while insisting that Aristotelianism nonetheless preserved its cardinal tenets. Aristotelian theology speaks of the "supreme thought thinking itself," instead of the "One" that is beyond all thought. Aristotelian epistemology is oriented towards abstraction from the data of sensory perception, rather than towards the "remembering" of Platonic ideas. The intellectual-eudaemonic character of the Aristotelian system is maintained despite the religious aspirations to draw close to God that were absorbed from the Neoplatonist school.[80] This preface enables Guttmann to portray the intellectualist Aristotelian school as a distinct spiritual world in opposition to Biblical personalism. Yet even this thesis is not presented by Guttmann unequivocally but in dialectical fashion. For if the two orientations differed so drastically from one another, how could Jewish philosophers such as Ibn Daud regard Aristotelianism merely as a kind of philosophic confirmation of the tenets of Judaism, without recognizing the deep conflicts between it and Biblical personalism? To explain this phenomenon Guttmann finds it necessary to list those elements in Aristotelianism that appeared, with some degree of justification, to approximate known components of the Biblical worldview. Aristotelianism appears sympathetic to ideas such as the unity of God, the ethical-teleological orientation of the order of creation and the immortality of the soul. From a normative point of view, Aristotelian ethics also requires the intellect to control human desires.[81] However (and here the second aspect of Guttmann's dialectic reveals itself), on these very same subjects there is a significant gap between the two points of view. As Guttmann puts it, "The God of philosophy, whether in the

Neoplatonic version of the highest unity or in the Aristotelian version of the highest thought, is radically different from that of the personal, willing, and ethical God of the monotheistic religions."[82] The teleology of Aristotelianism is grounded in a dynamic-deterministic lawful pattern, such that "A Divine providence, if it is to mean anything at all, can only mean the purposive causality of all processes as grounded in God." Even the immortality of the soul becomes "intellectually and not morally determined."[83]

From here Guttmann proceeds to discuss the ways in which the Arab Aristotelians addressed these significant conflicts prior to Maimonides' time. The Islamic thinkers' method for reconciling the premises of Biblical revelation with the Aristotelian system is also depicted in bipolar dialectical fashion. On the one hand Islamic philosophers expounded Biblical perspectives in Aristotelian terms; yet Guttmann does not believe that they merely adopted an idiomatic Aristotelian terminology in order to express Biblical ideas in the language of the time, as Wolfson maintains. In Guttmann's evaluation, the Islamic sages exchanged Biblical articles of faith for Aristotelian doctrines without feeling that in so doing they were deviating from the original import of personalism. The most prominent example of this trend is related to the subject of providence: The purposiveness of the Divine will is transformed by the Islamists into the inner purposiveness of the dynamic lawfulness of nature, which imbues matter with forms in keeping with a Divine principle of form.[84] From Wolfson's standpoint this does not constitute a deviation or innovation on the part of medieval thought vis-à-vis the original scriptural philosophy. To his way of thinking, Philo had already understood the Divine will to be active primarily through the establishment and preservation of the laws of nature. The proof text for this assumption was God's promise to Noah after the flood. As we have seen, Wolfson did not believe that any real development took place in religious thought from the foundation of scriptural philosophy until the present. Guttmann, in contrast, did not flinch from pointing out significant departures from Biblical personalism that could be discovered in medieval religious thought, in keeping with his developmental-evolutionary view.

On the other side of the dialectic, we find that the Islamic sages tempered certain Aristotelian doctrines in order to render them as similar as possible to personalist religious ideas. Ibn Sina, for example, insisted that the limitation of Divine knowledge to the laws governing the forms does not mean that God is unaware of individuals. Alfarabi, for his part, argued that Aristotle's theory of the eternity of the world is less than absolute.[85] Yet Maimonides and his Jewish philosophic successors did not consider it sufficient to take the naturalistic sting out of the Aristotelian system. Maimonides preferred to present the Aristotelian position on the eternity of the world in all its severity, rather than resolving the conflicts between personalism and metaphysics by way of mutual adaptation and by ignoring difficulties. Guttmann depicts Maimonides and his disciples as thinkers who made an original and universal contribution to the philosophy of religion, through their aspiration "to formulate the problem [of the relation between religious and scientific thought] in all its sharpness and to seek a solution that would overcome it from within."[86] On the basis of the pure philosophic criteria of consciousness and systematic method, then, medieval Jewish Aristotelian thought is revealed to be the most profound of the medieval religious philosophies.

IBN DAUD

The philosopher Ibn Daud was "the first Jewish Aristotelian,"[87] and he serves a parallel function to that of Isaac Israeli in the Neoplatonist school. Just as Isaac Israeli grafted the Neoplatonist system onto Jewish soil without grasping the depth of the conflict between the Biblical creation doctrine and the theory of emanation, so Ibn Daud brought Judaism and Aristotelianism into contact without being aware of the systematic contradictions inherent in his approach. Yehuda ha-Levi, who was active after Israeli, was aware of the huge gap between the Biblical, personalist orientation to God and the philosophical natural-intellectual orientation. Through him Jewish philosophy attained a high level of self-awareness, by becoming alert to the disharmony between the two religious postures that served as the basis for its deliberations. Ibn Daud's writings, however, show no indications that the polemic of al-Ghazali and ha-Levi with Aristotelianism had influenced him, and "Like most Jewish Neoplatonists, he simply approximated or equated philosophic theories and religious ideas, circumventing rather than solving the problem of their difference."[88] Nevertheless, he enjoys the same credit awarded Isaac Israeli as he "has all the interest attaching to the beginnings of all great historical processes."[89]

In contradistinction to the philosopher Ibn Daud who blurred the opposition between the world of personalism and that of metaphysics, Maimonides absorbed the legacy of Yehuda ha-Levi and "threw the opposition between Aristotelianism and Biblical revelation into bold relief in order to overcome it by a genuine synthesis."[90]

MAIMONIDES

Maimonides' originality, in Guttmann's view, does not consist in the invention of new ideas. His strength lies instead in the ability to make creative syntheses between existing worldviews.[91] The portrait of Maimonides that emerges from Guttmann's scholarship, however, is largely at odds with this contention. Admittedly, Guttmann articulates Maimonides' epistemology and theory of religion in synthetic terms; the level of one's philosophic understanding determines the level of one's attainment of religious certainty. Unlike ha-Levi, Maimonides does not regard religious certainty as an inner conviction independent of intellectual attainments. A person's inner religiosity, his conscious sense of connection to God, is contingent upon the depth of his philosophic understanding. From ha-Levi's standpoint, the immediacy of the religious experience requires that it subsist in an entirely different dimension than through the agency of the intellect. Maimonides, on the other hand, contends that precisely the attempt to grasp physical and metaphysical concepts through cognitive means enriches the religious experience directly, while a reliance on authoritative historical tradition connects humans with religious objects only indirectly. For Maimonides, then, philosophic knowledge is both a foundation and a precondition for religious knowledge.[92]

Even if Maimonides' basic epistemological approach as depicted by Guttmann can be characterized as genuinely synthetic, this is not the case with regard to other classic issues in religious philosophy. When we inquire into such topics as theology, the theory of creation and the theory of prophecy, there seems at times to be a contradiction between the historical role Maimonides plays within Guttmann's developmental scheme and the manner in which Guttmann characterizes Maimonides' actual positions on these subjects.

For instance, with regard to theology Maimonides adopts the strict Neoplatonic doctrine of the unity of God as it was internalized by medieval Arab Aristotelianism. Maimonides' theoretical contribution to buttressing this theory of unity is systematic rather than substantive. He articulates the theory and grounds it systematically and with marked consistency, demonstrating in the process his unparalleled philosophic virtuosity. Yet Maimonides fails to introduce any Jewish content into the theory that could fuse with the Aristotelian elements. The Jewish aspect of Maimonides' theology is expressed not in the content of the doctrine, but in his motives for enhancing it. In Guttmann's evaluation, Maimonides considered the purgation of corporeal elements from the God-concept to be a religious obligation.[93] This combination of motivation and sense of obligation stemming from the Jewish side with the philosophic acuteness of the Aristotelian system does not constitute any real blending of the contents of the two traditions.

With regard to the theory of attributes as well, Guttmann distinguishes between the formal side of Maimonides' arguments and the expressive-religious side. Formally speaking, Maimonides adopts the Neoplatonist doctrine that the Deity is a perfect unity and consequently unknowable. On the other hand, Maimonides' God is the creator God of the Bible, a personal

God whose vitality and connectedness to his creation are not consistent with a unity that is always sufficient unto itself.[94] According to Guttmann, Maimonides' negation of all divine attributes actually enables him to establish a thoroughly personalist religious relation. Admittedly, by denying the existence of knowledge, will or power in God, we eliminate the possibility that He could have qualities of a type familiar to us in physical or human life. Yet in so doing we hint at the possibility that hidden within Him are mysterious, unknown qualities analogous to human qualities, which afford the Deity a positive, active character. Accordingly, the formal side of Maimonides' theory becomes the foundation for the expression of a religious relation. Here too, however, we find no actual substantive synthesis.[95]

Similarly, with regard to Maimonides' creation theory, Guttmann is unable to justify his claim that Maimonides' historical role was to reconcile two extremes whose battle lines were sharply drawn by Yehuda ha-Levi. Maimonides did indeed make a critical philosophic contribution of the first order on this issue. He argues that the intellect is capable of determining truths only concerning the lawfulness operating in the universe since its inception; it is not, however, competent to describe the process of transition from the non-existence of the world to its creation and the establishment of these lawful patterns. Accordingly, the intellect cannot decide the question of the eternity or creation of the world. In the absence of philosophic certainty, Maimonides tilts the scales in favor of the traditional religious doctrine of creation. Here too, then, he produces no substantive synthesis; he rather creates the philosophic conditions that permit a decision in favor of religion.[96]

With regard to the theory of prophecy, Maimonides makes a point of rescuing prophecy, understood as a divine commission, from the naturalist imperialism of philosophy, just as he saved voluntaristic creation from the supposed universality of Aristotelian causality. In Guttmann's view, Maimonides adopted the Aristotelian view that prophecy is the natural outcome of human cognitive development directed towards the intellectual apprehension of the Deity. Yet according to *The Guide of the Perplexed*, God can deny a person prophecy despite the fact that the latter has fulfilled all of the natural conditions for receiving it. While admittedly God does not select prophets directly, and the prophet's mission does not stem from the will of God alone, the Divine prerogative to deny prophetic illumination even to persons who have prepared themselves for it always remains intact. If this is Maimonides' real opinion, and Guttmann believes that it is, then again there is no synthesis here, only an artificial and arbitrary obstruction of naturalist imperialism when it happens to pose a threat to Biblical personalism.[97]

Both Maimonides' theory of creation and his theory of prophecy, then, reveal Maimonides to be a thoroughly Aristotelian thinker, whose substantive positions and discursive style were drawn largely from Greek-Arab metaphysics. Guttmann defines Maimonides' teachings as "theistic Aristotelianism," depicting him as a thinker who succeeded in establishing a place for the creator God of the Bible within the framework of Aristotelian cosmology.[98] In other words, Maimonides produced not a synthesis of personalist and metaphysical-causal positions, somehow staking out a middle ground between the two traditions, but a somewhat tempered version of Aristotelianism. Although Guttmann does not claim that Maimonides achieved a synthesis on every theological issue he addressed, he nevertheless sums up Maimonides' historical contribution, particularly with regard to creation theory, as a "true fusion," metaphysically speaking, between Biblical religion and Aristotelianism.[99]

Guttmann, then, portrays medieval Jewish philosophic development before Maimonides as a schema of dialectical evolution according to the criterion of self-awareness. Isaac Israeli implants Neoplatonist ideas in Jewish soil without any awareness of the fundamental conflicts involved. Ibn Gabirol represents systematic progress, although he accepts Neoplatonism unequivocally, with no attempt to stage a systematic confrontation between personalism and metaphysics. Bahya Ibn Pakuda also neglects to make any such attempt: His thought represents a watered-down version of Neoplatonism that is subordinated on cardinal points to traditional Jewish religiosity grounded in faith, humility and submission. With Yehuda ha-Levi, who pointed out the fundamental oppositions between the two religious orientations, Jewish philosophy develops further and becomes conscious of its own conflicting foundations. Within the framework of Neoplatonist religiosity, however, these conflicts are not sufficiently sharp to stimulate an attempt at synthesis between metaphysics and personalism. It was necessary for Ibn Daud to come along and initiate an encounter between the more scientific brand of Aristotelianism and Judaism. Yet only Maimonides, aware as he is of the deep conflicts between personalism and metaphysics, can establish a place for the creator God of the Bible within the framework of Aristotelian cosmology by way of fully-self-conscious reflection.

We are faced, then, with a historiosophic scheme that portrays the process of the ascent of Jewish philosophy to self-awareness through a series of necessary stages.[100] Although Guttmann adopts a critical-external stance towards the authoritative status of the idea of development prevalent among nineteenth century Jewish thinkers, he himself seems to describe the history of religious Jewish philosophy according to a developmental telos that leads to "spirit knowing itself" (in the sense of religious spirit).[101] In Wolfson we have seen that the encounter between Biblical religion and Greek philosophy concluded with the triumph of Biblical principles, as Western philosophy was shaped by Biblical tenets.[102] For Guttmann, by way of contrast, the very texture of Judaism itself was deeply influenced by this encounter, which brought Judaism to reflect upon its own unique personalist elements. His assumption is that a reflective awareness of the uniqueness of the Jewish religious orientation is attainable only through dialectical engagement with an opposing, but also profound, religious worldview. Personalist Judaism, however, paid a heavy price for this encounter. Maimonides, for all his awareness of the difference between creation and emanation, did not acknowledge the extent to which he deviated from the ideals and religious values of the "original" Judaism. Maimonides transferred the emphasis in Jewish religiosity from the awareness of a personal relation to God contingent upon an active moral imperative, to intellectual inquiry. In so doing he infused Jewish culture with Aristotelian ideals, without recognizing the conflict between these ideals and the religious values of Biblical and rabbinic Judaism.[103] The implication of all this was that medieval Jewish philosophy at its peak remained in an important sense alienated from itself, in the grip of an intellectualist religiosity foreign to it. Only in the modern period, through the neo-Kantian influence of Hermann Cohen, would reflective Jewish philosophy return to the ethical-activist underpinnings of Biblical religion.

THE TRANSITION FROM THE MEDIEVAL TO THE MODERN PERIOD—WOLFSON'S SPINOZA AND GUTTMANN'S SPINOZA

Before Guttmann launches his discussion of the modern period of Jewish philosophy, which in his view brought Judaism to a reflective awareness of its ethical and personalist foundations, he devotes a chapter to the subject of "The Influence of Jewish Philosophy on the System of Spinoza." Guttmann regards Spinoza as a kind of transitional figure between the middle ages and modernity. Despite the fact that Spinoza liberated discourse on the religious phenomenon from its subjugation to historical religions based on unique revelations,[104] he still persists in identifying final religious truth with the conclusions of theoretical metaphysics and is not yet able to treat ethics or religion as domains of consciousness with independent validity.[105] We will now address Spinoza's place in Guttmann's historiosophic scheme, while comparing it with the key role Spinoza plays in the subversion of Biblical philosophy in Wolfson, in order to further elucidate the systematic differences between the two scholars.

In Wolfson's evaluation, "significant time" in the history of philosophy was that period when full commitment to Biblical doctrines prevailed, and when philosophy served to articulate the Biblical faith most clearly and systematically. Tensions arose in medieval religious philosophy from the need to reconcile logical contradictions between fundamental Biblical premises regarding the independence and freedom of God and human beings from nature, and the systematic-naturalistic aspiration of philosophy to encompass both God and man in a unified cosmological order. So long as Western philosophy maintained its commitment to Biblical doctrines, it was willing, as a matter of deliberate choice, to bear the logical tensions that sometimes arose between these doctrines and the quest for philosophic totality. Spinoza, the Jew who was intimately acquainted with Philonism but rejected the authority of the Bible, developed motifs and concepts that already existed in scriptural philosophy in order to refute that very framework. Spinoza did not advance religious philosophy, nor did he introduce new content into it. Quite the contrary: He returned religious philosophy to its pagan pre-history, when philosophy did not regard the Bible as an authoritative source of metaphysical knowledge. To Wolfson's way of thinking, that philosophy which is called modern, which arose in the aftermath of Spinoza, is an expression not of progress but of regression. It merely clothes ancient Greek heresy in a different conceptual garb.[106]

Guttmann ordains a different task for Spinoza in his historiosophic scheme: not that of the dismantler of the tradition alone, but that of heir and innovator. Aristotelian Jewish thought, which founds the religious connection to God upon the happiness inhering in knowledge, was Spinoza's philosophic starting point.[107] Nevertheless, Spinoza purged Aristotelian intellectualism of its teleological elements, transforming the content of human knowledge into a causal-mechanistic system devoid of all value distinctions.[108] Wolfson, characteristically, stresses Spinoza's roots in the past, construing his mathematical formulations as merely an expressive mode for the transmission of quintessentially medieval philosophic concepts.[109] Guttmann, in contrast, discerns innovations and genuine development in the history of thought, and he acknowledges the impact of contemporary, extra-philosophic streams of thought and culture on Jewish thinkers. From his vantage point, then, to the same extent that Spinoza's teachings were influenced by the medieval heritage, they were also influenced by the scientific vision of the seventeenth century, namely, "to comprehend science as a mathematical-causal nexus . . . and [Spinoza] transferred this ideal from the science of nature to the knowledge of the whole of reality. For him, the notion of law in the natural sciences became the axiom of metaphysical knowledge."[110] Thus the mathematical form of Spinoza's exposition is no mere explanatory mode, as Wolfson alleged, but the faithful reflection of a worldview that strives to cast a logical-mathematical web over all manifestations of cognitive and physical reality.

In this frame of reference it is also significant that according to Guttmann Spinoza is not merely the profound and systematic heretic we find in Wolfson; Wolfson measures a person's faith or heresy ("paganism") according to the criterion of his concurrence or non-concurrence with Biblical tenets of faith. Consequently, Spinoza's rejection of the revelatory status of the Bible—and in the process, of Biblical doctrines such as creation, providence and prophecy—renders him pagan in Wolfson's eyes. Wolfson is not interested in religiosity as a state of soul. To the extent that he has a religious orientation, it consists in the readiness (which in his view has rational force as well) to assent to articles of faith offered to humans by way of a heteronomous revelation. Spinoza's unwillingness to accept articles of faith that autonomous reason cannot sustain makes him a heretic. Given that his particular heresy issues specifically from an intimate acquaintance with scriptural philosophy and its problems, he is the most suitable figure to have concluded the period of pure religious philosophy and to clear the philosophic way for the old-new "modern" heresies.[111]

Guttmann's position, in contrast, is that religiosity is not measured by the acceptance or non-acceptance of heteronomous articles of faith. Religiosity is a longing, issuing from emotional sources as well, for an object to which sanctity is ascribed. This longing is a universal and autonomous human phenomenon. There are different types of religiosity, such as the aesthetic, the intellectualist and the ethical, yet generally speaking there is no major philosophic system that is devoid of religious motivation.[112] Accordingly, in Guttmann's conviction, Spinoza's attempt to exorcise value distinctions (aside from the value residing in theoretical comprehension) from the realms of cognition and nature is not an expression of religious neutrality or of a secular consciousness. By denying the existence of value distinctions and value hierarchies in the structure of the cosmos, Spinoza seeks precisely to ascribe an equal and all-encompassing value to reality in all of its manifestations. In Guttmann's words, "For him, the denial of all differences in value, which is implicit in the scientific world view, becomes a religious affirmation of existence, which by reason of God's activity is extended equally to all beings. The value of a perfection which is indifferent to all valuation becomes the bearer of religious affirmations of value, implanted in all beings. . . . God, who in accord with his logical content can be labeled the concept of being of the natural sciences, becomes the object of a mystical divine feeling."[113]

From Guttmann's standpoint, then, Spinoza is not a heretic but the paradigm of an intellectualist religious type. For medieval Aristotelians, theoretical understanding was not the only activity of consciousness; volition and emotion were also considered to be independent phenomena. In Spinoza, by comparison, all aspects of consciousness are derived from the theoretical impulse to create images (whether physical or conceptual).[114] In Guttmann's opinion, this intellectualist religiosity is unaware of the fact that its emotional, volitional and even epistemological origins are to be found in a unique religious domain of consciousness that is not merely an aspect of the theoretical. Medieval Jewish philosophy, which led to the growth of a theoretical Jewish religiosity while distancing itself from its personalist Biblical origins, had much in common with Spinoza, who fathered the purest and most extreme kind of intellectualist religiosity. With Spinoza, however, religious intellectualism exhausted itself, and in so doing created an opening (contrary to Wolfson's opinion) for the continuing growth of religious thought in the modern period. As Guttmann puts it in the last sentences he devotes to medieval religious Jewish philosophy: "Spinoza pursued the intellectualizing of the moral and religious consciousness to its logical extreme. The impossibility of grasping the nature of religion and ethics in terms of the presuppositions of a strict intellectualism necessarily became obvious in his system."[115] Spinoza, then, not only marks the conclusion of an era; he also brings religious philosophy to the point at which it is compelled, out of inner teleological necessity, to embark on a new era. Henceforth, Jewish religious philosophy will be constrained to move beyond intellectualism and to clarify, in evolutionary-incremental fashion, the independent foundations of religion and morality. Spinoza was not aware of the independent religious sources that prompted him to sanctify the scientific worldview. Such a level of consciousness could be achieved only after additional cumulative reflection, which was to conclude with the insights of Hermann Cohen and Julius Guttmann himself.

THE MODERN PERIOD: THE SIGNS OF MODERNITY IN RELIGIOUS JEWISH PHILOSOPHY

We have noted Wolfson's ambivalence regarding modernity. On the one hand, he recognized the contribution of the modern period to the progress of science and politics in the empirical and social realms. He considered the Copernican revolution an achievement of the first order and was even willing to accord a qualified legitimacy to the theory of evolution in the field of biology. With regard to matters of state, Wolfson valued the contributions of democracy and federalism. Yet in metaphysical matters, in all that concerns the nature of the Deity and His relation to humans and to the cosmos, Wolfson doggedly criticized the presumption of the modern period in allowing limited human reason supreme authority in place of Divine revelation. Wolfson praised the medieval thinkers for their fidelity to fundamental Biblical premises, their ascription of a genuine transcendence to God and their deep, sincere motivation to undertake the work of reconciling the contradictions between the unifying monism of philosophy and the ontic pluralism of the Bible. Wolfson regarded the modern period as a period of decline, a regression that prompted the revival of classic Greek heresies and the establishment of false gods who represent human ideals and aspirations.[116]

For Guttmann, on the other hand, the modern period advanced Jewish philosophical discourse from several points of view. At first glance this assertion might seem surprising, for in the modern period, according to Guttmann himself, the unity of Jewish culture disintegrated. In the middle ages most areas of cultural activity, such as commentary, poetry, homiletic discourse and even philosophy, were rooted, at least in part, in traditional religious culture. In Europe of the modern period, most cultural fields—including the aesthetic, literary and philosophic realms—were overtaken by the surrounding non-Jewish culture.[117] Yet Guttmann contends that "Despite the fact that the medieval thinkers were, in their total personalities, far more deeply rooted in the tradition and substance of Jewish life, and that belief in the Divine authority of revelation was self-evident to them, the modern thinkers, in their theoretical explanation of Judaism, upheld with greater staunchness the true meaning of its central religious doctrines."[118] How so? It was precisely the liberation from an unequivocal commitment to a unique, authoritative and heteronomous revelation—a liberation that is one of the hallmarks of modernity—which enabled the universal and autonomous human consciousness to attain untrammeled self-awareness and to recognize the religious relation as embedded in the very core of its being. This awareness, mediated by theoretical and moral knowledge, is itself a Divine gift, though given precisely so that it might be autonomous.[119]

Modernity enables the autonomous religious consciousness to become fully aware of itself since the spirit is liberated from the bounds of a given legal tradition. Furthermore, the reflective discussion of religion is liberated from its identification with metaphysics. Kantian philosophy destroyed all faith in the ability of metaphysics to provide theoretical proof of the fundamental tenets of faith. The search for a rational justification and grounding for religion was transferred to the realm of ethics. Religion in general and Judaism in particular were perceived to contain the necessary postulates of the ethical life—the existence of God, providence and the immortality of the soul. The premise that the Jewish religion reflects the universal truth of a rational, ethical religion in its purest historical form, and that Judaism is the spiritual core of a universal human faith, furnished a solid basis for religious self-awareness.[120] The definition of the essence of the religious relation in ethical terms, as a relation with a Deity who makes ethical demands upon us, returned Judaism, this time by way of a reflective awareness, to the original ethical-activist orientation from which it had strayed in the middle ages. Yet this evolutionary movement was also gradual. Despite Guttmann's contention that Jewish thought in the modern period is characterized not by sequential development but by a series of discrete phenomena,[121] a developmental framework is recognizable in his discussion of the modern period as well.

MENDELSSOHN

Moses Mendelssohn is the first thinker whose philosophic work was regarded by Guttmann as having been undertaken within the framework of modern assumptions. His philosophic activity is based on the presupposition that cultural life in all of its manifestations is autonomous, rather than the expression of a particular religious tradition. Mendelssohn identifies with the modern aspiration to create an interreligious cultural community founded on common religious and ethical beliefs that are free of ecclesiastical particularity.[122] Guttmann depicts Mendelssohn's teachings as an unreconciled mixture of medieval and modern elements. On the one hand, Mendelssohn's understanding of the relation between reason and revelation is close to the medieval model, a model that was in consonance with the "conservative enlightenment" of his time. The authenticity of a given religion is measured not according to the criterion of miracles, but according to the degree of correlation between its beliefs and the judgments of reason. In the spirit of Maimonides, it is reason that grants validity to revelation, not miracles. Mendelssohn also supports Maimonides' statement in the *Mishneh Torah* that the validity of the revelation at Sinai derives not from its status as a miracle, whether private or public, but from the fact that it constituted a direct revelation of the Divine presence to an entire people, an event that was passed down through the testimony of one generation to the next. In subsequent generations the theory of particular, historical revelation was subject to much scientific criticism; in Mendelssohn's age, however, belief in revelation was not considered to involve a lack of intellectual honesty.[123] In other fields, however, Mendelssohn departs from medieval thought-frameworks, thereby revealing himself to be the first genuinely modern Jewish thinker. From his standpoint, the rational foundations of religion are not to be found within esoteric metaphysical frameworks reserved for philosophers alone. The universal nature of natural religion derives not from its being moored in philosophic thought-patterns that recognize no cultural boundaries, but from the fact that it can be apprehended by the natural healthy intellect of every rational being. While metaphysics is justly grounded in rigorous processes of logical discourse, religious knowledge is not contingent upon metaphysical erudition, but upon the unmediated certainty of simple, unbiased reason, along the lines of "Behold who created all of these." Along with the severance of the necessary connection between religion and philosophic metaphysics, we find here a democratization of the religious consciousness. For Guttmann both these developments are signs of progress in the understanding of the essence of religion.[124]

Mendelssohn's premise that religious truth is accessible to the common sense of every person, regardless of culture or origin, led to two additional principles. First, the unmediated religious truth of "the heavens proclaim His glory" is not subject to historical or developmental stages. While theoretical reason progresses cumulatively, the basic religious and moral certainties are not merely the outcome of professional metaphysical discussion, and they remain eternal in nature.[125] This position is consistent with

Guttmann's own aspiration to create typologies of religiosity that are independent of historical development (although, as we have seen, he himself is not free of an evolutionary orientation concerning religious phenomena). Mendelssohn's democratic principles help him transcend medieval conventions in portraying the relation between reason and revelation. Saadia Gaon and Maimonides postulated that metaphysical truth, which is also religious truth, can in principle be attained through reason without the assistance of revelation. Revelation serves to publicize and educate, since, without an authoritative revelation from on high, few human beings would succeed in attaining such truths through their own powers. In Mendelssohn's view, by comparison, revelation does not serve to disseminate the eternal truths, since these can be attained without the aid of revelation not only by philosophers, but by all human beings who have eyes to see.[126] The unmediated religious relation to the creator and providential God existed among the children of Israel before the Torah was given, and it constitutes a precondition for revelation, rather than being part and parcel of it. Revelation includes laws, which protect the religious relation from the corrosion of idol worship and remind us of eternal truths by creating common experiences of remembrance and devotion, yet revelation is not itself identical with these truths.[127]

Within the framework of Guttmann's scheme, Mendelssohn's transformation of revelation into pure (or almost pure) law is a first stage in the weakening of heteronomous revelation as a component in the religious consciousness of the modern Jew. The denial of rational and religious significance to the laws of the Torah—although this was not absolute even in Mendelssohn himself—was perceived by his students to be a devaluation of heteronomous revelation, similar to the kind that occurred in the wake of later deistic and scientific-scholarly critiques of historical religion.[128] In Wolfson, to recall, this process was deemed regressive, for Wolfson did not believe that scientific critique had succeeded in subverting faith in the revealed character of the Bible.[129] Guttmann, however, as a liberal Jew, definitely shifted the category of revelation from its textual, historical sense such that it might signify the gift of autonomous religious consciousness. From Guttmann's point of view this reorientation seems to have begun already with Mendelssohn, who focused his inquiry into the truth of religion on the independent consciousness of the ordinary person, while according the Torah the function of a mere law code. Mendelssohn's fidelity to the commandments of the Torah stemmed, Guttmann surmises, from the religious sentiments he inherited from his forefathers, and from a certain pessimism regarding the ability of the religion of reason to survive in pagan surroundings without the support of a legal code. Yet this connection to his forefathers' tradition did not fuse into a synthesis with his assumptions regarding the autonomy of the human religious consciousness.[130]

According to Guttmann's theory, then, Mendelssohn represents a first encounter between traditional Jewish religiosity and the fundamental premises of the Enlightenment. This encounter did not yet produce any real tension, for two reasons. First, the Enlightenment itself had not yet arrived at metaphysical conclusions hostile to the Biblical faith, as would occur in the nineteenth century, when religious philosophy was influenced by German speculative idealism.[131] Second, Mendelssohn himself assigned his loyalty to the commandments and his identification with the natural religion of reason to different compartments of his consciousness.[132] Both his simple religiosity[133] and the conservatism of the surrounding Enlightenment[134] precluded his becoming a synthetic figure who could harmonize the conflicting elements within himself. Thus from the standpoint of Guttmann's historiosophic scheme, Mendelssohn is a sort of "Isaac Israeli" or "Ibn Daud" of the modern period: the type who effects an encounter between two worlds, yet without bringing them into self-conscious, systematic interaction.

FORMSTECHER AND HIRSCH

We have seen that in Guttmann's view the modern period in Jewish philosophy can be characterized by two primary developments:

1. Liberation from the heteronomous and particularist revelation-concept, and the construal of the religious consciousness as a domain of perception engaged in by the autonomous, universal human spirit.
2. Liberation from the identification between religious perception and the apprehension of metaphysical truth, and a return to the identification between the religious consciousness and the reception of absolute ethical imperatives. In this fashion religious thought returns to the original ethos of the Bible, despite, or perhaps even because of, its alienation from the Bible's external legal authority.[135]

After Mendelssohn these two processes intensified, though not to the same extent. On the one hand, faith in a particularist supernatural heteronomous revelation eroded. One could no longer encounter detailed interpretive attempts to create absolute identity between the contents of the revelatory message and recognized philosophic theories on the part of systematic philosophers in the modern period. Instead, efforts would be made to create a more general identification between the principles of the ethical religion of reason and those of Judaism as an evolving historical faith.[136]

In Guttmann's evaluation, however, the Kantian critique of the objectivity of metaphysics did not immediately take root. Post-Kantian idealism deviates gravely from Kant's teachings, in his view. This speculative idealism does not ascribe to spirit the modest and fitting role of deriving absolute moral imperatives, but rather the presumptuous role of deriving all of being from dialectical logical rules. This turnabout could not fail to have an impact on the course of development of Jewish religious philosophy. Just as in medieval times Jewish thinkers operated within the framework of the major external schools of Islamic philosophic culture—the Kalam, Neoplatonism and Aristotelianism—so in the modern period the philosophers Formstecher, Hirsch, Krochmal and Steinheim were decisively influenced by the German idealism of Fichte, Schelling and primarily Hegel.[137]

It is illuminating to find in Guttmann's writings, a definite analogy between the roles of nineteenth-century thinkers and those of the medieval period. We have already seen that Mendelssohn was assigned the role of creating "an unconscious encounter of two spiritual worlds," as Isaac Israeli does in the middle ages. Within the framework of the Hegelian school, Formstecher and Hirsch fill the role of R. Saadia Gaon, Krochmal the role of Solomon Ibn Gabirol, Steinheim the role of R. Yehuda ha-Levi and Hermann Cohen the role of Maimonides. Evidently, then, despite Guttmann's observation that Jewish philosophy of the modern period does not exhibit the same kind of continuity that prevailed in medieval times, he portrays a fairly continuous development in Jewish thought by way of progressive and almost necessary stages.

Solomon Formstecher and Samuel Hirsch approach the idealistic school from a Saadian-theological perspective. According to Guttmann, Saadia Gaon was the first Jewish philosopher to explicitly belong to a well-known external school, and he adopts both fundamental positions and structure of discourse from this school. Nevertheless, Saadia stakes out an explicitly theological stance, expressed through his independent criticisms of beliefs that in his mind contravene the Biblical worldview.[138] By the same token, Formstecher and Hirsch follow in the footsteps of prominent representatives of the German idealism of the early nineteenth century (Schelling and Hegel, respectively), both from a substantive point of view and in the style of their argumentation. Nevertheless, they institute changes in those elements of the idealistic system that could potentially threaten fundamental Biblical tenets.[139]

Samuel Hirsch, for instance, adopts the Hegelian approach on two central issues. On the question of the relation between religious and philosophic knowledge, he argues like Hegel that the mission of philosophy is not to supply new spiritual content, but to raise the content of the religious consciousness from the unmediated sphere of emotion and images to the sphere of the logical-necessary link between concepts. Similarly, his historiosophical discussion is undertaken according to a dialectical Hegelian scheme, with paganism being led stage by stage to an awareness of its limitations, and consequently to self-negation.[140] Yet fundamental Hegelian premises, as well as historiosophical methodology, are arrested at the stage at which they begin to endanger the basic tenets of Biblical religion.

Hegel maintained that philosophy is only a more abstract version of religious knowledge, and that the content of the knowledge itself undergoes no substantial change in the process of conceptual refinement. Guttmann, however, argues that in practice Hegel essentially transformed the contents of religion. In Guttmann's opinion, the genuine religious consciousness as presented in the Bible treats humans as possessed of absolute free will, and not as a function of some process of self-realization on the part of reason. Hegel and Hirsch concur that the uniqueness of humans lies in their ability to say "I" to themselves and in so doing to grasp themselves as standing over and against the world rather than being part of it. The two of them call this ability "abstract freedom." We see here that Hegel and Hirsch both begin at the same starting point and employ a common philosophic terminology. Yet for Hegel, "the logical pantheist," a person's abstract freedom necessarily turns into "actual freedom" when he participates in the self-realization of reason. While in Hirsch, the Biblical Jew, progress towards abstract freedom must be made not through some necessary developmental transition (from finite to infinite reason), but by preserving the possibility of choice. Hirsch understands the supreme ethical value of humans to consist not in participation in the self-articulation of reason, but in the choice between passive surrender to one's sensual nature or the active subordination of the senses through the activation of free will.[141]

Hirsch's tendency to constrain the Hegelian system in order to prevent it from threatening the ethical personalism of the Bible surfaces again in his historiosophic scheme. In Hegel, a dialectical lawfulness encompasses all phenomena of the spirit, within whose framework a transition takes place from "transcendent" Judaism (in which the spirit is still understood to be divided into infinite Divine spirit and finite human spirit) to "immanent" Christianity, which represents the principle of the inclusion of the infinite spirit within the finite spirit. According to Hirsch, in contrast, this necessary dialectical development applies only to paganism, namely, to the subjugation of freedom to nature and the transformation of sensual nature into a Divine principle. The necessary stages of the development of paganism lead from within themselves to the revelation of the inadequacy of sensual nature as a Divine principle. Judaism, however, is immune to this dialectical lawfulness. Every person, at any time, who has attained active ethical freedom and does not passively subject his freedom to his sensual nature, can grasp the content of an ahistorical religious truth.[142]

Formstecher and Hirsch, then, are active within the framework of the German idealist school in similar fashion to R. Saadia Gaon's activities within the framework of the medieval Kalam. Both have a thoroughly Biblical worldview, namely: They understand the essence of the religious consciousness to be more connected to ethical freedom than to the contemplation of theoretical truth. This Biblical insight is dominant for them, and the manner in which they adapt their school's defining concepts ("abstract reason," "actual freedom," "spirit becoming conscious of itself," etc.) as well as the scope to which they employ the historiosophic categories characteristic of the school (the unfolding of spiritual phenomena through necessary stages) are conditioned by their commitment to the fundamental tenets of Biblical religiosity.

RABBI NACHMAN KROCHMAL

R. Nachman Krochmal adopts a different position towards the idealist school, a position that suggests an almost complete internalization of its premises and modes of discourse. In this Krochmal parallels R. Solomon Ibn Gabirol, who belonged entirely to the Neoplatonist school, and in whose theory Jewish voluntarism is only barely perceptible. Contrary to Formstecher and Hirsch, who accepted the terminology and the schemata of the idealists yet limited them in relation to Judaism,[143] Krochmal held the conclusions of German idealism to be identical with the inner truth of Judaism.[144] After the fashion of the medieval Arab Neoplatonists and in the spirit of nineteenth-century German idealism, he believed that religiosity at its peak aspires to intellectual identification and communion with the "Absolute Spiritual."[145] His religious orientation was thoroughly intellectualist. He considered the world to be derived from the Deity through a necessary causality and deemed the "Absolute Spiritual" to include and comprehend limited spiritual ideas that exist in their own right and are reflected in the reciprocal relations between phenomena in the material and historical world. The creation narrative for him was merely a concrete and vivid way of expressing the philosophic theory of emanation. In his perspective, the religious impulse to unite with the source of being is identical to the philosophic impulse to know the abstract and most comprehensive truth.[146]

Krochmal, then, adopts the religious and intellectual values of idealism; in so doing he betrays the influence of the medieval tradition of Ibn Ezra and Maimonides.[147] Maimonides, however, adhered to the voluntaristic Biblical creation doctrine, justifying it philosophically within the framework of the Aristotelian school.[148] Krochmal, by comparison, is closer to the Arab Neoplatonists and to Ibn Ezra, as he judges the Biblical creation narrative to be merely an imaginative way of expressing the philosophic truth of emanation.[149]

As already noted, the historical function Krochmal serves in Guttmann's theory resembles that of Ibn Gabirol. Krochmal internalized the Neoplatonist theory of emanation almost completely, and he therefore expresses the stage in which the external school is appropriated in full. Just as in Ibn

Gabirol scarcely a trace remains of Biblical voluntarism, so too with Krochmal we find only vestiges of the volitional dimension of the Deity. Hegel, when describing the transition from the self-sufficient Deity to the world, portrays this transition as governed by a necessary dialectical lawful process. To his mind the process itself is sovereign, and the movements of both God and the world are conditioned upon it. Krochmal, in contrast, believes that the emanation of the world from its Divine source stemmed from a voluntary act of self-contraction on the part of the Deity. Nevertheless, Krochmal's worldview remains emanational-determinist at heart. It is ruled by a necessary structure of emanational connections between concepts, with the voluntary Divine self-limitation constituting a kind of voluntaristic "island" of little import in the context of the theory as a whole.[150]

STEINHEIM

The thinker Solomon Steinheim, who lived some time after Krochmal, argued that every rational worldview is indeed controlled exclusively by the principle of causal determinism. The theoretical explanation of reality is predicated on the assumption that for every effect there is a cause. Whether we are faced with a primitive theoretical outlook such as that of mythology, or with a more sophisticated attempt to understand reality, reason is unable, by its very nature, to relinquish a uniform determinism as the ruling principle in the interpretation of reality.[151] Yet in so doing reason betrays not only itself, but also empirical reality, human self-awareness and the concept of God Himself.

Reason betrays itself, for on the one hand reason demands uniformity, universalism and necessity in everything concerning the application of its concepts and rules to reality. On the other hand, as Kant demonstrated, reason bears within itself fundamental schemata that conflict with that uniformity, universalism and necessity, namely, the categories of time and place. The categories "here" and "there" and those of "before" and "after," upon which the activity of reason itself is predicated, create fissures in the necessary uniformity to which it aspires. The all-embracing stasis which is the final resting point of theory, coupled with the dynamism underlying the process of logical thought itself, is one of the "antinomies" of reason as such.[152]

Reason betrays reality by denying it any dynamic and emergent elements. By its very nature, reason transforms the "becoming" character of experience into a static matrix of concepts that are subsumed within ever more abstract concepts. Neither does reason provide a satisfactory explanation for the place of matter in the cosmos. By virtue of its assumption that there are no effects without causes, it is constrained either to transform matter into an absolute (namely, to claim that matter is in effect its own cause) or to deny the real existence of matter in order to defend the principle of causality. For reason has no way of explaining the causal transition from thought to material reality.[153]

Reason also betrays the unmediated self-understanding of human beings, which testifies to the existence of an absolutely free will, independent of the influence of external or internal-psychological factors.[154] And finally, it betrays the concept of the absolute Deity that it itself establishes, by subordinating the Deity to the rational principle of necessary causality, or to the eternal existence of matter.[155]

In the course of this critique Steinheim, like R. Yehuda ha-Levi in the middle ages (though perhaps with greater severity), contends that reason is inadequate to grasp the truth, not only religious truth but also the truth concerning empirical reality. Thus we are obliged to turn to another source of knowledge—revelation—which articulates fundamental truths that reason is incapable of formulating on its own. While reason by its very nature entails a deterministic worldview, revelation presents us with a voluntaristic worldview. The cosmos was not produced by a Deity subject to the law of causality or to the principle of the eternity of matter. It was created entirely out of nothing, through the infinite and benevolent will of God. Human beings are not swallowed up within a necessary lawfulness, but are free beings, who through the freedom they are granted achieve a moral communion with the commanding God. These axioms are not accessible to reason as such; consequently we infer that the writings through which they have reached us are not the fruit of the human intellect or of any autonomous moral or religious consciousness. Over and against the arrogance of reason in attempting to articulate a comprehensive worldview, we are witness not to an alternative human consciousness, but to a heteronomous revelation. Ultimately, *critical* reason will be constrained to acknowledge the limitations of *dogmatic* reason which presumes to ascribe an ontic status to its presuppositions, and to thereby acknowledge the supremacy of revelation.[156]

From a historiosophic point of view, Guttmann's scheme again features a parallel between the medieval and modern periods. An "intellectualist" figure marks the near total assimilation of the external non-Jewish school. Ibn Gabirol's spiritual world was shaped by emanationist Neoplatonism, and R. Krochmal's spiritual world was shaped by a German idealist version of this theory, which posits the emanation of reality from spiritual essences. In opposition to this theory there arose "personalist" figures, who sharpened the awareness within Jewish thought of the gap that obtains between Biblical voluntarism, which demands the submission of a free human will to the heteronomous decree of a free Divine will, and pagan intellectualism, wherein religiosity is expressed by way of theoretical cognition.

In sum, the encounter between Biblical voluntarism and metaphysical intellectualism is conducted in both the medieval and the modern periods according to the following formula: (1) a formal encounter between the two orientations (Isaac Israeli and Moses Mendelssohn); (2) the formulation and justification of Biblical doctrine within the framework of the conceptual world of metaphysics, while defending fundamental Biblical tenets (Saadia Gaon, Formstecher and Hirsch); (3) the overwhelming of Biblical doctrine by the metaphysical-pantheist perspective (Ibn Gabirol and R. Krochmal); (4) a reaction against this submission by way of a return to an unadulterated, assertive Biblical stance (R. Yehuda ha-Levi and Steinheim).

The next stage, in both the medieval and modern periods, was the attempt to achieve a genuine synthesis between the two archetypes of religious faith through a monumental systematic-philosophic effort. In the middle ages it was Maimonides who undertook this task, and in the modern period it was Julius Guttmann's teacher Hermann Cohen. Just as in Maimonides this project was accompanied by the sacrifice of some of the central features of the Jewish religious consciousness (namely, the transition from a practical, activist value-system to a contemplative one),[157] so in Hermann Cohen the systematic project of synthesis undermined the independent, reified status of God as well as the personalist quality of the religious relation.[158]

HERMANN COHEN

In his exposition of Hermann Cohen's teachings, Guttmann ventures beyond the classic issues of religious philosophy, such as theology or creation theory. First, he describes two developmental stages in Hermann Cohen's own philosophy. These stages are then made to lead ultimately to a third and final stage, namely, the religious philosophy of Guttmann himself. Guttmann's own thought is positioned at the end of his historiosophic structure and is characterized as correcting the tensions and distortions that can be found in Cohen's teachings.[159]

In the first stage, Cohen's understanding of religion is wholly contingent upon his interpretation of Kant. Here, as with previous thinkers, the presuppositions and conceptual frameworks of the external school determine the approach to religious faith in general and to Judaism in particular.[160] With the decline of Hegelian German idealism (which in Guttmann's view was a metaphysical digression from Kant's theory),[161] German philosophy in general (especially the Marburg school) and Jewish religious philosophy (in the guise of Cohen, who was also the leader of this school) returned to Kant's original teachings.[162] Kant himself grasps God as a postulate of practical reason, an axiom that serves to guarantee the future harmony of moral perfection and happiness. Cohen regards this theological position as a concession to eudaemonism and as subversive of Kant's own morality of duty.[163] God, in his view, is the principle that guarantees the possibility of realizing ethics in nature. In the same vein, ethics is unable to express its essence as the eternal task that aspires to future realization without a natural context that can serve as a platform for this realization. Ethical teachings, then, require, in and of themselves, a transcendent principle which guarantees the realization of morality in nature.[164] This does not mean a transcendent reality that by its very nature is beyond human apprehension. In Cohen's philosophy, the Deity itself is placed within the structure of human consciousness. God's transcendence is expressed by the fact that the God-concept cannot be confined either to the realm of cognitive understanding nor to that of practical reason. As a principle that promises a future connection between the two domains, it stands outside of both of them.[165]

Even in this first stage of his theory, Guttmann contends, Cohen echoes a number of classic Jewish teachings. While the transcendence he describes is not the existential transcendence of the Bible, it precludes the reduction of the Deity to a mere ethical ideal or theoretical-metaphysical concept. Cohen is particularly careful to distinguish his theology of transcendence from Spinoza's pantheism, that identifies the Deity with nature and denies the independent status of ethics. Cohen's God is effectively the guarantor of a moral order in the world. Cohen thereby reveals his affinity with the messianism of the Jewish prophets, who envisioned a future in which absolute morality would be realized in universal human history.[166] Guttmann demurs here in characteristic dialectical fashion. The bid to implant Biblical monotheism within the framework of a rational ethical system is necessarily conditioned upon the forfeiture of a cardinal Jewish perspective regarding the relation to God. Cohen's God remains a postulate, a sort of necessary foundation for the ethical system that exists in order to ground its definitions and accomplish its imperatives. He is still only an idea and a principle, never attaining the status of a living existential being. Cohen speaks of this principle with genuine religious enthusiasm, yet the Deity, for him, remains an ideal being rather than a real one. In a somewhat critical tone, Guttmann stresses that Cohen's own premises actually require him to ascribe full ontological status to God. If God is indeed the guarantor of the realization of ethical ideals within the framework of the concrete natural world of events, it would seem to be more consistent to conceive of Him as a sublime reality possessed of decisive powers, rather than merely as an idea conditioning the attainment of the ethical ideal.[167]

The status accorded religion as a phenomenon of the human spirit in Cohen's early theory also elicits Guttmann's criticism. Religion is the historical source of ethics, yet it is philosophic ethics that refines and corrects religion, says Cohen. Philosophy is obliged to recognize and honor its cultural sources and to appreciate the importance of the prophecy of Israel, which gave birth to ideas such as "humanity," "messianism" and "universal history." Ultimately, however, it is ethics that affords the religious God-idea autonomous status within the framework of human consciousness. Guttmann admits that Cohen's emotional connection to the Jewish faith is religious in character, meaning that it is suffused with commitment and pathos. But there is no doubt that Cohen ultimately expects religion to give way to philosophic ethics (if not in the immediate future, then at later stages of spiritual development).[168]

This observation brings us to the second stage in the development of Hermann Cohen's theory, according to Guttmann. In his late philosophic works Cohen assigns religion a more exalted place in human consciousness. Moreover, the content of his God-concept undergoes a significant transformation. Religion is still not accorded the status of a truly distinct domain, alongside ethics and cognitive knowledge, nor is it perceived as an independent perspective that sustains the other fields of knowledge, as Guttmann himself argues in his lectures on the philosophy of religion.[169] Nevertheless, religion is presented as an aspect of ethics characterized by its own special virtue.[170] While ethics treats the human individual merely as a formal-external unit, as the subject and object of the universal ethical ideal, religion bestows self-worth upon the individual as a flawed sinner in need of the love and compassion of his fellow. The suffering individual, who does not always embody the ethical ideal, requires confidence in God's forgiveness, which now represents not only the ethical ideal, but the archetype of the love and compassion one is supposed to feel for one's neighbor. This development in Cohen's thought is a systematic validation of the feeling of compassion. Admittedly this validation is conferred not from a phenomenological standpoint, as an inseparable part of the structure of human experience, but from a deductive standpoint, as a vital element in assuring the personal and communal solidarity required to implement universal ethics.[171]

Even in their later version Cohen's teachings did not develop sufficiently, in Guttmann's view, to grant religion a genuine methodological autonomy or to ensure that the Deity would be grasped as an existential reality who maintains a personal connection with concrete human beings. Man's love for his fellow and God's love for man are still subordinated from a methodological point of view to the requirements of universal ethics. There is no question that Cohen exhibited an original Jewish religiosity, and that he made ample use of personal religious images in describing the relations between God and man. Ultimately, however, Cohen's God remains an idea. Cohen's commitment to autonomy and to the exclusive prerogative of human cognition to derive the ideals of the spirit prevents him from ascribing to God any kind of existential, personal or heteronomous status.[172] Only the phenomenological perspective of Guttmann himself, which makes its appearance at the conclusion of the history of religious philosophy, enables a reflective return to the original Biblical religiosity that relates to God as a live existential reality who makes demands upon human beings. These demands admittedly receive rational and moral validity only by virtue of the autonomous human intellect, for Guttmann is not willing to relinquish the human role in shaping and validating revelation. Yet the connection between God and man is, by his conviction, a personal-moral connection between two independent, existential beings.[173]

A SUMMARY OF THE HISTORIOSOPHIC
THEORIES OF WOLFSON AND GUTTMANN

We will now sum up the principles of Guttmann's historiosophic theory that emerged from the above analysis, while comparing them to the historiosophic premises of Wolfson. For both Wolfson and Guttmann Jewish philosophy as a whole is constructed from two elements. For Wolfson, the one element is a series of metaphysical doctrines that emerge from the narratives, laws and exhortations of the Bible. The other is the logical-conceptual form of philosophic discourse, which articulates the fundamental Biblical tenets in a clear and systematic way. According to Guttmann's theory, one element is the personalist Biblical faith, while the other is the pantheist intellectual faith.[174] In the view of both thinkers the two elements move within time; yet with regard to the direction and character of this movement, they have diametrically opposite positions. The main way stations along the path also differ for each of the thinkers. And finally, each thinker's theory regarding the source of energy for motion within time is also distinct from that of the other.

THE DIRECTION OF MOTION IN TIME

As noted earlier, Wolfson's perspective can be characterized as an "orientation by origins." While his theory admittedly features a movement of graduated development that continues until the advent of Philo's thought, once Philo empties philosophy of its pagan presuppositions and renders it the systematic mouthpiece of the Biblical worldview, there are no more innovations or real developments in Western philosophy. All of the theological issues treated in the various conceptual systems advanced during the course of the history of religious thought ultimately reflect an original, fixed catalogue of issues which are generated by the primordial tension between the unifying impulse of reason and the divisive impulse of Biblical transcendence. There is no real development and no real progress as far as the substantive doctrines of scriptural philosophy are concerned. The significant content of scriptural philosophy had already been established at the founding moment. Time, Wolfson asserts, unfolds, articulates and applies a primordial, eternal ideational content in diverse cultural and linguistic contexts. To the extent that change is discernible in scriptural philosophy, it is primarily a change in form in conformity with the conceptual systems and dominant problems of the various philosophic schools. So long as scriptural philosophy holds its own, and remains in a certain tension with reason's "mythological" tendency to encompass all of reality within a coherent system, scriptural philosophy will continue to work through its classic problems in various cultural contexts. The moment that one of the basic elements is removed, Western philosophy will decay, regressing to its prehistoric pagan origins. From Wolfson's standpoint, a philosophic system is judged by the extent to which it reflects an early archetypical stance; the original Biblical worldview serves as a perennial touchstone for fidelity, deviation or betrayal.[175]

It goes without saying that Guttmann's opinion regarding the direction of the movement of Jewish philosophy is entirely different. To his way of thinking, Jewish philosophy possesses a necessary inner telos that leads to a valued end attained through completion of a process of advancement. At the outset of the process, the personalist Biblical faith emerges as a spontaneous, living reality, yet one devoid of self-consciousness. Deprived of the encounter with religious intellectualism, it would lack the foil against which it would set off its own uniqueness. It would also lack the requisite rational tools to draw crucial conceptual distinctions. Without these tools it could not attain consciousness of its own special essence. The philosophic religious ethos, then, provides the Biblical faith not only with a language for self-expression, but with a worthy religious rival. It helps Biblical personalism to "raise its consciousness" through rational confrontation. The conceptual language of Western philosophy serves not as a means of expression, but as a matrix for the understanding of the parameters of Jewish uniqueness.[176]

Guttmann can hardly be considered an extreme evolutionist, one who considers all early phenomena primitive and all later phenomena highly developed. Spontaneous personalist religiosity, as expressed in the Bible and the Talmud, is considered worthwhile in its own right. Yet over the course of the generations it becomes more refined (for example, its morality of obligation divests itself of utilitarian and authoritarian elements) and more profound (in that it is able to give a conscious account of the quality of the personalist religious relation as opposed to intellectual religious communion). The phenomena considered by Guttmann, then, are judged not according to the degree to which they reflect or deviate from an early archetype, but according to the extent to which they advance the evolutionary process towards its completion at the end of historical time.[177]

For Wolfson, who considers faith to be the expression of assent to revealed doctrines, scriptural philosophy declines together with the decreasing willingness to accept the authority of the Bible at the end of the medieval period. For Guttmann, who conceives of faith as part of the autonomous structure of human consciousness, Jewish religious philosophy continues to develop in the modern period, until the present day, as an expression of the perpetual striving of human beings—who are creatures characterized by a religious consciousness—for self-knowledge.[178]

THE QUALITY OF MOTION IN TIME

Wolfson and Guttmann have opposing historiosophic orientations not only with regard to the *direction* of philosophic motion in historical time, but also with regard to the *quality* of this motion. In Wolfson's view, the phenomena at issue are pure ideas that assume and discard expressive languages. These pure ideas, by virtue of their status as rational-logical transhistorical essences, are immune to the vicissitudes of time and place. In general it can be said that Wolfson did not ascribe genuine forward motion to the history of Western philosophy, in the sense of significant substantive change that is cumulative and progressive over time. This is not to imply, however, that in his view religious philosophy remained in a condition of total stasis throughout its history. The motion of religious philosophy in Wolfson's historiosophy can be characterized as a deductive-expository movement that both applies and corrects. Over time, corollaries and sub-corollaries are derived deductively from basic articles of faith. There is a further elaboration of certain topics that serves to extend and clarify the ramifications of archetypical concepts for new types of problems. In addition, old ideas are applied to new arenas of controversy that arise in different cultural surroundings. All of this takes place without any real substantive departure from the basic tenets of scriptural philosophy.[179] Slight deviations from the Biblical worldview are sometimes detectable, whether in the "mythological"-pagan direction (those positions that present the logos as born rather than created),[180] or in the "primitive" direction (such as the Islamic Asharia's denial of the rationality of God's will).[181] Yet scriptural philosophy soon corrects itself, returning to the "orthodox" fold. Wolfson's historiosophic theory does not concede to particular time periods, schools of thought or individual thinkers an originary role in the course of religious philosophy. The fact that a given philosophic discussion took place at a certain period (the tenth or the seventeenth century), within the framework of a certain school (the Kalam or the scholastics) or within the framework of the teachings of a certain thinker (Clement of Alexandria or Leibnitz) is a matter of indifference to him. Neither the period, the school nor the thinker serves as an agent of change possessed of independent initiative. They all function as passive fields that await the application of the Biblical worldview to their universe of discourse.

Guttmann's position, by comparison, is that movement in the annals of religious philosophy is not deductive but dramatic and dialectical. It is dramatic because it is based on an encounter between elements between which there exists real substantive and qualitative tension. Wolfson maintained that philosophy is indeed an appropriate medium for expressing the Biblical worldview, and it thereby continues the rabbinic midrashic effort to interpret original content through the use of different sets of concepts.[182] Admittedly, at times the systematic and comprehensive nature of the rational matrix hampers the expression of Biblical doctrines, since they entail a strict distinction between Creator and created. This produces a certain degree of tension.[183] Such tension, however, ultimately contributes to the Bible's expressive capacity: It elicits controversy and sharpens arguments, through which "the law is elucidated."[184] Guttmann, on the other hand, views this as an encounter between two independent elements, each of which is liable to gain an advantage over the other.[185] There are also cases in which thinkers seek to create a synthesis, yet comprehensive syntheses are very rare (Maimonides and Hermann Cohen), and they effectively leave the essential tension between personalism and intellectualism intact, without resolving it fully.[186]

The dialectical drama described by Guttmann develops by way of historical periods, philosophic schools and the activity of individual thinkers. The thesis at issue on the stage of history is the Biblical personalist faith, that originally lacks self-consciousness. This thesis continues to maintain itself through Talmudic Judaism until the medieval period, although at times it is drawn in contemplative and ascetic directions that reach full development only in the middle ages. The antithesis is medieval intellectualism. From R. Saadia Gaon to Maimonides, the trend to allow reason autonomy in interpreting the Bible (through internal dialectical movements) gathers force. Moreover, the intellectualist religious faith that aspires to comprehend God in thought also intensifies and supersedes the moral activism of early Judaism. Upon the conclusion of the medieval period, Spinoza exemplifies the inability of personalist religiosity to develop itself and attain self-awareness within the framework of a consistent intellectualism devoid of all value distinctions.[187]

It could be argued that for Guttmann the modern period has the status of a synthesis, though not a full synthesis. First, philosophy becomes more congenial to the ethical personalism of the Bible, while shaking off (again through an inner dialectical movement) intellectualist metaphysics and accepting the influence of Kantian morality.

The universalist and autonomist trends that Guttmann sees as character-istic of modernity also free the Biblical faith from the bonds of authoritar-ianism and exclusivity. This enables religion to express itself as an au-tonomous and universal dimension of the human spirit.[188] Reason, however, still constrains living religious faith in the web of its concepts—even in Hermann Cohen—until Guttmann himself appears to free religion from the limits of reason, through the vigorous and principled application of the distinctions of reason itself. In this manner Guttmann confers legiti-macy upon reason and upholds its specific role, while bestowing rational and ethical validity upon the religious experience.[189]

The classic division into periods, therefore (ancient, medieval and mod-ern) bears a totally different significance in the theories of Wolfson and Guttmann. It should be noted that these distinctions are pagan-Hegelian at base: The Bible and Greek philosophy are treated as "anticipatory" phe-nomena, which lead to Christianity. The "Teutonic" philosophy of Hegel re-fines Christianity and articulates a systematic and comprehensive theory, one that establishes Christianity on the basis of a final union between the cognition of limited human beings and the infinite cognition of God.[190] Wolfson, on the other hand, treats these categories merely as a foci for com-munication with the academic world of his time. From his vantage point, there is essentially only one time period, that of scriptural philosophy, which begins with Philo and concludes with Spinoza. This period repre-sents "meaningful time" in history, compared with Greek "pre-history" and modern "post-history," and within this one period there are no turning points and no progress.[191] Guttmann, by comparison, regards the middle ages as a major turning point in the annals of religious philosophy. It brings real innovation in its train, as Judaism is exposed to intellectualist meta-physics and is almost overcome by it (although important personalist as-pects, that are protected and elaborated, are always preserved). The modern period brings with it another genuine turning point, as moral activism at-tains a preferred status in the philosophic world, and personalist faith achieves autonomy vis-à-vis cognition and ethics, though only through their assistance.[192]

The classification of periods in the two thinkers can be examined not only by means of conventional theoretical categories, but also by examining the place of the Bible in each philosopher's theory. From Wolfson's standpoint, pre-history presents us with a worldview that cannot communicate with Western humanity (the Biblical vision), and a language which might some-day be employed to disseminate that worldview— philosophy. Only upon the conjunction of these two elements does true history begin. The middle ages is a period in which the Bible is enhanced through the employment of philosophic language, while the hallmark of the modern period is the aban-donment of the Bible and a return to pre-historic paganism. Guttmann, in contradistinction, maintains that the ancient period bequeathed us the living Biblical faith, devoid of self-consciousness, along with Greek philosophy, that is energized by an intellectualistic religiosity without recognizing religion as an independent source of truth. The middle ages feature an increasing alienation from the Bible, rather than its empowerment. This alienation, however, is the price the Biblical faith must pay for its exposure to a competing faith and a challenging conceptual system. Finally, in the modern period Jewish philosophy reclaims the Biblical ethos (in contrast with the kind of abandonment suggested by Wolfson), this time by means of a self-consciousness acquired through exposure to philosophy. Concurrently, philosophy becomes aware of the methodological limitations of cognition and is willing to recognize religion as an autonomous domain of consciousness characterized by a unique, even paradoxical, phenomenological structure.

The historical drama articulated by Guttmann is composed of sub-narratives that are also of a dramatic and dialectical character. In every period there are certain thinkers and schools of thought that continue the story line and move it forward. In the middle ages, for instance, the Neoplatonist school was not the appropriate platform for bridging the gap between personalism and religious intellectualism. Neoplatonist intellectualism was itself too religious to serve as a foil for the Jewish faith. As a result, the historical-developmental telos had to bring forth the Aristotelian school, whose intellectual eudemaonism was the framework that could bring the oppositions into greatest relief.[193] In the modern period, so long as Hegelian idealism held sway, Jewish philosophy had to content itself with a theological-polemical stance. The Christian presuppositions that sustained the Hegelian school prevented Jewish thinkers from relating to it as a framework for the systematic reconciliation of religious faith and reason. Only the neo-Kantian school, that embodied philosophy's renunciation of the quest to know the infinite via the finite human intellect, could serve as a frame of reference for Hermann Cohen's attempt to create a new synthesis.[194] This time it was not the school's distance from Biblical personalism that equipped it for the task, but precisely the proximity between the two. This is because in the modern period we find that religion and reason acknowledge each other's respective domains, while in the middle ages the conflict concluded with the triumph of one of these two elements, namely, a thoroughgoing intellectualism. Furthermore, within the framework of every period the division of labor among the major thinkers repeats itself: There is a figure who effects the initial encounter (Isaac Israeli or Moses Mendelssohn), the "theological-polemical" figure (Saadia Gaon or Formstecher and Hirsch), the figure who identifies with the external school (Ibn Gabirol or Krochmal), the figure who reacts to what he deems to be a surrender of Jewish specificity (ha-Levi, Crescas, Steinheim or Rosenzweig) and finally the synthetic figure (Maimonides and Hermann Cohen).

To the question, "Does Jewish philosophy exist?" Wolfson would probably respond, "Certainly, and was there ever any other philosophy?" The religious principles of Biblical Judaism are the active, guiding and dynamic
force in the unfolding of Western philosophy. Consequently, any distinction between "general" and "Jewish" philosophy is meaningless. Judaism
was always self-confident and proactive and was never forced into any kind
of defensive posture. On the contrary, its influence is apparent far beyond
the boundaries of its religious and national-cultural parameters.[195]

In comparison, for Guttmann the driving element in the history of religious philosophy is the non-Jewish one. The Biblical religion is prodded
into reflection by metaphysical schools that invade its cultural sphere. The
pantheist ethos underlying the Western philosophic heritage penetrates the
spiritual world of the major Jewish thinkers. Since Guttmann does not deal
in pristine ideas that are immune to the influence of culture, but rather in
different types of human religiosity that are exposed to the "Zeitgeist" of the
surrounding culture, Judaism, in his view, is forced to struggle for its religious character. Judaism does not initiate the engagement, nor does it
choose its timing or location. The major schools of Western philosophy—
Neoplatonism, Aristotelianism, speculative idealism and Kantianism—
pose successive challenges to the Biblical faith. Judaism responds to these
challenges, rather than posing them to itself.[196]

Western philosophy exists in its own right and is nurtured by a profound
religious ethos distinct from that of Judaism. Yet towards the end of the
scheme, there is a crucial turning point within the framework of Western
philosophy itself. A transition takes place from speculative metaphysics to
activist ethics, a change that brings about a rapprochement between the ethical personalism of the Bible and Kantian morality. It is precisely this rapprochement that allows the Jewish religious faith to attain both independence and self-consciousness.[197]

NOTES

1. Julius Guttmann, *The Philosophies of Judaism* (New York: Jewish Publication
Society of America, 1964), 3–18.
2. Guttmann, *Philosophies of Judaism*, 3–18.
3. Guttmann, *Philosophies of Judaism*, 3–18.
4. Guttmann, *Philosophies of Judaism*, 5–7.
5. Guttmann, *Philosophies of Judaism*, 6–7.
6. Guttmann, *Philosophies of Judaism*, 9–11.
7. Guttmann, *Philosophies of Judaism*, 6–8.
8. Guttmann, *Philosophies of Judaism*, 115–17.
9. Guttmann, *Philosophies of Judaism*, 5–7.
10. Guttmann, *Philosophies of Judaism*, 15.

11. Guttmann, *Philosophies of Judaism*, 2.
12. Guttmann, *Philosophies of Judaism*, 30–31.
13. Guttmann, *Philosophies of Judaism*, 18–22.
14. Guttmann, *Philosophies of Judaism*, 21–22.
15. Guttmann, *Philosophies of Judaism*, 22–24.
16. Guttmann, *Philosophies of Judaism*, 24–25.
17. Guttmann, *Philosophies of Judaism*, 414–15, note 48.
18. I am indebted to Prof. David Hartman on this point, as he directed my attention to this element of Guttmann's scholarship in one of his lectures.
19. Guttmann, *Philosophies of Judaism*, 25–26.
20. Guttmann, *Philosophies of Judaism*, 27–29.
21. Guttmann, *Philosophies of Judaism*, 27–29.
22. Regarding Philo's concept of the logos, Guttmann states on p. 26 of *The Philosophies of Judaism*, "This combination of Stoic, Platonic, and Jewish notions has resulted in a complicated mixture riddled with contradictions."
23. Guttmann, *Philosophies of Judaism*, 62–65.
24. Guttmann, *Philosophies of Judaism*, 414–15, note 48.
25. Guttmann, *Philosophies of Judaism*, 30; Guttmann states there: "Jewish Hellenism was a transitory phenomenon in the development of Judaism." In note 48 as well (pp. 414–15), Guttmann expresses reservations about what he deems to be Wolfson's exaggerated idea of Philo's enduring influence.
26. Guttmann, *Philosophies of Judaism*, 207–12.
27. In *The Philosophies of Judaism*, p. 3, Guttmann makes the following observation about all of Jewish-Hellenistic philosophy, of which Philo was the most prominent representative: "[The first absorption of these ideas] took place during the Hellenistic period. Judaeo-hellenistic philosophy is so thoroughly imbued with the Greek spirit, however, that it may be regarded, historically speaking, as merely a chapter in the development of Greek thought as a whole."
28. Guttmann, *Philosophies of Judaism*, 29.
29. Guttmann, *Philosophies of Judaism*, 24–28.
30. Guttmann, *Philosophies of Judaism*, 81–85.
31. Guttmann, *Philosophies of Judaism*, 30–32.
32. Guttmann, *Philosophies of Judaism*, 32–34.
33. Guttmann, *Philosophies of Judaism*, 33–37.
34. Guttmann, *Philosophies of Judaism*, 37–40.
35. Guttmann, *Philosophies of Judaism*, 36–38.
36. Guttmann, *Philosophies of Judaism*, 38–40.
37. Guttmann, *Philosophies of Judaism*, 42–43.
38. Guttmann, *Philosophies of Judaism*, p. 60, as he puts it: "With the end of the ninth century, the prehistory of Jewish philosophy came to an end and its true history began."
39. Guttmann, *Philosophies of Judaism*, 47.
40. Guttmann, *Philosophies of Judaism*, 55.
41. Guttmann, *Philosophies of Judaism*, 47.
42. Guttmann, *Philosophies of Judaism*, 64–67.
43. Guttmann, *Philosophies of Judaism*, 327–29.
44. Guttmann, *Philosophies of Judaism*, 15.

45. Guttmann, *Philosophies of Judaism*, 59–60.
46. Guttmann, *Philosophies of Judaism*, 82–83.
47. Guttmann, *Philosophies of Judaism*, 3.
48. Guttmann, *Philosophies of Judaism*, 62–63, 152–53, 182–83, 230–32.
49. Guttmann, *Philosophies of Judaism*, 3.
50. Guttmann, *Philosophies of Judaism*, 42–43.
51. Guttmann, *Philosophies of Judaism*, 61–63.
52. Guttmann, *Philosophies of Judaism*, 42–43.
53. Guttmann, *Philosophies of Judaism*, 72–74.
54. Guttmann, *Philosophies of Judaism*, 62–63.
55. Guttmann, *Philosophies of Judaism*, 41–43.
56. Guttmann, *Philosophies of Judaism*, 62–64.
57. Guttmann, *Philosophies of Judaism*, 63–64.
58. Guttmann, *Philosophies of Judaism*, 63–64.
59. Guttmann, *Philosophies of Judaism*, 67–71.
60. Guttmann, *Philosophies of Judaism*, 70–71.
61. Guttmann, *Philosophies of Judaism*, 67–68.
62. Guttmann, *Philosophies of Judaism*, 72.
63. Guttmann, *Philosophies of Judaism*, p. 70, in his words there: "[According to Saadia], the main purpose of revelation is thus not theoretical but practical, and even the theoretical truths taught by religion merely serve as presuppositions to the ethical content of revelation." Clearly there is no real correspondence between this theory and Kant's metaphysical critique. From Guttmann's vantage point, however, it seems that the establishment of ethics as the core of revelation in Saadia anticipates an emphasis that will reach its full systematic significance only in the modern period.
64. Guttmann, *Philosophies of Judaism*, 89. In the preamble to his discussion of the teachings of Ibn Gabirol, Guttmann states: "It took one hundred years [after Isaac Israeli, designated by Guttmann as the first Neoplatonist] before Solomon Ibn Gabirol inaugurated a new succession of Jewish Neoplatonists. . . . [Only now] was the Kalam displaced by Neoplatonism. . . . With Solomon Ibn Gabirol, Spain became the center of Jewish philosophy [from the eleventh century on]."
65. Guttmann, *Philosophies of Judaism*, 84.
66. Guttmann, *Philosophies of Judaism*, 84.
67. Guttmann, *Philosophies of Judaism*, 85.
68. Guttmann, *Philosophies of Judaism*, 85–87.
69. Guttmann, *Philosophies of Judaism*, 89–90.
70. Guttmann, *Philosophies of Judaism*, 90–91, 104.
71. Guttmann, *Philosophies of Judaism*, 104–5.
72. Guttmann, *Philosophies of Judaism*, 106–10.
73. Guttmann, *Philosophies of Judaism*, 120.
74. Guttmann, *Philosophies of Judaism*, 126, 130–33.
75. Guttmann, *Philosophies of Judaism*, 135–36.
76. Guttmann, *Philosophies of Judaism*, 124–25; as Guttmann states there: "Yehuda ha-Levi felt this fundamental distinction between philosophy and religion more radically than appears from its somewhat formal presentation. The philosophers' god rests unmoved in himself; he knows nothing of man and does not care for him. . . .

The God of religion, on the other hand, desires to elevate man to himself. . . . For the philosopher, God is merely an object of knowledge towards which he adopts the same theoretical attitude as he does towards other objects of knowledge. . . . [Ha-Levi's view of the relationship of philosophy to God] certainly applies to science as such, and correctly describes the attitude of science to its objects and its utter indifference to all non-theoretical distinctions of value. . . . Yehuda ha-Levi is enabled to place philosophy as mere knowledge of God, in fundamental opposition to religion, which is life with God."

77. Guttmann, *Philosophies of Judaism*, 143.

78. Julius Guttmann, "Religion and Knowledge in Medieval and Modern Thought," in *Religion and Knowledge* (Jerusalem: Magnes Press, 1955) [Hebrew translation from the German], 20. See also the entire discussion of Yehuda ha-Levi there (pp. 13–21, particularly pp. 19–21).

79. Guttmann, *Religion and Knowledge*, 20–21, 43. The change that has taken place in the modern concept of religion is articulated by Guttmann as follows: "To the extent that in modern philosophy as well the relation of reason to revelation is the nexus of every effort to attain religious truth, the idea of universal religious truth is inextricably bound up with it from the start. Once the ability to attain religious truth is also attributed to autonomous thought, this idea inadvertently leads us to the proposition that religious truth is the joint possession of humankind."

80. Guttmann, *Philosophies of Judaism*, 134–36.

81. Guttmann, *Philosophies of Judaism*, 136–37.

82. Guttmann, *Philosophies of Judaism*, 138.

83. Guttmann, *Philosophies of Judaism*, 139.

84. Guttmann, *Philosophies of Judaism*, 140–42.

85. Guttmann, *Philosophies of Judaism*, 142–43.

86. Guttmann, *Philosophies of Judaism*, 143.

87. Guttmann, *Philosophies of Judaism*, 143.

88. Guttmann, *Philosophies of Judaism*, 143.

89. Guttmann, *Philosophies of Judaism*, 85.

90. Guttmann, *Philosophies of Judaism*, 152.

91. Guttmann, *Philosophies of Judaism*, 152–53.

92. Guttmann, *Philosophies of Judaism*, 155–56.

93. Guttmann, *Philosophies of Judaism*, 158–59. See also Guttmann, "Religious Motives in the Philosophy of Maimonides," *Religion and Knowledge*, 91.

94. Guttmann, *Philosophies of Judaism*, 151.

95. Julius Guttmann, *On the Philosophy of Religion* (Jerusalem: Magnes Press, 1976), 41–42. See also the following passage in Guttmann, "Maimonides' Theory of God," *Religion and Knowledge*, 108: "The paradoxical nature of the essence of God is also reflected in the knowledge we possess about it. The positive becomes negative, except that this is directed towards something definitely positive. Instead of mandating the existence of God we negate absence from Him, yet in so doing we are aiming at something positive that is beyond reality in the positive sense of that which we can apprehend. In negating His absence we are not able to mandate His presence. But in so doing we imply that there is something in His ineffable essence that corresponds to that which we recognize as reality in its most sublime form."

96. Guttmann, *Philosophies of Judaism*, 168–69.

97. Guttmann, *Philosophies of Judaism*, 171–73. Also in this matter of the artificial restriction of Maimonides' naturalism through the designation of the Divine will as a constraint, I am grateful to Prof. Eliezer Schweid, who directed my attention to it.

98. Guttmann, *Philosophies of Judaism*, 182.

99. Guttmann, *Philosophies of Judaism*, 182.

100. Guttmann appears to have been influenced in this orientation by Hegelian trends in the philosophy of history. On the ineluctable dialectical stage-by-stage development towards the self-consciousness of spiritual phenomena in Hegel's historiosophy, see: Georg Wilhelm Friedrich Hegel, *Introduction to the Lectures on the History of Philosophy* (Oxford: Clarendon Press, 1985), 79–81, 126–32; W. H. Walsh, *Philosophy of History* (New York: Harper & Row, 1967), 135–43.

101. Guttmann, *Philosophies of Judaism*, 304–5.

102. Guttmann, *Philosophies of Judaism*, 85–86.

103. Guttmann, *Philosophies of Judaism*, 182.

104. Guttmann, *Philosophies of Judaism*, 281–82.

105. Guttmann, *Philosophies of Judaism*, 285.

106. Guttmann, *Philosophies of Judaism*, 72–73.

107. Guttmann, *Philosophies of Judaism*, 277–78.

108. Guttmann, *Philosophies of Judaism*, 272–73.

109. Guttmann, *Philosophies of Judaism*, 96–97.

110. Guttmann, *Philosophies of Judaism*, 267.

111. Guttmann, *Philosophies of Judaism*, 69–73.

112. Guttmann, *Philosophies of Judaism*, 124–26.

113. Guttmann, *Philosophies of Judaism*, 273–74.

114. Guttmann, *Philosophies of Judaism*, 276–77.

115. Guttmann, *Philosophies of Judaism*, 285.

116. Guttmann, *Philosophies of Judaism*, 73–76.

117. Guttmann, *Philosophies of Judaism*, 47–48, 289–91.

118. Guttmann, *Philosophies of Judaism*, 349.

119. Guttmann, *Philosophies of Judaism*, 123–24.

120. Guttmann, *Philosophies of Judaism*, 278–79.

121. Guttmann, *Philosophies of Judaism*, 290–91.

122. Guttmann, *Philosophies of Judaism*, 291–92, 298–99.

123. Guttmann, *Philosophies of Judaism*, 293–97.

124. Guttmann, *Philosophies of Judaism*, 296–98.

125. Guttmann, *Philosophies of Judaism*, 298. In his words: "One must not introduce into this process [of the progress of theoretical reason] the ultimate moral and religious certainties. Of necessity, such must be the heritage of all generations; the portion allotted to earlier generations must be the same as that given to later ages. It is this interest in the universality of religious truth which is opposed to the idea of its evolution in the course of history."

126. Guttmann, *Philosophies of Judaism*, 296–98.

127. Guttmann, *Philosophies of Judaism*, 298–301.

128. Guttmann, *Philosophies of Judaism*, 296–97, 304–5.

129. Guttmann, *Philosophies of Judaism*, 36–37.

130. Regarding the compartmentalization in Mendelssohn's consciousness, Guttmann states (*Philosophies of Judaism*, 300): "Both aspects of his consciousness

stand next to each other, although they do not stand over against one another. He was thus saved from inner turmoil, because he separated the two sides of his existence, the two bases of his consciousness."

131. Guttmann, *Philosophies of Judaism*, 306–8.
132. See note 130 above.
133. Guttmann, *Philosophies of Judaism*, 293–94.
134. Guttmann, *Philosophies of Judaism*, 296–97.
135. Guttmann, *Philosophies of Judaism*, 175–76.
136. Guttmann, *Philosophies of Judaism*, 304–6.
137. Guttmann, *Philosophies of Judaism*, 305–8.
138. Guttmann, *Philosophies of Judaism*, 156–58.
139. Guttmann, *Philosophies of Judaism*, 308–21.
140. Guttmann, *Philosophies of Judaism*, 313–17.
141. Guttmann, *Philosophies of Judaism*, 314–16.
142. Guttmann, *Philosophies of Judaism*, 316–18.
143. Guttmann, *Philosophies of Judaism*, 178–81.
144. Guttmann, *Philosophies of Judaism*, 323: "His philosophic views . . . leave no doubt that Krochmal viewed German idealistic metaphysics as identical with perfect truth. . . . He insisted that the doctrines of modern philosophy were in complete agreement with Judaism."
145. Guttmann, *Philosophies of Judaism*, 323–25.
146. Guttmann, *Philosophies of Judaism*, 331–34.
147. Guttmann, *Philosophies of Judaism*, 328–29.
148. Guttmann, *Philosophies of Judaism*, 168–70.
149. Guttmann, *Philosophies of Judaism*, 321–33.
150. Guttmann, *Philosophies of Judaism*, 333, in his words: "Of the Biblical idea of creation, only the notion that the self-limitation of God is a spontaneous act of Divine freedom remains."
151. Guttmann, *Philosophies of Judaism*, 346–47.
152. Guttmann, *Philosophies of Judaism*, 345–46.
153. Guttmann, *Philosophies of Judaism*, 346–48.
154. Guttmann, *Philosophies of Judaism*, 348–49.
155. Guttmann, *Philosophies of Judaism*, 346–47.
156. Guttmann, *Philosophies of Judaism*, 344–45, 348–49.
157. Guttmann, *Philosophies of Judaism*, 170–71.
158. Guttmann, *Philosophies of Judaism*, 366–68.
159. Guttmann's book admittedly ends with a presentation of Franz Rosenzweig's theory, rather than with that of his teacher Hermann Cohen. This might be considered problematic for our thesis regarding a theoretical developmental continuity between Cohen and Guttmann, without Rosenzweig serving as a link in the development. The fact that the analysis of Rosenzweig was inserted into the Hebrew version of *The Philosophies of Judaism* as a supplement to the original German work is not in itself sufficient to exclude Rosenzweig from the continuum. The discussion of R. Krochmal was also a later addition to the Hebrew version, and we have seen that his position in the division of labor among the modern thinkers was entirely appropriate. It appears that Guttmann felt obliged to report on the new orientation represented by Rosenzweig's theory, yet did not see fit to include it in the continuum

of schools that generally serve as the framework for his historiosophic discussion. With regard to Rosenzweig he observes, on p. 367, that "on no account can he be designated as the leader of a school with views held in common," and on p. 397, "He left no school behind him, in the formal sense of the term." Guttmann credits Rosenzweig with sparking an interest in Judaism among the younger generation through his "original and striking" interpretation of Judaism as a "single whole," but not with long-term philosophic influence. Guttmann's remarks about Rosenzweig should be compared with what he says about Cohen, specifically in the preface to his discussion of Rosenzweig (p. 367): "The great achievement of Hermann Cohen will long remain in the center of Jewish religious philosophy, despite many adverse criticisms. His influence is felt in every aspect of philosophic work carried on within Judaism since his day, despite the shifting of philosophic interests brought about by time and the inward life of the Jewish people." As demonstrated below, Guttmann regards himself as Cohen's successor, the person who amended and enhanced his vision in order to grant religion its proper place.

160. Guttmann, *Philosophies of Judaism*, 353, in his words: "His understanding of the basic principles of religion is unconditionally dependent upon the fundamental extension which he gives to the Kantian transcendental philosophy."

161. Guttmann, *Philosophies of Judaism*, 305, in his words: "Post-Kantian German philosophy, which had developed—in various directions—far beyond the simple ideas of Enlightenment rationalism, as well as beyond Kant's practical religion of reason. . . . [It] developed the transcendental philosophy of Kant into a metaphysics of the spirit, which derived the world-whole from the self-initiated movement of the ultimate spiritual principle."

162. Guttmann, *Philosophies of Judaism*, 353.

163. Guttmann, *Philosophies of Judaism*, 353–55.

164. Guttmann, *Philosophies of Judaism*, 354–56.

165. Guttmann, *Philosophies of Judaism*, 356–57.

166. Guttmann, *Philosophies of Judaism*, 355–57.

167. Guttmann, *Philosophies of Judaism*, 356–58.

168. Guttmann, *Philosophies of Judaism*, 358–59.

169. Guttmann, *Philosophies of Judaism*, 360–61, 111–14.

170. Guttmann, *Philosophies of Judaism*, 242–46.

171. Guttmann, *Philosophies of Judaism*, 361–62.

172. Guttmann, *Philosophies of Judaism*, 365–68.

173. Guttmann, *Philosophies of Judaism*, 116–17.

174. Guttmann, *Philosophies of Judaism*, 61–63, 137–38.

175. Guttmann, *Philosophies of Judaism*, 93–96.

176. Guttmann, *Philosophies of Judaism*, 122–26.

177. Guttmann, *Philosophies of Judaism*, 174–79.

178. Guttmann, *Philosophies of Judaism*, 116–18, and also Guttmann, *Philosophy of Religion*, 81: "The religious consciousness is of a unique character, since it has no source in other phenomena. What then, we may ask, is the significance of this fact? It does not mean that there is truth in religious consciousness. All that we have established is that in the human spirit there is present a consciousness which is the religious consciousness proper." However, in the conclusion to the last chapter Guttmann adds a prescriptive statement to this descriptive statement (p. 130):

"From the combining of that aspect which is based on absolute certainty and of that which results from postulates it emerges that religion need not and cannot remain exclusively a postulate but should, and indeed can, also serve as a guide in life."

179. Guttmann, *Philosophy of Religion*, 45–47.

180. Guttmann, *Philosophy of Religion*, 145–51.

181. Guttmann, *Philosophy of Religion*, 68–70.

182. Guttmann, *Philosophy of Religion*, 82–84.

183. Guttmann, *Philosophy of Religion*, 66–69.

184. I use this expression according to its sense in the Babylonian Talmud, Baba Metziah 84a, in the tale about R. Yohanan and Reish Lakish. For an instructive commentary on this aggadic narrative, see Jonah Fraenkel, *Iyyunim be-Olamo ha-Ruchani shel Sipur ha-Agadah* (Tel Aviv: HaKibbutz HaMeuhad, 1981), 73–77.

185. Fraenkel, *Iyyunim*, 174–75.

186. Fraenkel, *Iyyunim*, 167–69, 170–71, 184–87.

187. Fraenkel, *Iyyunim*, 173–74.

188. Fraenkel, *Iyyunim*, 174–76, 177–79.

189. Fraenkel, *Iyyunim*, 116–17.

190. Regarding Wolfson's polemic with Hegelian historiography, see Harry Austryn Wolfson, *Philo*, vol. II (Cambridge, MA: Harvard University Press, 1947), 440–43.

191. Wolfson, *Philo*, 78–81.

192. Wolfson, *Philo*, 174–75.

193. Wolfson, *Philo*, 164–66.

194. Wolfson, *Philo*, 178–88, 184–87.

195. Wolfson, *Philo*, 85–86.

196. Wolfson, *Philo*, 159–62, 164–71, 177–83, 183–87.

197. Wolfson, *Philo*, 185–87.

6

Guidelines for the Interpretation of Jewish Philosophical Texts

The divergent perspectives of H. A. Wolfson and Julius Guttmann in matters of epistemology and historiosophy find expression in the interpretive modes they adopt as well. Our examination of Wolfson's writings revealed that for him, the text is actually a mask cloaking a deeper reality. Outwardly, there appear to be contradictions in the text; yet these contradictions are merely illusory. A harmonizing exegesis reveals the text to be consistent and systematic. This exegetical principle stems from the epistemological premise that human thought on the highest level is monistic and coherent. Ostensibly the text contains innovations in the form of novel concepts, problems and topics. This is also illusory, however, for every new thing is actually old. The "historiosophy of beginnings" requires that everything new be understood as an echo or reflection of the old. Ostensibly the text exhibits diverse forms of literary expression: sermons, commentaries and even geometrical deductions. Yet the careful investigator detects that there is no substance to these forms, as they merely serve to camouflage pure eternal ideas that transcend differences of form and genre. Ostensibly the beliefs and opinions expressed in a given text are shaped by its historical context, yet the perceptive commentator understands that the historical and empirical context, while interesting, is not decisive—as theological ideas are not influenced by historical or cultural developments. There is only one significant original context, and that is the pristine archetypal reservoir of fundamental positions that articulate the basic gestures of faith or heresy. The text seems to persuade the reader that the phenomena it contains derive from proximate causes, whether historical or cultural. Scholars of Wolfson's ilk, however, lay bare what they consider to be the inner reality of the text, demonstrating that all the surface phenomena that catch the attention of the reader are mere epiphenomena—deriving ultimately from pagan or Biblical motivations.[1]

GUTTMANN'S APPROACH TO CONTRADICTIONS WITHIN THE TEXT

With regard to every single one of these subjects, Guttmann's exegetical orientation differs from that of Wolfson. In the case of contradictions within the text, for instance, the categories of "surface" and "inner reality" take on an entirely different significance.

"Surface" for Guttmann signifies the sincere aspiration of Jewish philosophers across the generations to reconcile the contradictions between scientific and religious truth.[2] Yet if from Wolfson's vantage point scriptural philosophy succeeded in providing a systematic and consistent account of the Jewish tenets of faith, for Guttmann this objective remains unrealized. None of the philosophic worldviews discussed in Guttmann's oeuvre is depicted as free of contradictions. Quite the contrary: In his view, the inner contradictions that appear in a religious philosophic text are part of its essence. Biblical personalism and metaphysical pantheism cannot ultimately be harmonized. There is no suggestion here that syllogistic argumentation has been merely used to articulate fundamental Biblical or pagan doctrines. According to Guttmann, what we have here is an encounter between two religious orientations whose differences are of great moment. The personalist relation to the Deity, expressing as it does a live connection between two real existential beings mediated by reason, cannot be fully and systematically reconciled with an intellectual religiosity that views the Deity as an object of theoretical reason or as a postulate of practical reason. Moreover, the conceptual-systematic language of philosophy, which brooks no contradictions, is not always adequate to describe the phenomenon of religious faith, fraught as the latter is with paradox and contradiction.[3]

Wolfson, who views philosophy as the handmaid of the Bible, regards Biblical theology as a coherent work of reason. Most of his scholarly enterprise was directed to defending the systematic coherence of ancient texts against the attacks of critics who looked upon them as a non-systematic admixture of temporal and cultural influences.[4] Guttmann, on the other hand, adopts a critical stance towards the texts he studies. He views himself as the final station in a historical process, a process that has endowed him with a higher degree of self-consciousness than that of his predecessors. Thus, instead of defending the integrity of Philo or Spinoza's teachings, for instance, he analyzes their systems with a view to exposing dialectical tensions that he believed were largely unknown to the thinkers themselves.[5]

In Guttmann's view, the teachings of Jewish philosophers over the generations have always been characterized by inner contradictions. While Wolfson used Talmudic forms of reconciliation between conflicting cases in order to create inner harmony in Philo's system,[6] from Guttmann's standpoint Philo's writings are far from consistent. On the one hand, says Guttmann, Philo's theology lacks any personalist character. His concept of God is exalted far beyond any perfections or values of which the human intellect can conceive, and certain elements in his teachings prefigure the theory of negative attributes. Nevertheless, he refers to the Deity in personal terms such as "Father" and "Creator," and remarks on His "mercy" and "goodness." Guttmann regards this not as a concession to contemporary modes of expression, but as simple inconsistency.[7] In concluding his exposition of Philo's doctrines, Guttmann seeks to understand the systemic flaws in Philo's "objective" concept of religion, as compared with his "subjective" relation to God. On the one hand, Philo was driven by a mystical longing to commune with God, who is beyond all positive content. From a logical standpoint, such a concept of the Deity excludes any possibility of a personal bond. Nevertheless, Guttmann contends, when Philo expresses what God means to him, he is unable to refrain from the use of personal expressions that bespeak a traditional Jewish faith. On the personal level, Philo is torn between two types of religious faith. The tension between them spawns two modes of relation to God, which are logically contradictory.[8]

Guttmann's deconstructive critical approach also emerges in his discussion of later thinkers, with complex, mature worldviews. For instance, the teachings of R. Bahya Ibn Pakuda of the eleventh century are depicted by way of a dialectical, discursive style whose aim it is to highlight both mystical Neoplatonist elements and personalist, Jewish modes of the religious relation. R. Bahya's emphasis on theoretical metaphysical knowledge as a precondition for the religious life, in Guttmann's opinion, reveals the influence of non-Jewish streams of thought.[9] His theology has a distinctly Neoplatonist cast, distinguishing as it does between the concept of absolute unity (which, logically speaking, conditions the existence of all beings) and that of relative unity (which serves as a way of characterizing all other phenomena). Bahya's Neoplatonist concept of the Deity is particularly stringent, as it logically excludes any possibility of ascribing positive attributes to God.[10] Yet his primary religious objective, of fostering a simple inner religiosity based on trust, humility and love, reflects a traditional Jewish faith. While his conceptual understanding of God denies Him any personal qualities, his religious sentiment is highly personal in character.[11]

Hermann Cohen, whose teachings represent modern religious philosophy at its best, also draws criticism from Guttmann for his inconsistency on certain issues. In this case, the inconsistency derives not from a grappling with two contrasting types of religious faith, but from the tension between

Cohen's personalist religious approach and his commitment to the methodological sovereignty of reason. Cohen's subjective faith was personalist, and his works are suffused with the love of God and trust in God's love for humans. Yet so long as religion remains for him a function of rational cognition, his concept of God can be no more than an idea. So long as religion claims no recognition as an independent domain of the human spirit, reason will be impotent to fully convey the personal relation between two real entities that characterizes the religious bond in its pristine form.[12]

Guttmann, then, employs the same exegetical technique to explain contradictions within the teachings of religious philosophers from different periods. To his way of thinking, logical contradictions in religious philosophy derive from two main causes. Either the thinker himself is caught up in an inner struggle between two types of religiosity, or the Jewish thinker's thoroughly personalist religiosity conflicts with the demands of metaphysics or ethics regarding the concept of God. This hermeneutic approach stems from Guttmann's epistemological and historiosophic premises, as described above: Jewish philosophy is a philosophy informed by religious faith, not a theology informed by doctrine, and it develops in historical time by way of a dialectical struggle between two types of religiosity. It is not surprising, then, that in the course of analyzing the works of various thinkers Guttmann seeks to *identify* contradictions rather than *resolve* them. He attributes these contradictions to the conflict between two types of religious faith that coexist in the spiritual world of a given thinker, or to the conflict between a Jewish personalist religious ethos and the logical requirements of the philosophic school from which the thinker took his bearings.

THE NEW AND THE OLD IN GUTTMANN'S HERMENEUTICS

Just as Guttmann recognizes and exposes contradictions, refusing to paper them over for the sake of coherence, so too does he not hesitate to focus on innovations as well. Since he believed that turning points in the development of Jewish philosophy are indeed conceivable, he declined to reduce everything new to something old. From Guttmann's standpoint Philo is not merely a systematic continuation of the Bible, and his views can be understood only in light of his Greek premises, which were drawn from his Hellenistic surroundings. His position regarding the ascent of the soul to a world beyond the senses, a process that concludes with communion with the Deity, is both an innovation and a deviation from traditional Jewish religiosity.[13] In a similar vein, Saadia Gaon is held not only to interpret the Biblical faith according to the terminology of the Kalam, but to pave the way for a new tendency to designate reason as the criterion for interpreting the Bible.[14] Mendelssohn as well, instead of conditioning the rationality of religion on adherence to, say, Aristotle's metaphysical method, chooses to ground it in the common sense of the average person, thereby giving voice to a greater universalism and a greater sense of democracy.[15]

This willingness on the part of Guttmann to valorize change within the framework of a teleological, developmental scheme leads him to highlight innovation and progress rather than subsuming the new under the old. Instead of assuming that everything new is actually old, he tries to identify the seeds of the new within the old itself. By way of example, he justifies the search for a universalist concept of religion in medieval sources, in which fidelity to a particularist revelation was taken for granted, as follows: "While one should tread cautiously in treating this potential attitude as the direct intention of the middle ages, we also have a right to consider problems from a historical perspective, in order to expose their potential connections as well."[16]

Guttmann believes that the medieval period already contained some intimations of the natural religion of the eighteenth-century Enlightenment. The openness of the Islamic world to numerous religious cultures lead to a somewhat relativistic ethos and to a slightly skeptical attitude towards claims of an exclusive historical revelation. Already by then an awareness had developed that all of the religions share a common moral core, that is compatible with autonomous human reason.[17] Although in the medieval era this ethos failed to develop into a full-fledged theory regarding the human source of religious faith per se, as occurred in the nineteenth century, numerous signs of this new idea were present in potential in the old. In highlighting the natural-cognitive character of prophecy, Arab Aristotelianism—as reflected in Maimonides' theory—manifests "preliminary signs of universalism."[18] Maimonides himself heralds the modern historical approach to the ritual laws of the Bible.[19] Already in the voluntarist critiques of al-Ghazzali and Yehuda ha-Levi against reason there "was embodied the figure, both the religious and the secular one, of modern 'irrationalism' that dismisses reason . . . in order to make room for a supra-rational concept of reality."[20]

Not only does Guttmann seek out and emphasize anticipatory elements in early theories. His "historiosophy of ends" directs him to judge early ideas critically, in keeping with the more "developed" concepts of the present. Certain Karaite thinkers are commended for their insistence on positing a rational concept of God as a prologue to revelation, a prologue independent of the authority of scripture. Moreover, they argue for the "inner evidence of our moral consciousness," with no concessions to utilitarianism at all.[21] Saadia Gaon, by way of comparison, combines the utilitarian principle he used to explain some of the commandments, with a recognition of the immanent rationality of the so-called "rational" commandments.[22] Nevertheless, the structure of the *Book of Beliefs and Opinions* (from teachings about God and creation to chapters on "commandment and admonition" that treat of practical matters) underscores the centrality of morality and action in Saadia Gaon's thought. The chapters on metaphysics are merely an introduction to the chapters on commanded actions; Saadia Gaon, then, approximates the Kantian scale of values embraced by Guttmann himself.[23] Guttmann goes so far as to fault Maimonides for subordinating morality to his social objectives, by treating it solely as a means for assuring the social conditions necessary for the pursuit of truth. Maimonides (to the dismay of Guttmann's Kantian sensibilities) failed to recognize the "innate value of the moral state of mind."[24]

TEXTUAL FORM AND CONTENT IN GUTTMANN'S HERMENEUTICS

Like Wolfson, Guttmann distinguishes between the form of the religious philosophic text and its content. Both scholars believe that the expressive modes of a text sometimes conceal a deeper stratum, where the true motives for a thinker's orientation can be found. However, they part company regarding the nature of this stratum. Wolfson believes that variegated textual forms all reflect a certain kind of content, namely, archetypal theological doctrines.[25] Guttmann, in contrast, believes that it is "religious motifs" that underlie the systematic and conceptual "surface" of philosophic works; different types of religious experience are the root cause of discrete formal conceptual articulations. Guttmann considers philosophy to be more than just a syllogistic language. The aim of reason is to participate in the establishment of a valid religiosity, conscious of its character and its uniqueness.[26] Coherent conceptual language, however, cannot fully express a religious relation that draws upon all of the human personality, including the realm of feeling. Thus unlike Wolfson, who strives to find pure ideas lurking behind the literary forms of the text, Guttmann seeks to discover diverse types of religiosity in it. Guttmann voices this aim explicitly in his article "Religious Motifs in Maimonides' Philosophy": "In fact, then, all of Maimonides' philosophy is fueled by religious motives. And if in the passages below we seek to emphasize the religious themes in particular, we mean by this only the following: We are not interested here in the details of the metaphysical disputations, concerning which a debate is conducted in Maimonides' work between Judaism and Aristotelianism; rather, we are interested in the deep motives underlying these disputations."[27]

Guttmann's approach is clearly illustrated in his analysis of Maimonides' philosophy. Maimonides' strict philosophic consistency with regard to the absolute unity of the Deity[28] stems not only from a formal logical necessity. He is driven first and foremost by "the religious requirement to purge the concept of the Deity of any trace of corporeality. This change in the way God is depicted should therefore in no way be viewed as a Maimonidean concession to science. Quite the contrary: He treats philosophy here as a means of divining the true meaning of religion itself. The philosophic purification of the depiction of God is simply a religious imperative for him."[29] Maimonides' penetrating criticism of the attempt to extend the domain of causal determinism beyond the boundaries of the created world also stems from more than sheer intellectual concerns. The energy that drives his logical consistency here derives from the attempt to support the conception of a God possessed of supreme will and displaying spontaneity and freedom in creating the world, as reflected in the personalist Jewish religious ethos from time immemorial.[30] In his creation theory too, Maimonides vigorously defends the voluntarist Biblical portrayal of God. The theory makes allowance in principle for the possibility of miracles (though only within the framework of a lawful system implanted in advance), of individual providence (though only in accordance with a lawful causality based on human progress in the field of cognition) and of prophecy by divine commission (that is preserved by virtue of the Deity's prerogative to deny prophecy even to one who has intellectually prepared himself to receive it).[31] All of these philosophic positions, in Guttmann's conviction, are ultimately sustained by deep religious motives, rather than by an external theological imperative to defend traditional articles of faith. Maimonides' views on these topics are also not the result of detached philosophic reasoning, but rather of a struggle between two spiritual orientations. His treatment of certain topics does indeed reflect his personalist inclinations, despite his Aristotelian frame of reference. Yet even when Maimonides displays his intellectualist predilections, "And the Deity is held to be the true and sublime object of metaphysical knowledge,"[32] the knowledge he speaks of is nurtured by a religious impulse. His is not a pure Aristotelian teaching in whose framework cognition itself is the source of happiness; rather, it is through cognition that a person is enabled to cleave to God. "It spawns the sense of loving God and the joy of intimacy with him. . . . The joy abiding in such a direct communion with God is attained by humans through cognition . . . The joy of perceiving God is the ultimate and most sublime aspiration of every religion according to this view."[33]

The book *Guide of the Perplexed* comes across at first as a compendium of multifarious metaphysical disputations. The entire book is written in an intellectualist mode lacking any direct relation to emotions and states of soul. In Guttmann's view, however, the text contains a stratum of religious feeling at its core, a stratum which is its deepest and most important dimension. The scholar is enjoined to penetrate beyond the theoretical form of the discourse, in order to uncover the religious impulses (which include emotional elements) that disclose the thinker's true spiritual orientation.

The quintessential expression of Guttmann's exegetical bent can be found in his analysis of what he considered to be Spinoza's religious faith. From a systematic standpoint, Spinoza is unwilling to relate to the cosmos as the medieval Aristotelians did, as a value-hierarchy of essences that extends from incorporeal intellects down to inanimate matter. The causality in the universe, to his way of thinking, is mechanistic-mathematical in character; it suffers no value distinctions, only distinctions concerning a kind of amplitude of being. Spinoza transforms the working assumptions of the new natural sciences, which strive to liberate themselves from teleological explanations, into a comprehensive metaphysical principle. Guttmann, however, deems this position as well a surface posture. If we attend to the deep religious layer of Spinoza's teachings, he argues, we will be persuaded that Spinoza's negation of all value distinctions with respect to being does not suggest a propensity to empty all reality of value. On the contrary, it emanates from a religious impulse that seeks to ascribe comprehensive value to all of being to the same degree.[34] The God of Spinoza, who from a logical standpoint constitutes the all-encompassing network of the mathematical laws of nature, is from a religious standpoint also an object of mystical longing.

Both Wolfson and Guttmann, then, discern a gap between the outward form of philosophical texts and the inner religious orientations they embody. Underlying the external mode or genre of expression Wolfson descries an engagement with key issues of medieval Biblical theology. Thus Spinoza's geometrical style of discourse is seen to be adopted for reasons of communication alone and to overlie typical themes derived from medieval theology.[35] For Guttmann, however, theoretical discourse necessarily masks religious longings, which take on various qualities and are oriented towards different objects.

CAUSALITY AND INFLUENCE
IN GUTTMANN'S HERMENEUTICS

Neither Wolfson nor Guttmann contented themselves with recording the chronology of religious thought. Both sought to create a comprehensive exegetical context for the specific objects of their inquiry, thereby associating them with a totality that endows them with significance. Wolfson felt he had attained hermeneutic meaning when he succeeded in characterizing a given item (such as a theoretical topic in the teachings of a thinker from a certain period) as the reflection of a primordial metaphysical position, whether Aristotelian, Epicurean, Philonic, and so forth.[36] What, then, was Guttmann's field of meaning? Did he also treat linguistic and cultural contexts and proximate horizontal streams of thought as worthless in ascertaining the theoretical field to which the item at issue should be related?

In this context let us return to Glatzer's distinction between "lower" and "higher" historicism, and to Shlomo Pines' scholarship as the prominent representative of these key trends in Jewish studies.[37] "Lower" historicism determines the relative value of events and even of spiritual attainments within the framework of the narrow context of the time and place in which they were produced. For Shlomo Pines, for example, Maimonides' teachings are the quintessential expression of a philosophic school that arose in a particular cultural region at a particular period in time.[38] His works should not be attributed to an internal Jewish tradition dating back to Saadia Gaon (and certainly not to Philo!) that strives to justify the Jewish faith, whether from a doctrinal or a religious standpoint, as Maimonides himself did not explicitly acknowledge the influence of such a tradition. Maimonides' philosophy should be regarded as belonging to a particular philosophic enterprise specific to that time and place, whose primary representatives were Avicenna and al-Farabi. No causal relationship or influence can or should be identified between conceptions distant from each other in time or place, such as the Bible and Maimonides, Plato and Maimonides, Saadia Gaon and Maimonides or Maimonides and Spinoza, Kant or Krochmal. The exclusive reference group for Maimonides' teachings is the circle of Aristotelian Arab philosophers who were his contemporaries in time and place[39] (and whatever Maimonides knew of Aristotle, he knew through them). Only with regard to such a reference group can scholarly inquiry detect close causal connections.

If we were to characterize Pines' approach from the standpoint of the higher historicism (that approach that ascertains the place of Jewish spiritual attainments within the overall spiritual creation of the West), he would not appear to credit Jewish philosophy with any influence on Western philosophy. While from Wolfson's viewpoint there really is no such thing as general philosophy, since all philosophy is actually Jewish scriptural philosophy, for Pines there is almost no unique Jewish philosophy, as this field of thought merely mirrors developments in the external schools.[40] Does Guttmann's approach, then, resemble that of Pines? Guttmann structures the chapters of his book *The Philosophies of Judaism* along the lines of the development of the external schools. Yet does he really limit his field of meaning to the narrow foci of region, period and external influence?

Guttmann does not seem to work on the assumption of a unilateral horizontal movement from the outside, in the sense that we find in Pines. Jewish philosophy is not merely the passive recipient of themes and conceptions from the external schools. On the other hand, neither does it shape the philosophic surroundings in the image of its own presuppositions, as Wolfson contends. Guttmann does believe, however, that Jewish philosophy absorbs fundamental premises and many important ideas from the external schools, and that the intellectualistic Jewish religiosity resulting from this encounter departs significantly from the personalistic religiosity of the Bible.[41] He further argues that Jewish philosophy responds in its turn to the influences it assimilates. Diverse thinkers in the annals of Jewish philosophy have articulated Biblical creeds within the framework of systematic schools of thought. There are those philosophers who defend Biblical tenets through polemics, and there are those who simply equate personalist and intellectualist elements while ignoring the yawning gap between them. The greatest of them, however, aspire to merge the two elements into one all-embracing philosophy (although even they—Maimonides and Hermann Cohen—are not able to overcome the immanent difficulties of such an endeavor).[42] In other words, Guttmann also posits a horizontal causal system, in addition to Wolfson's vertical one. Yet this horizontal causality is not entirely one-directional, like that of Pines. The challenge of the external schools arouses Jewish philosophy to inquire into the nature of the connection between religion and philosophy, thereby spurring it to make a singular contribution to the history of religious thought.

The principles of (1) significant dependence of Jewish philosophy on its horizontal surroundings contemporary in time and place, along with (2) the drive to illuminate the topics at issue in a special light, are both highlighted in Guttmann's spirited preface to *The Philosophies of Judaism.* "The Jewish people did not begin to philosophize because of an irresistible urge to do so. They received philosophy from outside sources, and the history of Jewish philosophy is a history of the successive absorptions of foreign ideas."[43] Up to this point Guttmann and Pines would seem to be in perfect accord. Guttmann, however, immediately appends the following telling addition: "Which were then transformed and adapted according to specific Jewish points of view."[44] As noted above, these transformations were effected in various ways, such as through polemics, claiming essential identity between metaphysics and religion or striving for synthesis. Moreover, different schools of thought were assimilated in different degrees. In any event, the causal system in Guttmann's scholarship is one of challenge and response. With respect to Saadia Gaon, for example, this pattern of challenge and response is portrayed as follows: "For his fundamental theses Saadia relied on the Kalam. Like other Jewish followers of the Kalam, he inclined towards its rationalist Mu'tazilite version. . . . Saadia followed Mu'tazilite convention even in the formal structure of his book. . . . But apart from this, he handled the traditional scholastic themes with great freedom. . . . Even where he agreed in principle with the tenets of Kalam, he frequently developed these notions in an independent fashion."[45]

With regard to Maimonides, the major impact of the external school is presented in the following manner: "In his understanding of the Aristotelian system, he followed the Islamic Aristotelians, al-Farabi and Avicenna."[46] Maimonides too was hardly passive, however, responding in an even more sophisticated fashion to the external philosophic influences he had internalized: He "threw the opposition between Aristotelianism and Biblical revelation into bold relief in order to overcome it by a genuine synthesis."[47] He possessed an "originality of creative synthesis" that he applied to the philosophic patrimony he had received from the tradition.[48] The pattern, then, is one of "creative synthesis" rather than the selection and rejection of philosophic ideas according to Biblical presuppositions, as was Saadia's practice. Yet both of these thinkers preserve the independence of their Jewish thought. Even the teachings of those thinkers who appear to have entirely surrendered to the dominant philosophic schools, such as Ibn Gabirol in the middle ages and Krochmal in the modern era, retain some degree of Jewish voluntarism.[49]

This pattern of "challenge and response," then, cannot be identified with the passivity and lack of originality with which Jewish philosophy was held to absorb external influence according to Pines. The difference between Guttmann and Pines goes beyond this, however. Pines' scholarship does not claim to place the individual themes of its investigations within a comprehensive theoretical scheme that extends over a lengthy period of time. His articles reflect an academic intellectual interest in local manifestations of Jewish philosophy,[50] with the divergence between the views of the different thinkers stemming entirely from external factors. The sources of changes in Jewish philosophy (such as the heightened influence of a particular Islamic thinker, or the transfer of a center of philosophic discourse from an Islamic cultural region to a Christian one) are also to be found outside of Jewish thought itself.[51] They do not belong to a unified causal system characterized by an all-embracing lawful pattern.

In Guttmann, by comparison, along with the horizontal causality of "challenge and response" operating independently in relation to every school of thought, religious thought is also characterized by a comprehensive scheme of vertical causality, from Biblical through modern times. This is not a rational trans-historical scheme like that of Wolfson. It comprises not only wholly logical tensions, detached from the influence of time and place, that stem from the adoption of a causal language to express a Biblical doctrine which exempts both God and human beings from any necessary causal system.[52] The all-encompassing framework that serves as the theoretical context for the particular subject at hand is not a set of principles unfolding its presuppositions and implications, but a sort of developing organism that realizes itself in dialectical stages.

Nevertheless, neither Wolfson nor Guttmann relates to the individual subjects of their study as valuable in their own right. Neither considers the accurate reflection of the historical situation at a particular point of place and time to be an end in itself.[53] For both scholars, the subject of study derives both its value and its hermeneutic significance from the fact that it partakes of a totality that is not confined to a narrow historical or geographical arena. The inherent question here is what role the item at issue plays in the totality that serves as its field of meaning. From Wolfson's standpoint, the item being studied serves only a reflective and expressive function. There is one given primordial totality, that of Philonic scriptural philosophy. The task of scholarship is to expose the expressions and reflections of the latter in different periods and places and among different thinkers. The item being studied serves no real function in constructing the totality or advancing it. The totality known as Philonism has persisted since the period of its inception, and every subsequent topic or discussion found in a Greek, Syrian, Arab or Latin manuscript is simply another version of that first fundamental worldview. Wolfson embarks upon his research with the structure of the totality already in hand, and he treats the items he studies as passive objects to be classified according to a table whose basic categories are already complete.[54] For Guttmann, in contrast, each item plays an active causal role in advancing the process of the construction of the totality. If we were to arrest the chronicles of Jewish religious philosophy at any stage, we would be faced with a totality-in-the-making as yet incomplete. Every topic in the corpus of a given thinker, every doctrine formulated, every school and every historical period plays a constructive role in the teleological dialectic of the organism's development to maturity.[55]

This teleological causal network, in which the individual contributes to the incremental establishment of the totality, can be examined on various levels. On the level of time, the ancient period is an "enabling factor" that exists "for the sake of" the middle ages. "By developing the notion of "revealed truth" [the Biblical canon] created what was to become later the main issue dividing religion and philosophy."[56] Judaism bequeathed to Christianity and Islam not a set of doctrines with a common content, as Wolfson alleges, but the very phenomenon of the integration of religious truth and religious life in submission to a particular document of revelation. This same claim to the exclusivity of revelational truth would later pose a challenge to medieval philosophy. Were it not for the encounter with the monotheistic religions, philosophy would never have addressed the problem of religion as a tradition that lays claim to an exclusive truth.[57] None of the medieval attempts to respectively circumscribe religious and philosophic certainty—either by rendering cognitive certainty a fundamental component of religious certainty (Maimonides), through a "two truths" theory (Albalag), or through theories that posit the superiority of religious apprehension over a discursive cognitive apprehension in metaphysical matters (al-Ghazali and Yehuda ha-Levi)—would have been possible had not the middle ages inherited scripture from ancient times. Prior to the middle ages philosophy had been nourished by the speculative religious ethos of Greek mythology,[58] and while it had developed its own critique and rational interpretation of mythology, it had not addressed the problem of revelation as a possible independent source of truth.[59]

In like fashion, the medieval period exists "for the sake of" the modern era. The signature of the medieval period is religious rationalism, yet almost every medieval Jewish philosophic system preserves personalist elements. The personalist ethos never dies out entirely, even in philosophic circles. However, the consistent and (ostensibly) value-free rationality of Spinoza that arose in the waning days of the middle ages demonstrates that it is inconceivable that a morally based religion retain its identity within the framework of a purely theoretical orientation, one that distinguishes between its objects solely by reference to the criterion of level of abstraction. The medieval encounter between personalism and metaphysics had to transpire in order for the organism of "Jewish philosophy" to become conscious of the impossibility of "grasping the nature of religion and ethics in terms of the presuppositions of a strict intellectualism."[60]

The final development of religious philosophy is achieved by modernity. Modern thought denies the exclusive authority of scripture, treating religion as a spontaneous universal phenomenon of the human spirit rather than as a phenomenon characterized by heteronomy, receptivity and exclusivity.[61] Only such an orientation can allow for the phenomenological-anthropological analysis that discloses the unique structure of the religious consciousness. Every historical period, then, makes its own singular causal contribution to the growing (or grown) organism of religious philosophy.

When we consider this kind of teleological orientation with respect to philosophic schools, we find every school acting to promote and coordinate the relation between religion and reason. The Mu'tazilite Kalam, for instance, spurs Judaism to employ an established rationalist teaching for the first time in order to articulate its own articles of faith. Nevertheless, Saadia Gaon "attempted to describe and establish the religious ideas of Judaism in a rational manner without altering their content."[62] In any event, the very fact of the encounter between Judaism and rationalism is necessary in order to pave the way for the Neoplatonist stage, in which "Greek philosophy was no longer the source of particular doctrines only, but the systematic foundation of their thought."[63] Here begins the attempt to maintain some degree of personalism within the framework of an overarching rationalist philosophic orientation, wherein "theoretical knowledge" is judged "a necessary prerequisite for the religious life."[64]

The attribution of such superiority to cognition enables the transition to an even more developed stage of medieval rationalism. While in both Neoplatonism and Aristotelianism "the true purpose of knowledge was now defined as the comprehension of the supra-sensual world, and the self-sufficient bliss of knowledge became the blessedness of communion with God," yet in Aristotelianism, "The intellectualist character of the Aristotelian ideal of life colored all religious formulations. . . . The blessedness of communion with God was, at least to some extent, conceived as a participation in the eudaemonism of divine knowledge."[65] As noted above, only a rarefied intellectualism such as this could serve as the backdrop for Maimonides' bid to stage a genuine confrontation between personalism and metaphysics.[66]

In terms of their relation to the totality under study—namely, the organism of Jewish philosophy, that grows in stages towards self-consciousness—schools of thought reflect even smaller units of development than historical periods. Yet every school also propels the process of mutual interaction between religion and reason to ever higher and more sophisticated levels.

An even smaller unit of development is that of individual thinkers and their teachings. We have seen that Guttmann appraises the various thinkers not according to, say, the degree of their individual originality, but rather according to how each thinker advances the encounter between the two elements that together make up the totality of Jewish philosophy. Within the framework of every school there arises a "figure who engages" metaphysics, who then enables the emergence of another, the "figure who surrenders" to metaphysics. The very presence of the "surrendering figure" serves as a catalyst for the advent of the "responding figure," who insists on the uniqueness of the religious relation in itself. The consciousness spawned by the responses of philosophers such as Yehuda ha-Levi, Crescas, Steinheim and Rosenzweig leads to the emergence of a "synthetic figure."[67]

Guttmann as a rule focuses on the mature crystallized theory of the individual thinker, rather than on the development of his thought over time. In contravention of this rule, however, the thought of his teacher and master, Hermann Cohen, is analyzed in terms of an inner teleological causality. According to Guttmann, Cohen's religious sentiment finds expression already in his early teachings on the absolute transcendence of the concept of God, a concept that is "placed" beyond the realm of epistemology and ethics, and in his esteem for the religious-historical sources of philosophic ethics. This same religious sentiment impels him, in the final stages of his philosophic development, to carry the religious dimension another step forward to full self-awareness. Without attaining to a complete methodological independence, religion does enjoy a certain separate status as a unique aspect of moral reasoning in Cohen's thought. It is the aspect that focuses on the individual sinner and on the feelings of compassion and love vital to the promotion of human solidarity.[68]

Guttmann, then, suggests a different exegetical-causal network than the one that emerges from Wolfson's scholarship. In Wolfson, a logical, transhistorical, vertical causality reigns supreme; the individual entity merely reflects and expresses an aspect of a static whole, without advancing it or substantively changing it. In Guttmann, however, we find a horizontal causality of "challenge and response" combining with a teleological-developmental vertical causality. The pattern of "challenge-response" that dominates a given period, following the ascent of a particular school of thought or a particular thinker (such as al-Ghazali, Avicenna or Hegel), is always made possible by certain preliminary theological groundwork. The individual thinkers or schools of thought, however, who differ in their substance and profile, play an active role in advancing the growth of the totality.

The two scholars' divergent perceptions regarding the character of the causal network that connects between individual objects of study, the network that endows these objects with hermeneutic meaning, stems from the differences between them in the realm of epistemology and historiosophy. In Wolfson's view, religious philosophy is always undertaken with reference to revealed doctrines. Religious knowledge is a knowledge that was disclosed through revelation from the start, and it remains for humans only to accept or reject it. The fundamental beliefs and opinions of scriptural philosophy enjoy a status similar to that of the Written Law in traditional Judaism; they require clarification, elucidation and application, but not completion or development. Religion, therefore, is not subject to evolutionary development, as every manifestation of theology in Western history is derivative, logically and deductively, from some ancient creed.[69]

In Guttmann's view, by way of contrast, the origin of religious knowledge is autonomous, not heteronomous. The religious consciousness is a specific kind of spontaneous human awareness, possessed of its own paradoxical structure, that is based on categories such as intimacy and alienation, concealment and revelation.[70] As a field of consciousness that is both naturally and humanly based, it is subject, like all other spiritual phenomena, to historical, dialectical, developmental laws.[71] While Guttmann strives to create archetypes of religious faith, such as personalism and intellectualism, that span all of history, the historiosophy of German idealism has left its imprint on his scholarship. Jewish religious philosophy develops in a dialectical-evolutionary fashion, and its discrete contents and elements are explicated in keeping with their contribution to the development of the human religious consciousness as a whole. Accordingly, these elements exert a driving force within the overall framework of a dynamic historical process.

NOTES

1. See above, pp. 201–28.
2. Julius Guttmann, *The Philosophies of Judaism* (New York: Jewish Publication Society of America, 1964), 4–5.
3. For an example of the paradoxical nature of the religious experience according to Guttmann, see *On the Philosophy of Religion* (Jerusalem: Magnes Press, 1976),

45: "Judaism believes that God is the God of justice and that at the same time there is in Him something that we cannot fathom. . . . Even though I am dust and ashes I feel that you [God] must do justice."

4. Guttmann, *Philosophy of Religion*, 91–94.

5. Guttmann, *Philosophy of Religion*, 148–52, 173–74.

6. Guttmann, *Philosophy of Religion*, 91–94.

7. Guttmann, *Philosophy of Religion*, 25, in his words: "Consistency was never Philo's strong point; if he occasionally seems to approach the Biblical conception of a personal God, this may more safely be considered inconsistency rather than the essential nature of his teaching."

8. Guttmann, *Philosophies of Judaism*, 28, writes: "Trustful submission to God is as important for [Philo] as the longing for mystical union with God. Philo probably did not realize the contradiction between the two ideals."

9. Guttmann, *Philosophies of Judaism*, 104–6.

10. Guttmann, *Philosophies of Judaism*, 106–7.

11. Guttmann, *Philosophies of Judaism*, 109–110, in his words: "In spite of the considerable Neoplatonic influence on Bahya's theoretical construction of the concept of God, the religious relationship of the soul to God, as conceived by him, is absolutely different. The basic religious categories are trust, humility, and love, and . . . simple piety."

12. Guttmann, *Philosophies of Judaism*, 367, in his words: "His book is full of the spirit of living religion, and he bends all of his conceptual, form-giving power to the task of integrating religion within the circle of his concepts; but in his most characteristic formulations he is still bound to this limitation. In his wonderfully religious structure, there remains an unbridgeable gap between the content of religion and the philosophic creation of concepts."

13. Guttmann, *Philosophies of Judaism*, 23, in his words: "The ideal of an ascent of the soul to the supra-sensual world, culminating in a union with God, is alien to the ethical religion of Judaism."

14. Guttmann, *Philosophies of Judaism*, 63–64.

15. Guttmann, *Philosophies of Judaism*, 296–98.

16. Julius Guttmann, "Religion and Knowledge in Medieval and Modern Thought," in *Religion and Knowledge* (Jerusalem: Magnes Press, 1955), 41.

17. Guttmann, *Philosophies of Judaism*, 52–55, and also in his article "Religion and Knowledge in Medieval and Modern Thought," *Religion and Knowledge* (especially pp. 9, 25–26).

18. Guttmann, "Religion and Knowledge," *Religion and Knowledge*, 26–27.

19. Guttmann, *Philosophies of Judaism*, 181–82, and also his article "The Religious Motifs in Maimonides' Philosophy," *Religion and Knowledge*, 101.

20. Guttmann, "Religion and Knowledge in Medieval and Modern Thought," *Religion and Knowledge*, 6.

21. Guttmann, *Philosophies of Judaism*, 77–79.

22. Guttmann, *Philosophies of Judaism*, 70–71.

23. Guttmann, *Philosophies of Judaism*, 70–71.

24. Guttmann, "The Religious Motifs," *Religion and Knowledge*, 95.

25. Guttmann, "The Religious Motifs," *Religion and Knowledge*, 66–68.

26. Guttmann, "The Religious Motifs," *Religion and Knowledge*, 116–17.

27. Guttmann, "The Religious Motifs," *Religion and Knowledge*, 87.

28. Guttmann, *Religion and Knowledge*, 91.

29. Guttmann, *Religion and Knowledge*, 91.

30. Guttmann, *Religion and Knowledge*, 92–93.

31. Guttmann, *Religion and Knowledge*, 92–94.

32. Guttmann, *Religion and Knowledge*, 95.

33. Guttmann, *Religion and Knowledge*, 95–96.

34. Guttmann, *Religion and Knowledge*, 172–74.

35. Guttmann, *Religion and Knowledge*, 95–98.

36. Guttmann, *Religion and Knowledge*, 92–96.

37. Guttmann, *Religion and Knowledge*, 96–101. See also Shlomo Pines' book, *Bein Machshevet Israel le-Machshevet ha-Amim* (Jerusalem: Bialik Institute, 1977).

38. With regard to "cultural regions," see Pines, *Bein Machshevet Israel*, 7.

39. See on this matter Pines' introduction to his translation of *Guide*: "The Philosophic Sources of *The Guide of the Perplexed*," in Maimonides, *The Guide of the Perplexed*, trans. and intro. by Shlomo Pines (Chicago: University of Chicago Press, 1963), especially lix–lxi, lxxxii–lxxxiv.

40. The following statement by Pines reflects his views on the subject: "The Jewish thinkers made use first and foremost of the books of Muslim thinkers, particularly of the most important thinkers. Any reference by them to the teachings of their Jewish predecessors is rare, and only secondary in significance." From "Ha-Skolastikah she-Aharei Tomas Akwinas, Mishnatam shel Rav Hasdai Crescas ve-shel Kodmav," *Divrei ha-Akademia ha-Leumit ha-Israelit la-Madaim* 1, no. 11 (1966): 4. Pines' student, Eliezer Schweid, takes issue with this thesis in arguing for the existence of a tradition of inner continuity in Jewish medieval philosophy. See his article "Ha-Im Kayemet Masoret Atzmait shel Filosofiah Yehudit?" on this topic, in his book *Ta'am ve-Haksheh*, (Ramat Gan: Masada, 1970), 12–36.

41. See above, pp. 170–71.

42. See above, pp. 169–71, 186–87.

43. Guttmann, *Philosophies of Judaism*, 3.

44. Guttmann, *Philosophies of Judaism*, 3.

45. Guttmann, *Philosophies of Judaism*, 62.

46. Guttmann, *Philosophies of Judaism*, 152.

47. Guttmann, *Philosophies of Judaism*, 152.

48. Guttmann, *Philosophies of Judaism*, 153.

49. Guttmann, *Philosophies of Judaism*, 160–62, 181–83.

50. Regarding Shlomo Pines' "intellectual" and "academic" approach to the subject of his scholarship, see his statement at the Symposium on Science and Faith in Jewish Studies, as recorded in *Ha-Universitah* periodical, 11, pamphlets 2–3 (October 1965): 24. A portion of his statement is also cited in Schweid's article, "Ha-Im Kayemet Masoret Atzmait shel Filosofiah Yehudit?" *Ta'am ve-Haksheh*, 35, note 13. Schweid expresses reservations there about conducting education or passing on a cultural heritage from within a stance of ethical indifference.

51. The following passage from Pines' article "Ha-Skolastikah," *Divrei ha-Akademia*, 2 (see note 40 above), conveys his view of the subject: "It is hardly plausible that people who were fairly well integrated into their foreign surroundings, who certainly knew the local tongue and some of whom evidently knew Latin as well,

would have been impervious to the moods, philosophic problems and sometimes stormy ideological debates that engaged these surroundings." Pines subsequently cites scholars he claims to have demonstrated the influence of Thomas Aquinas or Averroes on Jewish thinkers like Hillel of Verona and Yitzhak Albalag.

52. Pines, "Ha-Skolastikah," *Divrei ha-Akademia*, 72–73.

53. For an apt description of the view that deems the historical event itself worthy of study, see Nathan Rotenstreich's lecture at the symposium on "Hora'at ha-Filosofiah be-Veit-ha-Sefer ha-Tichon u-va-universitah," as recorded in *Iyyun* 23, no. 1 (Winter 1972): 33–34.

54. Rotenstreich, "Hora'at ha-Filosofiah," 98–101.

55. Rotenstreich, "Hora'at ha-Filosofiah," 169–71.

56. Guttmann, *Philosophies of Judaism*, 13.

57. In Guttmann's words: "Armed with the authority of a supernatural revelation, religion lays claim to an unconditioned truth of its own, and thereby becomes a problem for philosophy." *Philosophies of Judaism*, 4.

58. Guttmann, *Philosophies of Judaism*, 10–11.

59. Guttmann, "Religion and Knowledge," *Religion and Knowledge*, 1, in his words: "At the very outset of its development philosophy elevated itself so far beyond Greek popular religion that the latter could never again serve to confront philosophy with the problem of religion. Neither the ancient criticism of popular idolatry nor the late philosophic interpretation of this belief contained any hint of such a problem."

60. Guttmann, *Philosophies of Judaism*, 285.

61. Regarding this distinction see Guttmann, "Religion and Knowledge," *Religion and Knowledge*, 21.

62. Guttmann, *Philosophies of Judaism*, 73.

63. Guttmann, *Philosophies of Judaism*, 84.

64. Guttmann, *Philosophies of Judaism*, 105.

65. Guttmann, *Philosophies of Judaism*, 134–35.

66. Guttmann, *Philosophies of Judaism*, 163–67.

67. Guttmann, *Philosophies of Judaism*, 163–64, 182–85.

68. Guttmann, *Philosophies of Judaism*, 185–87.

69. Guttmann, *Philosophies of Judaism*, 98–101.

70. Guttmann, *Philosophies of Judaism*, 118–120.

71. Guttmann, *Philosophies of Judaism*, 116–18, 174–76, 177–80.

III

BEYOND TIME AND SOCIETY— PHILOSOPHY, JUDAISM AND HISTORY IN THE SCHOLARSHIP OF LEO STRAUSS

INTELLECTUAL BACKGROUND

Leo Strauss was born in Kirschhein, in the Hesse region of Germany, in 1899. He relates that he grew up in a "traditional, even orthodox, Jewish home, in a rural area of Germany."[1] He received his doctorate at the University of Hamburg in 1921. From 1925–1932 he served as research assistant at the Academy of Jewish Research in Berlin, when Julius Guttmann was its director. Strauss specialized there in seventeenth-century Biblical criticism, particularly the thought of Spinoza and edited the writings of Moses Mendelssohn.

During this period Strauss attended Guttmann's lectures in Jewish philosophy at the Academy for the Science of Judaism. Strauss was grateful to Guttmann for the vast knowledge he imparted to him, but took radical issue with his scholarly method. In 1932 Strauss left Germany for France (having received a stipend from the Rockefeller Fund), and from 1934–1938 he lived in England.

In 1938 Strauss immigrated to the United States, where he served as lecturer and subsequently as professor of political science and philosophy at the New School for Social Research in New York until 1948. In 1949 he was awarded the chair of professor of political philosophy at the University of Chicago, where he remained until 1968 (from 1954–1955 he was a visiting lecturer at the Hebrew University of Jerusalem). From then until his death in 1973 he taught at St. John's College in Annapolis, Maryland, where he held the position of resident scholar.[2]

During the years he taught in the United States Strauss developed a following of students renowned in the academic world—some of whom were even influential in the American government—who affiliated themselves with what came to be known as the "Straussian school." The school's proponents characterize it according to the following principles: a great attentiveness to the analysis of original texts, the disavowal of historical and contextual explanations in the exegesis of philosophic sources and the refraining from uncritical adoption of all of the elements of modern liberal democracy. The systematic origin of these tendencies in Strauss' writings will be elucidated below.[3]

Strauss himself testified to the evolution of his thought in his preface to the English edition of his book *Spinoza's Critique of Religion*,[4] testimony that, in the words of his student Ralph Lerner, constitutes a sort of intellectual autobiography. Strauss began[5] by examining the historical and cultural origins of the longing for medievalism that affected Germany during the Weimar Republic, explaining why the integration of Jews into German society and culture was fundamentally impossible. His grasp of the situation within the context of the liberal-modern view that every human problem is ultimately given to resolution initially inclined Strauss in the direction of the solution proposed by the political Zionist movement. However, in his view, despite the Zionist movement's achievement in restoring the "honor" of the Jewish people, it has failed to resolve "the problem of the Jews." The fact of a common origin was not a sufficiently broad basis for the establishment of a Jewish entity, and the Jewish people had perforce to ground its existence in a common spiritual culture as well. Yet his investigation of the cultural dimension of Zionism convinced Strauss that historically, Jewish culture has regarded itself not as the product of a "national spirit," but as a genuine Divine revelation. Religious Zionism as well finds itself to be first and foremost religious Judaism, and only secondarily Zionism. And even if the establishment of a Jewish state is the most significant event in the chronicles of the Jewish people since the redaction of the Talmud, this does not mean that it constitutes either an absolute solution to the Jewish problem or a sign of redemption. Strauss then proceeds to relate how the understanding of Judaism as a religion based on revelation caused him to reexamine modern Jewish ways of thinking about the concepts of commandment and revelation. Strauss criticizes the perspectives of Cohen, Buber and Rosenzweig, predicated as they are on modern presuppositions concerning the autonomy of spirit or the value of individualism. The above insights pushed Strauss towards the realization that orthodoxy might be the only possibility. At this point, by his own admission, he turned to Spinoza, for "A return to orthodoxy would have been conceivable only if Spinoza were wrong on every count."

Strauss' first book, *Spinoza's Critique of Religion*, the fruit of his scholarship from 1925–1928, was published in 1930. His final assessment regarding Spinoza is that the philosopher's system is essentially hypothetical and fails in its project of providing a clear account of totality of Being without being constrained to posit a mysterious God. Nevertheless, Strauss remarks at the end of his introduction that he did not allow himself to celebrate the "victory" of orthodoxy over rational philosophy in this matter. Both because Jewish orthodoxy has always claimed superiority over other orthodoxies by virtue of its superior rationality (*"for this is proof of your wisdom and your discernment in the sight of the nations"*—Deut. 4:6), and because of his wish to confront the new existential theories that rely on the "will to power," Strauss decided that it would be unwise to relinquish reason. At this juncture, relates Strauss, he turned to medieval rationalism, discovering there the theory of esoteric writing that so engaged him in his later work.

The question that arises here is: What drove Strauss to the investigation of medieval philosophy: the wish to find an answer, by way of reason, to the menacing implications of the radical historicization of thought that emerges from the philosophies of Nietzsche and Heidegger and of the doctrine of the "will to power," orientations that leave humans without any objective rational or moral anchor, or the wish to find a rational justification for Jewish revelation in particular? On this topic Strauss' students and collaborators differ. His student Ralph Lerner emphasizes Strauss' disappointment at the tendency of educated German Jewry to gloss over the contradictory demands of revelation (submission) and reason (unconditioned inquiry). Driven by embarrassment or convenience, prominent German Jewish thinkers had exchanged the simple faith of their forefathers regarding the creation of the world, the revelation at Sinai and the immortality of the soul for anthropocentric or individualist interpretations in the spirit of the modern enlightenment. Other thinkers sought to confine religion and knowledge to separate compartments of "truth." At some point Strauss reached the conclusion that the genuine radical choice was between an orthodoxy that mandates a belief in the God of the patriarchs, the Creator of the world, and a political Zionism that is atheist through and through. Says Lerner:

> Every self-respecting Jew, confronted with the quandary just described and unable to accept wholeheartedly either the simple ancestral faith or its faithless antagonist, could only yearn for an enlightened Judaism to which he might cleave with heart and mind. It is a measure of Strauss' liberation and calm daring that he could bring this question into the open: Must enlightenment perforce be modern enlightenment?[6]

In Lerner's opinion it was this question that led Strauss to investigate Maimonidean rationalism and medieval Jewish and Arab philosophy. By Strauss' own admission, he continued to study *The Guide of the Perplexed* all his life, even when he was publishing widely on issues of general political philosophy.[7]

According to Shlomo Pines, author of the authorized English translation of *The Guide of the Perplexed* to which Strauss wrote the introduction, Strauss' motives in studying medieval philosophy were of a different order. Pines holds that the fundamental influence operating on Strauss was not a Jewish one, although the view that Judaism is revelation rather than the product of the "national spirit" retained a central place in his thought. In light of his acquaintance with Strauss in late 1920s Berlin, Pines states that Strauss was first and foremost a philosopher "who had experienced the radical teaching of temporality and historicity in Heidegger, the anti-religiosity of Spinoza, the political theories of Machiavelli and Hobbes . . . and the focus of Nietzsche, according to Strauss' reading, on the teaching of the will to power, and possibly also on his sense of nihilism."[8] In Pines' view, although Strauss argued that philosophy is unable to refute orthodoxy, "He knew very well that this way was not for him." It was the thought that "subverts foundations and reveals the nakedness of the world and man" that exerted a decisive influence on Strauss, not the quest for an "enlightened Judaism." Strauss turned to medieval thought, says Pines, out of an awareness of the social destructiveness of modern nihilism, however profound and true it might be on the theoretical level. He was looking for a non-deleterious nihilism, and he found it in the work of the medieval thinkers. These philosophers, though they also did not believe in a benevolent Providence, knew how to camouflage the destructive implications of true philosophy. They paid lip service to the tenets of faith, both "out of fear for their own security, but also out of concern for the society to which they belonged." Hence Strauss' pursuit of the hidden meaning of texts with an "external" message, and his method of meticulous reading in the tradition of the medieval commentators on Maimonides, a method Pines deems unique in contemporary scholarship.

Lerner and Pines differ not only with regard to Strauss' motives for studying medieval Jewish philosophy, but also with regard to the period in which he began searching for the "exoteric" masks of texts. According to Lerner, the book *Philosophy and Law*, published in Germany in 1935, which is the product of scholarship Strauss conducted in the early 1930s, is essentially an early book that lacks any radical conclusions regarding Maimonides' worldview, conclusions that were the fruit of the developed "exoteric" method of reading.[9] Pines, by way of contrast, contends that already by the late 1920s Strauss was aware of the importance of Plato's *Laws* (that introduced the exoteric way of writing) in understanding Maimonides' views.[10] From Pines' standpoint, then, *Philosophy and Law* is the precursor of Strauss' mature approach, and only *Spinoza's Critique of Religion* represents his early perspective. From Strauss' own testimony one might conclude that the change in his orientation was first evidenced in an article he wrote in response to a book by Carl Schmitt that appeared in 1932, which was published in English as an appendix to the English edition of *Spinoza's Critique of Religion.*

In keeping with our approach above, we will not seek a definitive answer regarding the motives and contextual influences that impacted on Strauss' thought. Following these brief background remarks, we will proceed to an analysis of the components of Strauss' mature perspective that, by Pines' account, remained constant for the rest of his life.[11]

In light of the specific focus of our project, namely, the attempt to articulate different conceptions of the discipline of "Jewish philosophy," we will pay special attention to those writings of Strauss that address the works of philosophers for whom Judaism was a major component or reference-point of their thought, that is, Maimonides, Yehuda ha-Levi and Spinoza.[12] Concomitantly, we will analyze in depth passages from Strauss' major theoretical articles that concern themselves with the nature of religion and philosophy and the possible and impossible relations between them.[13] These were certainly not marginal topics for Strauss, given that he himself characterizes the struggle between revelation and philosophy as "the most important fact of the whole past."[14] Strauss emphasizes that his extensive engagement with the works of various political thinkers derives from the fact that he regards political philosophy as "the end and the conclusion, the crowning and seal, if one will, of metaphysics."[15]

Strauss' historiosophic perspective will concern us next. Despite, or perhaps because of, the fact that Strauss did not propose a comprehensive historical scheme along the lines of Wolfson and Guttmann, he draws a clear distinction between the ancient and modern worlds and elaborates on what he considers to be the unique characteristics of each.[16] Finally, as in the case of Wolfson and Guttmann, we will examine Strauss' hermeneutic method, so conclusively formulated and illustrated in his famous work *Persecution and the Art of Writing.*[17] The discussion will be supplemented throughout with comparative observations underscoring the profound distinctions between Wolfson, Guttmann and Strauss' grasp of "Jewish philosophy."

NOTES

1. Details of Strauss' early biography can be found in the article "Leo Strauss, On His Sixty-Fifth Birthday," in Joseph Cropsey, ed., *Ancients and Moderns* (New York: Basic Books, 1964), v–vi. Strauss' testimony is taken from a short article entitled "A Giving of Accounts" that appeared in *The College,* the periodical of St. John's University of Annapolis, in April 1970. It is also cited in John P. East, "Leo Strauss and American Conservatism," *Modern Age* 21, no. 1 (Winter 1977): 2.

2. Other biographical information can be found in East, "Leo Strauss and American Conservatism," *Modern Age.* Concerning the argument between Strauss and

Guttmann, see Fritz Bamberger, "Julius Guttmann: Philosopher of Judaism," *Leo Baeck Institute Year Book* 5 (1960): 19–20 (including notes 45, 48).

3. On the "Straussian" school as it is perceived in the academic and political worlds in the United States, see Werner Dannhauser, "Leo Strauss: Becoming Naïve Again," *The American Scholar* 44, no. 4 (Fall 1975): 636–42; Jacob Weisberg, "The Cult of Leo Strauss," *Newsweek*, Aug. 3, 1987, 46.

4. Ralph Lerner's foreword to Leo Strauss, *Philosophy and Law* (Philadelphia: Jewish Publication Society of America, 1987), ix.

5. The discussion in the passages below is based on Leo Strauss' preface to the English edition of *Spinoza's Critique of Religion* (New York: Schocken Books, 1965), 1–31. See also "Why We Remain Jews," a transcript of a lecture delivered by Strauss to the Hillel Foundation of the University of Chicago, prepared July 1964 by Werner Dannhauser & James Lane, pp. 6–8. (The lecture is included in a collection of Strauss' articles published and introduced by Kenneth Hart Green entitled *Jewish Philosophy and the Crisis of Modernity* (Albany, NY: SUNY Press, 1997), 311–56.

6. Lerner, foreword to *Philosophy and Law*, xii.

7. Leo Strauss, "How to Begin to Study *The Guide of the Perplexed*," introduction to Moses Maimonides, *The Guide of the Perplexed*, ed. and trans. Shlomo Pines (Chicago: University of Chicago Press, 1963), xi.

8. The citations and discussion in this section are taken from Shlomo Pines, "Al Leo Strauss," *Molad* 7, no. 37–38 (end of 1976): 455–57.

9. Lerner, foreword to *Philosophy and Law*, ix–x.

10. Pines, "Al Leo Strauss," 455. Interestingly, Guttmann himself, in an article written in response to the book *Philosophy and Law* entitled "Filosofiah shel ha-Dat o-Filosofiah shel ha-Hok?" in *Divrei ha-Akademiah ha-Leumit ha-Israelit le-Madaim 5*, no. 9 (1976): 190, 193, depicts the "revolution" in Strauss' thought in the direction of highlighting the exoteric nature of medieval philosophic works as manifesting itself in articles that appeared after *Philosophy and Law*, between 1936–1941 (according to Pines' calculation in his notes on Guttmann's statement there). Guttmann, however, does identify hints in this direction in the book *Philosophy and Law* itself.

11. According to Pines' account ("Al Leo Strauss," 455), "Many of the opinions Strauss espoused until the end of his life had already crystallized at that time [namely, 'in the late twenties or a little later'], and I remember things he said at the time which can be found in material written some thirty years later."

12. Our principal texts for this topic will be: On ha-Levi—Leo Strauss, "The Law of Reason in the *Kuzari*," in *Persecution and the Art of Writing* (Glencoe, IL: Free Press, 1952), 95–141; on Maimonides—Strauss, "The Literary Character of the *Guide for the Perplexed*," *Persecution*, 38–94; Leo Strauss, "How to Begin to Study *The Guide of the Perplexed*," introduction to Moses Maimonides, *The Guide of the Perplexed*, ed. & trans. Shlomo Pines (Chicago: University of Chicago Press, 1963), xi–lvi; on Spinoza—Strauss, "How to Study Spinoza's *Theologico-Political Treatise*," *Persecution*, 142–201.

13. Our chief texts for this topic will be: Strauss, *Philosophy and Law*, 1987, originally *Philosophie und Gesetz*, Berlin 1935; Strauss, *Persecution and the Art of Writing*, introduction, and the chapter called "Persecution and the Art of Writing" (7–37); Leo Strauss, "What Is Political Philosophy," address delivered at the Hebrew University, 1954, appearing in *What Is Political Philosophy* (Glencoe, IL: Free Press,

1959), 65–99; Strauss, *Spinoza's Critique of Religion*, preface to the English transla-tion, 1–31; Leo Strauss, "Jerusalem and Athens," in *Studies in Platonic Political Phi-losophy* (Chicago and London: University of Chicago Press, 1983), 147–73; Leo Strauss, "The Mutual Influence of Theology and Philosophy," *Independent Journal of Philosophy*, 3 (1979):111–18. It should be noted that those texts addressing specific thinkers often contain highly significant observations on the question of the con-nection between religion and philosophy, while the articles formally devoted to this topic contain highly significant remarks about the thought of the various philoso-phers. This state of affairs will naturally guide us in our analysis.

14. Strauss, "The Law of Reason in the *Kuzari*," *Persecution*, 107.

15. Strauss, *Philosophy and Law*, 50.

16. See particularly the first chapter of Strauss, *Philosophy and Law*, 23–58, titled "The Conflict of the Ancients and Moderns in the Philosophy of Judaism: Com-ments on Julius Guttmann's 'Philosophies of Judaism.'"

17. See note 13 above.

7

Epistemological Perspectives— Religious and Philosophical Knowledge

Their Character and Modes of Interaction

THE ESSENCE OF THE RELIGIOUS RELATION
AND RELIGIOUS KNOWLEDGE IN LEO STRAUSS

According to Wolfson's view, the "objective" content of religion (to use Guttmann's terminology) is embodied within a system of faith tenets originating in revelation. This content has a more reliably rational basis than religious knowledge that emanates from the human intellect. The "subjective" side of religion, that which expresses the believer's relation to the object of his belief, is merely the human prerogative to accept or deny this doctrinal order.[1] Guttmann, by comparison, views the religious consciousness as a quintessentially human epistemological category that partakes of the structure of human consciousness, together with and in interaction with theoretical and moral cognition. Guttmann does not entirely dismiss the heteronomous aspect of religion, of course; beyond the prism of human consciousness there is an actual God who reveals Himself to human beings and makes His word known. Guttmann's interest, however, is focused on the place of the religious consciousness within the human cognitive structure, and he considers the religious experience to be a spontaneous, volatile phenomenon. The attraction to and the fear of a God who is both hidden and revealed is fed by a self-sustaining certainty, independent of any revelatory or rational authority. Guttmann's religious persona is neither docile nor dependent, but is rather characterized by an emergent spontaneity informed by robust emotions.[2] Religion, consequently, is a matter that is "accessible to man as man," to use the language of Strauss.[3]

Leo Strauss characterizes the essence of the religious relation and the substance of religious knowledge differently. Strauss considers knowledge, among other things, to be a form of power,[4] that facilitates control. In his conviction, "the biblical solution . . . stands or falls by the belief in God's omnipotence,"[5] in relation to whom humans are helpless. God in the Bible, accordingly, is called "I shall be that I shall be," which from Strauss' standpoint signifies that "it is never possible in any present to know that what God shall be."[6] While for Guttmann the mysterious, concealed aspect of the Deity suggests a certain positive knowledge intimating sublimity and potency,[7] for Strauss all that humans can discern from the Bible about God is His mysteriousness. Only as a mysterious God can He be "truly omnipotent."[8]

This state of affairs begets the question of how God makes Himself known to human beings, and whether any connection between God and humans is possible. Strauss holds that "The biblical answer is the covenant, a free and mysterious action of love on the part of God."[9] This Divine overture demands a human response. The response, however, is not the experience of some kind of extraordinary certainty or validity, as depicted by Guttmann. Nor is it a matter of assenting to certain truths, as Wolfson understood faith to be. In Strauss' view the response is indeed a gesture of faith—not in the sense of receiving doctrines, but in the sense of trust. The Biblical believer surrenders himself, submitting unconditionally to the Divine will,[10] even if this will contradicts itself and every human concept of morality.[11] For Strauss the religious relation does not manifest itself as a type of evidence or inner certainty that can be compared, if only negatively, with evidence of another kind. There is also no real similarity between Wolfson's concept of "assent" and Strauss' concept of "trust." Wolfson considers philosophy's claim to the status of ultimate arbiter in matters of faith to be an act of "pride," while the willingness to accept revealed cognitive religious knowledge is a sign of "humility."[12] Strauss, on the other hand, ventures beyond the conflict between intellectual "pride" and "humility," preferring to examine the topic from the perspective of power and control. In Wolfson, reason attains partial intellectual knowledge of God and His attributes, a partiality stemming from the limitations of human cognition, depending as it does on the senses. Strauss, however, does not consider humans capable of attaining any theoretical knowledge of God. God's omnipotence and the negation of the possibility of any human intellectual control of God imply the absolute relinquishment of the cognitive knowledge of divinity. In Strauss' words, "The biblical God is known in a humanly relevant sense only by his actions, by his revelations."[13] Moreover, it is impossible to achieve prophecy "naturally" or to discern any kind of lawful pattern regarding these actions and revelations of God, as this kind of information is accessible only if God bestows it. This insight is also included in Strauss' understanding of the concept of "I shall be that I shall be." "The Bible is the account of what God has done and what he has promised. . . .

In the Bible . . . men tell about God's actions and promises on the basis of their experience of God."[14] This is not a manifestation of intellectual humility in the face of a perfect, transcendent intellectual authority. Nor is it a spontaneous eruption of certainty regarding the actual presence of a guarantor of a future moral order. It is a response of unconditional devotion to the loving call of God, who requires that humans love Him and only Him with all their hearts and all their souls and all their might.[15] The response to this call is not supposed to be some kind of subjective emotional inwardness, but a commitment to the revelatory text by way of which the call was first transmitted.[16] The Bible is the book that relates the narrative of human experience with God (not human knowledge of God), specifying what He demands of humans within the framework of the general requirement to love and serve only Him. The essence of the love and service required of humans in the Bible, says Strauss, is action, not the adoption of articles of faith or inner piety. Regarding the basic human duality of thought and speech on the one hand, and deeds on the other, "The Bible asserts the primacy of deed."[17] The "action" meant by Strauss, however, is not the moral activism of Guttmann. In Strauss' view, the Bible's demand for justice "means primarily obedience to law, and law in the full and comprehensive sense, divine law."[18] The sacrificial love required of humans in response to the Divine call, the implicit trust that comes from faith, is an obedient love, committed to the Divine laws prescribed in advance in a particular and unique revelatory message.[19] Guttmann, the liberal Jew, sought to distill from the Bible a personalist religious inwardness coupled with moral-social activism. He considered the personalist religious faith to be in the process of freeing itself from the fetters of a particularist external authoritarianism, and becoming, with the evolution of the philosophy of religion, a universal human possession. Wolfson, in contrast, chose to focus on the doctrinal tenets that can be distilled from the narratives, exhortations and precepts of the Bible and to treat these elements as the common underpinnings for what he termed the "scriptural philosophy" reflected in the three monotheistic faiths. Strauss, in contradistinction to the other two, was unwilling to turn his back on what he considered to be the heteronomous, legal and particularist character of the Bible and of the Jewish religion.

Strauss had already become interested in pre-modern Judaism, devoid of idealist and universalist elements, as Guttmann's student in Berlin in the 1920s and 1930s. Already in *Philosophy and Law* Strauss sharply criticizes Guttmann's theory that religion is a type of certainty originating in the human consciousness. In Strauss' view, monotheistic religion understands itself as bestowed from the outside, and not as a direction of consciousness or realm of certainty.[20] The definition of religion as an inner human phenomenon is a modern distortion that stems from the idealist tendency to derive both the world and God from human consciousness.[21] By way of comparison, in the ancient and medieval periods humans were considered to be citizens of the cosmos (even if endowed with a special status) who belonged to an objective, external natural order. This cosmos, along with its Creator, was understood to be self-evidently, ontologically real. Both creation, then, and revelation were grasped as ontological events that transpired in a genuine, external reality.[22]

If the authentic form of religion is external revelation rather than a spontaneous awareness of the human spirit, then neither the content nor the quality of religion are a "type of personalist religious faith," but rather—obedience to the law. The distinctions Guttmann draws between diverse types of religious orientations, and first and foremost between the mystical-pantheist orientation and the personalist one, stem from the pioneering work of Shleiermacher and others in the typology of the religious consciousness and of religious faith. However, says Strauss, these same distinctions between different types of religious inwardness originate in the descriptions of religious inwardness found in mystical literature, the very type of religiosity portrayed by Guttmann himself as opposed to Biblical personalism.[23] Just as the Bible should not be considered solely as an expression of the human religious consciousness but primarily as a revelatory document, at least according to its own understanding and that of the medieval commentators, neither should it be considered an expression of personalist religious inwardness while ignoring its character as externally imposed law. In Strauss' words, "even the medieval philosophers, despite their intellectual orientation, do not understand religion to be either a "domain of validity" or a "direction of consciousness," and least of all as a "domain of culture," but rather, as *Law*."[24]

It is the law, then, that constitutes the "objective" aspect of religion for Strauss, not articles of faith, as Wolfson contended, or the reality of God as the source of morality, as Guttmann understood the object of personalist religious faith to be. The "subjective" aspect of religion, that in Guttmann's mind expresses the relation of the believer to the object of his belief, is for Strauss surrender and obedience, in contradistinction to the "certainty" of Guttmann and the "assent" of Wolfson. The subjective experience of "certainty" in Guttmann expresses the unique inner conviction of the believer as to the presence of a transcendent moral reality, a conviction gained independently of rational or external-historical proofs.[25] The subjective gesture of "assent," as articulated by Wolfson, corresponds to the object of that assent, namely, theological doctrines meant to be accepted on the basis of authority.[26] In Strauss as well there is a correlation between the gestures that express the subjective-relational pole of religion—surrender, obedient love—and the objective pole of an articulated law imposed from without, a law that specifies God's demands for unconditional love from human beings.[27]

Aside from his early critique of Guttmann, Strauss' insights regarding the quality of Biblical faith are grounded in an attentive literary-philosophic analysis of the Bible itself. Strauss intimates his overall understanding of the biblical worldview already in the introduction to his book *Persecution and the Art of Writing*, published in 1952, and elaborates more fully in a lecture he gave in 1967, "Jerusalem and Athens—Some Preliminary Reflections."[28]

To Strauss' way of thinking, the first verse of the book of Genesis is already charged with one of the elements of the Biblical worldview: "In the beginning God created the heavens and the earth, and the earth was formless and void, and darkness was on the face of the deep. And a wind from God swept over the water." This verse does not clarify whether the earth existed before the act of creation, if only in a state of chaos, or whether the act of creation applied to this proto-earth as well. In any event, the verse addresses only the primordial state of the earth and not of the heavens. In other words, already in the first verse the Bible directs our attention to the goings-on on earth and distances us from speculation concerning the state of the heavens.[29]

The description of the six days of creation reinforces this thrust. Strauss discerns here an ascending order culminating in the creation of man, who alone bears the "image of God" in the world. The further we progress along the order of creation, the greater the value ascribed to the created phenomenon. The earth is created after the heavens, and accordingly it is of higher value. In the first three days the light, the heavens and the earth are created, and the earth is covered with oceans and plants. In the last three days the heavenly constellations are created (the sun, moon and stars), the fish and the fowl, the land animals and finally humans. All of the creations of the first three days are immobile, while all the creations of the last three days are mobile. The order of creation in the Bible is not a natural order, even according to the perspective of ancient humans. The plants are created before the sun, for the plants are the permanent coverage of the immobile earth, though even ancient humans knew they depended on the sun. The sun, in contrast, is grasped as mobile. A further comparison between the plants (the third day) and the sun (the fourth day) reveals that regarding the plants it is said that God summoned their appearance through His speech, but not that he made them, while regarding the sun it is said that God made it. Moreover, humans are said to be "created" rather than "made."[30] In other words, the higher one climbs in the hierarchy of value, the closer one comes to God.

Strauss also calls our attention to the fact that the sun, the moon and the stars are mobile, yet lifeless. This is why their appearance precedes even the most primitive species of animals. Movement takes preference over fixity, and life takes preference over simple movement. The creations of the first three days are immobile and cannot change their places. The heavenly constellations change their places but not their paths. The animals change their paths, but not their ways, and only human beings are capable of changing their ways. A preference is evident, therefore, not only for life over simple mobility, or immobility, but also for freedom of choice over determined, instinctual behavior. Already in the creation narrative the Bible confers a value on humans, namely on the human ability to change one's ways, and on vitality and movement, while downplaying the value of the sun and the heavenly hosts, which are lifeless and follow fixed trajectories, and were not created in the likeness of a "living God." Only human beings, possessed of the power of motion, choice and change, reflect the Divine vitality.[31]

The second chapter of the book of Genesis illustrates the direction that was laid down in chapter one, of emphasizing and conferring value on the earth, life, humans and their voluntary actions. At the juncture between the first and second chapters the Bible is faced with the question of good and evil. After the creation of humans, it is said concerning "everything that God had made" that "behold, it was very good." Accordingly, the evil that afflicts humans on earth is not part of the fabric of the Divine creation. Why, then, are humans subject to evil and suffering? Chapter two depicts a primeval state of affairs in which human beings did not suffer at all, thus attributing to humankind itself the responsibility for evil.[32]

Life often comes down hard on human beings. The earth does not always reward its tillers for their backbreaking labor, and the rains don't always come at the appointed time. Yet if the Bible were to tell us that things had always been this way, such an account would constitute an authorization for human cruelty and miserliness. If the reality surrounding human beings had always been one of harshness and deprivation, there would be nothing to advise them of their obligation to behave justly and compassionately precisely in such a reality. The human responsibility to behave justly and compassionately even under conditions of natural deprivation is stressed in chapter two, which portrays a more felicitous primordial reality. The conditions of human existence were meant to be otherwise: conditions of a childlike dependency and submission to a God who provides for all their needs. Humans were destined for a life of simplicity, ease and innocence, yet on account of their behavior they now find themselves in need of rainfall from heaven and forced to work for a living. Strauss derives this primordial human destiny not only from the reality in the garden of Eden (the flowing rivers and the vegetation), but also from the contrast between the life of humans in the garden and the prohibition against eating specifically from the tree of knowledge of good and evil, on pain of death. In other words, human life in those primordial times was a life devoid of the knowledge of good and evil (the kind of knowledge that serves to guide human life), such that humans were dependent on God to direct their lives and supply their needs. In that pristine reality, "knowledge of good and evil" meant the downfall of human beings, as they were not constituted for this kind of life. The Biblical ideal, then, was a life of innocence, simplicity and dependence.[33]

In fact, in the course of the Genesis narrative it becomes clear that this idyll cannot persist, nor are humans expected to restore it. After the expulsion from the garden of Eden humans are permitted to establish and develop civilization—in similar fashion to the permission granted the people of Israel in the days of Samuel to appoint themselves a king, although God is ultimately the father and king of all humans—despite the immanent conflict between pious devotion and the qualities required to found and cultivate a civilization. This permission represents a Divine concession to man's desires, which are "evil from his youth," and to the need of humans to enhance their status vis-à-vis a hostile nature, rather than an expression of a pristine ideal.[34]

The attempt to create a type of human life that subsists without "knowledge of good and evil" fails, therefore, because the serpent aroused the skeptical and inquisitive side of the first humans, causing them to overlook the fact that the quest for knowledge involves violating the Divine commandments. This is not a human revolt against the sovereignty of God, however; the skepticism and curiosity implanted in humans simply distracts them from the Divine command.[35]

Strauss here draws a connection, also alluded to in the introduction to his book *Persecution and the Art of Writing*,[36] between the "demotion" of the importance of the heavens and the heavenly constellations in chapter one and the prohibition of eating from the tree of knowledge of good and evil in chapter two. He does not articulate the substance of this connection, yet he seems to imply that according to the Biblical ideal, no supreme value should be ascribed to the attainment of theoretical knowledge about the cosmos or political knowledge enabling self-government. Speculative and political knowledge belongs to God, while humans are meant to content themselves with childlike submission to His sublime will. This is the most apt posture for created beings, while the quest for speculative and political knowledge spells disaster.

The knowledge that sparked the downfall of human beings, however, was actually part of their original nature. The fact of the Divine prohibition against the pursuit of the knowledge of good and evil suggests that to begin with humans possessed a certain knowledge of good and evil, and that they had some sense that this knowledge was bad for them. The absolute Divine prohibition attests to the existence of a certain potential in humans that might lead to a transgression of the prohibition. And in fact, this very human drive for the expansion of knowledge overcame Adam and Eve and led to their fall.[37] The complex conditions of this fall are what lead to a Divine response that consists not only of punishment. In the period after the fall, until the generation of the flood, humans enjoyed great longevity and refrained from eating meat and drinking wine. This was a sort of reminder of the lost possibility of eternal life through simplicity. The period is portrayed as a time of moral decline. Yet the covenant with Noah after the flood, and the covenant with Abraham, begins the narrative motion that eventuates in the Sinaitic covenant and the revelation of the Torah (which is both a "tree of knowledge," meaning the kind of knowledge that can guide one in matters of good and evil, and a "tree of life"). This motion appears to represent a beneficent Divine response to human failure, a failure which from a certain standpoint is inevitable, as it stems from a potential that had been implanted in humans since their creation.[38]

After the experience of a life of simplicity devoid of knowledge of good and evil, a life that is desirable but unattainable given the doubtfulness and inquisitiveness implanted in human beings, the Bible presents us with the picture of a kind of life that proceeds with knowledge of good and evil, but lacks any real laws or sanctions. The punishment of Cain, that he wander the earth unmolested by humans, is relatively mild. The judicial institutions and penalties that come into being in Noah's time, when it is decreed that "Whoso sheds man's blood by man shall his blood be shed" (Gen. 9:6), do not yet exist. Whether we hold that after eating from the tree of knowledge, humans fell, or whether we hold it is then that they came into their own, according to the Bible people are incapable of living without the restraint of law and punishment. The same progress that equips humans to cope more effectively with their natural surroundings (now the wild animals will dread humans) is accompanied by the advent of explicit laws against murder and severe punishment for their infraction. Cain was not commanded not to kill, and his punishment was not so severe. After the flood severe punishment is decreed for the shedding of blood.[39] The human relation to God, then, is no longer to be characterized by unmediated dependence. It rather involves a gesture of obedience, mediated by a heteronomous law.

The imposition of the law on humans is actually a benevolent act on the part of God. The law is not forced on human beings in a wholly unilateral fashion, but rather transmitted within the framework of a covenant. Although the covenant is not between two equal partners, the superiority of God is expressed not through any great show of force, but through supreme self-restraint. By law, if almost all humans on earth become corrupted, all the sinners deserve to be annihilated, as happened in the flood narrative. Yet now, despite (or perhaps precisely because of) the fact that God knows that "the devisings of a man's heart are evil from his youth" (Gen. 8:21), God promises never to wipe out all of life on earth. The survival of life on earth will not be conditioned on the obedience of most humans to the laws of God.[40]

Further on in the article Strauss describes the transition between the covenant with Noah and the covenant with Abraham. Here not only does the heteronomous and legal character of the Biblical religion come to the fore, but a rationale is provided for Biblical particularism. Disobedience to an unwritten law (when Ham gazes on his father's nakedness) again brings down punishment on man. In this case the penalty is not annihilation, but the division of humans into a cursed portion (Ham and Canaan) and a blessed portion (Shem and Yafet). When humans seek to overcome the Divine policy of division through the conquests of Nimrod and the attempt to build the Tower of Babel, God reinforces it by dividing the human race into nations that do not understand each others' language (Strauss observes ironically that this state of affairs is a "milder alternative to the flood"). With the advent of Abraham, God's response to the almost universal violence on earth undergoes an additional transformation. The creation of different nations enables a division between a holy and chosen nation and other nations. In Strauss' words, "The emergence of nations made it possible that Noah's Ark floating alone on the waters covering the whole earth be replaced by a whole, numerous nation living in the midst of the nations covering the whole earth."[41]

The election of the holy people, both whose birth (Isaac was born when Sarah was ninety years old) and continued existence (the sacrifice of Isaac, which culminated in a miracle) are miraculous in nature, begins with the election of Abraham. Abraham, more than any other Biblical figure, represents the ideal of Biblical religiosity. His righteousness is first expressed by his willingness to trust in God's promise that his progeny would be as plentiful as the stars of the heavens and would inherit the land of Canaan, a promise whose fulfillment he would not live to see, due to the short life span of post-diluvian humans. The argument Abraham advances to God that there may be a number of righteous people in Sodom is also understood by Strauss as an expression of Abraham's faith in God's righteousness, rather than as a doubt concerning that righteousness. It is not, in Strauss' opinion, a resort to an autonomous criterion of justice, a kind of objective standard by which even the deeds of God can be measured. Abraham's faith in God's righteousness is deeper than Noah's (who did not react at all to the news of the impending flood), as is his awareness that he himself is "only dust and ashes." Accordingly, in fear and trembling, he makes himself a human partner in God's righteousness, not one who casts doubt on that righteousness. Abraham displays involvement and takes responsibility, thereby participating in the righteousness of God Himself.[42]

The essence of Abraham's trust in God is that God will not do anything that is incompatible with His righteousness. While admittedly "nothing is too wondrous for the Lord," God limits His own ability to perform miracles on account of His righteousness. The greatest test of Abraham's trust is the binding of Isaac. The commandment to sacrifice Isaac contradicts God's own promise that the holy, chosen nation will descend from Isaac, as well as an explicit Divine prohibition against shedding blood. Why, then, doesn't Abraham ask for the decree to be rescinded this time, as he did in the case of

Sodom and Gomorrah? Strauss believes that with regard to Sodom and Gomorrah Abraham was not commanded to do anything himself; most importantly, he wasn't commanded to surrender to God, by rendering to Him that which was most precious to him. Abraham knows that God demands that humans love only Him unconditionally, not themselves, and not their most cherished hopes. Abraham loves God with all his heart, all his soul and all his might, Him and not the chosen people.[43] And as for the prohibition against spilling blood, while God is indeed the God of righteousness, Divine righteousness does not necessarily coincide with human righteousness. Only God is always unqualifiedly righteous, though often unfathomably so (this unfathomability also emerges from Abraham's argument over Sodom and Gomorrah, for ultimately Abraham accepts the decree regarding the city's destruction, even were it to contain nine righteous men).[44]

Abraham's faith, then, is a "simple, single-minded" innocent faith, resembling the faith of a child,[45] and he is rewarded precisely because he seeks no reward. For Abraham, the ideal Jew, the commandment itself is its own reward. Abraham is not characterized by a utilitarian morality, oriented toward objectives external to morality itself; he is willing to surrender his life "for the sanctification of God's name." Revelation claims human beings unconditionally, and the Jew's submission to the Torah represents the relinquishment of his theoretical and practical sovereignty in favor of the omnipotent power of God.[46]

In Strauss' opinion, only through this kind of unqualified surrender to heteronomous law, without hope of theoretical or practical gain, can ethics gain validity as a categorical morality distinct from human conventions. And only such a categorical morality, founded on pious submission to the Divine revelation, can transform human beings into "their brother's keepers."[47] This is the universal significance of the particular, chosen religion of Israel, for only he about whom it is said "And he put his trust in the Lord, and He ascribed it to his merit," can also be the one who keeps "the way of the Lord, by doing what is just and right" (Gen. 18:19). Neither speculative nor autonomous practical reason can confer validity upon revelation, as Guttmann alleged. The autonomy of cognition and of morality are not expressions of God's will. Only the forfeiture of autonomous scrutiny of the Divine will, whether according to the law of contradiction or according to supposedly autonomous moral imperatives, makes possible a morality of absolute validity.

THE NATURE OF PHILOSOPHY AND PHILOSOPHIC KNOWLEDGE ACCORDING TO LEO STRAUSS

The difference between Strauss, Wolfson and Guttmann consists not only in their view of religion but also in their view of the essence of philosophy.

Wolfson saw philosophy as a neutral intellectual activity involving logical deduction. Its fundamental premises can therefore be derived from either scriptural or pagan norms. Admittedly a certain tension arises at times between philosophy's methodological quest for logical unity and the split in substantive reality (God, world, human beings) that underlies the Biblical worldview. Yet Wolfson, who does not posit substantive connections between form and content in the world of the spirit, does not believe this tension should prevent philosophy from serving the Bible as a faithful, expressive tool. All significant philosophy in the Western world has been subordinated to the Biblical heritage, thereby transforming it into the theology of the Bible.[48]

Guttmann regarded philosophy as an aspect of the human religious longing to commune with the absolute. Aristotle, Plotinus, Spinoza and Hegel all strove as one for intellectual unification with the most abstract conceptual truth that encompasses all of being. In so doing they were giving expression to an intellectualistic religiosity of the mystical-pantheist variety. While, admittedly, on certain points Guttmann seeks to grant philosophy methodological independence and to treat it as an autonomous source of validity, ultimately, in his view, the orientation of the soul that fuels the philosophic endeavor is the wish to commune, by way of the intellect, with God.[49] However, in Strauss' view philosophy is not a religious gesture at all, but a thoroughly secular one.[50] Philosophy is neither a rational language nor a conceptual cloak for religious longings, but rather a fundamental posture that calls for the absolute independence of the human intellect and rejects submission to the will of a supreme power whose presence and revelation are not self-evident.[51] This position also claims human beings unconditionally, and so precludes any serious inner relation to revealed religion.

In order to explore Strauss' view in greater depth we will examine some of his writings that take up the question of the nature of philosophy. Already in his article "The Law of Reason in the *Kuzari*" (1943), Strauss calls philosophy "not a set of dogmas, but a method, or an attitude."[52] If so, what is the essence of such an attitude? What is the orientation or posture of the philosopher? Strauss replies that the philosopher is "a perfect man" by virtue of his activity as an "investigator."[53] This position is exemplified by the opposition Strauss creates between Socrates' response to the oracle and the king of the Khazars' response to his dream in Yehuda Halevi's *Kuzari*: "Socrates' attempt to check the truth of the oracle led him to the philosophic life; the king's attempt to obey the angel who had spoken to him in his dreams, made him at once immune to philosophy and ultimately led him into the fold of Judaism."[54]

If the religious person who experiences revelation arrives at an "attitude" of submission, the philosopher arrives at an "attitude" of inquiry. The philosopher, then, lives a life of investigation and scrutiny. What is it that the philosopher investigates and scrutinizes? Strauss defines the subject of the philosopher's quest throughout the introduction to his book *Persecution and the Art of Writing* in the following manner: "genuine knowledge of the whole . . . the science of the essence of every being . . .the science of the divine and of the natural things."[55]

From the philosopher's standpoint, human happiness consists in a life spent searching for theoretical knowledge regarding the essence of being. This knowledge does not come to man from the outside; "philosophy being a kind of knowledge accessible to man as man."[56] The philosophic pursuit is self-sufficient, not being contingent upon any external source. Thus, argues Alfarabi, whose writings in Strauss' conviction faithfully reflect Plato's viewpoint, and whom Maimonides called the greatest philosopher of his time:

> philosophy by itself is not only necessary but sufficient for producing happiness: philosophy does not need to be supplemented by something else, or by something that is thought to be higher in rank than philosophy, in order to produce happiness. . . . The praise of philosophy is meant to rule out any claims of cognitive value which may be raised on behalf of religion in general and of revealed religion in particular.[57]

Evidently, then, no unique religious certainty that complements philosophy or broadens its perspective, as Guttmann claimed, can be presented alongside philosophy or above it. Neither can philosophy be turned into theology, as Wolfson proposed. Theology, according to Strauss, is "the art of the explication and defense of every Divine law or positive religion."[58] Theology, as an art bound to a predetermined religious content, does not lead humans to the object of the philosophic quest, which is "the science of the essence of every being."[59]

Strauss agrees with Wolfson that theology is an "art of syllogism." Yet this syllogistic art that is bound to Divine law or positive religion has nothing in common with the secular orientation of philosophy, and accordingly theology does not encompass knowledge of any philosophic value. Strauss furthers hones his argument: "religious speculation, and religious investigation of the beings, and the religious syllogistic art, do not supply the science of the beings, in which man's highest perfection consists, whereas philosophy does supply it. He [Alfarabi] goes so far as to present religious knowledge as the lowest step on the ladder of cognitive pursuits, as inferior even to grammar and to poetry."[60]

On what grounds is this claim to exclusivity based? Why is the philosopher necessarily a heretic and a non-believer in revealed religion as a source of truth? In Strauss' opinion, both Biblical and Greek thought are based on the concept of justice and on the premise of the identity of the good with the ancient. The ancient concept of justice was obedience to Divine law, not an autonomous morality devised by human reason. Justice expresses a kind of balance or intrinsically desirable state, that exists in reality itself, beyond human conventions. This justice was assumed to exist in the form of laws, and it was up to humans either to accept or discover them, not to create them.[61]

This view that there are ancient, Divine laws embodying goodness and truth arouses a fundamental difficulty. For there are numerous codes of law that contradict one another, with each claiming to be the genuine Divine code. At this point the Bible and philosophy go their separate ways. The Bible claims that "one particular divine code is accepted as truly divine."[62] Since God is one, omnipotent and mysterious, He revealed His will in a certain book to a certain people, and the other books are sheer falsehood. The fundamental propensity of Biblical figures to self-surrender, piety and submissiveness is paradigmatic for this direction of life. The philosopher's penchant for searching, investigating and examining leads him in another direction. In Strauss' words, "The philosophers transcend the dimension of divine codes altogether, the whole dimension of piety and of pious obedience to a pre-given code. Instead they embark on a free quest for the beginnings, for the first things, for the principles. And they assume that on the basis of the knowledge of first principles, of the first principles, of the beginnings, it will be possible to determine what is by nature good, as distinguished from what is good merely by convention."[63] While humans don't create goodness and truth, they also don't receive them as pre-given. They attempt to ground the correct way of life for human beings in enduring "natural" principles that they seek to discover in the course of their inquiry.

The attitude of Biblical figures is characterized by openness to an unmediated encounter with a promising, active, loving and demanding God.[64] In contrast, the philosopher's free quest is mediated by "sense perception and reasoning based on sense perception."[65] The intellectual awareness the philosopher seeks is always linked to the senses and the mind, in contradistinction to the Biblical awareness of unmediated presence or the mystic consciousness of union without boundaries. Philosophy, then, should not be turned into a logical, syllogistic method subordinated to the premises of holy texts, for philosophy is "a free quest for the beginnings." Nor should it be turned into a type of intellectualist-pantheist mystical religiosity. Not only does philosophy lack the dimensions of surrender and devotion that are at the heart of religion, but philosophic enlightenment "is never divorced from sense perception and reasoning,"[66] which distinguishes it from the mystical enlightenment that breaches these epistemological boundaries.[67]

How does philosophy know that "free inquiry," bound to "senses and rational thought," is exclusively sufficient to determine the right way of life?

Philosophy's manner of exposing "primordial goodness" is different from that of the Bible, and it is based on one aspect of human nature, yet how do we know that it's the true one? What is to prevent the philosopher from examining revelation as a possible source of truth in the course of his search? Philosophers, Strauss would say, are willing to recognize the validity only of clear and evident knowledge, clear and proven knowledge according to sensual or logical criteria. According to the philosopher, revelation is at most accorded the status of "an indifferent possibility."[68] This begets the following question, however: Even the philosopher knows that human wisdom is imperfect. If so, why does he choose to rely on it alone? Philosophers like Socrates acknowledged that human wisdom is also not "evident." Strauss further insists that philosophy is incapable of proving the non-existence of revelation.[69] Thus the philosopher's heresy is tendentious and is not based on the philosophic ideal of selecting a way of life according to clear and distinct knowledge alone. Yet the philosopher's dismissal of revelation does not stem merely from a stubborn refusal to assent to a super-human truth, as Wolfson contended. The reasons for the philosopher's refusal to accept revelation should not be reduced to faults such as "pride" or "stupidity." The philosopher does indeed possess a certain evident knowledge: the awareness of the imperfection of the human knowledge at his disposal. This evidence and clarity, regarding his lack of knowledge of the whole, renders a way of life dedicated to the attempt to attain such evident knowledge cardinal and normative for him. Philosophy, then, is the "quest for knowledge regarding the whole."[70] This life of quest is generated and motivated by the evident situation of lack of knowledge. The life of quest is also the utter antithesis of the life of submission to specific laws through relinquishment of knowledge concerning "what is above, what is below, what is before, and what is behind."[71] The philosopher would be unable to conduct a free inquiry regarding beginnings, if "God owns nothing in His World except the four cubits of the Halakhah."[72] Accordingly, by virtue of his own positive ideal the philosopher is unable to accept the way of life dictated by the Bible. The heresy of the philosopher is not wickedness. It is a principled heresy, based on the only evident knowledge he possesses: the knowledge that he does not know and that he must question and search. Moreover, any solutions the philosopher finds can and should continue to be challenged in the future. Philosophy, then, as a questing activity, should not be identified with any given substantive cluster of solutions, or "system."[73] Philosophy is the act of pursuing clear knowledge of the whole. In its own right, it constitutes an all-embracing way of life driven by the thirst for knowledge, rather than a tool or a partial realm.[74] From Strauss' standpoint, Wolfson distorted Western philosophy when he changed it from a way of life dictated by an independent ideal into an instrument for the articulation and justification of something foreign to it, namely, the Biblical faith. By the same token, Guttmann distorted the nature of philosophy as well, rendering it into merely a partial realm, a "compartment" of the human consciousness that exists alongside religion, or that constitutes a way of thinking nurtured by religious impulses.

Just as Strauss' conclusions regarding the Biblical faith were shaped by an attentive reading of the Biblical text, so his characterization of philosophy derives from a profound scrutiny of the works and lives of the ancient philosophers.[75] On the face of it, observes Strauss, Plato's philosophy resembles the Biblical worldview. Plato also teaches that the heavens and earth were created by an invisible god called the "Father," who exists eternally, is essentially good and created a world that is also good. The created world is dependent both for its constitution and its preservation on the will of the Creator, and He intervenes in the acts of justice and injustice committed by human beings. However, unlike Wolfson, Strauss was unwilling to content himself with this external similarity. Strauss' inspection of the contexts in which Plato's theology is articulated (in the *Republic* and the *Laws*) persuades him that these are merely useful beliefs for the propagation of elementary education and the maintenance of a system of justice and punishment. Even in these exoteric writings of Plato, we find hints that the real gods are cosmic gods, in contrast with the traditional gods of Greek mythology. These cosmic gods reveal themselves to humans not in accordance with their own autonomous wills, but perpetually. They "are accessible to man as man," to his observations and calculations made in the course of his quest for "natural or rational causes."[76] The God of the philosophers is the final object of the human intellectual pursuit of founding principles. The heroic human figure that symbolizes the pure philosophic life, in Strauss' view, is Socrates. Just as Abraham was willing to sacrifice that which was most precious to him for an unfathomable God, Socrates was willing to sacrifice himself for the sake of clarity. Philosophy claimed all of him.[77] Yet just as the innocent dependence of the garden of Eden was replaced by a covenant based on law and punishment, due to the "devisings of the human heart" and the imperatives of building a civilization, so Socrates' overt quest for evident knowledge, a quest cruelly trampled upon by the ignorant masses, was replaced by the covert quest of Plato and his successors. Theirs was a clandestine quest conducted by way of esoteric writing, to which Strauss devotes considerable attention.[78] In the final analysis, the Biblical concession that established a legally mediated relationship with God made a life of reverence and dependence possible for humans, even under the pressure of the cruel civilizational struggle for survival. And the philosophic concession that led to clandestine inquiry allowed the philosophic way of life to persist within the framework of a hostile human society, one devoted solely to its own self-preservation through myth and superstition.[79] Genuine philosophers were often compelled over the course of history to surrender their bodies, by acting and speaking on behalf of the ruling society, in order to forestall the relentless persecution of heretical philosophy. Yet so long as they remained philosophers in the original sense, they continued to direct their souls to the quest for evident knowledge.[80]

THE POSSIBILITY OF RECIPROCAL INFLUENCE BETWEEN PHILOSOPHY AND RELIGION

An examination of Strauss' understanding of the nature of Biblical religion and the nature of the philosophic quest discloses that each of these orientations incorporates within itself a polemic against the other. On the one hand, according to Plato, the cosmic gods, those abstract entities that serve as the object of human inquiry, are loftier in character than the traditional deities of Greek mythology. The traditional gods are accessible only through the (particularist) traditions of Greece, while access to the cosmic gods is the birthright of every "barbarian" (i.e., non-Greek, namely, they are universally accessible). Before he creates the world, the Platonic God looks to the ideas, the principles of rational necessity within which the natural good is contained—ideas that are higher than God.[81] On the other hand, we find that Strauss reads the Bible as an explicit polemic against philosophic speculation. It is forbidden to gaze up at the heavens and valorize them as a focus for contemplation. The value of the earth is greater than that of the heavens. Eating from the "tree of knowledge of good and evil" spells death for humankind.[82] Humans must not seek to control God by striving to know Him, for he is "I shall be what I shall be": indefinable, shrouded in thick clouds and appearing to his chosen ones only by way of promises and actions that are not knowable in advance. It is forbidden to quest far afield for the good, seeking it in either the heavens or across the ocean, "for the thing is very near to thee, in thy mouth and in thy heart, that thou mayst do it" (Deut. 30:14). For "He has told thee, O man, what is good; and what does the Lord require of thee, but to do justly, and love mercy, and walk humbly with thy God?" (Mic. 6:8) The Divine Law that embodies the primordial good is right beside you in the one and only Divine law, and it cannot be discovered through a free quest for beginnings.[83]

This illustrates why Strauss does not believe in the possibility of genuine spiritual interaction between philosophy and religion. To his way of thinking there can be no "religious philosophy," namely, a philosophy animated by religious feeling or a religious ethos, as Guttmann believed. Moreover, Strauss sees no possibility of a "philosophic religion" a la Guttmann, a religion influenced by the contemplative ethos that understands philosophic certainty as a component of religious certainty.[84] There is philosophy founded on the autonomy of reason, and there is religion founded on the omniscience and omnipotence of God. These elements are not given to mutual fusion, or even to mutual complementarity. Furthermore, neither element has ever been subordinated to the other, contrary to Wolfson's claim. "No man can be both theologian and philosopher, or for our purposes, a creature who is beyond the struggle between philosophy and theology or the fusion between the two. . . . Philosophy and Bible are the alternatives or the antagonists in the drama of the human soul. Each of the two antagonists claims to know or to hold the truth, the decisive truth, the truth regarding the right way of life. But there can be only one truth. . . . Each of the two opponents has tried since millennia to refute the other."[85] According to Wolfson, there has been only one philosophy—the Jewish-scriptural one—and it has persisted in all three monotheistic faiths. In his view, Western philosophy is ultimately nothing other than Jewish philosophy.[86] According to Guttmann, since both the Bible and philosophy were sustained by either a personalist-religious or a pantheist-mystical ethos, an encounter between the two was entirely plausible. This encounter led to a mutual influence: Personalist elements were introduced into the contemplative metaphysics of Arab philosophers, while Jewish religiosity was penetrated by the ideal of moral purification as a means of contemplating God to the extent of human ability.[87] According to Strauss, however, philosophy is philosophy and Judaism is Judaism. There never has been either a Jewish philosophy or a philosophic Judaism, but only "theologians who suspect[ed] philosophers and philosophers who [were] annoyed or [felt] annoyed by the theologians."[88]

The question then arises of how Strauss relates to those medieval thinkers whom various scholars perceive as synthetic figures, or at least as figures who integrated both Biblical and philosophic elements within their spiritual world.[89] R. Yehuda ha-Levi employed philosophic thought categories in order to defend a "despised" religion. Is it plausible that his worldview remained unaffected by the philosophy he drew on? Maimonides, in Guttmann's words, sought "to implant Aristotelianism" in the cultural soil of Judaism and to arrive at a "fusion from within" between metaphysics and Biblical personalism.[90] Strauss' perspective, however, allows for only one question: Was Maimonides a "Jew" or a "philosopher"?

In his close analysis of the *Kuzari* by R. Yehuda ha-Levi, Strauss explores the question of the reciprocal influence between Judaism and philosophy from a particular angle. In contradistinction to Guttmann, his focus is not on the religious trends prevailing in communities of believers. From his standpoint it makes no difference whether a few philosophic influences have penetrated certain branches of Jewish culture, such as commentary, homiletics, liturgical poetry, and so forth, as Guttmann contends.[91] Strauss' question is as follows: Can Judaism, as a posture and a way of life, and philosophy, as a posture and a way of life, dwell together within the spirit of a great thinker? The structure and content of the narrative framework in the *Kuzari* persuade Strauss that R. Yehuda ha-Levi was indeed a thinker of stature who had been exposed to philosophy on the most profound level. Yet precisely for this reason, he never combined the two classic positions within his consciousness simultaneously. Philosophy is discussed twice in the *Kuzari*: Once between the king of the Khazars and the philosopher, and once between the king and the Jewish scholar, but never between the Jew and the philosopher directly. Moreover, the disputants on the subject of philosophy are not of equal philosophic caliber. The Jew is well-versed in philosophy, but the king has only a superficial acquaintance with it, and consequently the dialogue between them is of insufficient depth. Ha-Levi refrains from staging a direct confrontation between the Jew and the philosopher, a confrontation in which the philosopher as well could have been portrayed as adopting Judaism. In Strauss' view, ha-Levi's restraint indicates that "[He] knew too well that a genuine philosopher can never become a genuine convert to Judaism or to any other revealed religion."[92] The Jew, by definition, is "a descendant from the witnesses of the Sinaitic revelation,"[93] while the philosopher is a person who has never tasted the "Divine thing." The Divine command did not touch him in the way that it touched the unmediated experience of the believer. The philosopher adheres uncompromisingly to human wisdom deriving from sensual or rational evidence, and therefore he cannot permit Divine wisdom to determine the truth.

This lack of an encounter due to the lack of agreement regarding fundamental premises, presented in literary form in the *Kuzari*, reflects, in Strauss' judgment, both the spiritual reality in the soul of R. Yehuda ha-Levi himself and the perennial relation between religion and philosophy across the generations. R. Yehuda ha-Levi, the Jew who had tasted the Divine thing, also penetrated the philosophic world, but not by partially embracing those philosophic theories that confirmed his religious beliefs. For when a person of Yehuda ha-Levi's stature strikes roots in the world of philosophy, he necessarily arrives at a full embrace of the critical and investigative posture of philosophy. Strauss offers the following observation here regarding the possibility of a spiritual fusion between religion and philosophy for a profound thinker:

What does influence mean? In the case of a superficial man, it means that he accepts this or that bit of the influencing teaching, that he cedes to the influencing force on the points where it appears to him, on the basis of his previous notions, to be strong, and that he resists it on the points where it appears to him, on the basis of his previous notions, to be weak. A confused or dogmatic mind, in other words, will not be induced by the influencing force to take a critical distance from his previous notions, to look at things, not from his habitual point of view, but from the point of view of the center, clearly grasped, of the influencing teaching, and hence he will be incapable of a serious, a radical and relentless, discussion of that teaching. In the case of a man such as Halevi, however, the influence of philosophy on him consists in a conversion to philosophy: for some time, we prefer to think for a very short time, he was a philosopher. After that moment, a spiritual hell, he returned to the Jewish fold.[94]

Great thinkers like R. Yehuda ha-Levi and Maimonides made no effort to overcome the conflict between philosophic critique and religious belief. Their greatness consisted primarily in the fact that they plumbed the depths of each position, using them as starting points from which to reflect on any given issue. Strauss emphasizes that ha-Levi's philosophic period was brief in the extreme, for an alienation from the Divine thing over time would have precluded his going back to being "Jewish." It is impossible for a great thinker to merge two conflicting fundamental premises within his spirit simultaneously. Making a temporary transition to another position, one that enables a critical perspective on one's original position, is the antithesis of harmony and synthesis and constitutes a "spiritual hell." The Wolfsonian theologian, who accepts or rejects doctrinal fragments according to their compatibility with his overarching doctrine, is a "superficial man," "confused" or "dogmatic." A great thinker is a person who embraces one comprehensive life ideal, free of contradictions, from among the conflicting possibilities that dwell in the human soul. And in fact, throughout the entire history of Western culture, while both theologians and philosophers sought to refute each other's arguments (unsuccessfully, from Strauss' standpoint), no dialogue was ever conducted between them.[95] A dialogue, or even a debate, is possible only if both sides share certain fundamental premises regarding the criterion of validity. But in the case of religion and philosophy, *Contra negantem principa, not est disputandum* (it's impossible to argue with one who disagrees with you on fundamental principles).[96] Philosophy's attempts to refute the validity of revelation are predicated on the assumption that there can be no miracles that deviate from rational necessity. The critical approach to revelation dismisses a priori the premise that the Creator performs miracles in His world, and that He revealed His will for the future to His chosen prophets. The rejection of these two premises constitutes the preemptive dismissal of the key premise of revealed religion: the absolute omnipotence of God.[97] By the same token, every attempt of the religious position to critique the pretensions of philosophy is doomed to failure. According to Strauss, religion correctly argues that philosophy has not succeeded in its attempt to demonstrate that the world and human life are subject to a comprehensive rational explanation without positing the existence of an unfathomable God.[98] The philosopher, however, would rejoin that the failure of a given system is no reflection on the philosophic quest per se, which to recall derives precisely from the evidence regarding such failure. Philosophic life is not tragic despite its lack of success, for it authentically reflects the human condition: a rational creature's search for clarity.[99] Over and against this one could argue that the decision to be a philosopher is based not on evidence, but on will or faith. The possibility that revelation does exist, a possibility that even the philosopher is compelled to acknowledge, renders the choice of philosophy non-evident.[100] The philosopher, however, would argue that without the objective evidence of reason, no particular revelation, by virtue of its status as particular, is capable of justifying itself vis-à-vis other particular revelations. Faith is prevented from adopting a critical-rational stance with regard to itself; it lacks the tools to corroborate itself vis-à-vis other faith positions that lay claim to exclusivity.[101] True, the internal conviction of the believer who has tasted the "Divine thing," is not based upon such an "objective" validity. Yet the believer is clearly incapable of conducting a genuine dialogue with competing approaches on the subject of the one truth on the basis of internal convictions alone.

Religion, then, does not complete philosophy by furnishing a higher level of cognitive knowledge, as Wolfson alleged, for religious faith is not at all cognitive, and philosophy has no need for its completions. The relation of religion to philosophy is not ambivalent, and it does not regard philosophy as a second revelation, but as unequivocal heresy. Religion has also not succeeded in vanquishing philosophy by transforming it into a handmaiden that services its dogmas. True philosophers across the ages have always refused to abandon their perennial quest, even if they conducted it surreptitiously or through esoteric writings. Philosophy has also not succeeded in undermining the basic posture of religion: "the need for divine mercy or redemption, [and] obedient love."[102] Contrary to Guttmann's opinion, philosophy did not afford religion an enhanced self-awareness beyond that existing within the Biblical text itself. It did not enrich religion, nor did it effect a change in the quality of religious belief. Those few individuals who were the authentic representatives of religion as a way of life and of philosophy as a way of life believed that these two foundations contradict one another and are in conflict with one another. According to Strauss, in *The Guide of the Perplexed* Maimonides "obviously assumes that the philosophers form a group distinguished from the group of adherents of the law and that both groups are mutually exclusive."[103]

Nevertheless, in certain periods instrumental relations have prevailed between religion and philosophy. Religion used philosophy for its purposes, and philosophy used religion for its purposes. Further on in his analysis of the framework narrative of R. Yehuda ha-Levi's *Kuzari*, Strauss adduces another reason why the Jewish scholar and the philosopher never confront one another. Ha-Levi, who had been a philosopher for a brief moment, understood how tempting and dangerous "non-contingent reflection" is. Had he staged a radical, unbridled confrontation between the Jew and the philosopher, he would have had to present the philosopher's arguments against revelation in their full power and glory. And even if revelation is capable of repelling these claims, as Strauss maintains, such a full exposure to philosophy is liable to cause the reader irreparable damage.[104] The theological defense of the despised religion can only sway one who has already experienced the Divine thing and leans towards "obedient love" to begin with. The king of the Khazars, who is both a dreamer and inclined to religious faith, is unquestionably the archetypical reader to whom the *Kuzari* is addressed. Yet even such a person is not immune to the dangerous influence of philosophy. The philosophic claims presented in the *Kuzari* are therefore of a depth that is subject to refutation through counterclaims that will be convincing only to one who is pious by nature. R. Yehuda ha-Levi, then, no longer has any inner spiritual connection to philosophy.[105] His book is an example of the "art of the Kalam," that employs logical argumentation to refute heretics and substantiate belief. Rational argumentation is for him merely a constraint, and fortunate is the one who is blessed with an innocent faith that has no need for such argumentation.[106]

Spinoza takes the opposite route and uses religion to legitimize philosophy. While R. Yehuda ha-Levi's book is addressed to "potential believers," Spinoza's book, *Theological-Political Treatise*, is addressed to "potential philosophers," educated readers who are not easily deluded. They are enlightened Christians, and they still accept the authority of scripture. Spinoza accordingly commends the Christian religion for being a more universalist and spiritual religion than particularist and sensual Judaism, and thus a more fitting starting point for philosophizing. An attentive reading of his writings, however, reveals that Spinoza draws no distinction between Judaism and Christianity with regard to cognitive status.[107]

To corroborate his philosophic worldview that miracles are impossible, Spinoza resorts to scripture itself. Not daring to argue openly against the very existence of a revelatory meta-rational Divine wisdom, he contends merely that revelation was not transmitted in a miraculous fashion. Spinoza has no wish to distance himself from his readers, who accept the authority of scripture as an infallible guide. He nevertheless pushes potential philosophers to draw the broadest possible conclusions from the principle that for him is so cardinal, the non-existence of miracles. On the surface level, therefore, he argues that scripture itself teaches us, whether directly or indirectly, that miracles are not within the bounds of possibility. As for those miracles that became the cornerstone of the Christian tradition, such as the resurrection of Jesus, Spinoza explains them as late "anti-religious" additions that were appended to the original scripture.[108]

This distinction between later additions and pristine scripture, which could be discussed only in Protestant Holland, serves Spinoza's declared objective as well: the liberation of philosophy from the fetters of theology. He identifies original Christian love with the quality of tolerance, that opposes persecuting people on account of their beliefs. In his words, the original New Testament taught just such a universal love, yet the apostles were constrained to compromise with conventional opinion in order to spread the gospel. This paved the way for the subjugation of philosophy to theology and the persecution of philosophy in the name of religion. Spinoza voices the hope that his era will restore the gospel to the original teaching of the evangelists, thus liberating philosophic thought from its status as the "handmaiden" of theology.[109] Spinoza therefore exploits the authoritative status of scripture in order to defend philosophy against persecution. His recourse to the Christian religion obviously does not derive from an inner connection to religious faith. In the *Theological-Political Treatise* he uses utterly negative expressions to refer to the fundamental characteristics of religion (especially since they appear in the form of the Jewish religion, which his readers in any case despise):

> [Moses] left nothing to the free choice of individuals . . . the people could do nothing but remember the law, and follow the ordinances laid down at the good pleasure of their ruler; they were not allowed to plough, to sow, to reap, nor even to eat; to clothe themselves, to shave, to rejoice, or in fact to do anything whatever as they liked, but were bound to follow the directions given in the law; and not only this, but they were obliged to have marks on their doorposts, on their hands, and between their eyes to admonish them to perpetual obedience . . . and should continually confess by their actions and thoughts that they were not their own masters, but were entirely under the control of others. From all these considerations it is clearer than day that ceremonies have nothing to do with a state of blessedness.[110]

It is more difficult to ascertain Strauss' opinion of Maimonides, whom certain scholars of Jewish philosophy deem the most "synthetic" figure.[111] Was he a "Jew" who used philosophy to bolster the faith of the perplexed, or was he a philosopher who used the Bible and the commentaries to legitimize philosophy? Strauss' early work *Philosophy and Law* (1935) leaves the impression that from his standpoint, both Maimonides and philosophers such as R. Levi ben Gershon, who were more radical than he, philosophized only within the framework of a predetermined commitment to the authority of revelation. Admittedly there were sharp disputes over the content of revelation, with some promoting it as a rational law that fosters human intellectual perfection in accordance with the philosophic perspective. Nevertheless, for the sake of legitimacy, philosophic activity itself had to appear to be sanctioned by the revealed law.[112] It is difficult to discern from this early work whether Strauss regarded such a justification vis-à-vis revelation to be an internal-spiritual need of thinkers like Maimonides and R. Levi ben Gershon, who accepted the fact of revelation as a given, even if they interpreted it in far-fetched ways. Or was it perhaps an exoteric gesture, designed to confer legitimacy upon their activity?[113] On the one hand, Strauss reiterates that these thinkers considered revelation to be a given fact, even if they saw it as the constitution of the ideal state according to philosophy. Strauss needs to stress this point in order to distinguish between medieval and modern philosophy, which is not beholden to revelation.[114] On the other hand, the reader may still legitimately interpret Strauss to mean that this justification before the authority of revelation stemmed from the thinkers' wish to legitimize philosophy in the eyes of the public.[115]

The article "The Literary Character of the *Guide for the Perplexed*" (1941) and Strauss' introduction to the English translation of *The Guide of the Perplexed* (1963) already address Maimonides primarily as the author of esoteric teachings that he conceals from the multitude by way of a certain "art of writing." In the external layer of the *Guide*, Maimonides, like R. Yehuda ha-Levi, is an adherent of the Kalam who seeks to defend the faith of the Torah. Ha-Levi, however, in contradistinction to traditional Kalam thinkers, preferred a simple faith to philosophic speculation. Maimonides, on the contrary, criticizes the traditional Kalam for beginning its discourse on religion from easily defensible propositions rather than from free speculation. Notwithstanding this point, however, Strauss writes that Maimonides' exoteric professions, particularly his avowed identification with the followers of the Torah rather than with the adherents of philosophy, identify him with the Kalam teachings, even if this is an enlightened version of the Kalam.[116] Moreover, his characterization of *The Guide of the Perplexed* as an exegetical work whose aim it is to interpret "the secrets of the Torah" renders it a "Jewish" book, that interprets a pre-given text, rather than a philosophic work that is its author's creation.[117]

Nevertheless, once Maimonides' dissimulations have been penetrated by Strauss' analysis, the positions that emerge are highly heterodox in nature. Maimonides evidently does not believe that the institution of sacrifices is of an eternally binding nature. He also holds that prophetic wisdom is likely to develop over the course of history, such that Isaiah may have been a prophet of a higher order than Moses. Furthermore, Maimonides fails to mention the belief in the immortality of the soul in the place where it would naturally have been expected.[118] Admittedly, prominently featured in the middle chapter of the book is a long defense of the creation theory against the proposition that the world is eternal, containing both a justification of miracles and of the fact of revelation itself.[119] Strauss insists any number of times, however, that such public declarations, whether with regard to creation or to the singularity of the Mosaic prophecy, are not to be trusted, as the heterodox opinions that appear obliquely and diffusively conform more closely to Maimonides' true convictions than those that are explicit and repeated.[120]

Notwithstanding the above, however, it would appear that Strauss affirms in all seriousness (and not merely as a starting point from which he distances himself over the course of the article) that Maimonides considered the Bible to be the most perfect esoteric work ever written, as authentic Divine truths underlie its precepts and narratives.[121] While Spinoza dismissed the Bible as the work of a hyperactive imagination,[122] Maimonides seems to have found a rational esoteric layer within it reflecting opinions "closely akin to" those of Aristotle.[123] Maimonides presents this hidden philosophic teaching as an ancient inner Jewish tradition that has long since disappeared from the world, and that he has undertaken to disclose anew. Viewed from this perspective, Maimonides did not appear to be importing Greco-Arab cultural elements into Judaism, but rather to be returning to an ancient Jewish philosophic tradition that had served as the basis for philosophy in Greece and the Arab lands.[124]

There were two faces, then, to Maimonides' religious worldview, with considerable tension obtaining between them. The "contradictions" in *The Guide of the Perplexed* reveal Maimonides to be a philosopher and free thinker unencumbered by conventional opinions, and his esoteric writing style enabled him to disguise opinions that were dangerous for conventional religion. Moreover, in Strauss' view Maimonides numbers among the elite for whom philosophic contemplation is the ultimate human end, an end that both completes and transcends morality, as emerges from the following statement: "the general principle underlying his entire work and nowhere contradicted by him [is] that knowledge of the truth is absolutely superior in dignity to any action."[125]

Such an understanding of Maimonides' worldview is not consistent with viewing him as a "Jew." We might therefore expect Strauss to contend that Maimonides holds the Hebrew Bible to be merely of instrumental value, rather than possessed of inner spiritual worth. Surprisingly, however, Strauss maintains that Maimonides' relation to the Bible is not merely instrumental in nature. Maimonides treats the Bible as an essentially unitive book whose internal contradictions are intentional, a book that hides a philosophic truth that is conveyed by way of multiple meanings, parables and riddles.[126]

This is not to suggest that Maimonides considers the Bible to be a fusion of Judaism and philosophy. The correct understanding of his opinion, according to Strauss, would seem to be that the Bible itself already relates to itself in instrumental fashion. To rephrase: The Bible, as an esoteric philosophic work, uses its own outer layer to cloak its inner meaning: The outer layer serves "for the proper condition of human societies," and the inner layer, for "knowledge of the truth."[127]

Consequently, the validity of the Bible for Maimonides derives from its status as an exemplary philosophic work, a work that relates to its own outer layer as a means for individuals to achieve emotional balance and for the community to attain social stability, in order to create the external conditions for the practice of theoretical contemplation. The idea that the life of action is merely a means to the life of contemplation does not induce Maimonides to detach himself from the Bible as Spinoza did. From his point of view, the Bible itself already displays an instrumental relation to the ideal of obedience and does not tout obedience as its ultimate message—as Spinoza wrote.

For Strauss, then, Maimonides was not a synthetic figure. He did not fuse philosophic certainty within himself as a component of his religious certainty, as Guttmann claimed. Neither was he characterized by "superficial," dogmatic" or "confused"[128] beliefs, and he therefore refrained from subordinating philosophy to theological premises in the manner that Wolfson claimed, at least in his own inner consciousness. Maimonides was not merely a follower of the Kalam who employed philosophy to defend religion, as R. Yehuda ha-Levi was. Nor was he merely a philosopher along the lines of Spinoza, who used the Bible itself to smooth the way for potential philosophers who still accept the authority of the Bible. Maimonides, in contrast, staked out his own independent approach, while in terms of his public "persona" he had to remain a "Jew" who adheres to the halakhah and confronts the "rival" philosophic sect.

Strauss characterizes this aspect of Maimonides' position as follows: "Maimonides doubtless subordinated his own views to those of the Jewish tradition."[129] It therefore follows that Maimonides had his own independent opinions that diverged from the Jewish tradition. Moreover, we learn that in order to continue being Jewish in terms of his public affiliation, he had to subordinate his views to the conventional ones. As a Jew in his public life, Maimonides used philosophy to defend cardinal elements of Judaism such as the creation theory and the uniqueness of the Mosaic prophecy. In Strauss' words, "A Jew may make use of philosophy and Maimonides makes the most ample use of it."[130]

Nevertheless, Maimonides is also a philosopher, and thus he seeks to bring potential philosophers, who still rely on authority in matters of beliefs and opinions, to the gates of philosophizing and to develop in them the "critical faculty"[131] so necessary for philosophizing and so antithetical to the Jewish ethos. The student of *The Guide of the Perplexed* is "a man regarding whom it is still undecided whether he will become a genuine man of speculation or whether he will remain a follower of authority."[132] Maimonides therefore employs his authority as a commentator to induce such a person to accept his philosophic reading of Biblical verses in place of the literal meaning. From these readings the student can learn the principles of physics, a science that he skipped over in his hasty course of study, although this science can only properly be acquired by means of independent reason.

Such students, then, receive rationality from Maimonides in the guise of authority.[133] Yet even a person who has studied philosophy in depth and whose critical faculties are as well developed as those of Maimonides himself, can still learn from *The Guide of the Perplexed*.[134]

In sum, R. Yehuda ha-Levi, Maimonides and Spinoza all testify to the utilitarian rather than substantive relations that have always subsisted between religion and philosophy among the great thinkers. Theologians employed philosophy to defend the foundations of religion, but without adopting contemplation as a fundamental posture. To the same extent, the philosophers used religious scripture and conventional religious doctrine to corroborate certain views they wished to promote, while concealing their other opinions. For ultimately the religious approach is self-sufficient; it requires no more enrichment or enlightenment than it had to begin with. And by the same token, philosophy is also a self-sufficient enterprise, that wants no knowledge to complete it beyond that provided by autonomous reason.

NOTES

1. See above, pp. 83–86.
2. See above, pp. 254–56.
3. Strauss uses this phrase to characterize philosophy, not religion. See Leo Strauss, "The Law of Reason in the *Kuzari*," in *Persecution and the Art of Writing* (Glencoe, IL: Free Press, 1952), 106.
4. Leo Strauss, "The Mutual Influence of Theology and Philosophy," *Independent Journal of Philosophy* 3 (1979): 112.
5. Strauss, "The Mutual Influence," 112.
6. Strauss, "The Mutual Influence," 112.
7. Strauss, "The Mutual Influence," 256–57.
8. Strauss, "The Mutual Influence," 112.
9. Strauss, "The Mutual Influence," 112.
10. Strauss, "The Mutual Influence," 111–12.
11. Leo Strauss, "Jerusalem and Athens," *Studies in Platonic Political Philosophy* (Chicago and London: University of Chicago Press, 1983), 160–61.
12. Strauss, "Jerusalem and Athens," 90–94.
13. Strauss, "The Mutual Influence," 112.
14. Strauss, "The Mutual Influence," 112.
15. See Strauss, "Jerusalem and Athens," 160–61, and also Strauss' preface to the English translation of *Spinoza's Critique of Religion* (New York: Schocken Books, 1965), 8–9.
16. Strauss, preface to *Spinoza's Critique*, 9.
17. Strauss, "The Mutual Influence," 112.
18. Strauss, "The Mutual Influence," 111.
19. Strauss, "The Mutual Influence," 112.

20. Leo Strauss, *Philosophy and Law* (Philadelphia: Jewish Publication Society of America, 1987), 24.

21. Strauss, *Philosophy and Law*, 5–6, 13.

22. Strauss, *Philosophy and Law*, 29. Strauss characterized the distinction between the medieval and modern orientations towards religion as follows:

> Modern 'philosophy of religion' is distinguished from the earlier kind in that it no longer has its foundation in metaphysics but in epistemology. This means that modern philosophy no longer (indeed, less than ever) understands man as a member of the cosmos, as a natural being (even if an outstanding one) among other natural beings. Rather, and oppositely, it understands nature from man, or, more precisely, from consciousness as that which constitutes nature. Just for that reason, it cannot "discover" God as the Creator from the cosmos, but rather only from consciousness. Under the sway of the cosmological orientation . . . the 'reality,' the 'absolute actuality' of God, was self-evident; hence just this reality becomes fundamentally incomprehensible once the modern orientation has fully established itself.

23. Strauss, *Philosophy and Law*, 34–35.

24. Strauss, *Philosophy and Law*, 40.

25. Strauss, *Philosophy and Law*, 117–18.

26. Strauss, *Philosophy and Law*, 36–38, 50–52, 92–95.

27. Strauss, "The Mutual Influence," 111–12.

28. See note 13 of Leo Strauss' "Intellectual Background" (introduction to part III).

29. Strauss, "Jerusalem and Athens," 152.

30. Strauss, "Jerusalem and Athens," 152–53. Strauss is referring here to Genesis 1:27. Admittedly the term "created" appears in Genesis 1:21 as well, with the creation of the "large sea-monsters" and "all the living creatures that creep," but Strauss does not relate to this.

31. Strauss, "Jerusalem and Athens," 153.

32. Strauss, "Jerusalem and Athens," 151.

33. Strauss, "Jerusalem and Athens," 155.

34. Strauss, "Jerusalem and Athens," 158. Strauss notes there that "civilization and piety are two very different things."

35. Strauss, "Jerusalem and Athens," 156–57.

36. Strauss, *Persecution*, 20–21.

37. Strauss, "Jerusalem and Athens," 157.

38. Strauss, "Jerusalem and Athens," 158.

39. Strauss, "Jerusalem and Athens," 158–59.

40. Strauss, "Jerusalem and Athens," 159.

41. Strauss, "Jerusalem and Athens," 160.

42. Strauss, "Jerusalem and Athens," 160–61.

43. Strauss, "Jerusalem and Athens," 161–62.

44. Strauss, "Jerusalem and Athens," 162.

45. Strauss, "Jerusalem and Athens," 162.

46. Strauss, preface to *Spinoza's Critique*, 26–27, 29.

47. Strauss, "The Law of Reason," *Persecution*, 140–41.

48. Strauss, "The Law of Reason," *Persecution*, 41–43.

49. Strauss, "The Law of Reason," *Persecution*, 124–26.

50. Strauss, in the wake of R. Yehuda ha-Levi, asserts that the philosopher is by definition a heretic; see Strauss, "The Law of Reason," *Persecution*, 107, note 34.

51. Strauss, *Persecution*, 105–7, particularly notes 29, 30, 33.

52. Strauss, *Persecution*, note 29.

53. Strauss, introduction to *Persecution*, 17.

54. Strauss, "The Law of Reason," *Persecution*, 106.

55. Strauss, introduction to *Persecution*, 7, 12, 16.

56. See note 3.

57. Strauss, introduction to *Persecution*, 12–13.

58. Strauss, introduction to *Persecution*, 12–13.

59. Strauss, introduction to *Persecution*, 12.

60. Strauss, introduction to *Persecution*, 13.

61. Strauss, "The Mutual Influence," 111–12.

62. Strauss, "The Mutual Influence," 112.

63. Strauss, "The Mutual Influence," 111–12.

64. On this topic see also Strauss, preface to *Spinoza's Critique*, 8–9.

65. Strauss, "The Mutual Influence," 112.

66. Strauss, "The Mutual Influence," 112.

67. Gershon Scholem considers "intuition" and "paradox" to be orientations that contribute to the understanding of the mystical experience, orientations that the philosopher according to Strauss is prevented from employing. See his book *Major Trends in Jewish Mysticism* (New York: Schocken, 1946), 3–7.

68. Strauss, "The Mutual Influence," 115.

69. Strauss, "The Mutual Influence," 117, and also Strauss, preface to *Spinoza's Critique*, 28. In the second passage he says, "The orthodox premise cannot be refuted by experience or by recourse to the principle of contradiction."

70. Strauss, "The Mutual Influence," 113. In his article "What Is Political Philosophy" (p. 11), Strauss formulates the matter thus:

> Philosophy, as quest for wisdom, is quest for universal knowledge, for knowledge of the whole. . . . Philosophy is essentially not possession of the truth, but quest for the truth. The distinctive trait of the philosopher is that "he knows that he knows nothing," and that his insight into our ignorance concerning the most important things induces him to strive with all his power for knowledge.

71. Strauss, introduction to *Persecution*, 20. The citation is from tractate Hagiga of the Mishna, chapter 2, mishna 1.

72. Strauss, introduction to *Persecution*, 21. The citation is from the Babylonian Talmud, tractate Berachot, p.8a.

73. Strauss, *Persecution*, note 29.

74. Strauss, "The Mutual Influence," 113–14.

75. Strauss, "Jerusalem and Athens," 165–66.

76. Strauss, "Jerusalem and Athens," 166.

77. Strauss, introduction to *Persecution*, 16. See on this subject Plato's *Apology* and *Critias*.

78. Strauss, introduction to *Persecution*, 17.

79. Strauss, introduction to *Persecution*, 16–18.
80. Strauss, introduction to *Persecution*, 21. He has the following to say on the subject:

> The precarious position of philosophy in the Islamic-Jewish world guaranteed its private character and therewith its inner freedom from supervision. The status of philosophy in the Islamic-Jewish world resembled in this respect its status in classical Greece. It is often said that the Greek city was a totalitarian society. It embraced and regulated morals, divine worship, tragedy and comedy. There was however one activity which was essentially private and trans-political: philosophy. Even the philosophic schools were founded by men without authority, by private men. The Islamic and Jewish philosophers recognized the similarity between this state of things and the one prevailing in their own time. Elaborating on some remarks of Aristotle, they compared the philosophic life to the life of the hermit.

81. Strauss, "Jerusalem and Athens," 166.
82. Strauss, "Jerusalem and Athens," 153–55.
83. Strauss, "The Mutual Influence," 111–13; see also Strauss, introduction to *Persecution*, 20.
84. See above, pp. 166–68.
85. Strauss, "The Mutual Influence," 114.
86. Strauss, "The Mutual Influence," 85–86.
87. Strauss, "The Mutual Influence," 161–62.
88. Strauss, "The Mutual Influence," 113.
89. Among the contemporary scholars who espouse this view are Isadore Twersky and David Hartman. David Hartman, for instance, in his book *Maimonides: Torah and Philosophic Quest* (Philadelphia: Jewish Publication Society of America, 1976), 26–27, has the following to say about Maimonides:

> [Maimonides'] total philosophic endeavor was an attempt to show how the free search for truth, established through the study of logic, physics, and metaphysics, can live harmoniously with a way of life defined by the normative tradition of Judaism. . . . Maimonides attempted an integration of philosophy and the teachings of his tradition.

90. Hartman, *Maimonides*, 166–70.
91. Hartman, *Maimonides*, 133–36.
92. Strauss, "The Law of Reason in the *Kuzari*," *Persecution*, 104–5.
93. Strauss, "The Law of Reason in the *Kuzari*," *Persecution*, 105, 112.
94. Strauss, "The Law of Reason in the *Kuzari*," *Persecution*, 108–9.
95. Strauss, "The Mutual Influence," 113–14.
96. Strauss, "The Law of Reason," *Persecution*, 105.
97. Strauss, preface to *Spinoza's Critique*, 28; and Strauss, "The Mutual Influence," 117.
98. Strauss, preface to *Spinoza's Critique*, 29.
99. Strauss, "The Mutual Influence," 113.
100. Strauss, "The Mutual Influence," 113, 117–18; see also Strauss, preface to *Spinoza's Critique*, 29–30, where Strauss muses: "But to grant that revelation is possible means to grant that the philosophic account and the philosophic way of life

are not necessarily, not evidently, the true account and the right way of life: philosophy, the quest for evident and necessary knowledge, rests itself on an unevident decision, on an act of the will, just as faith does."

101. Strauss, preface to *Spinoza's Critique*, 30.

102. Strauss, "The Mutual Influence," 111.

103. Strauss, "The Literary Character of the *Guide for the Perplexed*," *Persecution*, 43.

104. Strauss, "The Law of Reason," *Persecution*, 109.

105. Strauss, "The Law of Reason," *Persecution*, 111–12.

106. Strauss, "The Law of Reason," *Persecution*, 99.

107. Strauss, "How to Study Spinoza's *Theologico-Political Treatise*," *Persecution*, 162–63, 173. Strauss remarks there that "according to Spinoza, the doctrine of 'the Scripture,' i.e., of both Testaments, contains 'no philosophic things but only the most simple things,' and . . . he probably regarded his teaching, i.e., the true philosophic teaching, about God as opposed to all earlier teachings."

108. Strauss, "How to Study Spinoza's *Theologico-Political Treatise*," *Persecution*, 166–67.

109. Strauss, "How to Study Spinoza's *Theologico-Political Treatise*," *Persecution*, 162, 168–69.

110. Benedict De Spinoza, *Theological-Political Treatise—The Chief Works of Benedict De Spinoza*, trans. by R. H. M. Elwes (New York: Dover Publications, 1951), 75–76.

111. Strauss, "The Law of Reason in the *Kuzari*," *Persecution*.

112. Strauss, *Philosophy and Law*, 39.

113. Strauss' statements on this topic are sometimes fraught with ambiguity. Take, for example, the following (Strauss, *Philosophy and Law*, 39): "Every medieval philosopher must explicitly or at least silently, frankly or at least outwardly, take *account* of Revelation in the treatment of all important questions."

114. Strauss has the following to say on the subject (Strauss, *Philosophy and Law*, 39): "No dispute is possible about the reality of Revelation and about the duty to obey it. . . . [T]he acknowledgment of the authority of Revelation is '*self-evident*.'" (The emphasis on the last word evokes, with a certain irony, the voice of Guttmann.)

115. For instance, on p. 40 of *Philosophy and Law* he says the following: "Their 'exoteric' writings have the function not so much of 'persuading' or 'inciting' men to philosophizing but rather by means of a '*legal speculation*' of showing that philosophizing is a duty, and that in its form and content it corresponds to the opinion of Revelation."

It would appear, then, that doubt should be cast on Ralph Lerner's contention in the introduction to the English version of *Philosophy and Law* that the book is "an early attempt, that was rapidly set aside in favor of more profound works and a more mature understanding" (pp. ix–x). It may be that in this book, which was published in 1935, Strauss was still reading Maimonides too literally and had yet to come to terms with the more radical message that appears between the lines and casts doubt on the traditional concept of revelation. Nevertheless, already in this work there seem to be explicit indications of the radical distinction between esotericism and exotericism that would characterize Strauss' later works. Strauss testifies about himself (preface to *Spinoza's Critique*, 31) that this change in his orientation first found expression in an article appearing at the end of *Spinoza's Critique of Religion*, which was first published in 1930. In either case, it is not possible to reach a final verdict on the matter within the framework of this work. An interesting discussion of the evolution of Strauss' thought in the direction of the "esoteric" stage can be found in Kenneth Hart Green's book, *Jew and Philosopher: The Return to Maimonides in the Jewish Thought of Leo Strauss* (Albany, NY: State University of New York, 1993), 93–134.

116. Strauss, "The Law of Reason," *Persecution*, 99; Strauss, "The Literary Character of the *Guide for the Perplexed*," *Persecution*, 40–43.

117. Regarding this distinction by Strauss between the two types of books, see Strauss, "The Mutual Influence," 112–13.

118. Strauss, "The Literary Character," *Persecution*, 40.

119. Strauss, "The Literary Character," *Persecution*, 40.

120. Strauss, "Persecution and the Art of Writing," *Persecution*, 22–26; Strauss, "The Literary Character," *Persecution*, 66. In the second source Strauss affirms that "his intention in writing the *Guide* was that the truths should flash up and then disappear again. . . . [A] considerable number of statements are made in order to hide the truth rather than to teach it."

121. Strauss, "The Literary Character," *Persecution*, 60–61, 65–66.

122. Strauss, "How to Study Spinoza's *Theologico-Political Treatise*," *Persecution*, 176, 178.

123. Strauss, "The Literary Character," *Persecution*, 60.

124. Strauss, "The Literary Character," *Persecution*, 50–52.

125. Strauss, *Persecution*, 92.

126. Strauss, *Persecution*, 60–61.

127. Strauss, *Persecution*, 72.

128. Strauss, "The Law of Reason," *Persecution*, 108–9.

129. Strauss, "The Literary Character," *Persecution*, 84.

130. Leo Strauss, "How to Begin to Study *The Guide of the Perplexed*," in Moses Maimonides, *The Guide of the Perplexed*, ed. and trans. Shlomo Pines (Chicago: University of Chicago Press, 1963), xiv.

131. Strauss, "How to Begin to Study," xix.

132. Strauss, "How to Begin to Study," xix.

133. Strauss, "How to Begin to Study," xxiii.

134. Strauss, "How to Begin to Study," xix.

8

Historiosophical Elements

On Religion, Philosophy, Pseudo-Philosophy and Time

In order to understand the historiosophical outlook of Leo Strauss, we must take a different approach from that which guided us in evaluating the historiosophic schemes of Wolfson and Guttmann. First, the focus of our project, confined as it is to the realm of Jewish thought, excludes the possibility of a comprehensive discussion of Strauss' work on the sources of Western political philosophy. We will limit our discussion to Strauss' perception of the historical struggle between theology and philosophy in the works of outstanding Jewish thinkers. Even from within this frame of reference, we can extrapolate a unique historiosophic perspective from Strauss' writings, one that can profitably be compared to the views of Wolfson and Guttmann.

It should be noted that the declared intent of Strauss' work is different from that of Wolfson and Guttmann. Wolfson and Guttmann explicitly set out to provide their readers with a comprehensive historical survey. Wolfson undertook to chronicle Western religious philosophy, and Guttmann the history of Jewish religious philosophy from Biblical times to Hermann Cohen and Franz Rosenzweig. Their work presents a systematic overview of philosophic activity during the historical periods in question.

Strauss, in contrast, did not consider himself bound to give an account of the ongoing history of philosophy on the basis of mere historical interest; he sought instead to engage in a literary-philosophical analysis of the textual masterpieces of the greatest thinkers. His main preoccupation was not historical research, in the sense of recording the events of different periods simply because they occurred, or uncovering a lawful historical pattern in the form of a set of causes and effects located within the dimension of time.[1] Strauss himself attests to the fact that his motivation for studying the thought of the past was specifically philosophic in character, motivated by the quest for the one truth.[2] He turned to past works after having examined the greatest works of modern theologians and philosophers and having found them wanting. Strauss was not interested in Jewish-philosophic compositions per se, nor did he seek out rare texts or arcane sources of Jewish philosophy. He had no use for brute facts alone, of the type pursued by those whom he called the "curious fact and cause chasers."[3] He turned to major Jewish thinkers such as R. Yehuda ha-Levi, Maimonides and Spinoza because their works embodied, on the most profound and self-conscious level, the perennial struggle between revelation and philosophy over the one truth. In order to approach an understanding of a great past work, argued Strauss, the reader must assume that the book in question might possibly contain the one real truth.[4] In his view, modern Jewish thinkers such as Mendelssohn, Cohen and Rosenzweig blurred the fundamental rivalry between revelation and philosophy, thereby preventing a clear grasp of the nature of that rivalry.[5] Strauss therefore returned to the "old books" written by thinkers of exceptional philosophic profundity and intrepidity, wherein the classic rivalry found expression, in order to search them for the one unclouded truth.[6]

In light of the above we can comprehend why Strauss refrained from articulating overarching historical schemes or delineating the lawfulness of the movement of thought through time, and why he refused to explore causal connections between the systems of the various thinkers. Strauss' principled arguments justifying this refusal are actually historiosophic messages in their own right. Strauss took issue, again for principled historiosophic reasons, with Wolfson's and Guttmann's assertions regarding the existence of a "beginning of time" and an "end of time" in the history of the relations between religion and philosophy. Notwithstanding this position, however, he distinguished unequivocally between ancient and medieval thought and modern thought, treating modernity as a turning point. We will address these issues more extensively below.

THE CRITIQUE OF GUTTMANN'S HISTORIOSOPHY

Strauss was Guttmann's student at the Academy for the Science of Judaism in Berlin of the 1920s, studying Jewish philosophic works under his tutelage. Strauss' respect for Guttmann's vast erudition did not restrain him from judging his book *The Philosophies of Judaism* severely, however.[7] According to Strauss, Guttmann assumes in his book that modern philosophers grasped the major insights of the Jewish religion with greater profundity than their medieval counterparts, despite the fact that the moderns were less immersed in the Jewish way of life.[8] Medieval thinkers staged a substantive confrontation between personalist Biblical religion and mystical-pantheist metaphysics, regarding both as authoritative traditions imposed from without. The development of the confrontation into a substantive encounter, however, led to a severe distortion in the quality of Jewish religious inwardness (from an activist personalism to a contemplative ethos), and Judaism thereby became largely alienated from itself. In the modern period, however, the exchange of the heteronomous conception of religion for one which treats it as a projection of human consciousness, and as characterized by a unique mode of perception, led to a more adequate understanding of the character of Jewish religious inwardness and of the central insights of Judaism.[9] By these central insights Guttmann was referring, among other things, to the free will animating the Divine governance of the world (voluntarism) and to the absolute moral demands that God places upon human beings.

Strauss contends that Guttmann's approach reflects an excessive adherence to modern presuppositions, causing him to prefer the achievements of modern Jewish philosophy over those of the middle ages and to create a developmental scheme in which the medieval era is merely a stepping-stone to the modern age.[10] We will first analyze the basic modern premises to which Strauss believed that Guttmann subscribed. Further on we will attempt to understand how these premises led him to devise his historiosophic scheme. Finally we will turn to the historiosophic principles that Strauss believes should replace those of Guttmann.

From Strauss' standpoint, Guttmann casts his lot with the moderns by endorsing several of the fundamental tenets of modern philosophy in general and of modern religious philosophy in particular. First, modern philosophy is characterized by an epistemological orientation rather than a metaphysical or a cosmological one. By this Strauss is referring to the assumption that human beings "construct" the natural world on the basis of their own thought categories. From Descartes on, and certainly from the time of Kant, external reality has been rendered contingent upon human consciousness for its very validity. By way of comparison, in the ancient and medieval periods it was taken for granted that there is an external nature in which humans also partake. Humans were considered to be one of the types of natural beings populating the cosmos, who live in the world alongside other beings.[11]

Furthermore, in modern idealist philosophy nature and morality are effectively divorced from one another. The "real" and the "ideal" are treated as two independent categories. While humans have the ability to legislate a categorical imperative in the realm of the "ideal," in the domain of the "real" they are confined, by virtue of their thought categories, to an objectivity that is essentially "inter-subjectivity." Humans are thereby prevented from apprehending absolute truths regarding the "thing in itself" and constrained to constructing a "natural" world on their own while connecting and classifying phenomena according to the manner in which they present themselves to human consciousness by way of human thought categories. In ancient and medieval worldviews, on the other hand, the good life was understood to be a life lived specifically in accordance with nature. The assumption was that an adequate understanding of the cosmos would furnish us with norms that should govern the good life.[12]

In accordance with his self-understanding as the creator of "natural" reality, modern man has taken two projects upon himself. First, he seeks to prove himself "theoretically and practically the lord of the world and the lord of his life."[13] Both Spinoza and Hegel, for instance, strove to construct comprehensive theories providing an adequate account of the whole without positing a mysterious Deity.[14] It was Bacon who called for the practical realization of this aspiration, namely, the taming of nature, including human nature, in order to improve the status of humans vis-à-vis nature. Nature would no longer be regarded as merely a "given" for human beings and would become more and more subject to human control. The boundaries of nature would gradually contract in both the theoretical and practical realms, with humans constantly progressing towards an ever-expanding freedom.[15]

The divergent perspectives of the ancient and medieval worlds on the one hand and the modern world on the other were naturally reflected in their views of religion as well. The Greek view, following Plato, along with that of Islamic and Jewish medieval philosophers, was that there is a Divine law directing humans towards their ultimate end, which is a rationally grounded understanding of the whole. The Divine law is meant to organize all of human life, and it applies to human thoughts, feelings and actions. However, the Greek understanding of "Divine law," namely, the patterns of ultimate beginnings to be investigated by human reason, and the biblical understanding of the law—as norms disclosed in a single unique revelatory document, were diametrically opposed to one another. Yet both of them identified the good with the primordial and treated the good as a fixed law.[16] Despite the rivalry between religion and philosophy in the ancient and medieval worlds, they shared a worldview wherein the external cosmos was regarded as pre-given. It was on the basis of this shared worldview that the classic debates regarding the creation or eternity of the world were conducted.[17]

The modern stance that everything is a human projection or construction affected the concept of religion as well. Emphasis shifted from consideration of the real relation obtaining between the Deity and external nature to the relation of human spirit to Absolute Spirit. For instance, the question of creation, which in ancient and medieval times was concerned with the very establishment of the real world underwent, in Hermann Cohen's work, a process of "internalization."[18] The creation idea is transformed from a cosmological assertion regarding the origin of the external world into a logical connection within a thought-system that posits a relation of contingency between an independent principle that enables creation and is not part of the creation process, and the process of creation itself. The real connection between God and the world is converted into an "internalized," logical connection of contingency between being and becoming.[19] Admittedly, Guttmann himself does not adopt this kind of rationalization of the content of the religious worldview, and he believes religion to have its own discrete structure of consciousness. He too, however, portrays the creation as a category relating primarily to the persistent inner connection between human beings and God ("createdness"), rather than as an explanation of the origin of the cosmos.[20]

Strauss holds that Guttmann's modern perspective led him to conceive of medieval thought in modern categories, thereby distorting its essence. Guttmann claims that the middle ages brought the question of the connection between religion and science to a point of crisis. To his way of thinking, Jewish medieval philosophy essentially identifies revealed religious truths with metaphysics. Two possible courses of action arise from this identification, both of which Guttmann rejects. One is that of mutual adaptation, and the other is what the medieval period termed the "two truths" theory. The first approach distorts the personalist basis of Jewish religion in favor of the contemplative ethos of metaphysics. The second—maintaining philosophy and religion in entirely separate dimensions—denies the possibility that the insights of philosophy might affect the self-understanding of religion, leading it to greater self-consciousness. In teleological fashion, then, a vital need arises for modernity, in which religion can discover itself to be both a dimension of human consciousness subsisting alongside cognition and morality on the one hand, as well as the orientation that guides and sustains them, on the other.[21]

Guttmann bases this claim on the premise that belief in the middle ages was concerned with revealed "truths." Since Guttmann is ultimately interested in arriving at a modern understanding of faith as deriving from a discrete, inner religious consciousness, and in distinguishing between such an understanding and the intellectualist understanding of religion, he is constrained to view the medieval period as a time of crisis that created the backdrop for this distinction through excessive identification between two "intellectualist" bodies of thought, namely, revealed doctrines and philosophic principles. Guttmann's position, argues Strauss, fails to do justice to the true medieval concept of revelation: revelation as a law that constitutes a society, or as a constitution that establishes a state.[22]

From Strauss' standpoint, then, Guttmann distorts the manner in which religion was understood in the past. He also ignores the substantive difference between the ancient and medieval worlds on the one hand and the modern age on the other, a difference that enables us to speak of distinct periods from a historiosophic point of view. Strauss holds that Plato was the first to espouse the idea of law as a uniform standard for ordering human life. Plato's thought centers around the idea of rational law, namely, law that is directed towards the possibility of human perfection. Only such a law can be termed a "Divine law," one that emanates from a "Divine source." According to Strauss, medieval Islamic and Jewish thought is not a stage on the way to modernity but the continuation of Plato's concept of the ideal state, albeit in altered form. While Plato considered a regime ruled by a philosopher-king to be an ideal for some unspecified future era, Islamic and Jewish philosophers saw the law revealed through scripture to be the embodiment of this ideal kingdom, an embodiment that had already once existed in times past.[23]

The starting point of the medieval philosophers for a philosophic understanding of revelation is Plato's framework, namely, the quest for the ideal regime. This framework is the legacy of the ancient world. In Strauss' view, the middle ages should not be treated as a new stage in which religion as an independent source of truth becomes a problem for philosophy. Admittedly, medieval philosophy needed to base its own legitimacy on the authoritative revealed law, something that was not mandatory in ancient times. Moreover, in the middle ages philosophers were not required to search for the ideal law, only to understand it with the aid of the philosophic disciplines to philosophically interpret a revelation that had already been granted. The ancient and medieval periods were nevertheless more similar than they were different. Both periods sought to understand the rational law, which is the only truly Divine law. The Platonic framework of the ideal state afforded medieval thinkers a starting point from which to grasp the essence, value and function of revelation from a philosophic standpoint.[24]

Strauss also insists that there is no teleological connection between the middle ages and the modern period, whereby the modern period solves a problem that arose in medieval times. Modernity is not an outgrowth of the middle ages. Quite the contrary: For Strauss the modern period constitutes a regression vis-à-vis the medieval period. This is not merely a Wolfsonian regression, that manifests itself in an alienation from revealed scripture as the source of a more perfect metaphysical knowledge, and a return to a metaphysics based on intellectual inference.[25] Rather, it is the repudiation of any objective external order, natural or supernatural, that could curb human theoretical sovereignty. The "hubris" of modernity does not consist in an unwillingness to accept the "yoke of the kingship" of supernatural revealed doctrines. Moderns, according to Strauss, go to much greater lengths: They are unwilling to treat nature as a given fact, even their own nature.

They lay claim, first, to the possibility of creating a "natural" worldview on their own, one dictated exclusively by their characteristic thought patterns. Second, they argue that it is possible to subjugate nature and succeed in the project of civilization. And finally, they are confident in their ability to extirpate those elements of human nature that contribute to violence and war. Most of all, to return to the concept of law, modern humans are unwilling to recognize the authority of any external law whatsoever, whether it originates in revelation or in a rational cosmological worldview. Any ethical or political legislation that obligates humans must necessarily, in accordance with the teachings of Kant, be "self-legislation."[26]

In a lecture he gave relatively late in his life, "Jerusalem and Athens," Strauss reiterates this claim: "the quarrel between the ancients and the moderns seems to us to be more fundamental than either the quarrel between Plato and Aristotle or that between Kant and Hegel."[27] This statement follows his pointed criticism of the modern faith as articulated by Hermann Cohen. To Cohen's way of thinking, argues Strauss, the one truth is a synthesis of Plato and the Jewish prophets. Cohen accepts Plato's teaching that the truth is first and foremost the truth of reason or science. The scientific truth, however, requires the completion and guidance of another, loftier idea, the idea of the good. This idea is not the Deity; it belongs to that realm of human rationality known as ethics. In contrast with Guttmann's interpretation of Cohen's later teachings, Strauss holds that Cohen did not posit two separate realms, as he believed that ethical truth must correspond to scientific truth. (Ethical truth must not contradict what we know from reason, including what we know about human nature, and it requires scientific truth as an arena of expression and realization.) Here Strauss asks: Why didn't Cohen content himself with this Platonic framework as his worldview? Why did he feel the need to complete the structure by creating a synthesis with the prophetic teachings? The answer to this question stems from Cohen's modern democratic optimism, namely, the belief that we can look forward to eternal progress that will bring a substantive transformation of human nature in its wake. If Cohen had adopted Plato's teachings consistently and systematically, he would have had to embrace the proposition that the ideal society is one ruled by a philosophic elite that enjoys exclusive possession of the scientific truth. This scientific truth is grounded in an understanding of nature, including human nature, as static and unchanging. Even in the ideal society governed by a philosopher-king, the good prevails only within the polis and not outside it. Plato takes it for granted that the polis will continue to be embroiled in an endless succession of wars necessitating a warrior class, a class deserving of a higher status than the manufacturing and commercial classes. Human nature, then, is fixed, and so long as there are human beings on earth, there will be wars.[28]

This vision of the future was insupportable for Cohen, and accordingly he deviated from Plato's teachings in favor of the optimism of the prophets, who foresaw a future messianic age involving the transformation of human nature and the end of war. The behavior of all human beings towards their fellows would undergo a radical change. In Strauss' opinion, this deviation of Cohen's is more than an arbitrary digression from Plato's teachings, a digression that could be set down to modern presuppositions concerning progress and democracy. From Strauss' vantage point, Cohen distances himself here both from his own concept of scientific truth and from the true meaning of the prophetic faith.

For one thing, the prophets had no relation whatsoever to knowledge in the rational-scientific sense. When they used the term "knowledge of God," they were speaking of "knowledge" in the metaphoric sense (meaning being governed by the will of God in a manner that affords close communion with Him). Strauss speculates that the fact that Cohen was incapable of adopting the prophetic model of knowledge, while he felt a kinship towards the Platonic version of scientific knowledge, explains why he calls Plato at one point "the Divine Plato," a term that he never uses in reference to the prophets. Yet it was precisely because the prophets lacked a fixed and self-sufficient theory of *physis* that they were able to envision a radical turning point in human nature. To recall, however, they viewed this turning point as the result of miraculous Divine intervention, not the culmination of an immanent natural process.[29]

Cohen's synthesis, then, would appear not to be a synthesis at all, but a distortion of Plato that he superimposes upon a distortion of the prophets. This incongruous combination originates not in a surrender to the spiritual authority of Plato or the prophets, but in the modern belief in the power of Western culture to effect the desired changes in nature and human nature. After the first world war, writes Strauss, and especially among the generation that experienced Hitler's Germany and Stalin's Russia, belief in the power of the "modern synthesis" to effect "progress" must necessarily founder. This leads Strauss to wonder whether each of the components of the modern synthesis is not perhaps more durable than the synthesis itself. To Strauss it appears that both Plato (and the ancient philosophic tradition that followed in his footsteps) and the prophets (and traditional Judaism in their wake) had a deeper grasp of the persistent and comprehensive evil that surrounds human life than do adherents of the modern belief in progress.[30] Strauss consequently devoted his life to the study of these ancient traditions, out of a clear understanding that the unredeemed character of the world and of human life is exemplified by the incessant, continuing rivalry between them. Instead of treating modernity as a solution to a substantive clash that arose in the medieval period between the sovereignty of God and the sovereignty of the cosmos with its deterministic laws, Strauss judges modern thought to be a negative innovation that disavows both poles of the conflict simultaneously. Modernity is nothing other than an exaggerated belief in the human capacity for self-redemption independent of God or nature. Strauss therefore demands that his readers go back and confront the contradictory claims that occupied the pre-modern world.

Strauss' approach generates the question of where these modern orientations that he attacks so vehemently come from. If modernity truly constitutes a negative turning point in relation to the past, how did this turning point come to pass? Is it possible to uncover causal elements that already existed in the past, elements that gave birth to modernity, or is modernity a wholly arbitrary repudiation of religious orthodoxy on the one hand and the authentic philosophic quest on the other? What is the origin of modern philosophy's trust in progress and its historicist-relativist view of the past as composed of functional stages leading inexorably to the present? Whence its derivation of the ideal from human reason alone, through the elimination of every human limitation, natural or supernatural?

Strauss evidently ascribes the above to the ascendance of modern science, and its connection to what he calls "the modern project."[31] The success of modern science in improving the status of humans vis-à-vis a hostile nature distracted philosophy from its original objective, the quest for the one ultimate truth about the whole.[32] From the perspective of the classic Straussian dichotomy—between thought in itself, with its disinterested quest for truth, and society in itself, that propagates superstitions and mythologies in order to guarantee its survival[33]—modern philosophy features not as genuine philosophy, but as a pseudo-philosophy or sophisticated superstition, whose purpose it is to validate science and the project of civilization.[34] Science enjoys tremendous social prestige due to its growing pragmatic success, but it still requires a supportive theoretical framework to secure its position, and for this it must turn to philosophy. Admittedly, science is successful, while philosophy has failed to resolve the problems on its agenda. Yet humans are still seeking a theoretical guarantee in order to assure themselves that scientific progress will continue in perpetuity. In Strauss' words, "there is an appalling discrepancy between the exactness of science itself, and the quality of its knowledge of its progressive character as long as science is not accompanied by the effort, at least aspiring to exactness, truly to prove the fact of progress, to understand the conditions of progress, and therewith to secure the possibility of future progress."[35]

The desire to assure the conditions of progress spawns the new discipline of developmental history, which consists primarily of the history of thought. Philosophy—whose aim it was to construct a coherent theory providing a final account of the whole while attempting to uncover beginnings and first causes—gives way to the history of thought: "Science in the present-day meaning of the term is therefore necessarily accompanied by history of human thought."[36] This statement parallels Strauss' assertion elsewhere in the same context that science and history are twin sisters.[37]

In past eras philosophy was an activity conducted in detachment from society and its interests, while history documented the annals of society. In the modern world, however, philosophy and history have been combined into a new discipline: the "history of human thought." According to Strauss' principles, this new discipline obviously cannot be considered a genuine combination, for authentic philosophy will always remain a self-sufficient activity, divorced from the successes and failures of human society in ensuring its physical survival vis-à-vis the forces of nature. The belief in progress and the historicism that developed in its wake are merely a "pseudo-philosophy" with a cognitive status similar to that of superstition.[38]

Modernity, then, does not lack for a causal explanation. What we have here is not a case of an inexplicable historical rupture. But from Strauss' writings on the subject, we gather that the explanation for the historical turning point does not seem to reside within the realm of philosophy itself. The pure philosophic orientation will remain forever eternal and ahistorical: "what unites all genuine philosophers is more important than what unites a given philosopher with a particular group of non-philosophers."[39] Developmental history pertains only to society and its mythologies. Pseudo-philosophy, therefore, which justifies modern society, should be treated as the theoretical superstructure of the modern project, namely, the taming of nature and the control of human nature through science.

SPINOZA AND MODERNITY

This principle applies not only to the historicist orientation of modern philosophy but to its epistemological orientation as well. In this connection, Spinoza marks the transition from the classical to the modern worldview.[40] On the one hand it can be argued, along the lines of Wolfson and others, that Spinoza unified God, man and nature, and consequently, for Spinoza, humans are not meant to legislate their own ends, but to bring themselves into a state of harmony with an all-embracing nature.[41] In this sense, Spinoza's worldview is "classic." Spinoza's nature, however, represents the metaphysical hypostasis of the modern scientific worldview that conceives of nature as devoid of teleological ends. Based on indifferent mathematical rules, it is not a nature that is likely to guide human destiny in accordance with a teleological theory of human nature. While in the view of the classical philosophers, a life based on the passions was a life contrary to nature, for Spinoza, everything that exists, exists in accordance with nature. In Spinoza there are no natural ends, and consequently there are also no ends that are natural to humans. What, then, is the origin of Spinoza's own ideal, an ideal so reminiscent of the classical pursuit of contemplation? Not nature, but the human *ratio*. And this end "is not natural, but rational, the result of man's figuring it out, of man's 'forming an idea of man, as of a model of human nature.' [Spinoza] thus decisively prepares the modern notion of the 'ideal' as a human project, as distinguished from an end imposed on man by nature."[42]

Evidently, then, the chief influence on Spinoza in this matter was not the classical tradition, which establishes contemplation as the natural human ideal. Certainly, Spinoza was influenced by this ethos and sought to realize it. He did not attempt in any way to negate the contemplative calling of philosophy by rendering it the handmaid of the sciences, as did Bacon.[43] Yet according to Strauss, the decisive influence on Spinoza's theory here was not the medieval tradition, as Wolfson maintained, but the modern revolt against that tradition. At first glance he seems more medieval than Descartes, Bacon and Hobbes, as he seeks to preserve philosophy's essentially theoretical character. Yet the cornerstone of his theory on human ends, the view of the contemplative ideal as the product of the human intellect rather than of nature or the cosmos, reflects above all the ethos of "the modern project."[44] Strauss uses the word "project" both to illustrate modern man's general aspiration to possess and dominate nature through science and civilization, and to express Spinoza's conviction that the ideal and appropriate life is essentially the "work" of the human intellect. Strauss here underscores the fact that Spinoza, while a great philosopher in the original sense of the word, meaning one who strives to construct a final, unified theory regarding the foundations of the whole,[45] paves the way for a modern "pseudo-philosophy" sustained by the "modern project." Spinoza, therefore, is part of the overall effort of enlightened man to prove himself "theoretically and practically the lord of the world and the lord of his life. The world he created had to make the world that was merely 'given' to him disappear."[46]

There are two faces to Spinoza: On the one hand, he numbers among the "genuine philosophers" who strive for ultimate truth rather than for insights of only historical and relative value, and who have a profound grasp of the rivalry between philosophy and religion. Plato, al-Farabi, Yehuda ha-Levi, Maimonides and Spinoza all belong to the same ahistorical elite, distinguished by its consciousness of the stark divide between religious submission and philosophic contemplation. The clash between these two postures is atemporal, representing a permanent conflict in the fixed nature of man. While induction into philosophy (for sophisticated persons who are still subject to the authority of religion) or induction into religion (for persons exposed to the influence of philosophy) necessarily changes in accordance with the superstitions or "pseudo-philosophies" of the time,[47] the religious gesture in itself and the philosophic gesture in itself remain fixed and atemporal.[48]

On the other hand, Spinoza is influenced by modern Western man's social interest in subordinating nature to his will. It is modern natural science, a pragmatic endeavor that grew out of this civilizing, self-interested impulse, that also informs Spinoza's worldview. This view is metaphysical: objective in the classical sense of the world and not conditioned upon human thought-categories in the manner of Kant. Yet it is no longer possible for a scientific-mechanistic worldview of this type, that has been elevated to a metaphysical status, to supply a fixed end for man. Already in *Philosophy and Law* Strauss states that "the 'goal- and value-free' nature of modern natural science could tell man nothing about 'ends and values,' that the 'Is,' understood in the sense of modern natural science, contains no reference whatsoever to the 'Ought' and thus that the traditional view that the right life is a life according to nature becomes meaningless on the basis of modern presuppositions."[49] Spinoza must therefore insist that the articulation of ideals be the task of the human intellect, a move that will ultimately lead to the Kantian philosophy and its German idealist successors. Spinoza exchanges the classical worldview, that was the backdrop for the debate between religion and philosophy regarding the right way of life, for the modern worldview, which is incapable of providing the context for such a debate.

The historicist and epistemological orientations of modernity, then, do not lack a causal background. Yet the causes for the emergence of these orientations seem to stem not from past philosophy, but from the modern belief in the human ability to create one's own physical, theoretical and ideal world. Such beliefs have a history, namely, a system of causes and effects that move within time. Human imagination and emotion (that seek to control nature in order to rid themselves of the fear of nature) and the beliefs that serve to confirm human aspirations (as an ideal of the civilization and culture)—all of these have a history. Pseudo-philosophy, that ultimately relies on ephemeral desires and fantasies lacking any eternal anchor in revelation or disinterested reason, is subject to development within time: "Of pseudo-philosophies there is an indefinitely large variety, since every later pseudo-philosopher can try to improve on the achievements, or to avoid certain blunders of his predecessors."[50] This temporal development, informed by "human interest" and not by "knowledge," is not necessarily characterized by an inner logic that would enable any kind of predictions as to its direction. "It is therefore impossible even for the most far-sighted man to foresee which pseudo-philosophies will emerge, and gain control of the minds of men in the future."[51]

In contrast, the classic rivalry between religion, that endeavors to mold all of human life in accordance with a particular, external revelatory law, and philosophy, that aims to mold all of human life in accordance with an external rational law derived from objective nature, is eternal and beyond time. This eternal struggle is rooted in the fact that these classic antagonists reflect two aspects of a fixed human nature: "Ultimately, I think, one would have to go back to a fundamental dualism in man [between thought and action] in order to understand this conflict between the Bible and Greek philosophy. . . . Philosophy and Bible are the alternatives or the antagonists in the drama of the human soul."[52]

This distinction of Strauss' between historical pseudo-philosophy and genuine ahistorical philosophy requires elaboration. Strauss' scholarly method with regard to R. Yehuda ha-Levi, Maimonides and Spinoza, great thinkers who honestly sought the truth, bears comparison with his remarks on the chronicles of the Epicurean critique of religion, which in his view derives from a hedonistic impulse. R. Yehuda ha-Levi, Maimonides and Spinoza each chose one of the two principal paths, revelation or philosophy, out of a profound awareness of the contradictions between them. Strauss is not interested in discussing the links between one thinker's choice and that of another. While in Guttmann, ha-Levi contributes the awareness of the gap between the God of Abraham and the God of Aristotle, Maimonides the effort to reconcile them from within on the basis of ha-Levi's awareness, and Spinoza the final proof of the ethical bankruptcy of medieval intellectualism,[53] in Strauss these thinkers do not fill these roles. Revealed religion has no need to perfect itself gradually over the course of time through thinkers with a continuous link between them, nor is philosophy in need of any such improvement. The religious and philosophic positions are exemplified in their pristine form by every great figure, of whatever era or school. Every great figure represents religion or philosophy at its very highest level; every great thinker serves as a distinct and independent atemporal model of the eternal struggle for the one truth. Great thinkers do not participate in particular schools, periods or traditions. Every one of them is a singular individual, a type of hermit[54] devoid of historical influence, who endeavors to engage in extra-historical communication with a select few like himself who are worthy of sharing his insights. The great philosophers retreat from history; they disguise their innermost thoughts by recourse to esoteric writing methods in order to avoid exposure. Philosophers' external writing methods reflect diverse ways of grappling with the assorted mythologies contingent upon time and place, yet this historical-political aspect of their writings only hides their inner, extra-historical views.[55]

Strauss opposes placing great thinkers within a given historical context on principle, whether in a context derived from modern categories (like Guttmann) or from those considered ancient (like Wolfson). Thinkers who lived the struggle between the philosophic quest and submission to the Divine law on the highest level should not be understood within any context

outside of their personal quest. For a scholar to contextualize a thinker in
such a fashion implies that the scholar understands the thinker better and
from a broader perspective than that from which the thinker understood or
presented himself.[56] The great thinkers did not perceive themselves as the
mouthpieces of a dogmatic tradition (as Wolfson assumed) or as responsible for promoting the self-awareness of religious philosophy (as Guttmann
believed). They did not consider their thought to be in the service of
processes that originated outside of themselves. They believed that they had
arrived, each by way of a single-minded, individual search, at the one truth
concerning the whole and its first causes. Spinoza believed he had succeeded through his own efforts in constructing a theory that provides an account of reality with no need for a mysterious God, and in refuting orthodoxy as well.[57] R. Yehuda ha-Levi believed he had succeeded in identifying
grave flaws in the philosophic orientation and in demonstrating that the
Bible is the only worthy guide for human life, despite the fact that the real
confrontation with the dangers of philosophy took place only between the
lines of the *Kuzari*.[58]

A responsible scholar of philosophical thought at its highest should not
be a mere historian, who assigns the thinker in question to a philosophic
tradition, school, "spirit of the time" or any other context. The study of a
philosophic classic cannot be an "objective" process of classification according to external categories. The first premise of Guttmann, and of other
scholars under the influence of the modern "historicist" orientation, is the
premise of sophistication.[59] Modern thought, suffused with its own self-
satisfaction, assigns all past philosophies their place in advancing the history of thought.[60] In the case of Wolfson, the tyranny of the past replaces
the tyranny of the present. This presupposition is, for Strauss, also dogmatic. All of the great answers to the great questions are understood to
have been given in the past. The questions and answers may be formulated
in new languages, but they cannot be reopened in any substantive way.
Here as well the historian engages in objective classification, not on a continuum of progress but nonetheless with regard to a pre-existing map of
pre-formulated doctrinary positions.

In contradistinction to the above, Strauss claims that there is only one
motivation likely to generate the requisite empathy between a contemporary scholar and a great thinker of the past, empathy of the kind that can
lead to understanding. As he writes on Spinoza:

> the strongest incentive for attempting to understand Spinoza's teaching as
> Spinoza himself understood it, that incentive being the suspicion that Spin-
> oza's teaching is *the* true teaching. Without that incentive no reasonable man
> would devote all his energy to the understanding of Spinoza, and without such
> devotion Spinoza's books will never disclose their full meaning. . . . if we open

our minds, if we take seriously the possibility that he was right, we can understand him.[61]

The scholar must strive to understand how a great thinker understands himself and how he presents himself. The great thinkers did not intend to write for their contemporaries alone, but mainly to bequeath a legacy to future generations.[62] Paradoxically, high-level thinking requires the historian to relinquish his role as a historian. In order to attain an inner understanding of a great work from the past, he must examine it in isolation, in its own right, as the potentially final truth. Strauss therefore adopts a textual, instead of a contextual, approach to R. Yehuda ha-Levi, Maimonides and Spinoza, and even towards the Bible. He believes that every book written with exceptional intelligence is a book whose meaning arises from within it.[63] Every such book represents a new apex in the atemporal debate between philosophy and religion. A thinker should not be treated as a receptacle for old dogmas in new, communicative languages, or as an actor in the drama of the evolution of religious thought. The work of a great thinker is not a means to an end but the objective of scholarship itself, if the possibility is taken seriously that the thinker himself, through his personal quest, can lead the scholar to the truth.

Strauss does not thereby mean to imply that a scholar has no need for the disciplines of history, philology or the history of thought. He needs philology in order to study the language of the thinker in question, the conceptual philosophic language of the times as he understood it, interpreted it and perhaps changed its meaning. For even a thinker oriented towards eternity could not create a philosophic language whose terms or concepts, in the way he used them, would remain static over time.[64] The history of thought is important to a scholar like Strauss, not in order to relativize the past as many modern historians do, but in order to relativize the present. In paradoxical fashion, historicism also grants scholars the possibility of looking from the outside at modern "pseudo-philosophy," the ideology that converted the pursuit of the one truth into a pragmatic relation to thought meant to confirm and ensure progress.[65] In the final analysis, however, philology and history are mere accessories that should serve to facilitate the identification, however temporary, between the inquiring scholar and the classic masterpiece.

Empathy between the individual scholar and the individual thinker is crucial according to Strauss for two reasons. First, the quest for the one truth by its very nature depends upon privacy and a disavowal of the historical process. Philosophy never enjoyed a high social status or broad historical influence among the public, even among the cultured elite. Communication between genuine philosophers was conducted not in public forums, but through the quiet reading and writing of great books by private individuals outside the flow of history.⁶⁶ Philosophers—together with theologians like R. Yehuda ha-Levi who engaged the philosophers on the highest possible level—are a rare breed with a common interest in the search for truth. Whoever likes to think, and the truth is dear to him, will feel a natural identification with exceptional individuals of his ilk who sought it in the past.

Second, the philosophic quest continues because the basic problems that fuel the quest have yet to be resolved.⁶⁷ The big questions—regarding the creation or eternity of the world, the existence of a natural telos or individual Providence, the immortality of the individual soul or merely of the acquired intellect, etc.—have never been decided. Religion has still not succeeded in refuting philosophy, and philosophy has yet to refute religion.⁶⁸ Every great thinker correctly reopens the great questions from their foundations, without generating normative precedents for the future or becoming part of a cumulative process.

Thus when the scholar-philosopher confronts the thought of a great truth-seeker, he does not view it from the outside as an illustration or as the reflection of a closed doctrinal tradition, as Wolfson would. Nor does he view it from the outside as a link in religious philosophy's evolution towards greater self-consciousness. For Strauss, Guttmann's modern, supersessionist "overcoming" of the substantive conflict between philosophy and religion in favor of a "more satisfactory" methodological demarcation between the two is not a solution but rather a retreat from the problem. The key question regarding the eternity or creation of the world remains open. Accordingly, if the scholar-philosopher is exposed to a figure gifted with intellectual superiority, who has experienced both the fundamental Biblical position and the fundamental philosophic position from the inside, has decided in favor of one or the other and seeks to defend the exclusive truth of his position while treating the rival position with the utmost seriousness, the scholar is commanded to become the temporary student of this figure. Perhaps the outstanding figure will direct him to the one real truth, by virtue not of his historical role, but of his personal intellectual quest. Ultimately, of course, the student must also exercise the right of critique on the basis of the law of contradiction or of experience (the two touchstones of the philosopher),⁶⁹ though not before he has utterly exposed himself to the all-embracing influence of the exemplary figure.

The scholar-philosopher, then, does not study a great thinker as part of a larger whole. The value of the latter's thought is not contingent upon its being the reflection of a broader historical phenomenon or playing a historical role. There is a non-contingent self-sufficiency to his thought, a self-sufficiency based on the fact that philosophic activity is carried out for its own sake. Only philosophy at its finest (or a theological engagement with philosophy on the highest level) creates a norm for the scholar-philosopher. The discovery of a philosopher who is completely detached from social-historical interests evokes a sense of obligation in the scholar. The use of philosophic tools in the books of superficial, unsystematic or dogmatic thinkers interests him not at all. Only those individual peaks of untrammeled thought, peaks devoid of any lawful-historical connection between them, each of which begins anew from the foundations, demand investigation, by virtue of their philosophic rather than their historical power.[70]

If Strauss had drawn a lawlike connection between the exceptional figures he studied, he would have created a historiosophic scheme situated within time, one that distributed value and meaning among the classic thinkers. Yet Strauss did not consider the value of the *Kuzari, The Guide of the Perplexed* or the *Theological-Political Treatise* to consist in their being the reflections of a scriptural philosophy that conquered history, or stages in the historical construction of religious philosophy in its modern configuration. It is precisely their detachment from the scriptural philosophy that was historically ascendant in the middle ages and the distance from the reigning "pseudo-philosophy" of the modern period that render these works, each in its own right, matters of vital interest to the scholar-philosopher.

While we are bidden to refrain from creating historical schemes that subordinate the great thinkers' quest to historical reality or to an objective other than the search for truth, in the case of "pseudo-philosophy" it is sometimes possible to trace a historical-developmental scheme. "Pseudo-philosophy" is so defined by Strauss not only by virtue of its status as the ruling conventional wisdom, but mainly because it is "conscripted" philosophy, catering to human fears and interests. Modern historicism, for instance, is a function of the human fear of the light that exists beyond Plato's cave. The fear of the search for the ultimate truth has attained such dimensions that humans have even dug themselves a tunnel under the cave.[71] Historicism is also a function of the need to demonstrate the principle of scientific progress, a project that has so assisted humans in overcoming the forces of nature. The critique of religion as well—a tradition that began with Epicureanism, continued by way of the enlightenment and has culminated in the new existential atheism—is also pseudo-philosophy from several important standpoints.

Epicureanism, in Strauss' view, originates in hedonism, in the human wish to cast off all restraints and devote oneself to worldly pleasures. It earns the designation of "pseudo-philosophy" because it is a theory in the service of human interests: "Epicureanism is so radically mercenary that it conceives of its theoretical doctrines as the means for liberating the mind from the terrors of religious fear, of the fear of death, and of natural necessity."[72] Epicureanism rebels against both religion and philosophy in its refusal to subjugate the human passions to external restraints, and in its attempt to eliminate the human fear of Divine law or natural necessity.

With the advent of the scientific revolution and the enlightenment, Epicureanism progressed to a new stage. While preserving its fundamental doctrine of the centrality of human pleasure in this world, it nevertheless underwent a significant transformation. Classic Epicureanism primarily sets itself against the frightening and menacing character of religion, although it also attacks its illusory character. The enlightenment critique of religion focuses mainly on the idea that religion is an illusion. As a fallacy offering redemption in the next world, religion robs human beings of the capacity to identify the genuine pleasures of this world and enjoy them. Political and religious leaders subsist on this fallacy, which they foster among the masses. It becomes an educated person's responsibility to shake off the illusion of religion and look our earthy reality straight in the face, namely, that a hostile nature habitually threatens our survival. Our task is to liberate ourselves by asserting sovereignty over nature and overcoming its restraints. The endeavor to assure humans of the earthly bounty to which they are entitled requires not only a scientific but a political revolution against the old order. The Epicurean who was once inclined to pursue serenity far from the madding crowd and who still exerts himself in the attainment of worldly pleasures, becomes henceforth a public figure. His theory is still mercenary, yet he himself is no longer quite so utilitarian, and he learns to die for his own truth and dignity.[73]

Just as the enlightenment stage in the development of the critique of religion is affected by historical conditions, namely, the scientific revolution and the possibilities that opened up in its wake, so the final stage in the critique of religion is also influenced by historical conditions. As Strauss writes:

> in proportion as the systematic effort to liberate man completely from all non-human bonds seems to succeed, the doubt increases whether the goal is not fantastic—whether man has not become smaller and more miserable in proportion as the systematic civilization progresses. Eventually the belief that by pushing ever farther back the "natural limits" man will advance to ever greater freedom, that he can subjugate nature and prescribe to it his laws, begins to wither.[74]

Evidently, then, the enlightenment stage of Epicureanism carries within itself, in typical dialectical fashion, the seed of its own destruction. Precisely when the "modern project" reaches fruition and succeeds in constructing human scientific and technological enterprises on a colossal scale, designed to dominate the environment and the means of production, precisely at this point humans are dwarfed. Precisely then they lose the freedom they so longed for.

At this historic juncture the critique of religion undergoes another transformation, one that culminates in total self-cancellation. The Epicurean position that rejects religion as an illusion that precludes a correct grasp of earthly reality no longer remains hedonistic in any sense. At this point religion is dismissed not for being a dangerous illusion, nor even for being a blinding illusion, but for being a comforting illusion. Humans must not deny their abandoned, exposed and hopeless state, a condition that no civilization is capable of righting. Rather than fleeing to the embrace of a religion that promises redemption, humans must gather their courage and look tragic reality squarely in the face. Admittedly, argues Strauss, these insights regarding human nothingness and abandonment in a Godless world can ultimately be traced back to the Biblical consciousness. The authenticity that rejects all escape and falsehood draws on the Biblical conscience as well. Consequently, then, the new critique of religion seeks to undermine the Biblical religion while simultaneously internalizing the Biblical consciousness itself. The new atheism conducts humans to the brink of the abyss, which the Bible itself understands life without God to be, and decides, without any consistent rational basis, against religion. This latest "pseudo-philosophy," specifically the property of intellectuals, reveals itself to be not only "anti-religious" but "anti-philosophic" as well; it is built on an inner contradiction and is therefore not consistent with reason.[75]

We have seen that with reference to outstanding theological works that grapple with philosophy, or outstanding philosophic works that grapple with theology, Strauss opposes the construction of any historical schemes whatsoever. A historiosophy that looks for patterns of development in historical phenomena, patterns driven by a certain lawfulness, is not applicable to an activity that by its very nature disavows historical processes, including the history of thought. By way of contrast, pseudo-philosophies that support human hopes or disappointments regarding earthly reality can sometimes be ruled by a certain dialectical logic. Historical conditions (such as the scientific revolution) that reach fruition at a given historical stage provide a stimulus that produces far-reaching changes in the Epicurean ethos. While the second stage of its development is fed by the fundamental trend of the first stage (the achievement of earthly well-being, and the view of religion as an illusion), the new conditions foster a "personality type" that is almost exactly the opposite: active, engaged and idealistic, instead of passive, private and down-to-earth. Yet once the second stage has reached maturity and run its course, an awareness gradually crystallizes of the self-contradiction inhering in the comprehensive aspiration for sovereignty and freedom. It is precisely the success of civilization that leads to an awareness of the incorrigibility of the human situation. This dialectical junction, that became possible only once circumstances were ripe, gives rise, through the power of disappointment and counterreaction, to the third stage: an atheism based on authenticity and integrity. Such an atheism is self-contradictory from the outset, grounded as it is in the same Biblical probity that it seeks, arbitrarily, to dismiss.

Thus the process of the "rise and fall of Epicureanism" takes the form of a stage-by-stage development, which instead of climaxing at the end of the process, attains, ironically, an outward success in the midst of the process and then ultimately annihilates itself. Here, in the case of a pseudo-philosophy, Strauss ascribes no inherent value to any stage in itself; rather, every stage fills its role in a historiosophic scheme. Further, Strauss is bold enough to assume that he understands the development of pseudo-philosophy better than the pseudo-philosophers themselves.

A SUMMARY OF STRAUSS' HISTORIOSOPHIC PERSPECTIVE IN COMPARISON WITH THOSE OF WOLFSON AND GUTTMANN

In seeking to draw historiosophical (or anti-historiosophical) conclusions from Leo Strauss' works, we found that he did not offer us schemes of historical causality or all-inclusive historical patterns. Strauss did not present his scholarship as a comprehensive history of religious philosophy, as we have seen, for reasons of principle. While Wolfson and Guttmann articulate their worldviews regarding the fundamental rules of historical continuity by way of comprehensive historical scholarship, Strauss has left us only essays concerning the relation between philosophy, religion and society, and various monographs that include both explicit and implicit historiosophic remarks. Moreover, Strauss believes that genuine philosophy lacks any principle of historical continuity. It is nothing other than a series of monumental attempts to ground the *autarkeia* of *theoria* as against those who would champion the exclusive claims of religious piety, and vice versa.

Strauss nevertheless adopts unique, distinct positions on the questions raised in the discussions of Wolfson and Guttmann. Considering the role of time as the arena wherein religious philosophy expresses itself, it seems that we can construct a basis for comparing the views of the three scholars. According to Guttmann, religious philosophy gradually attained self-awareness over the course of time. Periods, schools and thinkers who appeared one after another on the continuum of time played a constructive role in elevating the religious relation from its non-reflective state to a state of higher self-awareness.[76] For Wolfson, however, time appears to have no role whatsoever, as, in his view, the fundamental tenets of Philonic philosophy persisted unchanged over the generations, in this sense being "beyond time" (or more precisely, trans-historical). In a similar vein, the unfolding of the implications of scriptural philosophy transpired in accordance with a lawful pattern of application and self-correction that was immune to the influences of the spirit of the times, schools of thought or cultural trends. Political, scientific and even cultural history did not hinder the parallel history of theological doctrines from adhering to its own laws. Nevertheless, even if Wolfson's scheme was an anti-scheme, whose function it was to refute the Hegelian scheme that had been accepted by the scholars of religious philosophy, it was nonetheless a scheme that related to the dimension of time. A particular segment of historical time is a kind of preamble in which the primordial elements evolve and create the backdrop for the onset of Philonic "significant time." Scriptural philosophy makes its appearance on the stage of history at a certain point in time and then proceeds to dominate the chronicles of Western philosophy for a long period of time. During this period no real changes transpire in scriptural philosophy that can be attributed to the workings of time. Nevertheless, time is "friendly" to scriptural philosophy in the sense that it furnishes it with an expanse in which to unfold, clarify and articulate itself.[77]

Within the framework of the temporal dimension the scriptural perspective penetrates many conceptual languages and addresses many issues under discussion, further entrenching its dominance. The objections raised against scriptural philosophy in the course of its encounter with contemporary streams of thought serve to sharpen its messages and disclose its assumptions. And finally, at a given point in time, scriptural philosophy vacates the historical stage. From Wolfson's standpoint, then, the annals of doctrines represent a "parallel history," characterized by a singular lawfulness that is unaffected by historical change in other areas. Nevertheless, this thesis of Wolfson's does not imply that time is not a dimension in which ideas move. While this movement is deductive rather than developmental, time is nevertheless the expanse within whose framework this movement can take place.[78]

Strauss' concept of time as a catalyst of motion in the annals of thought is substantially different. While Wolfson distinguishes between the history of metaphysical doctrines that do not develop but only unfold and disseminate themselves within the dimension of time, and the history of scientific and political theories that develop in tandem with the course of events, Strauss distinguishes between the disinterested positions of religion at its best or philosophy at its best that have no temporal basis, and the "pseudo-philosophies" that are subordinate to human interests and develop in conjunction with earthly human fears and aspirations. In Strauss, religion and philosophy are first and foremost fundamental attitudes, postures and ways of life that lay claim to the entire human being. On a certain level there subsists a perpetual argument between the two on the basis of their common "cosmological" worldview. Yet on another level, the possibility of any substantive debate between them is precluded because they do not share fundamental premises, a situation that caused and causes their mutual relations to be conducted on an instrumental rather than a substantive basis, despite the theological syntheses proposed in the past in order to justify religion or to afford philosophy religious legitimacy. Moreover, the fundamental positions of philosophy and religion have been fully conscious of themselves and of the positions of their rivals since time immemorial. There was consequently no need for the dimension of time to provide them with an expanse for the development of self-consciousness. In addition, since what were at issue were attitudes or postures rather than systems with fundamental principles that must be applied to particular situations, there was no need for time to provide an expanse for application, illumination and clarification. Strauss' concept of the essence of religion and the essence of philosophy consequently denies time any role in the enrichment or enhancement of the two foundations. There isn't even a "parallel history" of ideas. In the quest for the one truth, and in the eternal conflict between the sovereignty of God and the sovereignty of the human intellect, the dimension of time is utterly meaningless.

This is also the reason why Strauss does not posit a "beginning" or an "end" to the history of philosophy. The antithesis between "thought" and "society" is eternal and radical, and accordingly there is no point in time at which philosophy as an activity (in contradistinction to pseudo-philosophic theories) appears on the stage of history and asserts its dominance. There is also no juncture at which it descends from the stage, as it never ascended the stage, but was always there, and to a certain extent it continues to exist, however hidden or beclouded it might be.[79]

From Strauss' pointed critique of Guttmann, Cohen and modernity per se we learn that that which is called religious philosophy today is neither religion nor philosophy. It is also arbitrary to claim that religion and philosophy reveal themselves at their highest levels, and in their most fitting mutual relations, precisely at the end of the historical "process."

Strauss would also seem to oppose the "orientation by origins" that characterizes Wolfson.[80] Admittedly he directs the contemporary student to search for the truth specifically in the past, in the ancient and medieval periods, rather than in the modern period or the future. In a similar vein, he himself tended to embrace the time-honored opinion that equates the good with the ancestral and considers memory the mother of wisdom.[81] Nevertheless, Strauss does not believe there is a given point in time when the ultimate truth is revealed, embodying all of its implications in advance; a point from which everything flows and to which everything refers. Perhaps Socrates and Plato can be said to have established the framework or direction of the quest: a law that is truly Divine, in that it promotes human perfection in its own right.[82] Yet no system has yet earned the right to become a normative model and to decide the great questions.[83] Philosophy is no mere homiletics, commentary or elaboration of a sealed truth that was bestowed from on high once and for all. The choice between investigative contemplation and pious devotion has not been decided once and for all; it is offered anew to the speculative powers of every great man in every age. Plato, in the wake of Socrates' execution, charted the secret and "political" course of philosophy. Correspondingly, Abraham is the first example of the Hebrew insight that "the reward for the commandment is the commandment."[84] Following these early figures, however, there arose other exemplary figures, whose importance was determined not to the extent that their conceptions could be reduced to earlier conceptions, but according to their own individual ability to free their spirits from social interests. R. Yehuda ha-Levi, for instance, cannot be subsumed under some biblical "system" (and certainly not under a "Philonic" system), yet from the standpoint of his fundamental position he follows the Bible, and his confrontation with philosophy, which he knows through and through, on the basis of the religious posture, is a spiritual pinnacle in itself. Maimonides, in the wake of Plato, sees *theoria* as the human end and ascribes only instrumental value to action. Many of the key parts of his theory can be identified with Aristotelianism. Nevertheless, the very fact of his intellectual quest, that took place in the heart of an authoritative religious culture, is a peak in itself. Socrates and Plato are not the beginning of a process; they are the first instantiations of the eternal, ahistorical rivalry that exists naturally and permanently within the human soul, by virtue of its very humanity.

It follows from the above that Strauss should not be characterized as subscribing to an "orientation of ends."[85] He does not view modern philosophy as the goal towards which philosophizing over the generations has been leading. Neither does he represent an "orientation of origins." A beginning in time does not confer value and provide clarification for all that subsequently takes place. Time measures social and political developments, along with developments within pseudo-philosophies connected with them. Strauss would be more accurately characterized as having an "orientation of eternity," with every point in time being suited in principle for instantiating the natural and abiding rivalry between religion and philosophy.

Thus we find significant differences between Guttmann, Wolfson and Strauss with regard to the question of "peaks" or "goals" in the history of religious philosophy. Their views on "turning points" in the relations between religion and philosophy diverge sharply as well.

In Guttmann's view, both Jewish personalism and pantheist metaphysics undergo a turning point in the middle ages. Judaism is faced for the first time with a type of contemplative religiosity that bears a unique substantive message. The impetus for the turning point is Greek metaphysics, which penetrates Jewish religious culture by way of Islamic culture. Biblical personalism adjusts itself in keeping with the intellectualist ethos, while preserving certain personalist elements. Pantheist metaphysics changes too, under the influence of the Islamic-Jewish world, largely adapting itself to the Biblical view of creation. Ultimately, religious intellectualism runs its course with Spinoza, when it becomes clear that an ethically-oriented religiosity is unsustainable within the framework of a worldview in which all distinctions are conceptual rather than value-based.[86]

From Guttmann's standpoint, modernity is a second positive turning point on religious philosophy's path to self-awareness. It is precisely the epistemological-autonomous approach of Kant that liberates religion from its connection to metaphysics, and henceforth religion need no longer be seen as a heteronomous revelation. The way is cleared for religion's recognition of itself as a spontaneous human awareness that perceives its objects by means other than intellectual cognition.

According to Wolfson, there was only one turning point, when Philo subordinated philosophy to scriptural doctrines, a turning point he terms a "revolution." In his view even Spinoza wrought no innovation in the chronicles of philosophy; he merely restored it to its pagan origins through the application and extension of pre-existing themes and elements. Yet even if Wolfson believed that the dismantling of scriptural philosophy by Spinoza was no innovation, he did definitely consider it to be a turning point. The condition for the existence of a philosophy worthy of the name (namely, theology) consists in a willingness to submit to the doctrinal authority of the Bible. Spinoza is the first thinker to seriously undermine this willingness, and in so doing he returns philosophy to its pagan pre-history. The regressiveness of modernity is expressed in the fact that it returns philosophy from a historical period of superior quality, in which philosophic discourse rested on scriptural foundations, to an earlier historical period of inferior worth, in which philosophic discourse derived from pagan premises.[87]

In Strauss' view, by comparison, the modern turning point in philosophy, with all its importance, and with all of his deep reservations concerning it, is essentially an "accidental" rather than a "substantive" development. From his vantage point, nothing happened in philosophy during the transition from the middle ages to the modern period. Philosophy did not cast off one of its spiritual components, as Wolfson maintains; instead, a certain pseudo-philosophy, possessed of an epistemological and historicist orientation, acquired almost universal hegemony by virtue of a social-pragmatic development external to philosophy: the rise of modern science.[88] This pseudo-philosophy turned the doctrine of progress into an absolute doctrine, thereby turning all of the attempts of the great philosophers over the generations to attain to a single ultimate truth into relative attempts. It erected an obstacle of unprecedented power, but not substance, to genuine philosophizing. While in the past a natural state of affairs prevailed wherein philosophy and religion fought over the right to guide human life, with each claiming the ultimate truth as its own, in the modern world a highly sophisticated superstition developed, one which mobilized philosophic tools for its purposes, and that denied the very possibility of the philosophic quest in its original sense. Entrenched thought patterns (historicism, relativism) blocked the way for numerous potential philosophers. Strauss nevertheless feels that a return to genuine philosophizing may now be possible, as this pseudo-philosophy has spent itself. The relativist approach to the past ultimately permits a relativist approach to modern pseudo-philosophy itself.[89]

Admittedly this development transpired in the modern period and as a result of the modern project in connection with modern science. Yet the fact that this obstacle was erected against philosophy specifically in the modern period is meaningless for philosophy itself. It is impossible to predict which pseudo-philosophies will attain hegemony in the various periods of human history, as there is no predetermined lawfulness in the history of ideas that would enable predictions. Certain social conditions developed, and a huge impediment was placed in the way of philosophy. Yet both genuine philosophy and biblical religion have not yet spent themselves and never will. True, it is definitely more difficult to engage in the philosophic quest today; people who find themselves in the tunnel under the cave must struggle first of all in order to reach the cave, and there is therefore no alternative for modern scholars than to pore over old books.[90] Yet this is one of the political developments that genuine philosophy has always confronted on its eternal path. In the middle ages it had to grapple with the belief in the unshakable authority of certain texts.[91] In the modern period it must confront the beliefs of a substantial portion of the "scientific" community, the new "priests," who impose their presuppositions upon the public at large.

A comparison of the views of Guttmann, Wolfson and Strauss on historical turning points also touches on the topic of the demarcation of historical periods. Guttmann, who regards historical time as the real dimension within which the phenomenon of religious philosophy comes into being and attains completion, ascribes great importance to distinctions between different periods. The distinctions between "the ancient period," "the medieval period" and "the modern period" are vitally significant for him in describing the development of religious philosophy. Periodization in Guttmann is undertaken according to the principle of the mutual interaction and mutual influence prevailing between personalist religious faith and the contemplative mode of religiosity. In the ancient period there is no interaction between these two types of religious belief, and they are still in the process of crystallizing. In the middle ages a serious encounter takes place, but the results are unsatisfying; the encounter leads to substantive compromises that detract from the uniqueness of each type. Only in the modern period is there a satisfactory mutual interaction, as religion, with the aid of the systematic and reflective thought of philosophy, becomes aware of its own unique paradoxical character and becomes capable of guiding the enterprises of epistemology and aesthetics on the basis of its own moral authority.[92]

In Wolfson, as we have seen, there is an "external periodization" and an "internal periodization." In his "external periodization," Wolfson adopts the conventional concepts of the "ancient, medieval and modern" periods. From this vantage point, the demarcation between periods is drawn according to philosophy's degree of willingness to subordinate itself to the Bible. In the "ancient period" philosophy has yet to encounter the Bible, and for lack of a better alternative it conducts itself on the basis of Greek-pagan religious premises. The medieval period is the satisfying one, when philosophy subordinates itself to the dogmatic control of the Bible. The "modern period," in contrast, is a type of "regression," as philosophy sloughs off the yoke of the Bible, returning to a pagan universe of discourse.[93]

Yet as noted above, all this is an "anti-scheme" constructed in opposition to those who judge the medieval period to be "obscure scholasticism" in comparison with the Greek and modern "enlightenment," or against those who view "Teutonic-Christian" philosophy as the final supreme synthesis between Greek paganism and Biblical transcendentalism. Only during the period between Philo and Spinoza does any meaningful philosophy (theology) take place. If the concept "period" is used to designate not only a formal-external segment of time but also and primarily an expanse of time that receives its character from significant and singular human activity or awareness, then only the expanse of time between Philo and Spinoza may properly be termed a "period" in Wolfson's historiosophy. The "inner narrative" of religious philosophy in the West is not considered to be a series of three distinct periods in Wolfson, but the crystallization, unfolding and disintegration of a single important period.[94]

The question arises: Is there any meaning to the concept "period" within the framework of Leo Strauss' worldview? There would seem to be two "periods" for him, the "ancient" and the "modern," and the "ancient" and "modern" thinkers appear to disagree fundamentally.[95] What all the "ancient" thinkers have in common is a "natural-cosmological" worldview that furnishes the context for the debate between religion and philosophy concerning the right life for human beings. Many thinkers whom he defines as "ancient" are classified by other scholars as "medieval." He designates philosophers such as al-Farabi or Maimonides as "ancients," because their quests for the single "metaphysical" truth were undertaken within the framework of the Platonic striving for an external "Divine" law that would guide humans towards their purpose. "Moderns," on the other hand, treat both reality and the ideal as human constructions, thereby pulling the rug out from under the traditional debate between religion and philosophy. There is no external reality to legislate ends, and human beings, the creators of reality, would fain legislate the moral law as well.

In light of the above it seems that these remarks are insufficient to characterize the historiosophy (or anti-historiosophy) of Strauss. To his way of thinking, the philosophic and religious approaches neither develop nor unfold themselves within the dimension of time. Every "period," that measures only human vanities and pseudo-philosophies, is potentially fit for both "contemplation" and "pious devotion." The "ancient," "medieval" and "modern" periods are distinguished one from another only in terms of the types of obstacles placed before the philosophic "life of inquiry" or the life of religious sacrifice: the authoritativeness of scripture in the middle ages and the myth of historicism in the modern period. All of this, however, is ultimately incidental from the standpoints of both philosophy and orthodoxy. Disinterested morality and the disinterested search for truth have no use for a "division into periods."

NOTES

1. For a characterization of diverse types of historical understanding, see Fritz Stern, ed., *The Varieties of History* (London: Macmillan, 1970); Edward Hallett Carr, *What is History?* (London: Macmillan, 1961); John Walsh, *Philosophy of History* (New York and Evanston, IL: Harper Torchbooks, 1967).
2. In his article "How to Study Spinoza's *Theologico-Political Treatise*," *Persecution and the Art of Writing* (Glencoe, IL: Free Press, 1952), 151–52, 154, Strauss writes the following:

The modern interpreter takes it for granted that in order to be adequate to its task, philosophy must be "historical," and that therefore the history of philosophy is a philosophic discipline. He presupposes then from the outset . . . that Spinoza's whole position as Spinoza himself presented and understood it, is untenable because it is manifestly not "historical." He lacks then the strongest incentive for attempting to understand Spinoza's teaching as Spinoza himself understood it, that incentive being the suspicion that Spinoza's teaching is *the* true teaching. . . . Our argument implies the suggestion that today *the* truth may be accessible only through certain old books.

3. Leo Strauss, *Philosophy and Law* (Philadelphia: Jewish Publication Society of America, 1987), 44.
4. See note 2.
5. See preface to Leo Strauss, *Spinoza's Critique of Religion* (New York: Schocken Books, 1965), 13–15, 18–28; Strauss, *Philosophy and Law*, 5, 26; Leo Strauss, "Jerusalem and Athens," *Studies in Platonic Political Philosophy* (Chicago and London: University of Chicago Press, 1983), 167–68.
6. In "How to Study Spinoza's *Theologico-Political Treatise*," *Persecution*, 142–143, Strauss writes as follows: "the most fundamental issue—the issue raised by the conflicting claims of philosophy and revelation—is discussed in our time on a decidedly lower level than was almost customary in former ages."
7. Strauss, *Philosophy and Law*, 23.
8. Strauss, *Philosophy and Law*, 26–27.

9. Strauss, *Philosophy and Law*, 25–26, 33–34.

10. Strauss, *Philosophy and Law*, 34.

11. Strauss, *Philosophy and Law*, 29.

12. Strauss, *Philosophy and Law*, 31.

13. Strauss, introduction to *Philosophy and Law*, 13.

14. Strauss, preface to *Spinoza's Critique*, 29.

15. Strauss, preface to *Spinoza's Critique*, 30; Strauss characterizes modern belief there as follows: "the belief that by pushing ever farther back the 'natural limits' man will advance to ever greater freedom."

16. Leo Strauss, "The Mutual Influence of Theology and Philosophy," *Independent Journal of Philosophy* 3 (1979): 111–13.

17. Strauss, *Philosophy and Law*, 14.

18. Strauss, *Philosophy and Law*, 5–6.

19. See Hermann Cohen, *Religion of Reason: Out of the Sources of Judaism*, trans. Simon Kaplan (New York: Frederick Ungar, 1972), 59–65.

20. For example, see the following passage in Julius Guttmann, *The Philosophies of Judaism* (New York: Jewish Publication Society of America, 1964), 17:

> Nature here has [no] substantial life of its own, but is conceived as inanimate and subordinate to the purposes of God. . . . Man himself, the end and purpose of creation, is not conceived solely as part of nature. . . . This anthropocentric conception . . . redirects all religious feeling from nature towards the transmundane God.

21. Guttmann, *Philosophies of Judaism*, 173–74.

22. Strauss, *Philosophy and Law*, 20, 52–53, 58.

23. Strauss, *Philosophy and Law*, 50–55.

24. Strauss, *Philosophy and Law*, 55–56.

25. Strauss, *Philosophy and Law*, 72–73.

26. See Strauss, preface to *Spinoza's Critique*, 15, where the "modern project" is presented as the human aspiration to master and rule over nature. See also p. 16, where Spinoza is portrayed as the forerunner of this modern orientation. See also p. 22, where Strauss presents Kant as the one who asserts that morality is not anchored in natural law, but grounded in the premise that "morality is self-legislation." Regarding Strauss' critique of the possibility of effecting a fundamental change in human nature, see his criticism of Hermann Cohen in "Jerusalem and Athens," 167–68.

27. Strauss, "Jerusalem and Athens," 168.

28. Strauss, "Jerusalem and Athens," 168.

29. Strauss, "Jerusalem and Athens," 167.

30. Strauss, "Jerusalem and Athens," 168. See also Strauss, preface to *Spinoza's Critique*, 21–22. Strauss there contrasts Cohen's "optimism" with Spinoza's "hardheartedness," characterizing Cohen as confident of "the ultimate victory of the good," while Spinoza believes that "there will be vices as long as there will be human beings."

31. Strauss, preface to *Spinoza's Critique*, 15.

32. Strauss concludes his lecture in *What Is Political Philosophy?* (Glencoe, IL: Free Press, 1959), 55, with the following statement: "For oblivion of eternity, or, in other words, estrangement from man's deepest desire and therewith from the primary issues, is the price which modern man had to pay, from the very beginning, for at-

tempting to be absolutely sovereign, to become the master and owner of nature, to conquer chance."

33. Strauss, introduction to *Persecution*, 7.

34. Regarding the concept of "pseudo-philosophy" in Strauss, see "How to Study Spinoza's...," *Persecution*, 155.

35. Strauss, "How to Study Spinoza's...," *Persecution*, 157.

36. Strauss, "How to Study Spinoza's...," *Persecution*, 157.

37. Strauss, "How to Study Spinoza's...," *Persecution*, 156.

38. Scientific progress depends on the belief that modern thought eclipses all of its predecessors. Strauss terms this belief a "dogma." See Strauss, "How to Study Spinoza's...," *Persecution*, 158.

39. Strauss, introduction to *Persecution*, 8.

40. Regarding the concept of "world-image" in Strauss, see *Philosophy and Law*, 14.

41. Strauss, *Philosophy and Law*, 71–73.

42. See Strauss, preface to *Spinoza's Critique*, 16.

43. Strauss, preface to *Spinoza's Critique*, 15.

44. Strauss, preface to *Spinoza's Critique*, 15–16.

45. Strauss, preface to *Spinoza's Critique*, 29.

46. Strauss, *Philosophy and Law*, 13.

47. Regarding a new problem philosophers encounter in their dealings with society, see the citation from *Guide of the Perplexed*, vol. I, 37, that Strauss brings in his book *Philosophy and Law*, 38.

48. Strauss, "The Mutual Influence," 113–14.

49. Strauss, *Philosophy and Law*, 15.

50. Strauss, "How to Study Spinoza's...," *Persecution*, 155.

51. Strauss, "How to Study Spinoza's...," *Persecution*, 155.

52. Strauss, "The Mutual Influence," 112, 114.

53. Strauss, "The Mutual Influence," 163–64, 169–70, 173–74.

54. Strauss, introduction to *Persecution*, 21.

55. Strauss, introduction to *Persecution*, 17–18.

56. Strauss, "How to Study Spinoza's...," *Persecution*, 146, 159.

57. Strauss, "How to Study Spinoza's...," *Persecution*, 151–53. See also Strauss, preface to *Spinoza's Critique*, 29.

58. Strauss, "The Law of Reason," *Persecution*, 140–41.

59. Strauss, "How to Study Spinoza's...," *Persecution*, 156.

60. Strauss, "How to Study Spinoza's...," *Persecution*, 157.

61. Strauss, "How to Study Spinoza's...," *Persecution*, 151–52, 154.

62. Strauss, "How to Study Spinoza's...," *Persecution*, 159–60.

63. Strauss, "How to Study Spinoza's...," *Persecution*, 149.

64. Strauss, "How to Study Spinoza's...," *Persecution*, 154–55. Strauss remarks there in this regard: "elaborate historical studies may be needed which would have been superfluous and therefore harmful in more fortunate times."

65. Strauss, "How to Study Spinoza's...," *Persecution*, 158.

66. Strauss, introduction to *Persecution*, 21.

67. On the question of the creation or eternity of the world as a fundamental issue that distinguishes between Judaism and philosophy, see Strauss, *Philosophy and Law*, 44–45, 47; Strauss, "The Literary Character," *Persecution*, 40.

68. Strauss, "The Mutual Influence," 117–18.

69. See note 69 to chapter 7. See also Strauss, "The Mutual Influence," 112: "This quest for the beginnings proceeds through sense perception, reasoning. . . . this awareness . . . is never divorced from sense perception and reasoning based on sense perception."

70. For a clarification of the distinction between a scholarship that is driven by the duty to investigate every phenomenon simply by virtue of its occurrence, and the scholarly norm dictated by philosophic value, see Nathan Rotenstreich's remarks at the symposium on "Teaching Philosophy in High School and University," *Iyyun* 23 (Winter 1972): 33–37 [Hebrew].

71. Strauss, "How to Study Spinoza's…," *Persecution*, 155–56.

72. Strauss, preface to *Spinoza's Critique*, 29.

73. Strauss, preface to *Spinoza's Critique*, 29–30.

74. Strauss, preface to *Spinoza's Critique*, 30.

75. Strauss, preface to *Spinoza's Critique*, 30. This analysis of Epicureanism appears in Strauss, *Philosophy and Law*, 16–19.

76. See above, pp. 187–89.

77. See above, pp. 65–67.

78. See above, pp. 83–85.

79. The philosopher's life in every age is described in the introduction to Strauss' book *Persecution*, p. 17, as follows: "the secret kingship of the philosopher who, being 'a perfect man' precisely because he is an 'investigator,' lives privately as a member of an imperfect society which he tries to humanize within the limits of the possible."

80. Strauss, *Persecution*, 79–81.

81. Strauss, "The Mutual Influence," 112–13.

82. Strauss, *Philosophy and Law*, 55.

83. Strauss, "The Law of Reason," *Persecution*, 105, note 29.

84. Strauss, preface to *Spinoza's Critique*, 29. Strauss notes there that "traditional Jewish morality is not mercenary: 'The reward for [the fulfillment of] the commandment is the commandment.'" (from *The Ethics of the Fathers*, chapter 4, mishna 2).

85. Strauss, *Spinoza's Critique*, 186–88.

86. Strauss, *Spinoza's Critique*, 174–75.

87. Strauss, *Spinoza's Critique*, 72–73.

88. Strauss, "How to Study Spinoza's …," *Persecution*, 155–57.

89. Strauss, "How to Study Spinoza's…," *Persecution*, 158.

90. As Strauss remarks in "How to Study Spinoza's…," *Persecution*, 154, "On the basis of this assumption, *the* true teaching is accessible to us only through certain old books."

91. See Strauss, *Philosophy and Law*, 38.

92. Strauss, *Philosophy and Law*, 173–76, 177–79, 213–14.

93. Strauss, *Philosophy and Law*, 72–73.

94. Strauss, *Philosophy and Law*, 79–80.

95. See the first chapter of Strauss' book *Philosophy and Law*, 21–58.

9

Guidelines for the Interpretation of Jewish Philosophical Texts

In Wolfson and Guttmann we have seen that epistemological principles concerning the nature of religion and philosophy and the modes of interaction between them generate two different orientations to the interpretation of Jewish philosophical texts. Wolfson—who collapsed all of religion and philosophy into theology and treated theology as a coherent system of beliefs and opinions founded on Biblical doctrines—regarded every theological text as a systematic treatise devoid of contradictions. Hence his predisposition to resolve contradictions through harmonization.[1] Guttmann, who considered the major philosophic systems to be ultimately religious philosophies, or metaphysical systems fueled by diverse types of religious experience, did not attempt to reconcile contradictions, choosing to highlight them instead. In his view, contradictions within the thought of a great thinker testify to the tension subsisting between his type of religiosity and the demands of pure reason, or between two types of religious faith (the "personalist" and the "intellectualist") within himself.[2] We have further noted a connection between the historiosophical schemes of Wolfson and Guttmann with regard to the movement of religious thought in time, and the manner in which they derive hermeneutical conclusions from the texts they interpreted: Wolfson, whose work was characterized by an "orientation of beginnings," sought the echoes of ancient, archetypal doctrinal beliefs in every text he encountered.[3] Guttmann, guided by an "orientation of ends," sought "precursors" of modern worldviews among philosophers of the ancient and medieval periods.[4] It is worth investigating, then, whether in Strauss as well epistemological positions on the nature of religious and philosophic knowledge and historiosophic theories on the relation between religion, philosophy, society and time generated distinct hermeneutic principles.

In his book *Persecution and the Art of Writing*, Strauss treats at length of the relationship between the character of philosophy as a life of "investigation" and the writing methods of the major philosophers, a relationship that obligates the contemporary interpreter as well. In ancient and medieval times freedom of opinion and freedom of inquiry were held to undermine social stability.[5] Philosophy, the autonomous quest for the beginnings and essence of beings, led, by its very nature, to positions in conflict with the prevailing orthodoxy. Philosophy was therefore always perceived, not only by society's representatives but also by philosophers themselves, as a threat to society. Accordingly, critical contemplation that relies on reason and the senses alone and depends on no other authority has never enjoyed any official social status. When such a status was afforded theologians conversant with philosophic argument, in Christian societies in which philosophic expertise was required for the systematization of revealed doctrines, philosophy necessarily became tendentious and alienated from its true essence.[6]

Strauss articulates this fundamental conflict between philosophy in itself and society in itself, and the influence of this conflict on the writings of the great philosophers, in the following manner:

> Philosophy and the philosophers were "in grave danger." Society did not recognize philosophy or the right of philosophizing. There was no harmony between philosophy and society. . . . Persecution, then, gives rise to a peculiar technique of writing, and therewith to a peculiar type of literature, in which the truth about all crucial things is presented exclusively between the lines. . . . But how can a man perform the miracle of speaking in a publication to a minority, while being silent to the majority of his readers? The fact which makes this literature possible can be expressed in the axiom that thoughtless men are careless readers, and only thoughtful men are careful readers. Therefore an author who wishes to address only thoughtful men has but to write in such a way that only a very careful reader can detect the meaning of his book.[7]

The great philosophers sought to protect themselves. They also advocated social responsibility,[8] as an unstable society cannot produce philosophers or support them economically. They therefore strove to disguise their opinions in order to conceal them from the public at large. Their hidden esoteric message was encoded in such a manner that only the closest reader, who is willing to exert himself in comparing diverse statements scattered throughout the work, could detect it.[9] How, then, did the great philosophers craft their writings to include an "exoteric" layer that largely reflects the opinions of the reigning orthodoxy, and an "esoteric" layer discernible only to philosophers or potential philosophers? How did they gradually persuade young intellectuals to exchange conventional opinions for opinions approximating the truth?[10] In Strauss' view, one of the cardinal tools philosophers employed, along with theologians such as R. Yehuda ha-Levi who were mindful of the power of philosophy, was that of deliberate self-contradiction.

In his article "The Literary Character of the *Guide for the Perplexed*," Strauss describes the tool of deliberate self-contradiction and its use by Maimonides.[11] In the introduction to *Guide of the Perplexed*, Maimonides himself notes the need for writers to deliberately contradict themselves in order to hide the philosophic truth from the multitude.[12] Consequently, argues Strauss, modern commentators on Maimonides are not entitled to propose their own solutions to the contradictions found in the *Guide*. He warns, just as Wolfson warned, against attributing the contradictions to developmental stages in the philosopher's thought. He also cautions against explanations (familiar from Guttmann) that impute contradictions to the fact that a thinker's attempt to reconcile between the Biblical and philosophic traditions was less than fully successful. Moreover, it cannot be argued that contradictions arose within Maimonides' thought because he began to address problems that exceeded the bounds of the philosophic tradition from which he sprang, though he still felt bound by this tradition. These and similar readings all presuppose that the modern scholar perceives contradictions of which Maimonides himself was oblivious.[13] Yet even assuming that Maimonides was aware of the discrepancies in his works, discrepancies that appear to be internal contradictions, Strauss nevertheless refrains from adopting Wolfson's method of reconciling a given contradiction through theoretical harmonization. In contradistinction to all of these approaches Strauss maintains that "all important contradictions in the Guide may be reduced to the single fundamental contradiction between the true teaching, based on reason, and the untrue teaching, emanating from imagination."[14] Together with this key precept, the scholar must take into account that for Maimonides (as for numerous other philosophers), the true teaching is generally implicit rather than explicit. When Strauss endeavors to determine which of the two poles of a given contradiction represents the true meaning, and which the more "conventional" teaching based on imagination, he asks himself: Which of the two meanings is rarer or more concealed? Of two conflicting statements, that which appears with lower frequency or is presented less explicitly is the statement that the philosopher deems to be true according to reason.[15]

Following this rule Strauss concludes in his introduction to the English translation of *The Guide of the Perplexed* that perhaps we should not rely on Maimonides' repeated declarations that the Mosaic prophecy was the apex of all prophecy. It may be that his true position is to be found in remarks from which it can be inferred that Isaiah's prophecy was of a higher order than that of Moses.[16] And perhaps his ostensibly casual remark denying the mandatory character of the entire system of sacrifices more closely approximates his true opinion than the whole lengthy idiosyncratic discussion of the laws of sacrifices within the framework of the *Mishneh Torah*.[17] Even with regard to one of the most fundamental tenets of Judaism, the doctrine of creation, suspicion arises that Maimonides' extensive and detailed defense of it serves merely to camouflage some assertion, or an allusion to some assertion to be found elsewhere, from which it can be inferred that he thought the world was eternal.[18]

Strauss' reading of Spinoza's *Theological-Political Treatise* is far less esoteric than his reading of Maimonides' *Guide of the Perplexed*. In his works on Maimonides, Strauss details at length the rules for identifying assorted types of contradictions and for identifying that pole which expresses Maimonides' true opinion. Yet Strauss typically alludes to the content of the contradictions only by way of suggestion or in footnotes. In comparison, in his article "How to Study Spinoza's *Theologico-Political Treatise*," he devotes less space to the rules of exegesis per se and writes more explicitly about the content of the major contradictions. The "theological" portion of the *Treatise*, for instance, begins and ends (and note that these are the explicit sections of the text, which are exposed to the eyes of superficial readers as well) by positing the possible existence of revealed or prophetic truths that are beyond the reach of human reason. This assertion is reiterated, whether explicitly or implicitly, in "a considerable number of other passages in the work." Nevertheless, there are sections (presumably far fewer) in which Spinoza simply denies the possibility of the existence of supra-rational knowledge.[19] Aside from making a numerical comparison of the two types of statements, and from checking their location in the text (whether exposed or concealed) and the manner in which they are expressed (whether explicit or implicit), the sophisticated commentator must be "intelligent and perceptive in his own right." A person who genuinely believes in the existence of revealed and supra-rational teachings would not be capable of saying that no one has any access to the truth except through the senses and the intellect. Such a person would not affirm even once that reason or philosophy alone, as distinct from revelation or theology, has a rightful claim to truth, or that the belief in invisible things which cannot be proven through reason or the senses is devoid of all foundation. Spinoza, then, essentially denied the existence of supra-rational truths.[20]

Within the framework of his analysis of the *Theological-Political Treatise*, Strauss points out several other key contradictions which demand from the interpreter not harmonization, nor the portrayal of an individual torn in two "through no fault of his own," but that he seek out that pole of the contradiction that represents Spinoza's serious opinion, in contrast with the pole that is presented in order to avoid subverting the faith of the masses. On the one hand, Spinoza declares that from the moment theology and philosophy are separated from one another, they will no longer be rivals. Theology correctly aspires to obedience, which is its legitimate domain, while philosophy aspires to truth. He further alleges that the cornerstone of theology is the belief that obedience alone, without recourse to theoretical contemplation, suffices for salvation. On the other hand, we can infer that Spinoza held this belief to be fundamentally mistaken on the basis of two other assertions: (A) He terms this belief a "supra-rational truth." (B) He affirms that supra-rational truths are not within the realm of possibility. Without it being spelled out explicitly, we are necessarily driven to the conclusion that Spinoza believed not that philosophy and theology should be allotted separate legitimate spheres of existence in order to prevent from coming into conflict, but that an essential conflict subsists between the two disciplines, as each lays claim to the exclusive path to the one truth.[21] According to Strauss, there is no doubt that the position we reach by painstakingly piecing together various links dispersed throughout Spinoza's book is his true opinion, in contrast with the opinion that he professes in public.

Another type of contradiction, between an explicit statement and one constructed from diffuse remarks, comes to light concerning the topic of Providence. In one place Spinoza affirms that the Biblical and philosophic teachings regarding Providence are identical. Elsewhere, however, he argues that philosophy alone teaches the truth about Providence, as it informs us that the Deity is equally concerned about all human beings, that is, that the same fate befalls the righteous person and the sinner.[22] The person who is "intelligent and perceptive in his own right" grasps immediately that Spinoza has emptied the scriptural belief in Divine concern with the fate of individuals and nations of all content, by exchanging the doctrine of reward and punishment for that of indifferent fate. The perceptive person understands that, in effect, Spinoza is stating that according to philosophy there is no such thing as Providence. Finally, the necessary conclusion from this deduction is that a fundamental antagonism exists between faith and reason on this cardinal issue. Strauss has no doubt that that pole of the contradiction which requires an independent cognitive effort befitting careful, intelligent readers is the one possessed of greater validity, in contrast with explicit and overt assertions that require no such effort.

Strauss further sharpens his stance with regard to the identification of the true side of a given contradiction in the course of a lengthy discussion of the ostensible philosophy of the New Testament, when he elaborates the following rule:

> if an author who admits, however occasionally, that he speaks "after the manner of man," makes contradictory statements on a subject, the statement contradicting the vulgar view has to be considered as his serious view; nay, every statement of such an author which agrees with views vulgarly considered sacred or authoritative must be dismissed as irrelevant, or at least it must be suspected even though it is never contradicted by him.[23]

A worthy interpreter, therefore, approaches the text with the assumption that a fundamental opposition exists between opinions that have crystallized under the aspect of a disinterested philosophic stance and those that have been generated by disinterested obedience to a revealed law. This is why philosophers have been subject to persecution throughout the generations. The intensity of the persecution varied in different periods, from the Inquisition to simple social ostracism, yet the persecution of philosophers is a ubiquitous political phenomenon that is not disposed to full historical resolution.[24] This phenomenon compels the thinker to instruct potential philosophers (or even believers who have been exposed to philosophy) in private, and hence his true opinions can only be detected by exposing their hiding-place: in an ambiguous word, an imprecise citation and primarily in the contradiction that subsists between an explicit and reiterated statement and a rare or ostensibly neutral one, which nevertheless carries dangerous implications.[25] The reader must also assume the primacy of the law of contradiction, meaning that a great thinker, once he has decided between philosophy and faith, will at least be consistent with himself, and not maintain two divergent positions simultaneously within himself.[26] This principle prevents the interpreter from positing the possible existence of unconscious contradictions. Every contradiction will be considered deliberate, and the interpreter's task will focus on the attempt to reveal the most hidden and unusual pole of the contradiction, the one that represents the author's inner position.

In our discussion of the historiosophy and hermeneutic doctrines of Wolfson and Guttmann we investigated how a scholar identifies an external influence on the teachings of a particular thinker. We determined that Wolfson played down the importance of the horizontal influence of contemporary beliefs and opinions. All such influence on scriptural philosophers consisted, in his opinion, of the adoption of contemporary conceptual languages and expressive modes, a process that eased the way for theologians to express Biblical doctrines in a more idiomatic and effective manner. To the extent that he perceived any substantive external influence, he considered it a vertical one, namely, the perpetual and formative influence of primordial doctrinal tenets. From a hermeneutic standpoint, these premises found expression in Wolfson's quest for resonances of past concepts, past topics and past theories in the texts he studied. Moreover, Wolfson distinguished explicitly between the meta-historical ideational content of the works he studied and their literary forms, which he treated as ephemeral husks that needed to be mastered in order to be disposed of.[27]

In Guttmann we saw that the dimensions of this influence operated differently. In the horizontal dimension we found a lawful pattern of "challenge and response." We saw that in Guttmann's view the influence of external schools was profound indeed, both in terms of dictating the systematic framework of philosophic discourse and even in terms of defining the religious ethos. In contrast, the personalist Jewish response, at least for the bulk of the medieval period and part of the modern one, was less decisive and somewhat defensive. From a vertical standpoint, every thinker, every school and every period contributed to a progression that culminates at the end of the process. Guttmann therefore sought for the "precursors" and "seeds" of future insights in past works. With regard to the relation between form and content, he postulated that the great systems, while they endeavor to adhere to pure logic, essentially reflect fundamental types of religious belief. At times, then, he distinguishes between the systematic form that the thinker employed and the type of religious orientation that provided the impetus for his investigations.[28]

Strauss, as we have seen, did not ascribe any great importance to history as a causal factor when studying the great books of the past. He did not attend to the supposed resonances of specific, pre-given past doctrines in the works he sought to decipher, nor did he seek to trace each book's role in begetting the orientations of the future. True, Strauss considered Socrates to be the first representative of the position of philosophic quest, and Plato the first to point out the political character of the objective of this quest ("the Divine law") and of its "art of writing." Yet Strauss did not thereby intend to give the impression that the pioneering status of these two created a binding framework for those philosophic seekers who succeeded them. Every serious individual philosophic quest reopens the big questions and constitutes an apex in itself. Strauss' historiosophy, as we have seen, allows for historical schemes only with regard to pseudo-philosophy. The outstanding works of philosophers and theologians of stature stand outside of the dimension of time, which measures only the movement of society and its ideologies. The great books reflect the personal quests of private individuals lacking in power and historical influence.[29] Thus Strauss' unit of research is not the entire historical continuum, not a "period," "tradition" or "school," but the solitary book itself. His approach to every work is literary and not historical. He has no interest in viewing the work in a horizontal context, as the product of a certain period or the molder of the reality of that period. Neither is he interested in viewing the work in a vertical context, as the product of a tradition or as a catalyst for future development. His subject is the text itself, and the book is conceived as closed in principle to the past, present and future. The great books are closed not only towards the outside, but towards the inside as well. The substance and overall character of the book, along with its compositional design, supply almost the only context for imputing meaning to the specific statements that compose it.[30]

Strauss articulates these hermeneutic principles in several places in his works. Fundamentally, Strauss embraces a doctrine that he attributes to Spinoza: "Intelligible books are self-explanatory."[31] This rule applies to books with a coherent rational content, even if this content is presented in ways designed to obscure it. Admittedly, Strauss acknowledges, the modern scholar requires a more comprehensive historical knowledge for the understanding of "old books" than Spinoza deemed necessary for the comprehension of the works he considered important,[32] because in Strauss' view Spinoza dismissed past thought in a sweeping fashion. Those few works that he professed to admire were the writings of contemporary philosophers such as Descartes and Boyle.[33] Strauss, by comparison, asserts that the "one truth" may be embedded specifically in "old books," and that the modern scholar should approach them from a position of empathy. Nevertheless, in principle Strauss agrees with Spinoza that philological and historical knowledge should play a merely secondary and instrumental role in the study of philosophic texts.[34] Any information that a great author does not furnish directly himself, and which he thus does not consider relevant to comprehending his book, must be subordinated by the scholar to the literary framework and design provided by the author himself. Such secondary information might include:

> information regarding his life, character and interests, the occasion and time of the composition of his books, their addressees, the fate of his teaching and, last but not least, his sources. Such extraneous knowledge can never be permitted to supply the clue to his teaching except after it has been proved beyond any reasonable doubt that it is impossible to make head and tail of his teaching as he presented it.[35]

According to Strauss, the phrase "as he presented it" refers to the manner in which the teaching is presented, that in his opinion serves as the key to understanding the content of the teaching. The potential philosopher who studies a great book is gradually conveyed from practical popular beliefs to the theoretical truth, guided by certain obtrusively enigmatic features in the presentation of the conventional teachings—structural obscurity, contradictions, pseudonyms, inexact repetitions of earlier statements, strange expressions and so on.[36]

The expository style of a great thinker is not external to the content of his thought. It is not merely a technical tool, an efficient format (like tables and diagrams) used to clarify the substance of the argument, as Wolfson argued. Neither is the form a seemingly systematic mode of discourse animated ultimately by religious feeling, as Guttmann claimed. According to Strauss the formal-literary problems relating to the composition of the work have been deliberately planted by the author to stimulate the curiosity of the penetrating reader and to direct him to a hidden content that could not be transmitted directly and explicitly.

A philosopher may not give voice to the theoretical content of philosophy in an explicit discourse for two reasons, one substantive and one political. The substantive reason consists in the fact that the truth, by its very nature, is meant to be internalized by the philosophic reader, if he is a genuine philosopher, only after the intense intellectual effort of questing, decoding, connecting, analogizing and abstracting. The medium of direct, linear address carries a message that implies dogmatism and the imposition of external authority, not a message likely to encourage independent thinking. Thus explicit discursive writing is anti-philosophic, while only esoteric writing encourages an autonomous quest and educates toward it. The reader in training needs to experience the maxim that "all excellent things are as difficult as they are rare."[37] Ordinary people, by way of comparison, put their trust precisely in the reiterated assertion, so long as it is not coupled with a contradictory statement. Above all, if the assertion issues from the mouth of an authoritative figure, it is grasped by the multitude as a genuine truth. From the popular standpoint, the explicit repetition of conventional beliefs helps fortify the orthodox public against its detractors, thereby enhancing social stability.[38] In contrast, someone with a philosophic inclination knows that the number of times a given assertion is repeated has no bearing on its truth. A young person with an alert mind will be drawn precisely to the fleeting, one-time, hardly noticeable deviation from conventional wisdom that is expressed by way of the barest hint among a sea of banalities. He alone will judge a proposition according to its rational merit, rather than according to its persistence as a motif throughout the work.[39]

This binary form of expression, then, which offers recurring conventional formulations for the masses and select, subtle heterodox formulations for those who "love to think," is not just an external garb. It is the most fitting style for a multi-faceted content designed to be grasped by different audiences in different ways. Thus from Strauss' point of view, the reciprocal connection between form and content in great works is substantive, not incidental. The degree of esotericism is indeed contingent upon the degree of persecution to which the philosopher is exposed (Spinoza is more "daring" than Maimonides),[40] yet esoteric writing in itself is not just an outer husk reflecting a fleeting historical situation, but a substantive literary mode reflecting the genuine gap that obtains between the multitude and the philosopher.[41]

In order to better understand the essential mutual connection posited by Strauss between the contents of a great work and its form, as expressed by its literary character, its design and the art of its composition, let us take as an example his analysis of the narrative framework of the *Kuzari*. Strauss' hermeneutic system is displayed here in all its clarity, although certain principles, such as those determining the book's literary character or the status of every detail in the book's plan according to context are also employed in the exegesis of discursive works such as *The Guide of the Perplexed*.[42] We will come to see that the connection between a book's form and its contents in

R. Yehuda ha-Levi operates not only on the general level of "multi-layered" writing for diverse audiences, but also with regard to the substance of the exoteric message in itself and the esoteric message in itself.

Strauss' first step is to determine the literary type of the book, in its overt format, on the exoteric level. The *Kuzari* belongs to a class of the art of the Kalam designed to refute heretics by recourse to syllogistic argumentation. It is not, therefore, a philosophic book in the precise sense of the word, meaning an expression of the personal quest of an individual who seeks a comprehensive knowledge of all beings.[43] Moreover, this book of Kalam is presented in a unique form: not as a continuous and fully crystallized discourse brought in the name of its author, but as a series of conversations between fictional characters, in which the author does not participate. This framework of dialogues supplies the key to understanding the exoteric aim of the work, while also hinting at its esoteric aim.

Before Strauss addresses the exoteric meaning of the narrative framework, he underscores the exegetical doctrine guiding him: "In the case of an author of Halevi's rank, it is safe to assume that the connection between the content of his work and its form is as necessary as such a connection can possibly be: he must have chosen the peculiar form of the *Kuzari* because he considered it the ideal setting for a defense of Judaism."[44]

It would be easy to defend Judaism before a Jewish public, yet Judaism's success in defending itself against philosophy and the historical religions must appear to be difficult. Accordingly, the defense of Judaism is conducted before a gentile. It would be easier to defend Judaism before a monotheistic audience—Christian or Muslim—that accepts the principle of the Divine origin of the Jewish religion. Therefore the figure who ultimately converts to Judaism is a pagan. It might not be difficult to evoke sympathy for the oppressed Jews in a person who had himself suffered. Consequently the conversations in the *Kuzari* are conducted with an individual of exalted stature, a king. And if all this still leaves an opening for a sympathetic attitude to Judaism in the heart of a pagan king, the character of the king of the Khazars is presented as one who is prejudiced against Judaism. Furthermore, the narrative framework is not entirely fictional, but based on debates that actually took place in the past. R. Yehuda ha-Levi's defense of religion makes use of an impressive historical event.[45]

The order of the characters' appearance, however, and the king's inner personality traits, structural aspects that might have been interpreted by Wolfson as mere stylistic conventions, are also a key to understanding the limits of R. Yehuda ha-Levi's exoteric message. The *Kuzari* was not intended to inspire a genuine philosopher to convert to Judaism. A genuine philosopher, who is committed to human evidence alone and has not experienced the "taste" of the "Divine thing," would dismiss the possibility of revelation outright as non-evident. No debate can be held with him, for lack of shared fundamental premises. By his very nature as a philosopher he would have to reject the king's dream as irrelevant. An examination of the composition of the *Kuzari* would reveal that the book never presents a direct high-level debate between the Jewish scholar and the philosopher, thus exposing a hidden substantive message concerning the impossibility of dialogue between a religious believer and a philosopher. This fact was well-known to thinkers such as R. Yehuda ha-Levi and Maimonides, but they refrained from declaring it publicly, as the public must necessarily believe that such an interchange could take place, and that the believer would prevail.[46]

R. Yehuda ha-Levi drops hints not only regarding whom he does not intend to convince in his book, but also regarding whom he does intend to convince. The *Kuzari* is directed to persons who resemble the king, not merely with regard to his external qualities, which are "difficult" for Judaism, but also with regard to his inner qualities, which are "sympathetic" to Judaism. The king is a man who has been privileged to experience revelation, a man with a pronounced and authentic religious bent. People like the king who have been touched by the Divine, who are of a religious inclination yet are also not immune to states of mind that generate doubt, require R. Yehuda ha-Levi's "Kalam" to strengthen them in their faith. The exoteric content of the *Kuzari*, then, is aimed neither at the simply pious who are immune to philosophy on the one hand, nor at genuine philosophers on the other.[47]

We become convinced, then, that the external details of the narrative framework, which are easily grasped even by the average reader, are crucial to understanding the substantive exoteric orientation of the *Kuzari*. We further discover that a closer reading deepens our understanding of the king's inward personality and also supplies details concerning the order of appearance of the disputants. These particulars point to ha-Levi's awareness of the innate difficulty involved in any attempt to argue before a critical philosopher on behalf of religion. Are there other morphological hints in the *Kuzari* that point to a more serious grappling with philosophy, one transcending the attempt to persuade a person of religious inclination? Does R. Yehuda ha-Levi afford us a glimpse of his own confrontation with philosophy, a confrontation that transpired, in Strauss' view, on a much higher level than that accessible to the typical reader? The key, according to Strauss, is again to be found in the literary character of the work. The book's literary structure and its plan, rather than any historical context, provide the answer to these questions.

In a comment he makes in the opening preface, ha-Levi contends that he presents the discussions as they actually transpired before the king of the Khazars: "I resolved to write them down exactly as they had been spoken."[48] However, this is not strictly the case. Ha-Levi changed the framework of the discussions, and Strauss assumes that he did so consciously and deliberately (according to the letter of Yosef, king of the Khazars to Hasdai ibn Shaprut, there was no philosopher present in the discussions, and the interlocutors argued primarily with one another, rather than one after another, as portrayed in ha-Levi's book). R. Yehuda ha-Levi, then, constructs a literary dialogue that he presents as historical. Under these circumstances, Strauss maintains, the educated reader is required to translate "relative statements" (statements that are made at a certain point of the fictional conversation) into "absolute statements" (that reflect the author's positions).[49]

Let us consider an example of such a translation. In the first book of the *Kuzari* the Jewish scholar draws a comparison between "rational religions" and "a religion of divine origin."[50] The comparison is designed to demonstrate the superiority of "a religion of divine origin" over "rational religions." "A religion of divine origin arises suddenly. It is bidden to arise, and it is there, like the creation of the world,"[51] in contrast with "rational religions," which come into being gradually, following the evolution first of a small, cohesive group of believers and then a concerted effort to promote the religion's adoption by the multitude. In another section, however, the scholar speaks of "the rational laws" approvingly, not as a type of law that is by nature distinct from religious laws and of a lower order, but as a necessary foundation that serves as the precondition for the establishment of any revealed law: "For the divine law cannot become complete till the social and rational laws are perfected."[52] Strauss perceives a contradiction here between two assertions, the key to whose resolution lies in examining the distinct context in which each assertion is made in the dialogue. Yet before offering his interpretation, Strauss notes the possibility of a "harmonizing" exegesis that would resolve the contradiction on the level of content alone, through an interpretation ascribing a different meaning in each place to the concept of "the rational laws." Strauss, by way of comparison, prefers an interpretation that aspires "to understand the different attitudes of the scholar to *the* rational *nomoi* in the light of the different conversational situations in which they express themselves."[53]

In Part One, when the king still remains outside the Jewish community, and can still be suspected of doubting the veracity of Judaism, the scholar adopts a derogatory stance towards "rational religions." Only in Part Two and thereafter, once the king has overcome his basic doubts, is the scholar willing to speak of "rational religions" in a positive manner. Thus in order to try to discern R. Yehuda ha-Levi's own opinion we must refrain from identifying it with the scholar's assertion in one of the two places, or with some harmonizing version that reconciles the two contradictory assertions. We should weigh not only the scholar's statements but his deeds and general behavior as well, in diverse situations. The absolute statement that can be derived from examining the scholar's general behavior in every relative situation is that "only on the basis of faith can allowances be made for reason . . . it is hazardous, if not futile, to make reason the basis of faith."[54]

Although to Strauss' way of thinking we have yet to touch upon R. Yehuda ha-Levi's innermost position, we have arrived at a doctrine far transcending the exoteric position of the book of *Kuzari* in its opening presentation. The reader to whom the book is directed is supposed to think that the scholar succeeds, through force of argument alone, in proving, so to speak, the truth of the Jewish religion. The book's structure, however, suggests to us that the very fact of this endeavor is not only dangerous but pointless, for it is impossible to ground a belief in an omnipotent God within the framework of a position that affirms the sovereignty of theoretical reason. In contrast, a person whose faith is unshakable can acknowledge the proper role of practical reason in determining the framework of a well-ordered way of life for the community as a precondition for Divine revelation.

In summary, then, for Strauss the totality that endows the specific detail being investigated with hermeneutic meaning is not historical, but literary. The necessary causal connection subsisting between the form and content of a great book determines the commentator's field of meaning, which is an expanse of literary composition rather than of history. Strauss distances the interpreter from the dimension of time outside the text, limiting his field of vision to the topography of the text itself. In Wolfson, to recall, the solitary detail (which was often a theological topic) receives its meaning when positioned in the trans-historical context of typical Philonic problems. It receives its interpretation when it is possible to demonstrate that it contains tensions characteristic of a fixed primordial theological framework. A trans-historical rational lawfulness determines the influence of early rational structures on later rational structures, not because of any physical contact within the framework of the world of events, but due to trans-historical rational parallels over which events exercise no control.[55] In Guttmann, the solitary detail (which could be a specific topic, but also the overall system of a thinker, a school or a period) is ascribed a more active role. It receives its interpretation within the framework of teleological causality, as dynamically advancing religious philosophy's development towards self-awareness.[56] In Strauss, by way of contrast, the solitary detail, which is almost always a statement (a group of sentences, a single sentence, or even a sentence fragment) is not generally attributed to a totality existing outside the text, but to the author's overarching design within the text. The reason for the location of any assertion—conventional or exceptional—at a specific point within the continuum of a work lies in the esoteric strategy of a single individual. Any profound engagement with philosophy demands detachment from society and its historical entanglements, and therefore one should not search for the historical causes for the "absolute" assertions of a great thinker. The linear causality of history is set aside in favor of the circular causality of literature.[57] In the process of textual understanding, factors such as the literary form of a book and the characteristics of the protagonists help determine the meaning of the narrative and of the statements that are put into the mouths of the speakers. Concomitantly, we can approach the author's authentic position only through painstaking analysis of both the content and location of the individual statements that compose the work.

NOTES

1. See above, pp. 91–94.
2. See above, pp. 201–4.
3. See above, pp. 93–96.
4. See above, pp. 204–6.
5. Leo Strauss, introduction to *Persecution and the Art of Writing* (Glencoe, IL: Free Press, 1952), 21. Strauss writes: "The status of philosophy in the Islamic-Jewish world resembled in this respect its status in classical Greece. It is often said that the Greek city was a totalitarian society. It embraced and regulated morals, divine worship, tragedy and comedy."
6. Strauss, *Persecution*, 19.
7. Strauss, *Persecution*, 17, 25.
8. Strauss, *Persecution*, 36. Strauss writes: "they [the ancients] called 'lying nobly' what we would call 'considering one's social responsibilities.'"
9. See especially Strauss, introduction to *Persecution*, 18.
10. See also Strauss, introduction to *Persecution*, 17.
11. Strauss, "The Literary Character," *Persecution*, 68–76.
12. In the preface to Moses Maimonides' *Guide of the Perplexed* (Chicago: University of Chicago Press, 1963), 17–18, 20, Maimonides cites seven reasons for the creation of contradictions in any work. The fifth reason is "the necessity of teaching and making someone understand. For there may be a certain obscure matter that is difficult to conceive. One has to mention it or to take it as a premise in explaining something that is easy to conceive and that by rights ought to be taught before the former, since one always begins with what is easier. The teacher, accordingly, will have to be lax and, using any means that occur to him or gross speculation, will try to make that first matter somehow understood. He will not undertake to state the matter as it truly is in exact terms, but rather will leave it so in accord with the listener's imagination that the latter will understand only what he now wants him to understand. Afterwards, in the appropriate place, that obscure matter is stated in exact terms and explained as it truly is."
The seventh reason is "In speaking about very obscure matters it is necessary to conceal some parts and to disclose others. Sometimes in the case of certain dicta this necessity requires that the discussion proceed on the basis of a certain premise, whereas in another place necessity requires that the discussion proceed on the basis of another premise contradicting the first one. In such cases the vulgar must in no way be aware of the contradiction; the author accordingly uses some device to conceal it by all means." At the end of the preface Maimonides writes: "Divergences that are to be found in this Treatise are due to the fifth cause and the seventh."
13. Strauss, "The Literary Character," *Persecution*, 69.

14. Strauss, "The Literary Character," *Persecution*, 73.

15. Strauss, "The Literary Character," *Persecution*, 73.

16. Strauss, "How to Begin to Study *The Guide of the Perplexed*," introduction to Maimonides, *Guide of the Perplexed*, xxxiii.

17. Strauss, "The Literary Character," *Persecution*, 70. Strauss notes there that the "incidental denial" of the obligatory nature of the laws of sacrifices is brought in passing in the *Guide*, in the beginning of chapter 46, part III. Along with the historical-contextual reasons adduced there for the sacrifices, which depict them as protests against the idolatrous customs of the time, there appears the following assertion (from Shlomo Pines' translation): "Then [Scripture] explains to us that in regard to this kind of divine service, I mean sacrifices, no sin whatever will fall upon us if we do not perform it at all. For it says: *But if thou shalt forbear to vow, it shall be no sin in thee.*"

18. In the preface to his article "The Literary Character of the *The Guide of the Perplexed*," *Persecution*, 40, Strauss affirms that "in spite of his ruthless opposition to the assumptions and methods of the *Mutakallimun*, he professes to be in perfect harmony with their intention. The intention of the science of *kalam* is to defend the law, especially against the opinions of philosophers. And the central section of the *Guide* is admittedly devoted to the defense of the principal root of the law, the belief in creation, against the contention of the philosophers that the visible world is eternal." According to Strauss' division of the *Guide* into subjects (see Strauss, "How to Begin to Study," *Guide of the Perplexed*, xii), the defense of the creation doctrine takes up some 19 chapters of the second part of the *Guide* (chapters 13–31). The defense is overt and protracted. Yet Strauss also tells us ("The Literary Character," *Persecution*, 73) that "of two contradictory statements in the *Guide* or in any other work of Maimonides that statement which occurs least frequently, or even which occurs only once, was considered by him to be true." In light of a sentence like this, the suspicion arises that perhaps buried somewhere in the *Guide* is a statement that would seem to contradict the defense of creation. It is not possible within this frame of reference to decide this complex question one way or the other, yet from Strauss' standpoint such a suspicion is evidently plausible.

19. Strauss, "How to Study Spinoza's. . .," *Persecution*, 169. See note 34 there, in which Strauss designates the relevant portions of the *Theological-Political Treatise*.

20. Strauss, "How to Study Spinoza's. . .," *Persecution*, 169–70.

21. Strauss, "How to Study Spinoza's. . .," *Persecution*, 170, and note 36.

22. Strauss, "How to Study Spinoza's. . .," *Persecution*, 171, and note 38.

23. Strauss, "How to Study Spinoza's. . .," *Persecution*, 177.

24. Strauss, "Persecution," *Persecution*, 32–33.

25. Strauss, "The Literary Character," *Persecution*, 67–76.

26. See again Strauss, "The Law of Reason," *Persecution*, 108–9.

27. Strauss, *Persecution*, 94–96.

28. Strauss, *Persecution*, 206–9.

29. Strauss, *Persecution*, 282–85.

30. In "Persecution," *Persecution*, 30, Strauss expresses this exegetical principle as follows: "The context in which a statement occurs, and the literary character of the whole work as well as its plan, must be perfectly understood before an interpretation of the statement can reasonably claim to be adequate or even correct."

For the concept of "closedness" in literary terms, I am indebted to Prof. Jonah Fraenkel, a specialist in aggadic narratives from the Department of Literature of the Hebrew University, who addresses this concept in his article "She'elot Hermenoitiyot be-Heker Sipur ha-Aggadah," *Tarbitz* 47, no. 3-4 (Spring-Summer 1978): 139-72 (see particularly pp. 157-59).

31. Strauss, "How to Study Spinoza's. . .," *Persecution*, 149.
32. Strauss, "How to Study Spinoza's. . .," *Persecution*, 160-61.
33. Strauss, "How to Study Spinoza's. . .," *Persecution*, 152.
34. In Strauss' words ("How to Study Spinoza's. . .," *Persecution*, 159): "Contrary to what he implies, we need for the understanding of his books such information as is not supplied by him and as is not easily available to every reasonable reader regardless of time and place. But we must never lose sight of the fact that information of this kind cannot have more than a strictly subordinate function, or that such information has to be integrated into a framework authentically or explicitly supplied by Spinoza himself."
35. Strauss, "How to Study Spinoza's. . .," *Persecution*, 159. This literary approach of Strauss to the study of philosophic works is remarkably similar in its principles to the literary approach Prof. Meir Weiss espouses in his study of the Biblical text. See Meir Weiss, *The Bible from Within* (Hebrew University of Jerusalem: Magnes Press, 1984), introduction, 1-46. On pp. 11-12, Weiss states: "But even while we recognise (sic) the importance of historical knowledge, we must remember that historical erudition is not itself an interpretation but the preparation for one. Interpretation begins only where historical research leaves off. 'Interpretation,' Kayser warns, 'is concerned with the text itself.'"
36. Strauss, "Persecution," *Persecution*, 36.
37. Strauss, "How to Study Spinoza's. . .," *Persecution*, 183.
38. Strauss, "Persecution," *Persecution*, 23.
39. Strauss, "Persecution," *Persecution*, 24-25.
40. Strauss, "How to Study Spinoza's. . .," *Persecution*, 183.
41. Strauss, "The Literary Character," *Persecution*, 59. Strauss stresses there that "Esotericism, one might say, is based on the assumption that there is a rigid division of mankind into an inspired or intelligent minority and an uninspired or foolish majority."
42. Strauss, "The Literary Character," *Persecution*, 42-43, 75-77.
43. Strauss, "The Law of Reason," *Persecution*, 98-99.
44. Strauss, "The Law of Reason," *Persecution*, 101.
45. Strauss, "The Law of Reason," *Persecution*, 101-2.
46. Strauss, "The Law of Reason," *Persecution*, 103-10.
47. Strauss, "The Law of Reason," *Persecution*, 111-12.
48. R. Judah HaLevi, *Kuzari*, trans. Hartwig Hirschfeld (New York: P. Shalom, 1969), part I, 35.
49. Strauss, "The Law of Reason," *Persecution*, 101-2 and note 17.
50. HaLevi, *Kuzari*, part I, no. 80-81, 58.
51. HaLevi, *Kuzari*, part I, no. 80-81, 58.
52. HaLevi, *Kuzari*, part II, no. 48, 112.
53. Strauss, "The Law of Reason," *Persecution*, 118.
54. Strauss, "The Law of Reason," *Persecution*, 119.

55. Strauss, *Persecution*, 101–3.

56. Strauss, *Persecution*, 211–15.

57. Regarding the concept of the "hermeneutic circle" as applied in the study of the Bible and aggadic literature, see:

a. Weiss, *The Bible from Within* (note 35 above), 27, where he brings the following citation by Ernst Staiger, *Die Kunst der Interpretation*, (Zurich: 1957), 11: "We must interpret the whole on the basis of the details and the details in the light of our understanding of the whole work. This is the hermeneutic *circulus* about which we will no longer say that it is a magic circle from which we can't escape but rather we must strive to walk it with care and concern."

b. Fraenkel, "She'elot Hermenoitiyot" (note 30 above), 153. He states there: "Let us employ the old hermeneutic principle here of 'the hermeneutic circle': The details are interpreted by the whole and the whole is interpreted by the details. The coherence and internal synthesis of a work are the foundations of every creative act of understanding, and all interpretation is constructed upon them." For a discussion of the concept of the "hermeneutic circle" in Shleiermacher, see Hans-Georg Gadamer, *Truth and Method* (London: Sheed & Ward, 1975), 167, 258.

Bibliography

ON CONCEPTUAL FRAMEWORKS
IN HISTORY AND THE SCIENCES

Carr, Edward Hallett. *What is History?* Basingstoke: Macmillan Press, 1986.

Kuhn, Thomas. *The Structure of Scientific Revolutions.* Chicago: University of Chicago Press, 1970.

Scheffler, Israel. *Science and Subjectivity.* Indianapolis, IN: Bobbs-Merill, 1967.

Schwab, Joseph. *Science, Curriculum and Liberal Education.* Chicago: University of Chicago Press, 1978.

Stern, Fritz, ed. *The Varieties of History.* New York: Vintage Books, 1973.

DEFINING THE FIELD OF "JEWISH PHILOSOPHY"

Berkovits, Eliezer. "What is Jewish Philosophy?" *Tradition* 3, no. 2 (Spring 1961): 117–30.

Fackenheim, Emil. "An Outline of a Modern Jewish Theology." *Quest for Past and Future.* Boston: Beacon Press, 1970, 96–111.

Roth, Leon. "Is There a Jewish Philosophy?" *Jewish Philosophy and Philosophers,* edited by Raymond Goldwater. London: Hillel Foundation, 1962, 1–19.

Schwartz, Moshe, and Moshe Halamish, eds. "Filosofiah Yehudit—Mahi?" (Symposium with the participation of Prof. Y. Levinger, Prof. S. Rosenberg, and Prof. Y. Sermonetta), *Hitgalut, Emunah, Tvunah.* Ramat Gan: Bar Ilan University, 1976, 145–69.

Schweid, Eliezer. "Ha-Im Kayemet Masoret Atzmait shel Filosofiah Yehudit?" *Ta'am ve-Hakasha.* Ramat Gan: Masada, 1970, 12–36.

——. "Ha-Filosofiah ha-Yehudit ke-Echad ha-Zeramim ba-Filosofiah shel ha-Meah ha-Essrim." *Da'at* 23 (Summer 1989): 101–10.

ON THE PLACE OF TRADITION
AND INTERPRETATION IN JUDAISM

Rawidowicz, Simon. "On Interpretation." *Studies in Jewish Thought.* Philadelphia: Jewish Publication Society of America, 1974, 45–80.
Rotenstreich, Nathan. *Tradition and Reality.* New York: Random House, 1972, especially chap. 1, "The Meaning of Tradition in Judaism," 7–18.
Scholem, Gershom. "Revelation and Tradition as Religious Categories in Judaism." *The Messianic Idea in Judaism.* New York: Schocken Books, 1971, 282–303.

ON STREAMS IN THE "SCIENCE OF JUDAISM"

Glatzer, Nahum. "The Beginnings of Modern Jewish Studies." *Studies in Nineteenth-Century Jewish Intellectual History,* edited by Alexander Altmann. Cambridge, MA: Harvard University Press, 1964, 27–45.
Rotenstreich, Nathan. "Tochnitah shel Hochmat Israel." *Ha-Machshavah ha-Yehudit ba-Et ha-Chadashah,* Vol. 1. Tel Aviv: Am Oved, 1966, 35–51.
——. "The Science of Judaism," *Tradition and Reality.* New York: Random House, 1972, 21–35.
Scholem, Gershom. "Mi-Toch Hirhurim al Hochmat Israel." *Devarim beh-Go.* Tel Aviv: Am Oved, 1975, 385–403.
——. "The Science of Judaism—Then and Now." *The Messianic Idea in Judaism.* New York: Schocken Books, 1971, 304–13.
Wiener, Max. "The Ideology of the Founders of Jewish Scientific Research." *YIVO Annual of Jewish Social Science* V (1950): 184–96.

ON THE STUDY OF THE HISTORY OF PHILOSOPHY

Copleston, Frederick. *A History of Philosophy,* Vol. I. London: Burns & Oates, 1946, 1–22.
Mandelbaum, Maurice. "The History of Ideas, Intellectual History, and the History of Philosophy." *History and Theory—Studies in the History of Philosophy. Beiheft* 5 (1965): 33–66.
Passmore, John. "The Idea of a History of Philosophy." *History and Theory—Studies in the History of Philosophy. Beiheft* 5 (1965): 1–32.
——. "Historiography of Philosophy." *Encyclopedia of Philosophy,* Vol. VI, edited by Paul Edwards. New York: Quentin Macmillan Co., 1967, 226–29.
Rorty, Richard, Jerome B. Schneewind, and Quentin Skinner, eds. *Philosophy in History—Essays on the Historiography of Philosophy.* Cambridge: Cambridge University Press, 1984.

Rotenstreich, Nathan. "Filosofiah ve-Toldotayah," *Al Tchumah shel ha-Filosofiah.* Jerusalem: Hebrew University Press, 1969, 160–79.
Windelband, Wilhelm. *A History of Philosophy,* trans. James H. Tufts. New York: Harper & Row, 1958, 1–22.

HARRY AUSTRYN WOLFSON

Sources

Crescas' Critique of Aristotle. Cambridge, MA: Harvard University Press, 1929.
"How the Jews Will Reclaim Jesus." *Menorah Journal* 49, 1–2 (Autumn–Winter 1962): 25–31.
"Maimonides and Hallevi: A Study in Typical Jewish Attitudes towards Greek Philosophy in the Middle Ages." *Jewish Quarterly Review* II (1911–1912): 297–337.
"The Needs of Jewish Scholarship in America." *Menorah Journal,* VII, no. 1 (February 1921): 28–35.
Philo: Foundations of Religious Philosophy in Judaism, Christianity, and Islam. Vol. I-II. Cambridge, MA: Harvard University Press, 1947.
The Philosophy of Spinoza. Vol. I-II. Cambridge, MA: Harvard University Press, 1934.
The Philosophy of the Church Fathers. Cambridge, MA: Harvard University Press, 1970.
The Philosophy of the Kalam. Cambridge, MA: Harvard University Press, 1976.
Religious Philosophy: A Group of Essays. Cambridge, MA: Harvard University Press, 1961.
Repercussions of the Kalam in Jewish Philosophy. Cambridge, MA: Harvard University Press, 1979.
Studies in the History and Philosophy of Religion. Vol. I-II. Cambridge, MA: Harvard University Press, 1973–1977.

Scholarly Literature

Harvey, Warren Zev. "Hebraism and Western Philosophy in H. A. Wolfson's Theory of History." *Immanuel* 14 (Fall 1982): 75–85.
Rotenstreich, Nathan. "Mechkar Histori ke-Omanut Kohanim." *Iyyunim ba-Machshavah ha-Yehudit ba-Zman ha-Zeh.* Tel Aviv: Am Oved, 1978, 104–9.
Schwarz, Leo. "A Bibliographical Essay." *Harry Austryn Wolfson Jubilee Volume* I, edited by Saul Lieberman. Jerusalem: American Academy for Jewish Research, 1965, 1–46.
———. *Wolfson of Harvard.* Philadelphia: Jewish Publication Society of America, 1978.
Twersky, Isadore. Foreword to *Repercussions of the Kalam in Jewish Philosophy.* Cambridge, MA: Harvard University Press, 1979, v–x.
———. "Harry Austryn Wolfson: in Appreciation." In Leo Schwarz, *Wolfson of Harvard.* Philadelphia: American Academy for Jewish Research, 1978, vii–xxvii.

Wieseltier, Leon. "Philosophy, Religion and Harry Wolfson." *Commentary* 61, no. 4 (April 1976): 57–64.

JULIUS GUTTMANN

Sources

"Binyan Eretz Israel ve-ha-Yahadut." *Ptachim* 12 (Adar A, 1970): 19–26.

Dat u-Mada [*Religion and Knowledge*, in Hebrew], edited by Shmuel H. Bergman and Nathan Rotenstreich, (trans. from German by Shaul Esh). Jerusalem: Magnes Press, 1955 (a collection of articles and lectures from the years 1908–1943).

"Filosofiah shel ha-Dat o-Filosofiah shel ha-Hok." *Divrei ha Akademiah ha-Leumit ha-Israelit le-Madaim* 5, no. 9 (1976): 188–207 (from the bequest).

The Philosophies of Judaism, trans. David W. Silverman. New York: Jewish Publication Society of America, 1964.

On the Philosophy of Religion (From a lecture series given at the Hebrew University during the 1946/7 school year, transcribed by Shulamit Tov, preface by Nathan Rotenstreich). Jerusalem: Magnes Press, 1976.

Scholarly Literature

Bamberger, Fritz. "Julius Guttmann: Philosopher of Judaism." *Leo Baeck Institute Yearbook* 5 (1960): 3–34.

Harvey, Warren Zev. "Hebraism and Western Philosophy in H. A. Wolfson's Theory of History." *Immanuel* 14 (Fall 1982): 77–85.

Rotenstreich, Nathan. Preface to *On the Philosophy of Religion*. Jerusalem: Magnes Press, 1976, 7–9.

———. "Toldot ha-Toda'ah ha-Datit u-Mahutah." *Iyyunim ba-Machshavah ha-Yehudit ba-Zman ha-Zeh*. Tel Aviv: Am Oved, 1978, 132–38.

Roth, Haim Yehuda. "Yitzhak (Yulius) Guttmann Zal." *Iyyun* 2, no. 1 (January 1951): 3–10.

Schweid, Eliezer. "Ha-Filosofiah ha-Yehudit ke-Echad ha-Zeramim ba-Filosofiah shel ha-Meah ha-Essrim." *Da'at* 23 (Summer 1989): 101–10.

Slomovics, Peter. "Yitzhak Yulius Guttmann ve-Yehezkel Kaufman: Machshavah u-Mechkar ve-ha-Kesher Beineihem." Ph.D. diss., Hebrew University of Jerusalem, 1981.

Shmueli, Efraim. "Profesor Yulius Guttmann." *Hochmat Israel be-Ma'arav Eiropa*. in *Hochmat Israel be-Ma'arav Eiropa*, edited by Shimon Federbush. Jerusalem-Tel Aviv: Ogen Press, 1958, 148–65.

Shohatman, Baruch. "Kitvei Profesor Yitzhak (Yulius) Guttmann Zal (1903–1950)— Reshima Bibliografit." *Iyyun* 2, no. 1 (January 1951): 11–19.

Werblowsky, Raphael Jehuda Zwi. Introduction to *The Philosophies of Judaism*, trans. David W. Silverman. Philadelphia: Jewish Publication Society of America, 1964, vii–x.

LEO STRAUSS

Sources

"A Giving of Accounts." *The College* XXII, no. 1 (April 1970): 1–5.
"How to Begin to Study *The Guide of the Perplexed*," introduction to Moses Maimonides, *The Guide of the Perplexed*, ed. and trans. Shlomo Pines. Chicago: University of Chicago Press, 1963, xi–lvi.
"The Mutual Influence of Theology and Philosophy." *Independent Journal of Philosophy* 3 (1979): 111–18.
Persecution and the Art of Writing. Glencoe, IL: Free Press, 1952.
Philosophy and Law. Philadelphia: Jewish Publication Society of America, 1987 (originally published 1935).
Spinoza's Critique of Religion. New York: Schocken Books, 1965, especially the preface, 1–31.
Studies in Platonic Political Philosophy. Chicago and London: University of Chicago Press, 1983.
What Is Political Philosophy? Glencoe, IL: Free Press, 1959.
"Why We Remain Jews." *Jewish Philosophy and the Crisis of Modernity*, edited by Kenneth Hart Green. Albany, NY: SUNY Press, 1997, 311–56.

Scholarly Literature

Dannhauser, Werner J. "Leo Strauss: Becoming Naïve Again." *The American Scholar* 44, no. 4 (Autumn 1975): 636–42.
Green, Kenneth Hart. *Jew and Philosopher—The Return to Maimonides in the Jewish Thought of Leo Strauss.* Albany: State University of New York, 1993.
Lerner, Ralph. Foreward to Leo Strauss, *Philosophy and Law.* Philadelphia: Jewish Publication Society of America, 1987, pp. ix–xii.
Pines, Shlomo. "Al Leo Strauss." *Molad* 7, no. 37–38 (end of 1976): 455–57.
Rotenstreich, Nathan. "Bein Atuna le-Yerushalayim." *Iyyunim ba-Machshavah ha-Yehudit ba-Zman ha-Zeh.* Tel Aviv: Am Oved, 1978, 139–43.

References to Bibliographies of Strauss's Writings

Cropsey, Joseph, ed. *Ancients and Moderns: Essays on the Tradition of Political Philosophy in Honor of Leo Strauss.* New York and London: Basic Books, 1964, 317–22.
Nicorgski, Walter. "Leo Strauss: A Bibliography." *Modern Age* 26 (Summer–Fall 1982): 270–73.
Strauss, Leo. *Studies in Platonic Political Philosophy.* Chicago and London: University of Chicago Press, 1983, 249–58.

Supplementary Literature

Cohen, Jonathan. "Review Essay of *Jew and Philosopher*, by Kenneth Hart Green." *Modern Judaism* 16, no. 1 (February 1996): 81–91.

———. "Strauss, Soloveitchik and the Genesis Narrative: Conception of the Ideal Jew as Derived from Philosophical and Theological Readings of the Bible." *Journal of Jewish Thought and Philosophy* 5, no. 1 (1995): 99–143.

Gildin, Hilail, ed. *An Introduction to Political Philosophy: Ten Essays by Leo Strauss.* Detroit, MI: Wayne State University Press, 1989.

Green, Kenneth H. *Jew and Philosopher.* Albany, NY: SUNY Press, 1993.

———. "Leo Strauss as a Modern Jewish Thinker," in *Leo Strauss, Jewish Philosophy and the Crisis of Modernity,* edited by Kenneth Hart Green. Albany, NY: SUNY Press, 1997.

Himmelfarb, Milton. "On Leo Strauss." *Commentary* 58, no. 2 (August 1974): 60–66.

Jaffa, Harry V. "Leo Strauss: 1952, 1953." *Modern Age* 26 (Summer–Fall 1982): 266–69.

Jaffe, Martin D. "Leo Strauss as Judaic Thinker: Some First Notions." *Religious Studies Review* 17, no. 1 (January 1991): 33–40.

Luz, Ehud. "Yahaduto shel Leo Strauss." *Da'at* 27 (Summer 1991): 35–60.

Pangle, Thomas. Introduction to Leo Strauss, *Studies in Platonic Political Philosophy.* Chicago and London: University of Chicago Press, 1983, 1–26.

Pangle, Thomas, ed. *The Rebirth of Classical Political Rationalism: An Introduction to the Thought of Leo Strauss.* Chicago: University of Chicago Press, 1989.

Smith, Steven B. "Gershom Scholem and Leo Strauss: Notes Toward A German-Jewish Dialogue." *Modern Judaism* 13, no. 3 (October 1993): 209–30.

Strauss, Leo. "On Husik's Work in Medieval Jewish Philosophy." *Introduction to I. Husik's Philosophical Essays: Ancient, Medieval, Modern.* Oxford: Basil Blackwell, 1952.

———. *Liberalism Ancient and Modern.* New York: Basic Books, 1968.

———. "Philosophy as Rigorous Science and Political Philosophy." *Interpretation: A Journal of Political Philosophy* 2, no. 1 (Summer 1971): 1–9.

———. "On the Interpretation of Genesis." *L'Homme: Revue Francaise d'Anthropologie* 21, no. 1 (1981): 5–36.

———. "Progress or Return: The Contemporary Crisis in Western Civilization." *Modern Judaism* I, no. 1 (May 1981): 17–45.

Udoff, Alan, ed. *Leo Strauss' Thought: Toward A Critical Engagement.* Boulder, CO: Lynne Rienner, 1991.

Index

318

Index

psychoanalysis, 38, 112, 114–15, 117, 123, 133, 182
punishment. *See* reward

Rahner, Karl, 48–49, 57n76, 80
rationalism, 7, 63, 66–67, 70–72; in Guttmann, 149, 155–56, 198n161, 210; medieval, 155, 213, 221; in Wolfson, 40, 53, 74–75
reconstruction, 11–13
reductionism, 4, 112, 114–16
regime, ideal, 264
"Relation Between Religion and Philosophy According to R. Yehudah Ha-Levi" (Guttmann), 123
religion. *See* God; revelation; theology
Religion and Knowledge (Guttmann), 108, 110, 145, 195n79, 195n95, 218n59
religious clarity, 117–18, 124, 130, 134
"Religious Motifs in Maimonides' Teachings" (Guttmann), 206
Religious Philosophy—A Group of Essays (Wolfson), 37–38, 53, 55n8, 55n12, 78
Repercussions of the Kalam in Jewish Philosophy (Wolfson), 65, 69
Republic, The (Plato), 241
resurrection of the dead, 47, 66, 148, 152, 154, 157, 247
revelation, 163–64, 174–77, 215, 227–28, 237–41, 260–64, 294, 298–301; of the Bible, 61–62, 64, 67, 81, 154, 211–12, 229–30, 236; commitment to, 182, 186; in Copleston, 9; in Guttmann, 116–19, 124–26, 153, 157–59, 194n63, 195n79, 218n57, 282; and Islam, 132, 137, 165, 205; in Philo, 38, 40–41, 45–46, 62, 66, 75, 78–80, 150–51; rejection of, 79, 96, 155, 170–72, 213, 265, 270; at Sinai, 39, 82, 84, 96, 130, 221, 234, 244; in Strauss, 220–23, 244–49, 255n100, 256nn113–15, 271, 285n6, 289–90, 292–93; in Wolfson, 35–36, 38–40, 42–49, 52–54, 92, 112, 188. *See also* theology

reward, 152, 236, 288n84; and punishment, 68, 114, 132, 153–54, 232–35, 241, 281, 293
Rorty, Richard, 10–13, 16
Rosenak, Michael, 48
Rosenzweig, Franz, 108, 129, 191, 197n159, 214, 220, 259–60
Rotenstreich, Nathan, 2, 17, 21–22, 108, 139n10, 140n57; and Wolfson, 32, 68, 85
Runes, Dagobert, 53

Saadia Gaon, 69, 99, 178–79, 183, 191, 209–10, 213; and Guttmann, 107, 127, 131–32, 137, 156–59, 189, 194n63, 204–6
sacrifices, 96, 249, 285, 291–92, 303n17; self-, 113–14, 229, 235, 241
Santayana, George, 32, 75
Schelling, F., 129, 178
Schleiermacher, Friedrich, 108
Schmidt, Karl, 222–23
Scholem, Gershom, 18, 20–21, 28n46, 83, 87n2, 254n67
Schwab, Joseph, 23, 28nn53–54, 86n1
Schwarz, Lee, 32
Schweid, Eliezer, 1, 109, 142n98, 196n97, 217n40, 217n50
science, 14–15, 23, 39, 74, 276–77; and Guttmann, 171–73, 175–76, 195n76, 202, 207–8; historical, 36, 97–98, 101; modern, 76, 267–68, 282–83; and Strauss, 238, 251, 263, 265–70, 287n38; and theology, 48, 51, 65–66, 107–9, 114, 131–32, 135–36, 162–63, 166
"science of Judaism," 16–23, 97–98, 109
self-legislation, 265, 268, 286n26
self-preservation, 71–72, 138, 241
sensualism, 7, 179, 213, 240, 244, 247; and Guttmann, 114–15, 152, 161–62, 216n13
"Sermonette" (Wolfson), 75
Silverman, David, 148

sin, 63, 68, 92, 113, 115, 138n9,
303n17
Skinner, Quentin, 11
Slomovics, Peter, 131
social responsibility, 290, 302n8
Socrates, 237, 240–41, 280–81, 295
Sodom and Gomorrah, 235–36
Solomon's Wisdom, 149
soul, 24, 142n124, 150, 216n11,
216n13, 237, 242–45, 271; and
Guttmann, 112, 116, 120, 125,
135–37, 146, 161–63, 204;
immortality of, 84, 148, 152,
164–65, 174, 221, 249, 281;
individual, 28n54, 48, 133, 274;
and Wolfson, 42, 53, 71–72, 74,
172; of the world, 37, 44, 57n75,
149. *See also* "Immortality and the
Resurrection of the Dead"
Spinoza, Baruch, 10, 32–33, 79, 96–97,
213, 268–73, 284; in Guttmann,
120, 125, 127, 170–73, 184,
189–90, 208–9, 237; in Strauss,
250–52, 260, 262, 271–72, 281–82,
285n2, 295–97; in Wolfson, 63,
65–67, 70–76, 78–79, 83–86,
88n57, 202, 269. *See also* "How to
Study Spinoza's Theologico-Political
Treatise"; *Theological-Political Treatise*
"Spinoza and the Religion of the Past"
(Wolfson), 52–53, 72
Spinoza's Critique of Religion (Strauss),
219–23, 224n13, 255n100,
256n115, 286n15, 286n26, 286n30,
288n84
Steinheim, Solomon, 178, 181–83,
191, 214
Steinschneider, Moritz, 18–19
Stoics, 37–38, 40, 44, 51, 57n75, 73,
93, 100; and logos, 96, 149, 193n22
Strauss, Leo, 239–42, 259, 261–64,
266–68, 275–77, 298, 300;
background of, 1, 21–25, 28,
219–23, 224nn10–11; and
Guttmann, 234–36, 241–43, 246,
251, 278, 280–82, 291, 301; and
split in religion and philosophy,

269–70, 273–74, 281, 284; and
Straussian school, 220; and
Wolfson, 124–25, 137, 227–32,
227–30, 236–38, 278–84. *See also*
ha-Levi, Yehuda; Maimonides;
Spinoza, Baruch; *and individual
works*
Studies in Contemporary Jewish Thought
(Rotenstreich), 32
*Studies in the History and Philosophy of
Religion* (Wolfson), 53, 55n16,
87n15
substantive structure. *See* epistemology
syllogisms, 41, 51, 202, 206, 238–39,
298
syntactic structure of the discipline, 23

Talmud, 1, 148, 151–55, 158, 161,
187, 220; in Wolfson, 32, 36, 50,
83–84, 157, 203
tenets of faith, 38, 171, 202
Tertullian, Quintus Septimius Florens,
40, 47–48, 102
theodicy, 148, 152, 155, 159
Theological-Political Treatise (Spinoza),
247–48, 275, 292
theology, 66, 76, 159–61, 178, 206–8,
215, 245, 301; in Guttmann, 32,
50–54, 114, 116, 128, 135–37, 164,
183–84; in Maimonides, 130, 167,
169; philosophy and, 19–20, 48–50,
251–52, 274–75, 277–78, 282,
289–95; philosophy as "handmaid
of," 41–42, 47, 53, 123, 131, 157,
202, 246–48; in Strauss, 230, 238,
241, 243, 256n107, 259–60, 292; in
Wolfson, 80–82, 87n15, 91, 97–100,
102–3, 134, 186, 237. *See also*
Judaism
Thomism, 8–10, 16, 77
Timaeus (Plato), 43
Torah. *See* Bible
totem, 115
trinity, 64, 82, 127, 155
Twersky, Isadore, 1, 33, 34n11, 60, 69,
84, 255n89
two-truths theory, 212, 263

About the Author

Dr. Jonathan Cohen teaches Jewish thought and Jewish education as well as the philosophy of education and curriculum theory at the School of Education, Hebrew University of Jerusalem. He also serves as a faculty member at the Mandel Leadership Institute and a curriculum adviser at the Shalom Hartman Institute. His academic interests center on the hermeneutic dimension in modern Jewish thought, with special focus on the relevance of alternative hermeneutic orientations for issues of principle in Jewish education. He has written extensively on the translation of philosophy and academic research to educational theory and on issues in modern Jewish thought proper—most recently on the literary character of the Bible in the thought of Franz Rosenzweig and Leo Strauss. He is currently at work on a book comparing the Biblical hermeneutics of Leo Strauss with the interpretive approaches of other modern Jewish thinkers such as Freud, Fromm, Buber, Rosenzweig, Soloveitchik and Hartman.